SECESSION AND RESTORATION
OF LOUISIANA

A Da Capo Press Reprint Series

THE AMERICAN SCENE
Comments and Commentators

GENERAL EDITOR: WALLACE D. FARNHAM
University of Illinois

SECESSION AND RESTORATION OF LOUISIANA

By

WILLIE MALVIN CASKEY

DA CAPO PRESS • NEW YORK • 1970

A Da Capo Press Reprint Edition

This Da Capo Press edition of
Secession and Restoration of Louisiana
is an unabridged republication of the
first edition published in 1938.

Library of Congress Catalog Card Number 78-75302
SBN 306-71263-6

Published by Da Capo Press
A Division of Plenum Publishing Corporation
227 West 17th Street, New York, N.Y. 10011

Manufactured in the United States of America

LOUISIANA STATE UNIVERSITY STUDIES
Number 36

SECESSION AND RESTORATION
OF LOUISIANA

SECESSION AND RESTORATION OF LOUISIANA

By

WILLIE MALVIN CASKEY

with foreword by

FRANK LAWRENCE OWSLEY

LOUISIANA STATE UNIVERSITY PRESS

UNIVERSITY ∽ 1938 ∽ LOUISIANA

PRINTED IN THE UNITED STATES OF AMERICA
BY GEORGE BANTA PUBLISHING COMPANY, MENASHA, WISCONSIN

To

Frank Lawrence Owsley, Ph.D.
Professor of American History
Vanderbilt University

This Book is Affectionately Dedicated

CONTENTS

ILLUSTRATIONS

[ix]

FOREWORD

Fifty years ago Civil War and Reconstruction were no further removed in time than is the World War today. The bloody shirt was still the unofficial banner of the Republican Party, and the South was still bitter and apprehensive of being reconstructed again. There was, as yet, in the minds of a majority of Northerners a close relationship between the words "Democrat," "Copperhead," "rebel," and "traitor." Nor were the historians far removed in their attitudes from those of the public at large. Yet it was in this emotionally charged atmosphere that the youthful professor of political science and history of Columbia University, William Archibald Dunning, aside from his prolonged study of the history of political theory, commenced the study of the controversial and forbidding subject of Civil War and Reconstruction, out of which was destined to come the renaissance in the writing of Southern history. Professor Dunning drew about him in this particular field a group of able young Southerners who undertook and carried out a systematic and objective study of Reconstruction as it operated in the individual Southern States, while Dunning himself, in essays and in a book, assumed the task of making a synthesis of the different parts and presenting the general picture of Reconstruction.

The first study to come from this Dunning school was Woolley's *The Reconstruction of Georgia,* and it bears the earmarks of pioneering. Next was Garner's *Reconstruction in Mississippi,* a work which is marked by disinterestedness, thoroughness and insight, and one which may be supplemented, but hardly superseded, by later researches. Next in time and of wider perspective and greater importance was Walter Lynwood Fleming's *Civil War and Reconstruction in Alabama.* In succession he published several books on Reconstruction: *Documentary History of Reconstruction, The Sequel of Appomattox, The Freedmen's Savings Bank;* and scores of articles came from his busy pen, so that in the end Dunning came to regard Fleming as the historian of Reconstruction. The Dunning school definitely set out to write a history of Reconstruction state by state; and its objective was almost accomplished. After Fleming's *Civil War and Reconstruction in Alabama* there

[xi]

followed: Hamilton's *Reconstruction in North Carolina;* Davis's *The Civil War and Reconstruction in Florida;* Ramsdell's *Reconstruction in Texas;* Thompson's *Reconstruction in Georgia;* and Staples's *Reconstruction in Arkansas.*

The other reconstructed states, South Carolina, Virginia, Tennessee, and Louisiana, were dealt with by scholars outside but obviously influenced by the Dunning school, and with the exception of Louisiana these states have been studied more or less satisfactorily. But Ficklen's work on Louisiana was cut short in its preliminary stages by the author's death, so that Louisiana, *the* horrible example of Reconstruction, has remained—with the exception of Miss Lonn's work on the later phases—fallow ground, waiting the hand of patient scholarship. Perhaps this is fortunate since so much material inaccessible to former scholars has been made available within recent years.

With this great need and opportunity so obvious, Dr. W. M. Caskey began several years ago his study of the Johnson period of Reconstruction in Louisiana, which he considers, with good logic, to be reorganization rather than reconstruction. This volume had its inception as a Ph.D. dissertation at Vanderbilt University, but the author has continued his patient and thorough researches until now he has gone far past the original bounds. He has become convinced, too, that the work must go on into a second—or even third—volume until the entire period of Reconstruction in Louisiana has been restudied in the light of new and vital material now available. While Dr. Caskey's work at Vanderbilt University was nominally under my direction, he and I both must have felt, though the feeling was unacknowledged by either of us, the unseen hand of the great Walter Lynwood Fleming and of his master, William Archibald Dunning.

FRANK L. OWSLEY

June, 1938

CHAPTER I

THE PRESIDENTIAL ELECTION OF 1860

The opening of the presidential campaign in 1860 found the Democrats in a dilemma: whether to support a candidate of their own choice; or to accept the proffered candidacy of Douglas, and thereby harmonize the discordant and disintegrating elements in their party. It was plainly evident that there was a growing feeling of resentment against further compromises on the part of the orthodox Democrats, who, as so-called ultras, championed the Calhoun doctrine that the Federal government should protect slavery in the territories. This growing bitterness of the orthodox Democracy was manifested not only towards the "Black Republican abolitionists" of the North, but also towards the Squatter Sovereignty attitude of a comparatively large and aggressive group of Douglas Democrats in the South.[1] But the ultras were at first disposed to suppress the family quarrels as a matter of expediency, confessing that they were not yet strong enough to succeed with a candidate of their own choice, and admitting that by separation from the Douglas Democrats, they would in all probability saddle an abolitionist upon the country. They were, therefore, apparently in no mood to submit tamely to the ultras from other states in the Charleston Convention, a fact that is clearly evidenced by the repeated warnings in the local press against threatened dissensions and scandals in the Democratic ranks.[2]

Thus, according to press reports, it was apparently understood, at least in the early months of 1860, that the Louisiana delegation would be instructed by the State Convention to support Douglas,[3] because of the realization that a third party candidate could not be elected, and it would be no holiday sport for the Charleston nominee alone "to defeat the motley but thoroughly drilled organization," composed of the "rags, shreds, and patches of all parties, united in opposition to the South."[4]

But the old line Slidell Democrats, always jealous and suspicious of the new line Soulé Democrats and Americans who now advocated the nomination of Douglas, proved to be in the major-

[1]

ity in the State Convention; they rejected the overtures of these Douglas supporters for representation in the Charleston Convention. They, in fact, refused to form any alliance with the Douglas Democrats for fear that they might get control and transfer the vote of the delegation to Douglas, and thereby embarrass the regular Democrats.[5]

The Slidell Democrats, now designated as the Southern Rights party, also defeated resolutions which specified that the delegates should pledge themselves to support the nominee at Charleston, and that nothing should be said about slavery in the territories. By an overwhelming vote they adopted resolutions expressing confidence in the Administration, instructing the delegates to vote as a unit and adhere to the two-thirds rule in the Charleston Convention, and proposing Slidell for the Presidency. They furthermore pledged themselves to support the Southern Rights party nominee and to meet with their sister states in convention in case a "Black Republican" should be elected. In addition, they adopted a resolution which was known subsequently as the "Louisiana Resolution." It specified:

. . . that the territory belongs to the several States as common property and not to individual citizens, thereof; that the Federal Constitution recognizes property in slaves and as such the owner is entitled to carry them into any of the territories, and to hold them there as his property, and if the people by unfriendly legislation or otherwise, should endanger the tenure of such property, or discriminate against it by withholding that protection given to other property in the territories, it is the duty of the General Government to interpose by an active execution of Court Power to secure the rights of the slaveholders.[6]

The Louisiana delegates, headed by former Governor Charles Mouton, became active participants in the proceedings of the Charleston Convention. The idea seems to have obtained among them that their resolution, which purported to give Congressional protection to slavery, would be substituted for the Cincinnati platform. But it elicited only a protracted debate.

Since the resolution represented the extreme Southern attitude, it was of course firmly supported by that group who seemed to have lost, by the nomination of a Southern man, any apprehension, and who now seemed to have little fear of the triumph of a "Black Republican." They reasoned, if press reports are to be credited, that although there were eighteen free states and only fifteen slave states, at least two or three of the free states would not vote with the Republicans; that California and Oregon could certainly be counted on in the House, where the election must eventually be determined; and that under no circumstances, short of flagrant treachery, could a "Black Republican" be elected in that body.[7] Those who subscribed to these views were of course the more optimistic.

When the deadlock ensued, the Louisiana delegates, in obedience to instructions, withdrew. The information was received in Louisiana with varying emotions and anxious forebodings.[8] There were many who believed that the course pursued by the bolting delegation justified "the confidence reposed in them by their constituents." These agreed with the principles enunciated by ex-Governor Mouton, the spokesman of the delegation, when he said: "If we are to fight the 'Black Republicans,' in company with Northern Democracy, we must fight them with the same weapons and exhibit the same front." Since it was obvious to these that there had been a difference that "involved Cardinal and fundamental principles," this Louisiana faction was willing to admit that it no longer belonged to the same party as the Northern Democracy and it was of course unwilling to go through with the election in company with them.[9]

Those who accepted this disruption as being the only logical step to take under these circumstances now acted to express their approval. More than six hundred business and professional men, who were said to have represented practically the entire Democracy of New Orleans, therefore issued a call for a ratification mass meeting for May 12. These representatives of the commercial and industrial interests designated themselves in the call as "the friends of the Constitution, impressed with the necessity of upholding, within the Union, the Constitutional Rights of the several States as the only safeguard against the dissolution of the Confederacy."[10]

The response must have been indeed gratifying to the sponsors. The meeting, reported as the largest ever assembled in the city, was enthusiastic, and unanimous in its endorsement of Louisiana's seceding delegation. The sentiment expressed by the several speakers was that their "interests were indissolubly bound up with those of the planters" in the other states, whose delegates were opposing the doctrine of popular sovereignty to the disruption of the party; that New Orleans, "the great emporium of slave products," was determined to support those seven states which had bolted the Convention; and that their Constitutional rights and demands would be upheld regardless of the costs. As one speaker boldly proclaimed, "in the Union if we can; out of the Union if we must."[11]

The resolutions that were adopted were equally as bold and expressive. They endorsed the "demands of the slavery interests for protection in the territories," commended the Louisiana delegation for refusing to accept "temporary success at the price of principles involving the very existence of our institutions"; and deemed it inexpedient to reassemble the State Convention, since the Baltimore Convention was "not a new, but only an adjourned Convention of the Charleston Convention."[12]

But other contemporaneous events demonstrated that Louisiana did not wholeheartedly endorse the action of the convention delegates. Douglas still had a considerable following, who were not to be conciliated or silenced. This minority, which from the first had apparently opposed extreme action, upon receipt of word of the Charleston disruption, now issued a call through its official organ for a "Union demonstration meeting in opposition to the 'secession action' of the State delegation," and for the further purpose of filling the alleged vacancies.[13] This meeting was held on May 8, but it does not seem to have met with a hearty response. If the opposition press is to be credited, "most of those present were hostile to its purpose."[14] Colonel Isaac Morse, a former disunionist, presided and delivered the principal address, after which a resolution was adopted pledging opposition "to all parties, or fragments of parties, and all aspirants for public office whose claims to public confidence are in any manner identified with disorganization or disunion sentiments and designs."[15]

Meanwhile Pierre Soulé, another former secessionist, espoused the cause of Douglas. It was largely through his influence that another "popular sovereignty" opposition meeting was held on May 19. At this meeting resolutions were passed calling on all who were opposed to division in the Democratic ranks to join in a state-wide call to select delegates to go to Baltimore on June 18. This state convention was directed to meet at Donaldsonville, and each parish was assigned delegates according to the plans formulated by the executive committee.[16]

The Donaldsonville Convention assembled on June 6, with a hundred and forty-nine delegates present in person or by proxy. Twenty of the forty-eight parishes were represented by a membership that was constituted in a large measure of former Whigs and members of the defunct American party. And although it was claimed by the opposition press to be "as unrepresentative of the State Democracy as it was irregular," it elected delegates to Baltimore, and adopted a series of resolutions expressive of its sentiments.

In launching this new "Squatter Sovereignty" party the Douglas wing denounced the bolting of the "seceding delegates as an unwarranted rebellion against that great principle of Democracy and paramount rule of the party discipline, which pledges the assent and submission of the minority to the will and resolves of the majority." The party expressed its preference for the nomination of Douglas at the approaching Baltimore Convention; it subscribed to the doctrine of popular sovereignty; and it condemned the "Louisiana Resolutions," which had demanded protection of the slave interests by Congressional legislation as the "delusive hallucinations of political dreamers."[17]

The organization of the Constitutional Union party during the interval between the adjourned Charleston and Baltimore conventions seems to have met with a most favorable response from its inception. Louisiana had manifested enough interest to send a delegation to the National Convention; moreover, the fact that this Baltimore Convention was a representative body, and that the delegates themselves were men of character, position, and patriotism, seems to have inspired confidence, especially among the conservatives.

The opinion soon crystallized in Louisiana that if Democracy was to be hopelessly divided this Constitutional Union party might be the nucleus of a national party, North and South, composed alike of Whigs, Democrats, and Americans; and that it might be the instrumentality for disrupting and defeating the "Black Republicans."[18] The idea soon became deeply rooted in Conservative circles that this party offered the most attractive ticket to thwart "Black Republicanism," and that it would effect a cordial union of all elements of Democracy with the Union men in securing this much desired end of saving the country from the clutches of Republicanism.[19] Since all signs plainly indicated that the opposition to the sectional party would be divided into three different groups at a time when that party was powerful, aggressive, and confident, conservative friends of the Union in Louisiana apparently resolved to repudiate both wings of the "discordant and wrangling Democrats," and determined to concentrate on the Bell–Everett ticket. Their arguments were plausible: that they must have some ticket acceptable to the conservative sentiment of the country but not obnoxious to the prejudices—whether reasonable or not—of Northern men; and that the Bell–Everett ticket would certainly give victory in several Northern states, to which the united vote of the Southern states could be added, insuring victory over sectionalism and Republicanism. Convinced of the righteousness of their cause these Louisiana "Constitutional Unionists" appealed to the people of Louisiana, and to the South, to "think of the great possibilities in an enlarged spirit of patriotism, and combine."[20]

This appeal was not without its effect in Louisiana. It met with a spontaneous and most cordial response, which was amply attested in a "great outpouring" for the Bell–Everett ratification meeting. Christian Roselius and Randell Hunt, two highly respected citizens, delivered orations. The former spoke upon: "Our rights in the Union, if we can, out of the Union if we must." He reviewed the blessings of the Constitution, and paid his respects to the disturbing elements, North and South—"secession, nullification, abolitionism, and all"—which menaced the Union, under the one head of "demagoguism." Hunt, who followed, denounced the

[6]

corruption of the Democratic administration in what was reported to be an "earnest and impassioned speech." Previously prepared resolutions were then passed, heartily endorsing the Bell–Everett candidacy, and requesting that delegates be elected in all parishes to meet in Baton Rouge on the Fourth of July and there in state convention assembled to nominate a state electoral ticket.[21]

The Louisiana press manifested a keen interest in, and devoted much space to, the Chicago, Baltimore, and Richmond conventions, expressing pleasure, or disgust and contempt at the proceedings in these bodies.[22] It agreed that the "notorious David Wilmot" was an "appropriate choice at Chicago," and gloried in the reported fact that Louisiana was one of the Southern states honored with the storm of hisses and groans of "this insane rabble of traitors and fanatics."[23] Equal resentment continued to be expressed over the disruption of the Democratic party, which now "presented a melancholy spectacle of a house divided against itself, instead of dwelling together in peace and unity." One influential daily even suggested that since the fatal disruption had finally been consummated by the delegates themselves, "instead of patching up an acceptable platform" as they should have done, the most satisfactory solution of this whole difficulty would be the performance by "the entire strength of the company" of the "hari-kari, or happy dispatch."[24]

The Douglas delegation, which had participated in the Baltimore Convention,[25] failed to arouse any degree of enthusiasm upon its return to New Orleans. Nevertheless, the Douglas followers plucked up courage, selected Miles Taylor, a Louisiana congressman, for the chairmanship of the National Democratic Douglas Committee at Washington, and, heartened by the accession and support of former Governor Wickliffe, Mayor Herron, and other citizens of reputation, laid plans for an aggressive campaign.[26]

But they could no longer arouse the old enthusiasm; the name of Douglas had lost its charm. He was suspected of and charged with duplicity, for it was generally believed, according to press reports, that he had proposed to give adherence to the so-called "Black Republican" party in return for the support of that party in his late senatorial canvass for re-election. It was believed that

[7]

he had "attempted to barter away what little of his principles that were left," but that the Republicans had not considered the game worth the candle. Slidell, in the heat of the campaign, even charged that no single act of Douglas had ever been friendly to the South; he prophesied that within a year Douglas would be found inside the "Black Republican" ranks.[27] And, as was to be expected, his "squatter sovereignty doctrine" gained few adherents outside the city of New Orleans and its environs.

The Breckinridge–Lane candidacy was the last to get under way. It rallied to its support the men who no longer had "that tender regard for Northern prejudices." These men had ceased to advocate compromise, contending that all previous compromises had only "encouraged, nourished, and invigorated those Northern prejudices." They now came out boldly against the abolitionists, reasoning that:

If the States of the South were invaded, its citizens murdered, its property destroyed, and its cities delivered over to the merciless torch of the incendiary, while the government was still administered by a friendly Democratic party, what might not be expected in case an avowedly hostile party should secure the reins of government.[28]

Such militant appeal, based on state rights and Democratic principles, gave impetus to the candidacy of Breckinridge and Lane. The younger men in particular enthusiastically espoused the cause. Young Men's Breckinridge–Lane clubs were organized throughout the state, and were reported to have become a "tower of strength" during the closing weeks of the closely contested campaign. In addition, they adopted the militant slogan: "We will not surrender the rights guaranteed to us by the Constitution"; they sponsored many meetings, rallies, processions, and oratorical programs in their efforts to restore harmony in the Democratic ranks, and to inspire confidence in their cause.[29]

These young Democrats finally pressed Senator Slidell into service. His addresses, which were reported to have been marked by "good temper, fairness, justice, and keen analysis," must have influenced that great merchant and capitalistic class with which he was intimately associated. He reasoned that there was great

[8]

danger to the Union should Lincoln triumph, and clearly indicated that it was the duty of the South to secede in that event.[30]

That portion of Slidell's addresses suggesting secession was received with the greatest satisfaction by the young Democrats. But, considered as a whole, his speeches were conservative, in fact too strongly national, and it became necessary to invite William L. Yancey, the author of the "Alabama Platform," who was continually being charged by the Bell supporters in Louisiana with raising the "red flag of disunionism," and with being the prime instigator of secession.

This idea of importing the so-called "orator of secession" seems to have originated with the "Yancey Rangers," a political club organized in October. Such action did not of course meet with the approval of the Bell faction. Nor did it seem to meet with the approval of any considerable element in New Orleans. This fact is amply attested, both by the resentment reflected in the press, and by the results of the election in New Orleans.

In anticipation of Yancey's prospective visit the opposition press proclaimed to the country in defiant tones the intelligence that the "high peaks of our National Union, like the everlasting mountains, shall stand forever and undivided, and indissoluble . . . and this is a straight-out Union city, a city which would become a comparative desert in case a violent separation of the States occurred."[31]

This same press, maintaining its defiant attitude during the visit and after the delivery of the speech, declared that the speech was the "grandest failure of the day." On the contrary the Breckinridge followers and Yancey Rangers declared that Yancey spoke to the "largest audience ever assembled in New Orleans"; that "20,000 voices uprose in earnest plaudits in approval of his manly sentiments" and "in response to his noble appeals of patriotism and honor"; and that the Yancey meeting, and procession that marched through the principal streets, was the "largest and most popular demonstration ever made in New Orleans and the South."[32]

In contrast to this final spurt of the Breckinridge–Lane campaign, which had been up to this time listless and colorless, and in contrast to the apathy of the citizens towards Douglas during the entire election period, the Bell–Everett campaign was waged with vigor. This was especially true in the city, from the earliest to the closing days. Their cause was supported by practically the entire city press; in addition, *The Louisiana Signal,* a Bell–Everett paper, was established by the Louisiana State Central Constitutional Union party to arouse the electorate from its lethargy, and to promote the organization of Bell–Everett clubs.[33]

That the *Signal* accomplished its purpose beyond expectations is evidenced by the number of active political clubs that are listed in its club directory, and from the fact that practically all the prominent business men, and others of high standing and reputation eventually rallied to the Bell–Everett standard.[34]

The appeal of the Bell supporters was irresistible. They were indefatigable in staging processions, public meetings, public speeches, and demonstrations. Bell–Everett clubs were organized throughout the state, and sent in glowing reports of Bell–Everett strength. The central theme of their appeal was that the Union had been the product of the Constitution; that it was "a political edifice, which for wisdom, patriotism, and magnanimity" was without a parallel; and that it was "the strength and security against domestic treason and foreign invasion."[35] Their orators also made the usual effective appeal in the name of Washington, Jefferson, and Jackson for the preservation of the Federal Union. The following was the typical eleventh hour appeal:

Patriots of Louisiana! Patriots of the South! Are you ready to decide the most momentous question that has ever yet been submitted to you? But two short weeks remain. Are you prepared at all points? Have you thoroughly canvassed all your parishes? Have you made arrangements to bring every Bell–Everett voter to the polls? Has no neighborhood been neglected? Has every legitimate influence been brought to bear in favor of the Union cause? Has every solvent argument been employed? Have all you worked as patriots should work, in a crisis like this? If you have, the State of Louisiana is sure for Bell and Everett by a very large majority. But if you have not—if you have left anything undone—employ the next two weeks increasingly and diligently in behalf of your country. The time is short—the emergency is pressing and vital; and the Union

[10]

expects every man to discharge his whole duty. Do it, and earn the gratitude of your countrymen, and the blessings of your God.[36]

Such sensational appeals for the preservation of the Union unquestionably had their effect in Louisiana, and also in the North, in influencing and shaping the public opinion on the later Louisiana situation throughout the Civil War and reconstruction period.

With this paramount question of the preservation of the Union as its central theme the Bell–Everett group never faltered, but approached the end of the contest with supreme confidence that it would poll an overwhelming vote in Louisiana, unless frauds on a stupendous scale were practised. This confidence is clearly reflected in the final grand Bell–Everett demonstration on the night before the election, on which occasion all the score or more of "clubs paraded, banners waved, bouquets were presented, bands played, and cannons boomed."

The "memorable celebration" was made brilliant, according to the *Daily Delta*, by the fair sex who participated, by the illuminations, by illustrations, and by immense displays and floats. A platform had been erected in front of the Clay monument on Canal Street; crowds formed in four grand divisions and marched through the principal streets to this place of rendezvous where it is reported "the cheering and enthusiasm knew no bounds." "The crowds of ladies and gentlemen," according to press reports of this same daily, "waved handkerchiefs, threw wreaths of flowers, and expressed heartiest sentiments of approval." In short, it was described as "one of the most imposing and gorgeous processions that was ever witnessed in New Orleans," and the orator, Randell Hunt, was reported to have electrified the throngs as he "grew eloquent over the Union and figurative about the Stars and Stripes."[37]

The early election returns only served to increase the confidence of the Bell–Everett adherents, and to dash completely the hopes of the so-called disunionists. The city gave the Bell–Everett ticket a vote of 5,215, and the Breckinridge Democrats only 2,645 votes, or approximately a two-to-one lead for Bell, almost one-

[11]

tenth of the votes of the state, as the official votes were to reveal. Furthermore the Breckinridge–Lane ticket ran a poor third in New Orleans in this triangular race. (There was no Lincoln electoral ticket, and consequently no Lincoln votes.) Douglas polled 2,998 votes. The tabulation showed that the conservatives had swept the city, the so-called disunionists, or secessionist group, actually receiving less than 25 per cent of the total city vote. But belated returns gave the "disunionists" the state by a narrow margin, and turned the headquarters of the Bell supporters into a place of sorrow.[38]

But the sadness and joy of both winners and losers were said to have turned into "gloom" when the telegraph brought the intelligence that the Republican candidate had been elected. This information "cast a pall over the city," and the minds of all parties, irrespective of past differences and bitternesses, were reported to have been filled with "deep anxiety and forebodings."[39] In fact, in the common sorrow over this calamity, all past political differences apparently disappeared. But there was at first little outspoken secession sentiment. Instead, a disposition was manifested to deliberate and to adopt a watchful waiting policy.[40]

A large group was of course pondering and debating secession. Some asserted that the North would never permit such action; still others, guided by mercenary motives, opposed such a revolutionary movement on the grounds of expediency, and professed to see no danger of aggression on the part of the North. Such submission sentiments had been expressed by the more conservative press, which had sensed defeat even before the election,[41] and now its first impulse seems to have been, not to judge Lincoln too hastily, but to wait for any "overt act, after inauguration" and to believe that the administration of a "Black Republican" would not necessarily mean an aggressive policy toward the South. The more extreme conservatives even asserted that a policy of withdrawal under such circumstances was downright "iniquitous and fallacious"; that it would be "unprecedented, unjustifiable and without the shadow of an excuse" to act before the newly elected President should express his purpose; that the "wrongs were as yet only prospective"; that "in any event, disunion was a perilous, and desperate remedy to be invoked only against intolerable wrongs"; and that "Constitutional remedies should first be resorted to, to preserve the Union, and not gunpowder," at least "until it became plainly evident that the new regime aimed at Southern humiliation and destruction." In fine, the influential press of Louisiana, and a large majority of the people, while admitting the right of secession, were still strong advocates of conciliatory measures, remonstrances, and forbearance in order to save the Union. They would preserve and perpetuate it by pouring the oil of Unionism in the South upon the troubled waters of sectionalism in the North.

But this did not include all, for there was an aggressive minority, which had been cheered by an advance in the price of sugar and a steady cotton market in the face of such adverse election returns, and which was more than ever confident of controlling the cotton markets of the world. This group now boldly warned the North that it must look out for the whirlwind that it had sown.[42]

The official election returns, tabulated parish by parish, appeared four weeks later, and at a time when the minds of the Louisiana citizens were deeply absorbed in the more important problems of the impending crisis. For this reason their significance and their influence on restoration policies have generally been overlooked. But a study of the vote is highly illuminating. The appended map (No. 1) reveals that the victor carried thirty-six of the forty-eight parishes, but secured only 22,681 votes, a bare majority over Bell, who polled a total of 20,204 and carried only nine parishes. The conservative Douglas faction polled 7,625 votes, but led in only the three parishes of Ascension, Assumption, and Lafourche, all located in the former strong Whig slaveholding parishes. Approximately half of the Douglas vote can be attributed to his New Orleans strength. The Bell strength, which was also composed almost entirely of the so-called Unionists, was confined almost entirely to the city and the nearby river parishes where the conservative Whig planter elements resided. In fact, this Bell ticket carried only two parishes in the northern part of the state, Ouachita and Madison, both river parishes in which the Whig planter element predominated. It did, however, poll a heavy vote in all the parishes bordering on the Red, Ouachita, and Mississippi rivers, where the population was more compact.

The sparsely settled hill and pine-barren parishes in the northern part of the state between the rivers were as usual the Democratic strongholds. The same sentiment prevailed in the pine-barren and prairie parishes of the central, west, and south; the northern tier of sparsely settled pine flat Florida parishes was as usual in the Democratic column.

The total vote, 50,510,[43] is also significant, because it became the basis of Lincoln's ten per cent reconstruction plan. Of this total, the Bell vote was more than two-fifths of the state. If the conservative Douglas vote is added to this, the total becomes more than three-fifths of the entire vote. In other words the extreme Southern Rights element could lay claim to only two-fifths of the votes in the state.

Considered from another angle, the Constitutional Union party of Bell polled 5,216 votes in the city, which was approximately the required one-tenth vote under the Lincoln plan. If to this the Douglas city vote is added, the conservative total would be 8,213 of the 10,858 votes cast, or approximately eighty per cent of the city vote.[44] In fine, the Bell party attempted to make the issue union or secession, and on the face of these returns, it would appear that only the Douglas vote, which was heavily conservative, prevented the success of the Bell–Everett ticket in Louisiana. It did not prevent them from making the apparently logical claim that the majority vote was strongly for the Union.

The conclusion, based on election returns, was that New Orleans and all this southeast section of Louisiana bordering on the Mississippi River, where the majority of the Louisiana votes were to be found, was overwhelmingly Union in sentiment. The vote was interpreted as a moral Union victory.[45] On the basis of such interpretation President Lincoln later selected what seemed to be the most promising city and state in which to inaugurate his restoration policy under his ten per cent plan. A close study, however, of the votes cast for Bell, Douglas, and Breckinridge shows that union, or secession, was not the issue, and that Lincoln's position was based on false logic.

[14]

MAP No. 1

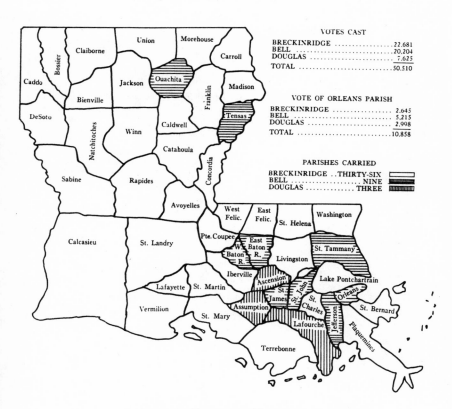

VOTES CAST

BRECKINRIDGE 22,681
BELL 20,204
DOUGLAS 7,625
TOTAL 50,510

VOTE OF ORLEANS PARISH

BRECKINRIDGE 2,645
BELL 5,215
DOUGLAS 2,998
TOTAL 10,858

PARISHES CARRIED

BRECKINRIDGE ..THIRTY-SIX
BELL ....NINE
DOUGLAS ....THREE

PRESIDENTIAL ELECTION IN LOUISIANA IN 1860

In Louisiana, and in the South as a whole, many Unionists *per se* voted for Breckinridge—as, for example, in East Tennessee, North Carolina, and Virginia; on the other hand, a majority of disunionists *per se* voted for Breckinridge. As for those who supported Bell or Breckinridge over the South as a whole, and in Louisiana in particular, the great majority—for example, Bell himself—later advocated secession or revolution when Lincoln failed to accept the Crittenden compromise, and similar compromises, which were considered as a just redress of Southern grievances.[46]

CHAPTER II

LOUISIANA SECEDES

At the beginning of the secession movement, Louisiana was without doubt the most conservative of the Gulf states. But a fact that has been generally overlooked is that this sentiment, especially in New Orleans, shortly underwent what appeared to be a tremendous change. Many of the so-called Union party now reversed themselves. Immediately following their defeat some of this Bell–Everett group emphatically declared that they had made the last compromise for nationality, and had cast their last conservative vote; that they would no longer be diverted, or seduced. And when the "Party of the South" was organized, a few days after the election, its auxiliary, a military organization which was given the title of "Minute Men," was said to have been largely constituted of members of the late Constitutional Union party. There were other signs of a change. It was observed that there were fewer expressions of devotion to the Union, and submissionists were no longer outspoken. Nor had the city, as was predicted, been precipitated into a frenzy of Unionism after the election. On the contrary public sentiment seems to have responded heartily to the decisive action of South Carolina.[1]

The North in particular seems to have failed to take two other factors into account. These were the character and temper of this highly volatile Latin population, and the extravagance of Louisiana's politicians, especially the Bell supporters, who had proclaimed in the heat of the campaign a devotion to Unionism and an animosity to secession, and whose actions were shortly to belie their words. These politicians had, it seems, for good or evil, unwittingly led the Northern press and Northern public to a belief. that Louisiana would not defend the institution of slavery; that she would not only submit, but, to employ a much used and abused quotation, "could not be kicked out of the Union." As a matter of fact, as has been said, the issue between Bell and Breckinridge was not union and secession, but a contest rather between radical or moderate groups who followed Breckinridge and conservative groups who followed Bell. The bulk of both groups agreed that the grievances of the South must be settled or the South would have to secede. The Bell followers were willing to exhaust every effort at a settlement in the Union; whereas many of the Breckinridge party, the ultras or Southern Rights men, considered that all efforts at settlement were exhausted by the election of Lincoln. Neither party was unionist or secessionist *per se,* though each party contained both unionists *per se* and secessionists *per se.*

The emergency contemplated by the legislature that had met in January, 1860, in Baton Rouge, had, in the opinion of many, now arisen. There was a persistent and growing demand to have the governor assemble the state legislature to secure co-operation on the part of Louisiana with the other Southern states. He was urged to make a special call so that the Louisiana representatives in Congress could be given full authority and instructions to act with other Southern representatives in the December session.[2]

Nor could this spirit be conciliated. Douglas, it was believed, might be able to do so; accordingly he was invited to come to New Orleans for the expressed purpose of convincing its citizens that there would be an anti-Lincoln majority in Congress, and that the Constitution afforded a remedy for every grievance. But his visit evidently added fuel to the flames. A feeling of hostility had been manifested toward him in the recent election, and it was once more reflected in a greater measure by the press, which declared that he was an "egotistic worn out political hack." The people were in fact at last demanding more heroic action, and his nostrums were dismissed with the declaration that "if the people of the South should adopt Mr. Douglas' recommendations and trust their cause to the nominal anti-Lincoln majority in Congress, they will consummate a long course of weak and unwise concessions and surrenders, by this crowning act of imbecility and pusillanimity."[3]

Louisiana, according to press reports, had another grievance at this time. It was the fact that the name of Louisiana was being omitted in almost all the lists of the states which were "paraded in the Northern journals" as co-operationists in the great Southern movements. Such action was denounced by the *Daily Crescent* as "a most pitiable delusion of the Northern press and people." The governor's action now announced to the country that Louisiana would not lag behind her sister states, and would not this time allow South Carolina to stand alone.[4]

Governor Moore had hesitated only a few days after the election, while waiting to see what the public sentiment of the state, its duties, and its interests required to be done.[5] The Louisiana constitution—and in fact the constitutions of all other slaveholding states—contained no specific provisions in regard to the calling of conventions, either as original exponents of sovereignty in political matters, or for the less grave functions of amending or changing the constitution itself. True, Louisiana and the other states had provided for submitting amendments, in a guarded form, to the people at a general election. But with these notable exceptions, no slaveholding state had provided any mode for the calling of conventions, nor had imposed any limitations on the general powers of the legislature. But the Louisiana Legislature had provided for just this contingency; and now, while the governor hesitated, and deliberated, he received petitions, signed by thousands, memorializing him to convene the legislature in special session. The following, which appeared in a local paper, seems to be typical and expressive of the predominating sentiment:

The undersigned, your memorialists, citizens of New Orleans, and of the State of Louisiana, deeply impressed with the conviction that the result of the recent election for President of the United States, in electing a Black Republican to that high office, is evidence of a deep seated hostility on the part of the North, towards our State in common with the other states of the South, and in view of the fact that many of our *sister States are taking counsel* through their Legislatures, as to what shall be done in this emergency, would respectfully request your Excellency to convene the Legislature of our State at as early a day as practicable, to take such measures as they may deem necessary and proper to vindicate and secure our rights.[6]

And now at last in obedience to what he conceived to be an overwhelming sentiment on the part of his constituency, the Governor issued his proclamation in which he incorporated the following reasons for convening the extraordinary session of the legislature:

And whereas the election of Abraham Lincoln . . . by a sectional and

[18]

aggressive anti-slavery party, whose hostility to the people and institutions of the South has been evidenced by repeated and long continued violations of Constitutional obligations and fraternal amity, now consummated by this last insult and outrage perpetrated at, and through the ballot-box, does . . . furnish an occasion . . . and the necessity for self-preservation requires us to deliberate upon our own course of action . . . I do convene the Legislature in extraordinary session. . . .[7]

During the interval between the issuing of this proclamation and the meeting of the legislature there were several signs to indicate the rapid concentration of public opinion around the point of resistance to the domination of what the press termed "Black Republicanism." This fact was demonstrated by the organization of "The Southern Rights Association of The State of Louisiana," and the establishment of a number of auxiliary branches over the state. Its membership seems to have consisted of the most substantial citizens, who proposed immediate secession.[8] Its roster showed that old party lines were now being ignored, and that old divisions and animosities were being forgotten in the eagerness of almost all to embrace the platform of the "Southern Rights party, Southern honor, and Southern independence." No group seems to have manifested this spirit in a greater degree than the late Bell–Everett Union clubs, notably the Mount Vernon Club, which had earned a reputation in the recent election for its energy, efficiency, and devotion to the cause of the Union.[9]

The influential ministers of the city also expressed what was now, at least to all outward appearances, the universal sentiments of their community. The Rev. Mr. Henderson, Dr. W. T. Leacock, and Dr. B. M. Palmer were the outspoken pulpit orators in the advocacy of Southern rights and resistance to the North. The latter unquestionably exerted a profound influence when he spoke "befitting . . . the solemnities of the judgment day," and upheld the institution of slavery as the foundation of all the material interests of the South. His appeal for Southern resistance on the grounds that the North was reaping all the profits arising from manufacturing and commerce seems to have been most effective.[10] This series of sermons was followed by the militant "address" of the executive committee of the Southern Rights Association to the people of Louisiana urging them to elect men of integrity to a convention, which would advocate the creation of a Southern Republic among the cotton states. It concluded with a warning that "vassalage, impoverishment and degradation will be the lot of all submissionists."[11]

The reaction, as was to be expected, was indicated by the apparent solidification of a spirit of resistance to Lincoln, and the formation and equipment of military clubs, rifle clubs, musket clubs, minute men clubs, and cavalry and infantry units by the parishes throughout the state. In short, if press reports are to be credited, the opinion was now fast crystallizing that the time for compromise had definitely passed.[12] This opinion seems to have been materially strengthened in Louisiana by the news that the Republican speaker had shown the "total insincerity of the entire compromise project" by appointing on the Congressional Committee of Thirty-three only Union men and the repudiated Douglas leaders, instead of men identified with the cause of the South.[13]

The extraordinary session of the legislature convened on December 10 and completed its labors in a harmonious three days' session. In addition to the call for a convention, it passed a bill appropriating $500,000 to be placed in the hands of a military board, which was authorized to arm the state and to organize, equip, and arm the militia. The convention act passed both houses by a unanimous vote after its sponsor, Senator Talbot of Iberville parish, explained on the floor of the Senate that "the object and aim of the Convention was secession."[14] There was noticeable the same division among the legislators that was shortly to be found among their constituents in regard to the comparative merits of separate and co-operative action; yet according to the records, not a voice was raised against secession.[15] Neither was a protest raised, nor a vote cast against a final resolution, which called for a "Union of the South for the benefit of the South."[16]

Preliminary meetings held shortly after the legislature adjourned clearly foreshadowed a spirited election for delegates. But the issue was not secession, that is, whether the state should or should not go out of the Union. That Louisiana would secede

[20]

seems to have been a foregone conclusion. The issue voiced in the press was the method of secession. This accounts largely for the two tickets: the "co-operationists," the large majority of whom favored secession but strongly advocated united Southern state action in the hope of attempting compromise before taking the final step; and the other secession group, composed of those who favored immediate action by the separate states, and who were designated as "immediate secessionists." This latter faction was dominated by the Southern Rights Association. Under its auspices they now not only selected a complete ticket of avowed secessionists, who were pledged to act without co-operation or consultation with the other Southern states, but also selected and enthusiastically unfurled from their headquarters the pelican flag of independent Louisiana, which signified their demands that the state resume her sovereign and independent rights.[17]

The co-operationist faction proceeded with more deliberation and counsel. It was composed, as has been noted, of those citizens who were as yet opposed to resorting to the extreme step of separate action. Its ticket was therefore selected in a caucus of the conservative leaders, but submitted to mass meetings for ratification.[18] The deliberations in these meetings revealed shades of belief that made any effective co-operative action impossible. The extreme right, which at heart opposed secession, feared to "close the mouths of that great inland sea to the interior commerce of more than a dozen great commonwealths, and thereby turn the commerce of this great Northwest towards the East,"—a fear that was to be realized. The members also feared that, as secessionists, they would never be allowed to hold the mouths of the Mississippi, —a fear which, as events soon demonstrated, was also not entirely groundless.[19] But most of this group of conservatives seem to have had no scruples against secession and revolution as the ultimate remedy, but opposed a policy of separate state action as both dangerous and too precipitate. Their position was best stated by Pierre Soulé, who presumed to speak for the more than seven thousand Douglas constituents. His card, which appeared in the local press during the canvass, not only denied the charge made in the heat of the canvass by the immediate secessionists that the co-operationists were submissionists, but clarified their position.

I am no submissionist [Soulé said], I hold that resistance to actual wrong is a paramount duty with States, as well as individuals. . . . There are, however, men who urge the expediency of separate action on the part of the States, and who advocate openly the policy of precipitating Louisiana of herself, and without seeking concert with other States, into the vo[r]tex of revolution!!

Having therefore to choose between ignominy or revolution, I am for revolution! . . . but not for an inconsiderate and dishevelled revolution.

I am for keeping Louisiana in concert and union with her sister states of the South. In other words, I am in favor of the State Convention sending discreet and experienced commissioners to commune with the other States, and adopt, in concert with them, such measures as may palliate, if not avert, the dangers which I see ahead of us in a proximate future.[20]

The attitude of other prominent Louisiana leaders just at this crisis merits consideration because of subsequently repeated charges of "a deep laid conspiracy" on their part to carry the state out of the Union. In a public oration Judge Charles Gayarré, a statesman, orator, scholar, and historian, revealed his position by explaining that just as concert before action had been impossible between the thirteen colonies, so was it now impossible between the Southern states, because events were crowding upon each other. "The fourth of March," he dramatically concluded, "is rushing upon the citizens like a fiery steed; and deliberation must now give way to action when Barbarians are at the foot of the capitol."[21]

The two Louisiana senators, the alleged leaders of the so-called conspiracy, also expressed their respective positions in no uncertain terms. Senator Slidell, alluding to the Congressional circular that was being distributed over the country, wrote to a friend as follows: "By speedy separation I mean the earliest possible declaration that our separation will take place on the fourth of March, this declaration to be unconditional."[22] Nor did Senator Benjamin, who wrote from Washington to the Louisiana Legislature, equivocate. He requested that the declarations of his opinions be given as wide publicity as possible, and in accordance with this

[22]

expressed desire his letter, the more pertinent parts of which follow, appeared in the New Orleans papers:

1. That the feeling of a very large number, if not a majority, of the people of the North, is hostile to our interests; that this feeling has been instilled into the present generation. . . .

2. That no just reason exists for hoping for any change in Northern feelings, and no prospect remains of our being permitted to live in peace and security within the Union.

3. That, therefore, the interest of the South, the very instinct of self-preservation demands a prompt severance of all connections with a government which has itself become an obstacle to what it was designed to effect, viz: "insuring *domestic* tranquility, and promoting general welfare!"

4. That to effect this purpose *separate State action is virtually necessary;* that all attempts at concerted action should be reserved for the work of reconstructing a government. . . . The emergency does not admit of this delay, unless the South is prepared to submit to the degradation of seeing Lincoln peacefully inaugurated as its President as well as that of the North. . . .

Indeed, if the faithful and persistent efforts of the present distinguished Chief Magistrate, so to administer the Government as to give us safety within the Union have been rendered fruitless by the operation of the causes above suggested, we must be blind indeed, if we entertain the remotest hope that widespread ruin, degradation and dishonor will not inevitably result from tame submission to the rule which our enemies propose to inaugurate. . . .[23]

Other forces, North and South, were contributing factors to this growing sense of hostility. The alarming telegraphic news from Charleston relative to the forts, and press reports on the feasibility of coercion were given great publicity in New Orleans and keyed up the populace to greater excitement and resentment. Articles in the more radical New York press in which the Southern people were branded as "a band of desperadoes, half-civilized, and half-crazed" were also given a greater prominence in some of the New Orleans journals than they merited; legal opinions to the effect that "Louisiana could not go out of the Union" also added some fuel to the flames. But the news articles that seem to have carried greatest weight were those alleging that the Federal forces were

[23]

about to be directed against the sovereign state of South Carolina, in which the Federal laws were considered as having ceased to exist.[24] Many doubting Thomases now became eleventh hour converts to the position that there was no longer any reason for delay. And it was at this time, a time when the populace of New Orleans was aroused to a high emotional state, that the election for delegates to the state convention took place. Representative and senatorial districts were used as units in electing delegates; this followed the pattern for electing the state legislature.

The result was most decisive for the immediate secession ticket in the city, where the election, according to press reports, was attended without undue excitement and with no difficulties. The entire senatorial delegation of five, and sixteen out of a possible twenty on the representative slate of New Orleans, were elected to the convention as immediate secessionists. But the vote on the issue of secession, that is on co-operative or immediate secession, or on the expediency of such action at all, is most difficult to ascertain. This difficulty is the more readily understood when it is recalled that the city was divided into five senatorial districts, that this same geographic division was subdivided into twenty representative districts, and that the electorate was voting for candidates in both districts at the same time. It was possible, however, to calculate the average majority for immediate secession in these districts by taking the votes for the individual candidates on the two tickets. The average majority was given as three hundred and ninety-seven in the city for immediate secession.[25]

A more detailed study reveals the hopelessness of arriving at any accurate totals on any issue for either the city or the state. In addition to senatorial districts, and the representative districts embraced in them, it must be remembered that each faction was entitled to more than one candidate in many districts throughout the state. This made it possible for the voter to vote a split ticket, and it is only reasonable to suppose that he did vote such a ticket, due doubtless to a misunderstanding of issues and the personal appeals of certain candidates.

Still another element that must be considered in any attempt to compute totals was the fact that several immediate secession candidates had no opposition. This of course resulted in a light vote being cast for such immediate secessionists. In many other parishes where sentiment appeared to be strong for immediate secession, and where the co-operationists had revealed little or no strength, the immediate secessionists did not poll their real strength, for the simple reason that there was no need to do so in order to win. This was certainly true in the many regular Democratic parishes.

But regardless of the results in the country parishes the fact remained—a fact that has generally been overlooked—that the great commercial metropolis of the Southwest had voted overwhelmingly for immediate secession and Southern independence only a few weeks after it had voted just as overwhelmingly for the Constitutional Union party of Bell;[26] and this city vote was at the time considered decisive. Even the *Picayune*, which was considered one of the most conservative daily papers of the South, concluded immediately after the city election results had been announced that "the city vote prefigures the vote of the State." In fact, the only hope of the conservatives had been in carrying the city. The same daily now reluctantly admitted that there was "no Union party left in Louisiana," and pessimistically concluded: "There is hardly a sacrifice consistent with honor and safety that ought not to have been made to avert the deplorable evil. But no chance is left."[27]

A tabulated parish by parish vote of the state seems to have been published in more than one New Orleans paper, and other sources give some election totals, but they probably are not official.[28] The vote of the co-operationists and the immediate secessionists was in fact so close in some instances, especially in the former Whig strongholds, and the means of determining the results in remote districts so meager, that it was some time before the official roster of delegates could be made public. Furthermore, the vote for each delegate elected and for each defeated candidate was not given at this time. Neither could any definite statement be given as to the actual sentiments of all the delegates because, as has been stated, several had no opponents, and a few who won were listed as doubtful or uninstructed where the issues had not

[25]

been clearly drawn.[29] The election results in the twenty-one senatorial districts, which elected thirty-one delegates, give what might
be considered at least a fair index to the real sentiment. Twenty-
one of these thirty-one delegates were listed in the press as "immediate secessionists," and the other ten as "co-operationists."[30]

A study of the data on map No. 2, which gives the senatorial
results, reveals the strength of the two factions of secessionists in
the various sections. It shows that the immediate secessionists carried thirteen and the co-operationists carried eight of the twenty-
one senatorial districts. It would also indicate that the immediate
secessionists carried twenty-nine parishes, including Orleans, with
its solid senatorial delegation, and that the co-operationists carried
nineteen parishes. This may or may not have been true, for, due to
grouping, a parish with a heavy majority could have overcome opposite majorities in other parishes in its group. But it does demon-
strate that all of the Western Louisiana parishes and all of the
North Louisiana parishes, except the six that sent only three delegates, and practically all the Florida parishes, together with the
city of New Orleans, voted for immediate secession, whereas the
old Conservative Whig, river, plantation, slaveholding parishes,
south and southwest of New Orleans, together with a few conservative central river parishes, and the six mentioned above, adhered
to the cause of the co-operationists. These old Whig parishes were,
as a rule, more populous, and usually cast a heavier vote than the
more numerous but less densely populated Democratic parishes.
However, the heavy majorities in the city would be expected to offset any majorities in these more densely populated parishes of the
southeast.

A study of the returns for the representative districts, which
elected ninety-nine delegates, reveals that the various sections of
the state voted almost as they did in the senatorial grouping. Map
No. 3 shows that the co-operationists carried nineteen, the same
number of parishes as in the senatorial grouping, and that the
parishes were, with but few exceptions, the same parishes as
before. The two factions, however, secured an equal number of
delegates in St. Landry and East Feliciana. The parish of Orleans also returned a split delegation, the co-operationists securing

MAP. No. 2

SENATORIAL DISTRICTS CARRIED

IMMEDIATE SECESSIONISTS 13
CO-OPERATIVE SECESSIONISTS 8

DELEGATES ELECTED

THE NINETEEN SHADED PARISHES
ELECTED TEN "CO-OPERATIVE SECES-
SIONISTS." THE REMAINING PAR-
ISHES ELECTED TWENTY-ONE "IMME-
DIATE SECESSIONISTS."

THE TWENTY-ONE SENATORIAL DIS-
TRICTS ELECTED THIRTY-ONE DELE-
GATES.

ELECTION RESULTS TO THE "SECESSION" CONVENTION ON A SENATORIAL BASIS

four, while the secessionists annexed seventeen more delegates, raising their total senatorial and representative votes to eighty; whereas the co-operationists claimed a total of forty-five; the other five were listed as doubtful.[31]

Press reports indicate that in the interval between this convention election and the convening of the delegates, a number of events occurred which still further stimulated enthusiasm for the secession movement and swept the state "towards the goal of secession." Perhaps no event contributed more to the solidification of this secession sentiment in Louisiana than a speech that Senator Benjamin delivered at this time in the United States Senate. "This telling blow," according to his biographer, was hailed "as the ablest speech ever delivered by this distinguished Louisianian." It did, in fact, create a profound impression throughout the country, and more particularly in his own state, where it was given wide publicity.[32] A minute description of his manner of delivery, and the effect, was given by a correspondent of the *Philadelphia Evening Bulletin,* and copied in the New Orleans papers. Benjamin was portrayed in this report as having read from a written paper in a measured, legal tone.[33]

It was, however, the eloquent conclusion that produced the alleged sensation. In it he summed up his argument, giving the causes of the differences, and spoke calmly of the approaching dissolution and conflict that he felt certain would ensue. He coolly enumerated the horrors of civil war, and alluded to the probability of the South's not being able to defend itself. As he came to his conclusion he had one hand in his pocket, the other negligently toying with a vest chain. He now balanced his head a little, to and fro, and his black eyes showed all the emotion he must have felt as he said:

. . . What may be the fate of this horrible contest, no man can tell, and none pretend to foresee; but this much I will say: the fortune of war may be adverse to our armies; you may carry desolation to our peaceful land, and with torch and fire you may set our cities in flames; you may even emulate the atrocities of those who in the war of the revolution hounded on the blood-thirsty savage to an attack upon the defenseless frontier; you may, under the protection of your advancing armies,

[27]

give shelter to the furious fanatics, who desire and profess to desire, nothing more than to add all the horrors of a servile insurrection to the calamities of civil war; you may do all this—and more, too, if more there be, but you never can subjugate us; you never can convert the free sons of the soil into vassals, paying tribute to your power; and you never, never can degrade them to the level of an inferior, and servile race, never! never!!³⁴

This repetition of the word "never" was reported to have been as free from emotion as if he had been insisting on some simple point of law, which could not possibly have been decided in any different way; but free from emotion as it was, it produced the greatest effect. The whole gallery on all sides "burst out as in one voice, in uncontrollable applause."³⁵

The belligerent tone of Governor Moore's message to the legislature, which met the day before the convention assembled, foreshadowed the action of that body upon the momentous question. After a brief allusion to the healthy condition of the treasury and the satisfactory condition of the railways and banking, he launched into his central theme: secession and war. He was convinced that the people of Louisiana had decreed secession, and he shared the sentiments of Benjamin, Slidell, and Beauregard (the last–named had recently returned from the North), that the "erring sisters" would not be allowed to depart in peace. He said:

. . . the vote of the people has confirmed the faith of the executive . . . that the individual sentiment of the state is for immediate and effective resistance, and there is not found within her limits any difference of sentiments, except as to minor points of expediency. . . . Throughout the borders of Louisiana we are one people . . . a people with one heart and one mind . . . who cannot be subdued.

He spoke of the cry in the North for coercion, and added that "the conflict shall come" as a result of "tyrannical purposes."³⁶

The concluding paragraphs of his message were an explanation and justification of his course in seizing with the state militia all the places recently occupied by Federal troops, a course that was promptly commended by the legislature in a resolution unqualifiedly approving of the "prompt, wise, and energetic action

MAP No. 3

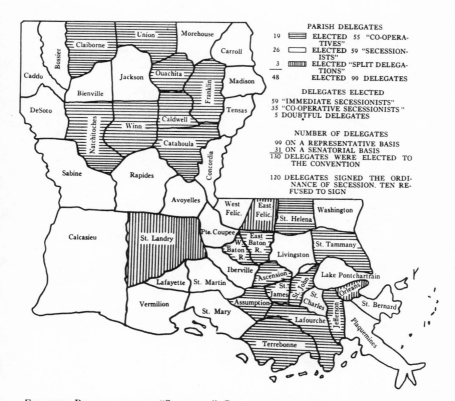

PARISH DELEGATES

19 [≡≡] ELECTED 55 "CO-OPERA-
TIVES"
26 [☐] ELECTED 59 "SECESSION-
ISTS"
3 [▦] ELECTED "SPLIT DELEGA-
TIONS"
48 ELECTED 99 DELEGATES

DELEGATES ELECTED

59 "IMMEDIATE SECESSIONISTS"
35 "CO-OPERATIVE SECESSIONISTS"
5 DOUBTFUL DELEGATES

NUMBER OF DELEGATES

99 ON A REPRESENTATIVE BASIS
31 ON A SENATORIAL BASIS
130 DELEGATES WERE ELECTED TO
THE CONVENTION

120 DELEGATES SIGNED THE ORDI-
NANCE OF SECESSION. TEN RE-
FUSED TO SIGN

ELECTION RESULTS TO THE "SECESSION" CONVENTION ON A REPRESENTATIVE BASIS

of the Governor" in securing to the state the possession of the arsenals and forts within the state.

Acting upon the Governor's recommendations the legislature passed several important acts which provided for transferring the regular military forces of the state to the Confederacy, for equipping and promoting the formation of military companies, and for providing for the general expenses of the state. It also again expressed its secession sentiments in a joint resolution, which declared that:

Secession is unquestionably reserved to the state to be exercised without molestation and any attempts to coerce or force a sovereign State will be viewed by the people of Louisiana, as well on her own account, as of her sister Southern States, as a hostile invasion and resisted to the utmost extent.[37]

Nor was there manifested, to any appreciable extent, any spirit of Unionism by the convention that now assembled in Baton Rouge on January 23, 1861, the day after the legislature convened. Only two weeks had elapsed since the election of the delegates, but, as appeared from the subsequent proceedings, a marked change had taken place during these few days as to the policy of immediate secession.[38] Whether this change can be attributed to a bold and industrious policy of organization on the part of the immediate secession group to create pressure of pretended public opinion, in order to commit co-operation delegates to their policy, as was charged later, it is impossible to say. But the fact remains that practically all visible elements of opposition to immediate secession had vanished.

With one hundred and twenty-three members present and seven absent the body organized by electing J. C. Perkins, of Lafourche parish, temporary chairman, and ex-Governor Mouton of St. Landry parish and J. T. Wheat of New Orleans, as permanent president and permanent secretary, respectively. If a spirit of division or of Unionism existed, it did not enter into this election, for Mouton was elected by an overwhelming majority and Wheat received a unanimous vote.[39]

The first matters of consequence to engage the attention of

the body were the reading of communications from the national delegation, the reception of the South Carolina and Alabama commissioners, and the appointment of a committee of fifteen to draft a suitable ordinance of secession. The two commissioners, ex-Governor Manning of South Carolina and Governor Winston of Alabama, who were waiting outside the bar, were invited to deliver addresses; both responded by soliciting the co-operation of Louisiana in the formation of a Southern Confederacy. They spoke in glowing terms of the future of such a Confederation, and urged the state to send delegates at once to the Montgomery Convention.[40] The "communication" was a joint letter from Senators John Slidell and J. P. Benjamin, and two of Louisiana's four congressmen, T. G. Davidson and John M. Landrum. It was addressed directly to the convention, and since it purported to give an authentic account of conditions at Washington, and suggestions as to the proper method of procedure on the part of the convention, it must have unquestionably influenced the deliberations and acts of that body. It also illustrated how rapidly the logic of events was precipitating the country into revolution by insisting that:

The time for argument has passed, that of action has arrived; we have now to deal with events as they are, not to discuss principles. . . . Scott is well known to have submitted to the Executive a plan of a campaign on a gigantic scale for the subjugation of the seceding states. . . . We recommend immediate and unqualified secession. . . . It is . . . a matter of expediency. . . . We firmly believe if our action is prompt and decided every slave-holding state will sustain us. This declaration should be accompanied by immediate action, and we recommend that all the seceding states shall meet at Montgomery, Alabama, on a day, not later than the 15th of February, for the purpose of forming a provisional government; and we invite you to pass in such form as you may deem proper, a recognition that the navigation of the Mississippi shall be free to the citizens of every State whose waters find their way to the Gulf of Mexico."[41]

The committee of fifteen, acting promptly, reported an ordinance on January 25, which remained unchanged, and shortly thereafter became the instrument that carried the state out of the Union. It follows:

[30]

AN ORDINANCE

To dissolve the union between the State of Louisiana and other States united with her, under the compact entitled "The Constitution of the United States of America."

We, the people of the State of Louisiana, in Convention assembled, do declare and ordain, and it is hereby declared and ordained, That the Ordinance passed by us in Convention on the 22d day of November, in the year eighteen hundred and eleven whereby the Constitution of the United States of America, and the amendments of the said Constitution, were adopted; and all laws and ordinances by which the State of Louisiana became a member of the Federal Union, be and the same are hereby repealed and abrogated; and that the Union now subsisting between Louisiana and the other States, under the name of "The United States of America," is hereby dissolved.

We do further declare and ordain, That the State of Louisiana hereby resumes all rights and powers heretofore delegated to the Government of the United States of America; That her citizens are absolved from all allegiance to said government; and that she is in full possession and exercise of all those rights of sovereignty which appertain to a free and independent State.

We do further declare and ordain, That all rights acquired and vested under the Constitution of the United States or any act of Congress, or treaty, or under any law of the State, and not incompatible with this Ordinance shall remain in force, and have the same effect as if this Ordinance had not been passed.[42]

But this ordinance did not pass unchallenged, for J. A. Rozier, a co-operationist and so-called Unionist, proposed a lengthy substitute, the pertinent parts of which follow:

Whereas, during many years past, associations and large bodies of citizens of the non-slaveholding States have evinced and carried out the steady purpose of assailing, by all the means they can employ, the peculiar institution of the Southern States, and have aided the attack by vituperative addresses, and speeches, by abolition petitions to Congress, by inflammatory discourses and by exaggerated appeals to the prejudices and passions of the ignorant and fanatical; and

Whereas, much sympathy has been exhibited and encouragement given in the non-slaveholding States, to bands of lawless ruffians, making attacks upon the slaveholding States, and endeavoring to incite insurrection among the slaves; and

[31]

Whereas, a formidable and powerful party, called Black Republicans, existing exclusively, with slight and insignificant exceptions, in the non-slaveholding States, has proclaimed that slavery shall be prohibited by action of Congress in the Territories. . . .

Be it ordained by this Convention, That all slaveholding States . . . are hereby invited and requested to assemble in Convention at Nashville, in the State of Tennessee, on the 25th day of February next . . . to take into consideration the relations which the slaveholding States shall hereafter occupy; . . . and also to fix upon and determine what amendments of the Constitution of the United States are necessary . . . and to finally settle and adjust all questions relating to the subject of slavery. . . .

Be it further Ordained, That in the event such amendments of the Constitution of the United States, and such measures for the protection of Southern Slave States, shall not be made and acceded to by the people of the non-slaveholding States promptly; then said Convention shall upon the call of the President thereof, re-assemble, and shall forthwith organize a separate Confederacy. . . .

Be it further Ordained, That six Delegates to said Convention, to be held on the twenty-fifth day of February . . . be chosen by this Convention to represent the State. . . .[43]

He made an eloquent defense of his resolution, speaking against what he called the "evil effects and injustice of separate secession," and pointing out how the Great West and South were closely bound together, commercially. He also showed more foresight than prudence, when he reasoned that Europe would not recognize the Confederacy; that it was impossible to establish a government founded on cotton states alone; that the tremendous expenses of an army would cripple the states; and that the states would eventually disagree among themselves. But his efforts proved futile; his resolution was defeated by a vote of one hundred and six to twenty-four.[44] But the matter of co-operative action was not dropped without still one more effort. James O. Fuqua presented a resolution and supported it upon the logical theory that separate action would prove disastrous to Louisiana's commerce. It, however, was also defeated in short order by a vote of seventy-three to forty-seven.[45]

Another interesting resolution that aroused acrimonious debate, especially later during reconstruction days, and has caused much speculation since, was introduced by C. Bienvenu, a co-operationist. It provided that the ordinance adopted must be submitted to a vote of the people on February 25th for popular approval. It was likewise defeated, the vote being eighty-four to forty-three.[46] John Perkins, a member from Madison, who had spoken in opposition to submission to popular vote, and who now brought the debate to a close, seems to have voiced the sentiment in favor of the necessity of an immediate decision on secession. He reasoned that the legislature, recognizing the great emergency, had called an election for a convention to pass on secession, and the delegates had been elected by the people with that object clearly in view. The speaker must have spoken with conviction for the original ordinance was again proposed and carried without further delay by a vote of one hundred and thirteen to seventeen.[47] All the delegates except ten then signed the ordinance.[48]

Before adjournment the Convention gave its attention to other matters of urgent importance. Acting on the advice of the commissioners it elected Alexander Declouet and John Perkins as delegates at large, and Charles M. Conrad, Duncan F. Kenner, Henry Marshall, and Edward Sparrow as delegates from the four Congressional districts to go to the Southern Congress which was to meet at Montgomery, on February 15, 1861.[49] In addition, the convention took over an aggregate of $418,311.52 in the United States mint in New Orleans, transferred $147,519.66 of Custom House funds to the Confederacy,[50] and specified an oath of allegiance. Finally the sovereign body passed resolutions endorsing the election of Jefferson Davis and Alexander H. Stephens,[51] and adopted a state flag by a unanimous vote "amidst the most intense enthusiasm and deafening applause."[52]

Upon receipt of an official copy of the secession act, Louisiana's senators, Benjamin and Slidell, requested that it be read to the Senate by the secretary of that body. Taking this ordinance as their text, both delivered dramatic valedictories, and departed from Washington on the day before three of their colleagues, Thomas J. Davidson, John M. Landrum, and Miles Taylor, retired from the House of Representatives.[53] Slidell's valedictory,

[33]

a vindication of the right of immediate secession, was delivered in a militant spirit. He hoped and wished to part amicably, but saw nothing to justify such expectations. Speaking of the possibilities of hostilities, he is reported to have shouted in an outburst of defiance:

This will be war, and we shall meet it with different but equally efficient weapons. We will not permit the consumption or introduction of any of your manufactured goods; every sea will swarm with our volunteer militia of the ocean. . . . Foreign nations will not let you blockade our trade. . . . We shall do with you as the French guards did with the English at the battle of Fontenoy. . . . Gentlemen, we will not fire first. . . . We separate because of the hostility of Lincoln to our institutions. . . . We now have no fears of servile insurrections. . . . His inauguration as President of the United States with our assent would have been considered by . . . our slaves as the day of their emancipation.[54]

Senator Benjamin's farewell address, which followed that of his colleague, was on this occasion temperate, logical, and no doubt effective in its defense of the legal right of revolution, the theme of the greater portion; it was received with "marked attention," both because of his former effort, and because he was now regarded as the so-called "arch conspirator," the chief exponent of the extreme Southern position. He reasoned:

Sir, it has been urged . . . that Louisiana stands on an exceptional footing . . . that whatever may be the rights of the states that were original parties to the Constitution . . . Louisiana can have no such right, because *she* was acquired by purchase. Gentlemen . . . speak of . . . the territory ceded by France as property bought. . . . I must conclude that they also mean to assert, on the same principle, *the right of selling for a price that which for a price was bought.*

I shall not pause to comment on this repulsive dogma of a party which asserts the right of property in free-born white men, in order to reach its cherished object of destroying the right of property in slave-born black men. . . . I simply deny the fact. . . . I deny that the province of Louisiana, or the people of Louisiana were ever conveyed to the United States for a price as property that could be bought or sold at will. . . . The archives of our State Department show the fact to be, that . . . *the sovereignty was not conveyed otherwise than in trust.*

We are told that . . . the South is in rebellion without cause, and

[34]

that her citizens are traitors. Rebellion! The very word is a confession; an avowal of tyranny, outrage, and oppression. It is taken from the despot's code, and has no terror for other than slavish souls. When, sir, did millions of people, as a single man, rise in organized, deliberate, unimpassioned rebellion against justice, truth, and honor?

Traitors! Treason! Ay, sir, the people of the South imitate and glory in just such treason as glowed in the soul of Hampden; just such treason as leaped in living flames from the impassioned lips of Henry; just such treason as encircles with a sacred halo the undying name of Washington![55]

There is still a generally widespread impression in the North, and even in some localities in Louisiana, doubtless handed down by tradition, that Louisiana was hurried into secession by such speeches; that the popular vote if allowed, would have been against secession; that the convention would never permit the publication of the vote for delegates to the convention, because it would thereby have thwarted the so-called "conspiracy" of the leaders, who, it has been alleged, were determined to "dragoon" the unwilling state out of the Union. All these charges, and more, were made in the press, even at that time, after it was reported that the convention had held several secret sessions;[56] and they were to be made again during reconstruction days, even by Louisianians, and the Louisiana press. But a close examination of the evidence connected with the calling of the convention and its subsequent proceedings does not seem to substantiate such conclusions.

The controversy over the election returns no doubt first gave color to such charges. The early returns, as has been explained, had indicated such an overwhelming majority for immediate secession that even the most conservative opposition had conceded defeat. The complete vote in every precinct was sent to the Secretary of State as the law required, but that official did not publish this return. Nor was publication a legal requirement. However, the roster of membership—but not the official vote—was obtained from that source by the press, and the individual names and their affiliation appeared in the news columns.[57] This count, as was explained above, gave the "immediate secessionists" eighty delegates, the "co-operationists" forty-four, and listed five as doubtful. This

[35]

at the time appeared to be convincing evidence of the prevailing sentiment. Some question, it appears, had arisen over the official count as the belated returns from remote precincts indicated a more conservative trend than was expected. But still no one seems to have seriously questioned the outcome until the following letter, addressed to the editor of the most conservative New Orleans daily, appeared over the signature of "C. B.":

I understand from a gentleman just from Baton Rouge that the popular vote was in favor of the co-operation ticket. Although the Convention has been in session for some time, I have not seen the official vote published, and as there can be no good reason for withholding the facts from the public, you will oblige many of your readers if you will give a full statement of the vote.[58]

This was apparently an innocent communication, doubtless written by a co-operationist, who may have favored secession, and who may have been motivated by a sincere desire for information only. But regardless of the motives, he set in motion a controversy that has never been settled satisfactorily. The editor, who opposed secession because of commercial reasons, now taking his cue from this correspondent, answered in the same issue that "an unsuccessful effort had been made to obtain the complete vote from the Secretary of State," and charged that it was being "shamefully suppressed." Continuing its thrusts at the immediate secessionists, the *Picayune*, which had a wide circulation both North and South, now, while the convention was still in session, began to advocate "the reconstruction of the old Union." Its editorials were soon reproduced by *The Philadelphia Bulletin*, and other Northern journals, all of which agreed with the *Picayune* that the trade of the Mississippi valley would in a great measure be deflected to the North and East.[59]

The broadcasting of such sentiment did not go unchallenged. It was not long before most of the Louisiana press was arrayed against the "hostile attitude" of the *Picayune*, and the agitation that now arose was soon reflected on the floor of the convention in the person of a determined minority leader, Bienvenu. He submitted a resolution to lay the results of the election before the

[36]

convention. The purport of such a resolution was of course to have the election results printed in the records. It was, however, decisively defeated on a motion to suspend the rules.[60]

The agitation would no doubt have ceased had not the *Daily Delta,* the most partisan of the immediate secession journals, conceived it as a duty to show its "loyalty" by answering the charges of the "submissionists and reconstructionists," as it inappropriately designated the "co-operationists" and their organ, the *Picayune.* And thus the family quarrel, the reverberations of which were to be felt beyond the state lines, went merrily on.

The editor of the *Delta* no doubt sincerely felt compelled to champion the course of the convention relative to the election returns, and at the same time to counteract or correct the impression that was getting abroad that the convention was not truly representing the popular will. To accomplish this task it repeatedly called the attention of the country—the whole controversy had now gotten into the border, and the Northern and Southern press —to the overwhelming vote for secession in the convention, which in itself it alleged to be sufficient evidence of unanimity. But the editor of the *Delta* now sought to crush his adversary, the *Picayune,* by charging that it was giving aid and comfort to "Black Republicans" by broadcasting that there was division in Louisiana ranks and that a healthy Union sentiment abounded therein. It would also completely disarm its "disloyal" adversary by producing the vote. The editor wrote: "We have determined to make up a complete, and as far as possible, an accurate tabular statement of the vote in all the parishes of the state. In New Orleans we have given the vote in round numbers. In Pointe Coupee and Avoyelles no 'submission' tickets were run, consequently the whole vote is necessarily placed in the Secession column. The result is, as will be seen, a handsome majority for secession."[61]

According to most of the daily papers the immediate secessionists were victorious by a majority of approximately 3,000.[62] Other sources give the vote as follows: immediate secessionist candidates, 20,448; co-operationists, 17,296.[63] It is highly probable that these other sources, especially the contemporary sources, obtained

[37]

the above results from a perfect copy of the *Delta* of March 27, 1864. But whether correct or not, there figures have been credited by subsequent Louisiana historians as authentic.

The *Picayune* was evidently not convinced by these "impressive figures," although it appears that the official figures were available, and would at any time have been made accessible. Contending that it, and not its opponents, was the real "guardian of the people's rights," the *Picayune* continued its attacks on the convention. The following editorial appears to be typical:

We charge that the Louisiana Convention in refusing to produce the official returns of the popular vote at the convention election, gave strength to the coercion party at the North and quickened its arrogant spirit. We charge that the Alabama, Georgia, and Louisiana Conventions by usurping the rights of the people to decide on the merits of the Constitution framed for their government, and by ratifying that Constitution, gave new and startling evidence of their distrust of the people, and thus furnished strong testimony to which the coercion party could appeal, in support of their position, that the South was divided, and that the movement in which we are now engaged, has not the sanction of the great body of the people. We charge that the conventions, and their aiders and abettors in this foul usurpation, have done all they could do, by showing distrust of the people, to encourage the belief entertained by the coercion party that the South would not present an united front. Attempts to coerce us in the main, if not alone, are owing to the criminal folly of the leaders, directors and prominent advocates of the Southern movement. . . .

Here, it will be seen, the distrust of the people which has characterized the whole movement of the leaders in the cause of secession, is adduced as a reason why recognition of the Confederate States should be delayed. When we are accused of giving strength to the Northern idea of coercion, and being instrumental in delaying the peaceful settlement of the questions between the new Government under which we live, we say that it is not we, but they—they who, assuming to be the guardian of the people's rights, have uniformly manifested distrust of the people's judgment.[64]

This editorial, and others of similar purport, reached a wider reading public than did those of the *Daily Delta* and other periodicals that attempted to refute the charges; and despite their apparent sincerity the editorials must have done the cause of the South incalculable harm since they conveyed the impression that there was division in the South. *The Cincinnati Gazette,* one of the Republican journals, after quoting the *Picayune,* carried editorials stating that if the ordinance had been submitted to the people, it would have been voted down; and that the effect of its adoption would be to destroy the commercial supremacy of New Orleans. This same journal, taking as its text the *Picayune* editorials, arrived at the same conclusion as did practically all the other Northern papers: that there was a strong reactionary party in the Confederacy that had definite and growing desires for reconstruction. Such sentiments were consistently expressed and persistently adhered to.[65] *The Philadelphia Press,* edited by Forney, taking its cue from the same source, published the following paragraph:

In Louisiana there is undoubtedly a strong national sentiment yet existing. A majority of the popular vote at the time of the election for delegates to the State Convention was against the candidates for immediate secession, and the course of events since that period has certainly tended to strengthen the Union sentiment.[66]

The Albany Evening Journal, edited by Thurlow Weed, *The New York Tribune, The New York Times,* and other Republican journals, including *The St. Louis Democrat,* using the series of editorials of the *Picayune* as their source, arrived at the same conclusion: that the acts of the Louisiana convention were a monstrous usurpation.[67] But the *St. Louis Democrat,* perhaps one of the most rabid abolition journals in the West, expressed extreme views in an article entitled: "Louisiana Opposed to Secession." It charged that the voice of the people had been silenced by the tyranny of the convention; that the people had been tricked; that there had been a brutal trampling down of their rights by the desperate and daring secessionists; and that this convention had resolved itself into a supreme power and had imposed upon the people a new government without their consent, since they had deliberately refused to submit their work to their constituents. For these reasons, it alleged that not only Louisiana, but also Alabama, Mississippi, and Georgia had been hurled out of the Union,

[39]

when the popular sentiment was in favor of continued attach-
ment to the Union. But in the case of Louisiana, it contended,
the action had been "most flagrant and despotic." This journal
even asserted that the popular vote cast for co-operation was a
three hundred majority; and that it expected to see the convention usurpers overthrown, and Louisiana brought back into the
Union.[68] And thus the work of industriously creating such a belief
in the North continued, and caused the crystallization of a sentiment that must have influenced Lincoln and the reconstructionists in the policies which they were to inaugurate in Louisiana
within a few short months.

The Louisiana convention did not refuse to make public the
official returns, although it did, perhaps, make a mistake by refusing to spread them on the minutes of its official journal. A
great clamor was made by some malcontents because the convention did not publish the returns from every precinct and parish.
But this does not seem to have been any legal business of the
convention, composed as it was of delegates whose election was
not contested. These returns were in the office of the Secretary
of State at Baton Rouge and were accessible to anyone who cared
to go to the trouble and expense of going through the returns.[69]
There was apparently no precedent to justify the convention in
adding to its expenses by publishing them in their records, and it
therefore legally, but as events proved, indiscreetly, refused. The
evidence would seem to show that only one editor took the trouble
to go through all the returns (as was indicated above) and that he
found a majority for the immediate secessionists. It would further
indicate that there was little unconditional Union sentiment in
the convention. This is substantiated in part by the fact that only
ten of the one hundred and thirty members finally refused to sign
the ordinance.

The truth seems to be that there was not a very large Union
party *per se* in Louisiana. Few of the "co-operationists" were "submissionists," at least in the convention, despite the fact that they
were so represented by the other faction of secessionists. But if
the popular vote had been in favor of the co-operationists, it would
not, it seems, have indicated that there was a strong Union senti-

ment in Louisiana. Apparently, the majority was for secession, when, after a consultation with all the slaveholding states, it was found impossible to obtain concessions from the North. This view is supported by the work of Denman, Shanks, and W. L. Fleming and other historians of the secession movement in the South.[70] Having voted thus, they gave most cordial allegiance to the Confederate Government; and all expectation that they would betray or desert the fortunes of the Confederates proved to be without foundation. To this cause the large majority of co-operationists remained loyal so long as that government could show a thread by which to hold the Southern people together.[71]

But if there was any considerable Union interest left after the convention acted, it either disintegrated or was driven underground after the fall of Fort Sumter, and after Lincoln's call for troops. The exploit of the native son, Beauregard, in connection with the former event fired the imagination of Louisianians. The military ardor, especially of the younger men, was reported in the press to have defied all restraint of the state authorities, who tried to prevent too great a number from leaving the state.[72] By June of 1861 more than 12,000, fully equipped by the State, had departed for the scenes of war, leaving too few, it was alleged, to man the Louisiana defenses. And before mid-July a detailed report on Louisiana's quota showed a grand total of 20,540 fully equipped men, most of whom were serving in the Confederate army, and outside the state. The parishes that had recently voted in favor of co-operation showed the same state loyalty as did the immediate secession parishes. East Baton Rouge parish which had returned a heavy majority for co-operation, was reported to have furnished more soldiers than any other in proportion to its white population.[73] When it is recalled that Louisiana's white population was only 295,151,[74] and that 980 companies were organized, the conclusion is that no state displayed greater loyalty to the South and greater military energy and enthusiasm in proportion to its resources and population than is revealed in these figures.[75]

Two grand military reviews in the year 1861 illustrate best the war spirit and the supreme confidence that prevailed. The first took place in April. New Orleans was described at the time as one long military camp. When Governor Moore inspected the troops in military review there was "one continuous public ovation." The press reported that "thirty thousand spectators witnessed this grand, gay, and imposing pageant. The windows, balconies, and streets were thronged and the enthusiasm was immense and beyond description."[76] But the war spirit evidently reached its highest tide on November 23 of this same year when "the grandest military review within the annals of the State was witnessed. Thirty thousand men marched in line, showing admirable military order and discipline, and making a most imposing exposition of strength." This review of Louisiana's military strength was again witnessed by the Governor, the generals, and their staffs, and by "20,000 of Louisiana's fair daughters," who again "thronged the verandas, balconies, and windows."[77]

It was to be expected that the citizens of Louisiana would undertake to show that New Orleans was the vital point at which the North would shortly strike; frequently reports and rumors served to deepen this conviction. The presence of a formidable squadron in the Gulf was reported as early as April, 1861, and rumors reached the city that the navy yards at the North were being employed to their utmost capacity with the city as the immediate objective. The New Orleans press also frequently quoted articles from the Northern press to the effect that a large fleet and army would be sent to New Orleans and that in so doing the North would only be acting on the defense with a two-fold purpose: to control and keep open the navigation of a river into which the "glorious valley poured its unexampled treasures," and at the same time to encourage the so-called "Union party"—which they asserted still existed in Louisiana—to make a demonstration of its reputed strength.[78] As this conviction of an impending attack deepened, the city and state made large appropriations, and strenuously demanded that the Confederate Government act in co-operation with them to make the city impregnable. The press suggested that the millions of idle capital [cotton] be used to build a sufficient number of the latest gunboats and floating batteries, and that this should be done with all possible speed in order to scatter the blockading squadrons at the mouth of the river.[79] It urged further that ample men and much material were then available for such a project, and that by continued delay the government was inviting disaster.[80]

But the co-operation of the agencies was never effected. In fact during all the months of suspense it appears that the military authorities were attempting to allay the fears and anxiety by lulling the citizens into a sense of security. General Lovell made inspections from time to time, and his reports carried the conviction that the city was prepared and could repel any invading army or fleet. Likewise the Governor's patriotic messages reiterated his conviction that the defenses of the city were in "a highly satisfactory condition."[81] In fact the military authorities had so far established confidence in their ability to destroy the "wooden fleet by the raking fire of Forts Jackson and Phillips"—if the press is to be relied upon—that it [the press] brazenly defied "Picayune Butler" and his large army "to come to town."[82]

Therefore, it is easy to understand the consternation of the citizens when the intelligence reached the city that the wooden fleet, "after the most furious and incessant bombardment that had ever been witnessed in modern warfare," had accomplished what was believed to be an impossible feat—it had passed the forts, and its guns now held the defenseless city at their mercy. There was now, of course, no alternative left but to bow to the inevitable ultimatum of Commodore Farragut, which occurred after several days of hesitation and fruitless negotiation.[83]

But when the circumstances which led to surrender were learned, consternation gave place to a bitterness and resentment against the authorities that the press made no effort to conceal or suppress. "The worst had happened," it bitterly complained, "because of the lamentable want of system, and energy on the part of the Confederate squadron in failing to co-operate at the critical moment," and in failing "to keep the river lighted at all times," thereby enabling the Federal boats to slip past the forts on a dark night; and it made the additional complaint that this unpardonable negligence had contributed most to another unpardonable and mortifying episode: ". . . the open and violent mutiny and subsequent surrender of the disspirited troops at the forts."[84] This re-

[43]

sentment deepened against the Richmond government when it was learned that the so-called "impregnable city" had been protected only by "wretchedly inadequate and contemptible armaments and defenses," and that in addition it had been "betrayed into the hands of the enemy by stripping it of its defenses, and defenders to protect distant, and less important portions of the Confederacy."[85]

CHAPTER III

BUTLER BEGINS RESTORATION

General Benjamin F. Butler, with several thousand United States troops, entered the city of New Orleans on May 1, 1862, unmolested by any demonstration, and made the St. Charles Hotel and Custom House his headquarters. His first act—the first of a series that have been considered oppressive—of his seven and one-half months' rule indicated that he had not been accorded the expected cordial reception; nor did this poor reception seem to augur well for the future of the inhabitants. *The Daily True Delta* had refused to print his proclamation, whereupon he promptly took it over, and made of this most loyal Southern journal an organ that was thereafter faithfully to reflect the policy of his administration.[1] *The New Orleans Daily Crescent,* whose principal proprietor was in the service of the Confederacy, was confiscated shortly thereafter for being a "treasonable journal," and was sold at auction for $3,200.[2] Such disciplinary methods had a most cowing effect on other publications, and their opinions became the echoes of the opinions of the chief military officers of the Department. In fine, the censorship completely cut off the city from all news, except "the authentic version" of such as the General permitted. This rigid censorship was not applicable to *The Daily Picayune,* a journal that was considered Unionist, and, with the possible exception of one or two issues, it continued its uninterrupted publication throughout the war and reconstruction days.[3]

Butler's first proclamation dated May 1, 1862, was plainly indicative of the fact that he had come to effect a speedy restoration of Louisiana. "Thrice before," he reminded the citizens,

has the city of New Orleans been rescued. . . . It has of late been under the military control of the Rebel forces, claiming to be the peculiar friends of its citizens. . . . All persons well disposed towards the Government of the United States, who shall renew their oath of allegiance, will receive the safeguard and protection of their persons and property. . . . All foreigners, not naturalized . . . will be protected. . . . All Confederates must give up their arms. Keepers of all public property, and all manufacturers of arms will report to the headquarters. . . . A sufficient

[45]

force will be kept in the city to preserve order, and maintain the laws.
. . . The armies came here to restore order.[4]

He followed this with a declaration of martial law, but announced that he would allow the city authorities to continue the
administration of city government without interference. Such permission was, however, to be revoked should any disturbances arise
to endanger the relations of the invading army and the citizens.
The currency, he promised, was to remain undisturbed, communications were to be kept open to procure ample food, and the army,
with the exception of·a small guard, was to be taken to the environs of the city.[5]

The press reported a deplorable state of destitution and hunger
among the mechanics and working classes. In addition, the city
was threatened with a really great catastrophe. The water stood
at the top of the levee, several feet above the city level, and there
was imminent danger of a crevasse and inundation. Furthermore
the deadly yellow fever season, which almost annually took a great
toll of human lives, was near at hand. All of these misfortunes now
gave Butler an opportunity to become a public benefactor, and
at the same time to resurrect and cultivate any spirit of Unionism
that might exist. Grasping the opportunity, he issued another proclamation, which was calculated to drive a wedge between the upper
and lower classes. It was addressed to the working men:

The deplorable conditions have been brought to the knowledge of the
Commanding General. . . . This hunger does not pinch the wealthy, and
influential, the leaders of the rebellion, who have gotten up this war.
. . . No relief has as yet been afforded by those officials. They have
caused, or suffered provisions to be carried out of the city for Confederate
service since the occupation by the United States forces. . . . Striking
hands with the vile, the gambler, the idler and ruffian they have destroyed
the sugar and cotton, which might have been exchanged for food for
the industrious and good, and regrated [sic] the price of that which
was left, by discrediting the very currency they had furnished, while
they eloped with the specie stolen from the United States as well as the
Banks, the property of the good people of New Orleans, thus leaving
them to ruin and starvation.

They have betrayed their country. They have been false to every

[46]

trust. They have shown themselves incapable of defending the State. . . .
They cannot protect those whom they have ruined. . . .
They will not feed those whom they are starving. . . .

MEN OF LOUISIANA, WORKINGMEN, PROPERTY-HOLD-
ERS, MERCHANTS, AND CITIZENS OF THE UNITED STATES,
of whatever nation you may have had birth, how long will you uphold
these flagrant wrongs, and by inaction suffer yourselves to be made the
serfs of these leaders? . . . We find, substantially, only fugitive masses,
runaway property burners, a whiskey drinking mob, and starving citizens with their wives and children. It is our duty to call back the first,
to punish the second, root out the third, and feed and protect the last.

Ready only for war, we had not prepared ourselves to feed the hungry
and relieve the distressed. . . . But to the extent possible within the
power of the Commanding General it shall be done.[6]

Such statements, according to Confederate sympathizers, were
more eloquent than truthful. Their evidence would seem to indicate that New Orleans had shown a spirit of charity and benevo-
lence towards its poor. The people, reports show, had maintained
for their destitute thousands a free market which had been successfully conducted, month after month, although trade was practically cut off and sources of wealth were fast drying up. In addition, fifty or more societies of benevolent ladies, according to these
same sources, had been laboring and devoting their resources to
clothe and feed the wives and children of this poorer class.[7]

But not all the acts of Butler were considered acts of charity
by his opponents, for subsequent prices quoted for almost all com-
modities for sale by the Commissary of Subsistence were considered extortionate. For example, a twenty-four pound sack of
flour was quoted at $1.80.[8] But there was some charity, for a report
on August 1, 1862, printed in an organ of Butler's, gave the information that during the preceding two months 234,710 pounds of
ham, 34,574 pounds of bacon, 65,775 pounds of crackers, 21,375
pounds of peas, 900 pounds of coffee, 4,579 pounds of fresh beef,
1,423 barrels of flour, and 958 barrels of pork were distributed
by the army.[9] Weekly reports thereafter by this official organ
indicated that these amounts were greatly increased. The total
number of persons receiving aid up to October 11, 1862, was listed

[47]

at 32,450, which included many of foreign extraction, the Germans and Irish being the most numerous.[10] But it must be borne in mind that Butler levied one assessment on the city, as will presently be shown, with the declared intention of feeding the poor, and providing public works.

Butler's achievements in sanitation during the summer of 1862 have been frequently referred to by Parton as little short of miraculous; the Butler press seems to have made a very great appeal to the poorer classes, because of these facts. He made stringent regulations and sternly enforced them. Contrary to general expectations and the "prayers of a malignant few" who would have invoked sickness and pestilence to sweep his "denizens" into a common grave with the inhabitants, as Butler alleged, conditions remained much more healthful than usual. The low death rate was pointed to with pride, and it no doubt compared favorably with any city of the North. The August death rate was indeed low for a sickly season. In fact, only two yellow fever cases were reported during this entire period. The highly satisfactory condition can, in a high degree, be attributed to Butler's sanitary measures.[11] But it should be recalled that the yellow fever epidemics were introduced as a rule from Havana, or other tropical countries; hence the blockades and stringent quarantine measures now made the possibilities of its introduction very remote. Furthermore, it was highly incumbent upon Butler to take all possible precautionary measures to protect his large army which was not yet acclimated and which, therefore, needed special safeguards to prevent its being swept away by the pestilence. Thus he incidentally safeguarded the health of the inhabitants by the enforcement of needed stringent sanitary measures for his army.

The original proclamation had promised the special protection of international law to foreigners. But one of Butler's earliest acts caused some of his critics to charge that this part of his proclamation was only so much high-sounding rhetoric. It seems that the Citizens' Bank owed Hope and Company of Amsterdam a large sum, due within the next few weeks, and upon the fall of New Orleans the directors concluded to place this amount in the hands

[48]

of the Holland Consul, for the payment of the debt. Butler, hearing of this transaction, claimed that the money still belonged to the Citizens' Bank, and forcibly took possession of and removed this large sum from the Consulate. He also placed federal soldiers as guards over the offices of the French and Spanish Consuls, from a belief that under similar circumstances similar sums had been deposited with these officials.[12] There were of course vigorous protests and intense excitement and rumors, which resulted in the removal of the soldiers, disavowal by the government, and restitution of the money on the part of the "Commanding General." But he now somewhat complicated international relations by making several other rulings. Charging that the foreigners as a whole were enlisted in the local militia and aiding the "Rebels," he ruled that a large class, who had been in the country over five years, were American citizens; that each of the other neutrals must take the special oath and register in order to get a passport through the lines; that if a foreigner intended to conceal rebellious and traitorous acts, he must get out; that if he did not like the laws he could go at once; and that no more protests, or arguments would be received from any subjects of a foreign country.[13]

But Butler did receive a lengthy and vigorous protest from the French Consul over a subsequent order requiring "all persons" to deliver up their arms. This Consul reasoned that the foreigners must retain their private arms, because the United States authorities could not extend adequate protection over them at "all times and in all places." He reminded Butler that the servile population was manifesting unmistakable signs of breaking its bonds, and insisted that in this event the foreigners would need these arms as a means of self-defense. Butler, however, remained obdurate in his determination to bring all foreigners to terms, as the following reply reveals:

I see no just cause of complaint against the order requiring the arms of private citizens to be delivered up.

You will observe that it will not do to trust to mere professions of neutrality. I trust most of your countrymen are in good faith neutral; but it is unfortunately true that some of them are not.

[49]

SECESSION AND RESTORATION OF LOUISIANA

Bonnegrass, claimed to be the French Consul at Baton Rouge and it was allowed him to keep his arms, relying upon his neutrality; but his son was taken prisoner on the battle field in arms against us.

You will also do me the favor to remember that very few of the French subjects here have taken the oath of neutrality, which was offered to, but not required of them, by my order No. 41. . . .

Of the disquiet of which you say there are signs manifesting themselves among the black population, from a desire to break their bonds . . . it would seem natural, when their masters have set them the example of rebellion against constituted authorities, that the negroes, being an imitative race, should do likewise.

Let me assure you that the protection of the United States against violence, either by negroes or white men, whether citizens or foreign, will continue to be as perfect as it has been since our advent here. . . .

I must require the arms of all the inhabitants, white or black, to be under my control.[14]

Nor was he disposed to show respect or deference to England. His official organ, taking cognizance of the fact that the English in New Orleans were in the habit of singing the "Bonnie Blue Flag" and occasionally displaying it, frequently reminded them that there would in all probability be an "after piece" to the struggle now going on; that the causes and justifications of such a contest were numerous; and that the "rebels," who had been deceived by the English hope of recognition, would not be unwilling to take part in the "new piece."[15]

Butler seems to have been equally unsuccessful in his relations with the citizens, whom he was expected to conciliate. Instead of ignoring the non-communicative attitude of a proud and highly sensitive people, and the petty offenses of a small minority, he elected to treat such conduct as an insult to himself and his entire army, and to begin a series of arrests and punishments that not only counteracted his efforts at restoration, but enabled him to earn for himself a most unsavory reputation. The first step was to set up a military commission for the trial of "all high crimes and misdemeanors."[16] His "woman order" soon followed. It seems that this sex incurred Butler's hostility by their persistence in playing the "Bonnie Blue Flag," and other secession airs, and by affecting nausea when passing the Yankees on the streets. Butler treated such incidents as grave offenses. For this reason he seems to have looked upon the following order as "well considered":

As officers and soldiers of the United States have been subjected to repeated insults from women, calling themselves ladies, of New Orleans, in return for the most scrupulous non-interference and courtesy on our part, it is ordered hereafter, when any female shall by mere gesture or movement, insult, or show contempt for any officers or soldiers of the United States, she shall be treated as a woman about town plying her avocation.[17]

And when Mayor Monroe protested that such an order would "give a license to the officers and soldiers of your command to commit outrages such as are indicated in your order, upon defenseless women," and that it was, in his judgment, "a reproach to civilization, not to say the Christianity of the age," the mayor was summarily arrested, and sentenced to Fort Jackson.[18] A number of arrests and imprisonments of men and women in all walks of life followed, including that of Pierre Soulé, who was placed in confinement, because he was said to be "a traitor and turbulent fellow."[19]

Nor did the ministers, who, he charged, had "put on the livery of Heaven to serve the Devil in," escape punishment. Practically all churches were closed, and their ministers sent North to distant prisons, when they "contumaciously refused" to pray for the President of the United States.[20] The clergy, as a matter of fact, had ceased to pray for the President of the Confederacy, or for the destruction of the Union or Constitution. Their chief offense, however, was that they had neglected or omitted to pray for President Lincoln and others in authority, thereby, in Butler's opinion, committing treason.

Butler also directed his efforts to purging the public schools, the alleged "nurseries of treason," of all disloyal teachers and tendencies. He charged that the teachers had diligently used, and were still using, every art to instill in the "ductile minds" an intense hatred towards the Government and "Yankee scum"; that that "vile jargon," the "Bonnie Blue Flag," had been substituted for that glorious anthem, the "Star Spangled Banner"; that the word "United" had been erased before the words "States" in the

[51]

textbooks; and concluded that the schools would be allowed to open as usual, but they would open "without the directors and teachers who encourage such sentiments." Acting accordingly, he replaced with loyalists the "disloyal" teachers, in the public and private schools.[21]

Butler also appointed an Education Bureau, visiting boards, and various committees to examine the teachers, to draw up elaborate manuals for their organization and government, and to guide the teachers, principals, pupils, parents, and even the lowly "porters" in all their respective duties.[22] The anticipated non-attendance did not materialize. On the contrary, the reports of Butler's agents conveyed the intelligence that the whole program was attended with unusual success, and that the primary, intermediate, and high school departments were filled up to their utmost capacity, and that all of the pupils were well equipped with new and improved school books from the North, instead of the torn and dilapidated books which had been left on hand.[23]

But the Commander devised another method whereby he apparently hoped to drive another wedge between the so-called wealthier and poorer classes. This was his assessment levied on one occasion by himself, and once by his successor, Banks. The reason for such action was "that the need of relief to the destitute poor of the city required more extended measures and greater outlay than" had hitherto been made. He, therefore, required that two classes pay: those who had "aided the rebellion with their means" and those who had destroyed the "commercial prosperity of the city," upon which the welfare of its inhabitants depended. The first class who had subscribed $1,250,000 for the defenses of the city, he now placed in schedule "A," and assessed each personal subscriber, corporate body, and business firm. From these he realized a total sum of $351,016.25. The second class, his schedule "B," constituted the cotton brokers, who had advised the planters not to bring their produce to the city, thereby bringing ruin, Butler alleged, to both producers and citizens. He caused both schedules to be published in the New Orleans press and provided that the sum set opposite each name be paid by a specified time, or the property of the delinquent be forthwith seized and sold at public auction. The money raised by this assessment was to be used, he explained, for the twofold purpose of providing employment and food for the deserving and starving poor.[24]

There were other acts of "renovation" during the early summer. The most sensational was the hanging of William B. Mumford before thousands, for taking down the United States Flag, an offense which had occurred, however, before the formal surrender of the city.[25] Butler next muzzled the *Estaffette du Sud,* a French journal, and *The Commercial Bulletin,* for printing language inconsistent with martial law, and for treasonable editorials.[26] He condemned several returning Confederate soldiers to be shot, but showed clemency by commuting the sentence.[27] He ordered that all captured so-called guerillas should be "tried at the drumhead by the Military Commission, every man shot, their houses burned, and their property destroyed."[28] He encouraged negro servants to give any desired information relative to their masters,[29] and finally he demanded that the Bank of Louisiana pay current funds for deposits of Confederate money.[30] In short, as one of his Northern critics put it: ". . . during all these months that he was laying the foundation of wealth which subserved his later ambition in politics, he was also acting the part of an avenger."[31]

The "irrepressible" negro problem was forced upon Butler from the first occupancy of the city by a constant influx of slaves within his lines; and his attempts to solve it do not seem to have enhanced his reputation. It appears that some owners, no longer able to provide for their slaves, actually encouraged them to go to the army, where they would be set free. To complicate matters, and ostensibly to embarrass the Commander, he was now urged by some of these same owners to arrest and return the slaves. Butler decided to treat such acts of owners as acts of emancipation[32] on their part, and promptly devised his negro enlistment scheme, whereby he organized them into military corps, placed muskets in their hands, and ordered that they serve on guard duty and work on the fortifications and public works. He provided further that they should be mustered into the United States army on an equality with the white troops; that is, they were to receive the same bounty upon enlistment, the same rations and equipment, and, upon their discharge, they were to receive a bounty of $100, or 160 acres of land, together with $13 per month during the term of service.[33]

These incentives met with a favorable response and there was soon a noticeable activity on the part of negro leaders to raise companies to serve in the army of the Republic. P. B. S. Pinchback, a negro leader, who was to be exalted to the Governor's chair in the stormy years that followed, was especially active. He complained, however, in a letter to his friends, published in Butler's official organ, that he was continually being "insulted by many so-called Union men."[34] In fact, a great hue and cry arose among white Unionists and Unionist journals in opposition to the employment of what they considered a servile and inferior race against men of their own race and blood. They reasoned that it was unsafe to entrust indolent, cowardly, and utterly unreliable Africans with muskets.[35]

The general dissatisfaction at such a policy was further made manifest in Butler's own camp. General Phelps became so incensed at being employed as a "slave driver," and at having to employ his army as a guard to protect the black laborers against "guerrilla forces," that he resigned.[36] Butler at first refused to accept his resignation, but it appears that he shortly after sent Roselius, a prominent Louisiana Unionist, who had great weight with the authorities at Washington, to make representations of General Phelp's movements. The result was his recall.[37] With the removal of this impediment, Butler proceeded to enlarge upon his negro policy by prescribing for them an oath of allegiance,[38] and encouraging, or at least tolerating, the formation of such negro clubs as the "Union Association of Free Colored,"[39] the "Louisiana State Colonization Society," and similar bodies, all of which naturally became inflated with a growing sense of their importance.

The fruits of Butler's policy in dealing with the negro population were soon made manifest. By September, certain classes of negroes began to insist on social equality, by forcing themselves into cars and on the seats set apart for the exclusive use of white patrons. Their conduct in general became quite boisterous, and

negro outrages were reported as common.[40] But still Butler persisted in his course, and even defended it in letters published in
Northern journals, and before the Committee on the Conduct of
the War. A letter was printed in the *New York Tribune* to the
effect that his two regiments of colored troops rendered him very
great services, and enabled him to accomplish much more than he
could have done without them. This same communication conveyed the intelligence that he had paid into the treasury three-
quarters of a million dollars, the proceeds of confiscation, and that
he was then feeding 30,000 whites and 10,000 colored.[41] He
claimed, furthermore, that he really resuscitated one of these
negro regiments that Governor Moore had raised and disbanded
in the early days of the war, and that, in no event, had he enlisted
other than free colored. The records would, however, warrant the
assertion that many were former slaves, even of French and British
subjects, whom he had freed after the slaves registered as French
and British subjects.[42]

Meanwhile, Butler, the politician, did not lose sight of the fact
that he was sent to "rescue and restore the State." This stupendous
task he would accomplish by a weeding out process—the separation of the sheep from the goats, as Parton expresses it.[43] In his
official journal on May 29 appeared an editorial that indicated
what the "plan of salvation" would be. The first requisite step
should be a declaration of obedience; and when the moment had
arrived when the Louisianians "could be judiciously trusted with
their own safety," they would be allowed to select their own rulers,
but not until then.[44] Those who would effect restoration almost
immediately took their cue. The Union Association sprang up as
if by magic, and promulgated its constitution. Its object was the
restoration of the Constitution and laws of the United States, and
of the State of Louisiana, as they existed previous to the act of
secession. Some of its more important articles provided for an
executive committee, for prominent speakers at regular stated
meetings, for all members to sign their names to this constitution,
and for eligibility of membership to four classes as follows: (1)
citizens of the United States, (2) citizens of Louisiana, (3) those

[55]

SECESSION AND RESTORATION OF LOUISIANA

who declare their intention of becoming a citizen of the United States, and (4) those who sign the Constitution and shall take the following oath of allegiance:

I,——, do solemnly swear (or affirm), that I will true and faithful allegiance bear to the United States of America, and shall support and maintain to the best of my abilities, the Union and the Constitution thereof. So Help Me God.[45]

The Executive Committee provided for a series of meetings at Lyceum Hall for the purpose of stimulating and cultivating a spirit of Unionism under the protecting wings "of the Union forces."[46] Its first real public meeting was appropriately called for July the Fourth, 1862. Others followed weekly or more often, and if the press reports are to be accepted at face value, the interest and enthusiasm grew by leaps and bounds during the summer and fall months. Such men as John E. Bouligny, Louisiana's conservative congressman, who alone refused to go out with his state, and Dr. Dostie, a radical, and many others of various shades of belief returned and espoused the movement. These men were pointed to as so many living indexes of a latent Union sentiment in the state, which needed only encouragement to make itself seen and felt. And as their numbers grew, and there were apparently a goodly number who identified themselves with the movement during the first few weeks, in like proportion did the press clamor for local power to be entrusted to the "faithful."[47]

On special occasions prominent speakers were imported to assist the local orators in educating the people; and, according to the frequent press reports, they spoke to most enthusiastic capacity audiences. Such speeches were usually printed in full. Almost all conveyed the same charges against the "Rebels," and professed sentiments of unswerving devotion and loyalty to the Union. The arguments were made that "ambitious men" had "influenced the popular mind," and caused the Union to be broken up; that a "mass of idle had been forced into the Confederate army" and were being held there after their term of service had expired; that many eminent Unionists had been forced to leave or were entirely suppressed. Their favorite contentions, however, were that the "rebellion" had been "sprung upon Louisiana," and that she never really went out;[48] that the secessionists had brought "desolation to New Orleans"; and that the criminal "manufacturers of public opinion" had caused the "cursed rebellion."

But the spirit of unanimity which the leaders showed in their wholesale condemnation of the secession movement and the prosecution of the war on the part of the Confederacy was not apparent in their discussions of methods of reconstruction and restoration. However, divisions in their ranks that became notorious, especially after the distribution of the "loaves and fishes,"—and the discovery that there would not be enough for all,—were not made manifest during the Butler regime.

The Unionists believed in the main—or professed to believe at this time—that there should be a cessation of civil war and restoration of the states to their "former position"; that Louisiana was still an "integral and inseparable part of the Union";[49] that there should be unconditional submission and the extension of clemency to erring men; that since the cause of the Confederacy was fast waning, and there was now a "chance to select good Union men," representatives should forthwith be elected to the National body; and that the state machinery of government should as quickly as possible be resurrected by the loyalists and reorganized on a popular basis of representation.[50] Thus was the appeal made to the old conservatives, to the poorer working class composed[51] of the "witty loyal of the Green Isle," and to that "grateful, thrifty, industrious German" element.[52]

That this movement in Louisiana was not altogether spontaneous can be ascertained from the press reports that Butler was occasionally present at these so-called "Great Union Demonstrations." The hand of Lincoln seems also to have made its influence felt. He is not mentioned in any of the resolutions, nor in the orations as yet, but he probably found, as in other central places, some indirect way to give the movement impetus and to direct its course, as the following letter which was written at this time, reveals:

The copy of a letter, addressed to yourself by Mr. Thomas J. Durant, has been shown to me. The writer appears to be an able, a dispassionate and an entirely sincere man. The first part of the letter is devoted to an effort to show that the secession ordinance of Louisiana was adopted against the will of a majority of the people. This is probably true, and in that fact may be found some instruction. Why did they allow the ordinance to go into effect? Why did they not exert themselves? The paralysis . . . the dead palsy . . . of the Government in this whole struggle is, that this class of men will do nothing for the Government, nothing for themselves, except demand that the Government shall not strike its enemies, lest they be struck by accident!

Mr. Durant complains that . . . the relation of master and slave is disturbed by the presence of our army. . . .

. . . I think I can perceive, in the freedom of trade which Mr. Durant urges, that he would relieve both friends and enemies from the pressure of the blockade. By this he would serve the enemy more effectively than the enemy is able to serve himself.

. . . there are a class of men who, having no choice of sides in the contest, are anxious only to have quiet and comfort themselves while it rages. . . .

Of course, the rebellion will never be suppressed in Louisiana, if the professed Union men there will neither help to do it nor permit the Government to do it without their help.

. . . the true remedy is very different from what is suggested by Mr. Durant. . . . The people of Louisiana who wish protection to person and property, have but to reach forth their hands and take it. Let them in good faith reinaugurate the national authority and set up a State government conforming thereto under the constitution. They know how to do it, and can have the protection of the army while doing it. The army will be withdrawn so soon as such government can dispense with its presence, and the people of the State can then, upon the old terms, govern themselves to their own liking. This is very simple and easy.

If they will not do this—if they prefer to hazard all for the sake of destroying the Government—it is for them to consider whether it is probable I will surrender the Government to save them from losing all. If they decline what I suggest, you scarcely need ask what I will do.[53]

Butler devised an oath for practically all classes and ages. The returned and paroled Confederates were required to register their names and residence and take a rigid oath; those who did not give their parole within one day after their arrival and take the prescribed oath to abstain from any Confederate activities whatsoever were to be treated as spies.[54] All others in the department who had ever claimed to be citizens of the United States, or any person "asking or receiving any favor, protection, privilege, or passport" were required to take and subscribe to an oath to "bear true faith and allegiance to the United States of America," and to "support the Constitution thereof." He ruled that all foreigners who had "been residents within" the United States for "the space of five years" should be treated as citizens of the United States, unless they could procure evidence to the contrary within sixty days. But should they succeed in establishing their foreign nationality within the limited time they must still take the oath required of all foreigners to "do no act, or consent that any be done, or conceal any that has been, or is about to be done that shall aid or comfort any of the enemies or opposers of the United States whatsoever."[55]

The order concerning foreigners caused much friction during his entire regime. Of the 5,000 paroled Confederate soldiers in the city, it was alleged that all but 300 not only took the original oaths required, but "chose the wiser part" by taking the subsequent oath of allegiance, and "cast their lot with the government of their birth, rather than be exchanged and resume their places in the ranks of the Southern Confederacy."[56] The first official figures on the "allegiance oath" and the foreigners' oath appeared in August and showed that the former had been administered to 11,723 male citizens, and that 2,499 male foreigners had complied with the requirements.[57]

The women and even the negroes were also brought within the purview of the President's confiscation proclamation on the ground that "all persons," included them. Butler had subsequently discovered that there was an "immense number" of women who held property separate and apart from their husbands, and that the women were the most active in "aiding, countenancing, and abetting rebellion." And his ruling that they must return to their allegiance by taking the oath, or suffer the penalty of the law,[58] greatly augmented the throngs of applicants during the closing days. The result was that there was a good deal of "swearing" done by persons of both sexes, and of all ages, conditions, and colors. The interpretation placed on "all persons" by Butler had indeed been most liberal when it also included the colored. But being elated at the idea of exercising their newly fledged privileges, these negroes literally thronged the Custom House and City Hall on the last day [September 23] to obtain their prized certificates as evidence of having had the oath administered.[59]

The grand total who took the oath was reported as 67,920, of whom 6,538 were "aliens."[60] This did not include the young men without property who were not urged to return to the faith, since they had no property worth considering.[61] Butler, however, had not allowed any other group, not even ministers, to remain neutral. For this reason it is impossible to conjecture the number that took the oath from pure motives. Butler's organ estimates it at fifty per cent. Other evidence would tend to prove that those who took it because of compulsion and only paid lip service to it far outnumbered those who were impelled by the purest motives.[62]

But the Confiscation Act was apparently enforced by Butler to the exact letter. He had from the first occupancy appropriated for himself and his officers the most imposing mansions of the absent Confederate generals. These were located in the exclusive residential sections of the city, and were occupied some time before the promulgation of the Confiscation Act.[63] His soldiers, according to reports, were also ravaging the countryside and hauling or driving away practically everything that the "rebels" possessed before it went into effect. Reports of such activities were not published; but the following account bears testimony to what was happening during the first few months' tenure in Louisiana:

> Last Saturday, by order, at one plantation of Captain Harry Harsel, a Confederate, we took forty negroes, sixty horses, two hundred head of cattle, forty bales of cotton, and burned twelve houses. . . . We also took $100,000 worth of property in twenty-four hours.[64]

Two preliminary confiscatory acts had in fact preceded the all-embracing Act of July 17, 1862. The first, which was passed by the Washington government on August 3, 1861, made provision for the confiscation of all property and forfeiture of all slaves used in any manner against the Federal Government.[65] As had been foreseen, the Confederacy countered with a retaliatory act, which made legal the seizure of all property, real and personal, of Northern subjects, including debts owed to Northern firms or individuals, which was to offset any losses incurred under the Federal act.[66] But the act under which Butler operated, and seems to have earned his unsavory reputation, was the Act of July 17, 1862.[67] It directed the President to cause the seizure of "all the estate and property, money, stocks, credits, and effects" of six classes of Confederates (all the civil and military officers); and it provided further for the seizure of all the property of any of the residue who, "aiding, countenancing, or abetting the rebellion, should not return to their allegiance within sixty days."[68]

Upon the expiration of the prescribed sixty days Butler promptly issued his "Order, Number 76." It required all, of both sexes, over eighteen years to list and describe all their property, and register themselves. This included the aliens and the loyal, as well as those who had not taken the oath of allegiance. All were provided with certificates defining their status. The latter class, that is, those who had not taken the oath of allegiance, were forced to register as "enemies of the United States," and received certificates to the effect that they had publicly declared themselves as such. For failure to comply with this registration order, a severe fine and imprisonment and confiscation of all personal and real property were decreed.[69] Some 4,000 irreconcilables, women as well as men, registered as enemies of the United States. These and others who so desired were provided with conveyance "to go within the rebel lines and not to return."[70] Such treatment of women was justified by Butler, who alleged that they were the most devout rebels, that they possessed much property, and that much more was being transferred to them to defeat the purposes of the Confiscation Act. However, many had no alternative but to take the oath. So, taking it under duress, as some authorities stated, they only paid lip service to it and compromised with their conscience by asserting that "a compulsory oath was not binding."[71]

The property of these registered enemies, together with much property of absentee Confederates who had no opportunity to take

[61]

the oath, if they had so desired, was forthwith seized and sold at auction to the speculators who followed Butler's army. These sales included not only the real estate, but the "furniture, gold, and silver plate" and personal effects.[72]

There appears to have been some unlawful entering of houses, and some unlawful seizures and sales in connection with the execution of this order. When the Unionists made loud complaints, Butler sought to curb this by announcing that the severest punishment would be administered upon his officers, or soldiers, who were guilty of unauthorized seizures.[73] But the sincerity of such a declaration was questioned, especially by his critics, in the light of his subsequent "Order, Number 91."[74] This order classed the population west of the river as disloyal, and served notice that "all property in this District of Lafourche is sequestered." This was explained to be all the parishes west of the river, except Plaquemines and Jefferson. The orders further directed that all this personal property be gathered and sold at public auction in New Orleans, after all army needs had been provided for. For the purposes of the order, all were to be treated as "rebels." It did, however, provide for reclamation; that is, loyal citizens, as well as foreigners, could put in claims for proceeds. Such treatment of many outspoken Unionists, whether they were sincere or not in their declarations, must have operated against the growth of a strong Unionist party in Louisiana. But it appears that "no distinction was to be shown between the loyal, and disloyal."

Butler became so deeply absorbed—or involved—in his confiscation schemes that he seems to have temporarily lost sight of the fact that he was sent to "rescue" and restore Louisiana. Nor does he make satisfactory explanation of the disposition of the proceeds that were realized from the confiscations. Despite the fact that much of the property was probably sold for a pittance to the speculators, considerable sums must have come into Butler's possession. Both Butler and his biographer claim that he "turned over to General Banks nearly $800,000 in cash and unsold property. . . ."[75] If this is true, it is strange that Banks did not mention it in any of his subsequent reports. Other contemporary sources would tend to disprove such allegations. The *Annual Cyclopaedia,* in fact, gives a much smaller sum. Butler's "defaulting quarter-master here turned over $75 as the net proceeds of the sales of all the splendid Paris-made furniture, gold and silver plates . . . taken from the houses of rich absentees and registered enemies."[76] Judge Durell, a Unionist, says:

> The net proceeds of property adjudged to the United States will be only $100,000. . . . Harpies . . . have done nothing but make money out of both parties during the war, and profit by confiscation; the government does not.[77]

In the meanwhile interest was aroused over the regular fall elections of congressmen from Louisiana to the Federal Congress. Lincoln unquestionably encouraged and stimulated this move-ment. He wrote a letter under date of July 31, 1862, stating that he was anxious to have Louisiana take her place in the Union as it was, "barring the already broken eggs."[78] Butler also later testified before the "Committee on the Conduct of the War" that he had been "informed from Washington that it would be very desirable to have Congressional elections in that part of Louisiana which was under our control."[79] Furthermore frequent use was made of the President's proclamation of September 22, 1862, to influence the electorate to participate in this election, on the ground that a state that was represented in the Federal Congress on January 1, 1863, would not be considered as being in a state of rebellion, but would come within his proclamation.[80]

But regardless of motives, the question was being agitated as early as the first weeks in August. The loyal German and French elements at this early date seem to have brought forward S. F. Glenn, a man of some prestige, and to have sponsored his elec-tion for the First Congressional District, lately represented by Bouligny.[81] Other arguments used to give impetus to the move-ment were that the registration showed some loyal sentiment, and that the early selection of good Union men, citizens of Louisiana, to represent the state in Washington, would help to defeat the "rebels."[82]

By November the movement had apparently gained enough popular support to warrant the issuing of a proclamation by the

[63]

military authorities for the elections in the two Congressional districts occupied by the Federals. The writs of election designated as the Second Congressional District: that part of the city above Canal Street known as the First District, and District Number Four, formerly the city of Lafayette, and the parishes of Jefferson, St. Charles, St. John the Baptist, St. James, Ascension, Assumption, Lafourche, Terrebonne, St. Mary, and St. Martin. The First District was to be composed of the remainder of the city, that portion of the Parish of Orleans lying on the right bank of the river, and the parishes of St. Bernard and Plaquemines. The oath of allegiance, and, in addition, the other qualifications prescribed by the laws of Louisiana, were the prerequisites prescribed for qualified voters by this writ. General Order No. 22, issued only a few days before the election, explained that registration was not necessary.[83]

The canvass was necessarily brief, but interesting in that it revealed at this early date a division in the ranks of the Unionist. All "Simon Pure Unionists," as the original Unionists were designated, agreed that the first requisite for a fit representative was "an untainted and unimpeachable fidelity to the Union." The Union association for this reason would not place its stamp of approval upon Bouligny, an aspirant and avowed Unionist. It did publicly endorse the candidacies of E. H. Durell and B. F. Flanders. The former was presented to the voters for his ability as a lawyer, his gentlemanly qualities, his ability, and his knowledge of the institutions and interests of Louisiana. The latter had "always been a patriotic, public spirited gentleman," and "fully acquainted with" the citizens and their interests.[84]

Others entered the race as independents, including a Mr. Barker, a Unionist candidate in the Second District, who boldly dubbed Butler and the army as "adventurers." Dr. Cottman, another independent Second District candidate, was said to have been persuaded to withdraw his name, and Michael Hahn was presented in his stead, by a group of Unionists, despite the fact that Judge Durell had already received the official endorsement.[85]

The spirited contest ended on December 2 with the election of "unconditional Union men in both districts" by large and decisive votes. The total vote cast in the First District was 2,543 against 4,011 in 1859. Bouligny, who also persisted in running independently, received less than 200 votes, while B. F. Flanders, the endorsed Unionist candidate, received 366 more than a majority of the whole number cast in 1859. There were no returns from four of the parishes in the Second District, but the total number of votes returned was 4,874, of which Hahn, the people's candidate and a German by birth, who had lived in Louisiana since childhood, received 2,581, a majority of 54 over his three opponents.[86] Judge Durell, the Unionist candidate, received a large vote, but was several hundred votes behind the successful candidate. The other two Unionists, Jacob Barker, who was designated as a "negro worshipper," and Greathouse, a conservative Unionist, received a few hundred each. Since the total vote cast in 1859 in this district was 8,944, and the total vote cast in this election was reported as 4,874, of which Hahn had received 2,581, he had made a creditable showing by polling not only a majority of the votes cast in his own election, but more than a majority of the votes cast in the similar election of 1859.[87]

Various causes had, however, operated to make the total vote light. The number of voters registered in the city was given at about 15,000 at this time, although registration was not, as has been mentioned above, a requisite qualification. But the average vote for the last five elections in the city had been only 7,310. Several thousand, enrolled in the army, were absent. Three thousand of these were reported to be in the Federal army, and were not present to vote on this occasion. Under these circumstances, a vote of 7,417 in both districts was considered as a signal triumph.

This first effort at reconstruction seemed to augur well for the future.[88] But there were signs of division, for the lukewarm Confederates and those who were formerly connected with the Confederacy had been outlawed by the "Simon Pure Unionists." These Unionists were, furthermore, not united as to what they wanted. It was already evident that there was a conservative faction who wished to save the Union, and, above all, to save slavery as it was. There was another group of Unionists whose ranks were being recruited, and who were indifferent or hostile to slavery, and would

[65]

throw it overboard. They would also make of the state a "white man's country." The negro did not as yet fit into their scheme of things.

The two newly elected congressmen started for Washington early in December. Both were, according to the Unionist organ, expected to "sustain Lincoln in every measure, which he proposes, which has for its end the salvation of the Union." This organ also reflected their attitude towards emancipation and the disposition of the negro, when it continued: "They will do this [support Lincoln] at any cost—not excepting the freedom of every slave in America."[89]

There was, however, considerable doubt as to whether they would be given an opportunity to support the President. The radical Republicans seem to have opposed their admission on the presumption that by so doing they might bring their district within the scope of Lincoln's emancipation proclamation, and the Democrats, because of an apprehension that, the door once open to the admission of members from the states in revolution, their party would be swamped with their Republican votes.[90] However, Lincoln's proclamation, declaring the freedom of all slaves within certain states and portions of states, seems to have removed some of the opposition of the ultras, and they were eventually seated.[91]

A rumor was current in August and the early part of September that General Butler was to be relieved. His official organ dismissed it with a statement that such an act "would give pleasure only to bitter secessionists, and to a few grumblers"; and it added that his administration had been so "marked by a spirit of wisdom and moderation" as to win "the good will of the unprejudiced," and "ultimately extort commendation."[92] But the rumors persisted until confirmation of his recall was received in early December.[93] He affected to be surprised beyond measure, and seems never to have been able to explain adequately the reason for his removal.[94] The reasons, however, seem obvious. The most urgent, as most authorities have agreed, was his treatment of the consuls and other foreigners. Foreign relations had, in fact, become so strained as a result that there was an almost unanimous demand of the ministers from those countries for his removal.[95]

[66]

MAP NO. 4

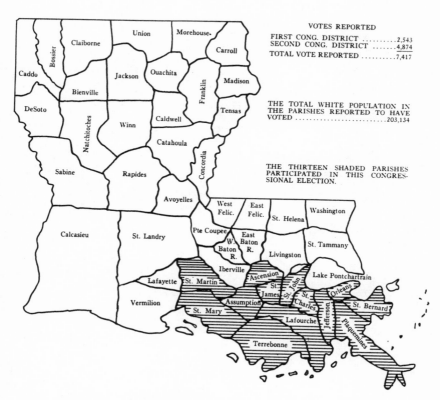

VOTES REPORTED

FIRST CONG. DISTRICT 2,543
SECOND CONG. DISTRICT 4,874
TOTAL VOTE REPORTED 7,417

THE TOTAL WHITE POPULATION IN
THE PARISHES REPORTED TO HAVE
VOTED 203,134

THE THIRTEEN SHADED PARISHES
PARTICIPATED IN THIS CONGRES-
SIONAL ELECTION.

THE FIRST ATTEMPT TO RESTORE LOUISIANA (DECEMBER 1862)

His "woman order" also seems to have met with general condemnation, especially in England, where it had been violently denounced in the House of Lords as "without precedent," and "infamous," and the hope had been freely expressed that it would be disavowed.[96]

The *New York World* also charges that General Butler "tortured New Orleans—a city where the Unionists were ready [for reconstruction] when first occupied by the Federals—into hopeless disloyalty"; that he exacted money from the captains of vessels before allowing them to clear; and that his tyrannical custom-house regulations and seizure of "custom-house deposits" had "disrupted . . . the whole system of exports, and imports."[97]

But the report of Reverdy Johnson, who came to New Orleans and made an investigation under Lincoln's commission, seems to have been the most incriminating. It charged that a number of the members of Butler's staff had been "guilty of fraud and corruption"; that his conduct in the financial transaction between the Bank of New Orleans and the French and Dutch consuls was indefensible; and, finally, that:

Unless the almost universal belief of gentlemen of intelligence and integrity in the city, having every means of knowledge, be wholly unfounded, and the reports of officers of the highest character in the service of the government, who have officially visited the city since it has been in the possession of the military, be also wholly unfounded, a state of fraud and corruption exists there that is without parallel in the history of the country.

Continuing his sensational charges against Butler, because of "aspersions" cast on himself, Johnson inserted the following card in a local New Orleans paper:

. . . But if he will exert the acuteness, and energy, which have heretofore had a different direction, into the investigation of some of those around him he will soon discover that the people of New Orleans, since they have been under his sway, have been perhaps as much sinned against as sinning; and he will also discover why (Rev. Johnson), who was acting under the immediate commission of the President, and who approves the results of the investigation, was assailed by some of these persons under his (Butler's) command. Their aspersions are utterly

[67]

false. Growing rich themselves on the necessities of the helpless people around them, by extortions offensive to decency, they seem evidently to be under the apprehension that my report, or knowledge of their conduct, may not only put an end to their career of plunder, but to subject them to the punishment due to their misdeeds.[98]

Charges of such sensational nature could hardly be ignored by the administration. But there were other, more serious, charges. It was alleged that he had unnecessarily sacrificed the lives of his soldiers and officers in private commercial ventures in which his brother, Dr. Andrew J. Butler, was growing immensely rich, and in which enterprises the Commander was to all outward appearances a silent partner. The still graver charge that he was guilty of treason because of his trade with the Confederates[99] made some action on the part of the Government absolutely imperative. The entire matter, it appeared, must be thrashed out and the guilty parties punished, or it should be hushed up. "The Committee on the Conduct of the War" evidently deemed it expedient to choose the latter course, for after a protracted session at Washington, it published what was purported to be "the entire testimony," according to which Butler was apparently exonerated.[100]

The final episode was the dramatic leave-taking, which required several days, and caused quite a stir.[101] Butler had announced that he would be happy to see his officers and those citizens who wished to call upon him. It is reported that quite a number came forward to participate in the elaborate ceremony, and to hear his farewell address. He had previously addressed the Army of the Gulf, reminding them that "a handful had compelled submission of the Queen City of the rebellion," and that they had not only "brought order, law, quiet, and peace," and enriched the government by "nearly one-half million," but had "fed the starving," won the confidence of the "oppressed race," "taught them to fight," blotted out "pestilence," and "met double numbers of the enemy and defeated him in the open field."[102] But he reserved his consoling words for the recalcitrant, or disloyal, citizens in his "farewell," in which he revealed what might have happened had he been inspired by less "nobler sentiments." This "farewell address" shows Butler's apparent lack of a sense

[68]

of humor, and it breathes a spirit of hatred towards the foreign countries that had no doubt been chiefly instrumental in his removal. The pertinent part follows:

CITIZENS OF NEW ORLEANS:—It may not be inappropriate, as it is not inopportune on occasion, that there should be addressed to you a few words at parting, by one whose name is to be hereafter indissolubly connected with your city. . . . You might have been smoked to death in caverns, as were the Covenanters of Scotland; or roasted, like the inhabitants of Algiers during the French campaign; your wives and daughters might have been given over to the ravisher, as were the unfortunate dames of Spain in the Peninsular war; or you might have been scalped and tomahawked as our mothers were at Wyoming by the savage allies of Great Britain in our own Revolution; your property could have been turned over to indiscriminate "loot," like the palace of the Emperor of China . . . your sons might have been blown from the mouths of cannons like the Sepoys at Delhi; and yet all this would have been within the rules of civilized warfare as practiced by the most polished and the most hypocritical nations of Europe. For such acts records of the doings of some of the inhabitants of your city towards the friends of the Union, before my coming, were a sufficient provocative and justification."[103]

Butler's "farewell address" was evidently delivered with the purpose of emulating that of the Father of his Country, for this "great deliverer" seems to have believed that he was playing a similar role in history. He has not as yet, however, been accorded a place as a soldier and statesman alongside that of his illustrious predecessor. But he did excel him as a prophet in his farewell address, for he has gone down in history, at least in Louisiana history, as a prophet of no mean ability. His name, as he has correctly prophesied, has been "indissolubly connected" with the city of New Orleans, where he still enjoys the unenviable sobriquets of "Picayune Butler," "Spoon Butler," and "Beast Butler."

CHAPTER IV

BANKS PREPARES LOUISIANA
FOR RESTORATION

The new Commander, General N. P. Banks, who enjoyed the full confidence of the administration, was apparently well fitted to the task of restoring the Constitution and the laws. He had served as a state legislator, member of Congress, Speaker of the House, and governor of his native state of Massachusetts; and in contrast to his predecessor, he was "a man of striking appearance and graceful manners."[1] The war had recalled him from his retirement in Illinois, and his recent impressive Shenandoah Valley record and Cedar Mountain achievement had greatly enhanced his reputation and prestige. He had, in short, come to be recognized as a capable warrior and able statesman, and was being prominently mentioned for the War Department portfolio.[2]

In his first proclamation Banks gave evidence of his political ability and purpose in Louisiana. "The duty with which I am charged," he said, "requires me to assist in the restoration of the Government of the United States." He promised to protect all, to consider liberally the claims of all, to eliminate all private and public suffering; and asked the co-operation and counsel of all in effecting this program with the following appeal:

People of the South-west! Why not accept the conditions imposed by the imperious necessity of geographical configuration, and re-establish your ancient prosperity and renowns? Why not become the founders of a state which as the entrepots and depots of your own central, and upper valley, may stand in the affluence of their resources without superior and in the privileges of the people, without a peer among the nations of the earth?[3]

This declaration of intentions to pursue a policy of liberality, conciliation, and magnanimity was followed shortly by another address that was even more reassuring. Speaking on the subject of emancipation, he declared that the State of Louisiana was "not in rebellion against the United States," because it was at that very time represented in Congress, and in addition he held out promises of pecuniary aid to all the loyal "for losses by acts of the United

[70]

MAP No. 5

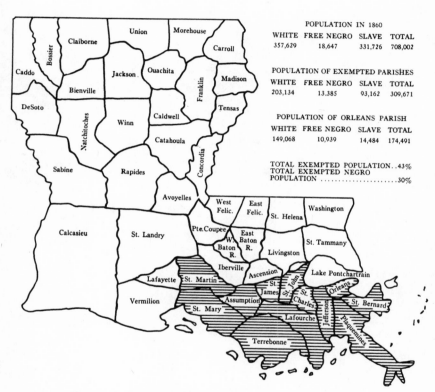

POPULATION IN 1860

WHITE	FREE NEGRO	SLAVE	TOTAL
357,629	18,647	331,726	708,002

POPULATION OF EXEMPTED PARISHES

WHITE	FREE NEGRO	SLAVE	TOTAL
203,134	13.385	93,162	309,671

POPULATION OF ORLEANS PARISH

WHITE	FREE NEGRO	SLAVE	TOTAL
149,068	10,939	14,484	174,491

TOTAL EXEMPTED POPULATION..43%
TOTAL EXEMPTED NEGRO
POPULATION 30%

LINCOLN'S EMANCIPATION PROCLAMATION IN LOUISIANA
(EXEMPTED PARISHES SHADED)

States, including slaves." It would not be his policy, he asserted, to encourage the laborers to desert, and neither was the war being waged for the "overthrow of slavery." Such statements, however, must have been most difficult to reconcile with subsequent ones: that he had no authority to compel the slaves to return to their masters, and that "the first gun at Fort Sumter proclaimed emancipation."[4] Furthermore his promulgation of the emancipation proclamation, which forbade the officers of the army and navy to return slaves to their owners,[5] even in the exempted parishes of St. Bernard, Plaquemines, Jefferson, Assumption, Terrebonne, Lafourche, St. Mary, St. Martin, and Orleans, was not calculated to arouse much additional enthusiasm for the Union cause.[6] However, General Banks was, in the beginning, personally popular with the masses, for he was a gentleman, dignified and respectful to all, and his demeanor, in contrast to that of Butler, was quiet and unobtrusive.

This early policy of attempted conciliation and liberality is reflected in his several "General Orders." He ordered that all sales of property on account of the government must be suspended until further orders, indicating very clearly his attitude towards "the ignoble army of speculators, confiscators, and devastators."[7] He commanded that all houses which had been taken possession of for the Government must be given up, and that such houses were no longer to be occupied for military purposes, except by special assignment;[8] that the order closing certain churches be provisionally suspended; and that the prisoners be released.[9] He added that no permits would be given to travel or trade beyond the lines;[10] and that registered enemies would be permitted to withdraw themselves as such, but would first be given ample opportunity to take the oath of allegiance.[11]

The Banks policy, however, seems to have been considered weak, timorous, and hesitant, especially by his associates, and he was soon compelled to adopt a more rigorous one.[12] Whether it would have succeeded, if continued, is doubtful. But his subsequent orders of May 1—that all registered enemies within the Department must depart within fifteen days; that no further transfers of property would be tolerated; and that "no persons, not loyal citizens of the United States" would be permitted "within the limits of the Department"—are evidence of the fact that his policy of conciliation had undergone a radical revision.[13] A rigorous enforcement of the "Enemy" clause resulted in a general exodus for the Confederacy of "Rebels," most of whom were in abject poverty.[14] He also decreed the death penalty for all who furnished "supplies to the enemies of the United States in arms."[15] But his special ire seems to have been aroused against the schoolmasters, schoolmistresses, and church officials. In the case of those who "propagated treason under the *mantle of religion,*" he was unsuccessful in his attempts at suppression. But many teachers, even in private schools, were heavily fined during the month of May for having Confederate flags and emblems in their possession, and for teachings that were considered to be of "insulting and seditious character."[16]

The movement for the re-establishment of a civil state government was in large measure contingent upon the decision of the House of Representatives as to the status of the two recently elected congressmen, Hahn and Flanders. The Louisiana election case had been referred to the House Election Committee, and there seemed little doubt all along that it would decide in favor of seating the two gentlemen. According to the evidence submitted the elective franchise had been freely exercised, and the voters had been unhampered by the "rebel" forces; nor did the evidence show that the election had been interfered with by the military authorities. The principal point in doubt appeared to be that the time of election fixed by the military governor, Shepley, differed from that of the law of Louisiana. It was contended, however, that the Constitution of the United States guaranteed to every state a republican form of government, and that this made it necessary and incumbent upon him to assume to fix the time.[17] The question of recognition, however, was debated at intervals for several weeks, in the course of which it was further alleged that President Lincoln had usurped his powers in appointing a military governor.[18] In answer, Noell stated that "our armies" had been sent to Louisiana "to subjugate the rebels, and to restore the Union," and that since Louisiana had elected the two congressmen in good faith on the basis of the "proclamation," that good faith on the part of the

House demanded the recognition of the State by seating the two members.[19] But the case was not decided, and Louisiana was kept in suspense, until about two weeks before the close of the session. At that time (February 17, 1863) Hahn, who had the privileges of the floor, delivered a telling speech in which he contended that New Orleans was a Union city, and not a hotbed of secession, and that Louisiana had contributed thousands of loyal soldiers to the Union army.[20] He was evidently most convincing, for the final vote for seating the two members was 92 to 44.[21] Whereupon Hahn was duly sworn, but Flanders, who was absent, was not sworn at this time.

Heartened by this recognition of the State by the acceptance of its duly elected congressmen, an active movement was now launched by certain groups to effect complete and speedy restoration of civil government within the state. This movement was sponsored largely by the Union Association and its auxiliary clubs, which had been reorganized with the approval of General Banks, and with Dr. J. L. Riddell, president, James Graham, vice-president, and S. G. Boner, secretary, and other prominent Unionists participating.[22] The general meetings were held weekly at Lyceum Hall. Press reports indicated that there were large and enthusiastic crowds in attendance to hear the "stirring and effective" speeches of the orators. They also gave the information that the roster of membership showed that thousands were signing the roll.[23] It was not, however, until after the receipt of the favorable action by the House that a resolution was introduced in one of these regular meetings memorializing the governor to order an election of delegates to frame a new constitution and to organize a new state government. This resolution was debated at many meetings, but laid over from time to time, for various reasons. Some opponents of immediate action voiced the sentiment that the time was not yet opportune, but that they should wait until all the state had been redeemed.[24] On the other hand, some urged immediate action, contending that no disrespect was meant to the military authorities; that such action would prove to be the salvation of the state; and that thousands of the Union men in New Orleans were ready to make a bonfire of the Constitution of 1852,

[73]

and to make a "free State" of Louisiana by at once "abolishing forever the curse of slavery."[25] But no definite action could be reached until Mr. Durant read a letter from Honorable M. Hahn, stating that in a conversation held with President Lincoln upon the subject of organizing a civil government for Louisiana the President heartily approved of the reorganization of the state and promised to send instructions to the military authorities in New Orleans to favor the movement. Hahn had evidently convinced the President by his argument that 13,000 square miles of the state and 350,000 of the population of 1860 were within the Union lines. This communication from Hahn no doubt was instrumental in bringing to a vote in the Union Association meeting the long-deferred question of holding a Convention. Upon the motion of Dr. A. P. Dostie it was decided affirmatively by a vote of 95 to 73.[26]

But action on organizing a state government was delayed partially because General Banks was just then beginning his 1863 campaign, and it was confidently believed among Unionists that the entire state would be in their possession in less than a month. Such sentiments were expressed by Hahn before the Union Association upon his return from Washington. He also asserted that in his last interview with Lincoln, the President had continued to express the hope that a state government would speedily be organized, and that he had given assurances that the military would be instructed to render all the necessary assistance.[27]

But still another factor which must also have cautioned delay was the lack of unanimity among the Unionists themselves as to any definite method of restoration. The heated debates among the leaders, who persisted in rousing interest through the frequent Union meetings, revealed at least two distinct, and opposing, schools of thought. All citizens, it appeared, wished to terminate the burdens of martial law, and all must have been stimulated in their efforts at restoration by the hope of "loaves and fishes."

Still, one group, which consisted largely of the conservative Unionist slaveholders, was honestly striving to maintain as far as possible the *status quo*. This group, which had most at stake, was ready to repudiate secession, and to preserve the Union.

[74]

However, they earnestly hoped to preserve slavery, not only in the exempted portions of Louisiana, but elsewhere, upon the termination of hostilities. Their chief spokesman frankly admitted in a subsequent address[28] that such was their intention and motives, although they appear to have cautiously concealed at this time the idea of the possible restitution of slavery. They were willing, and no doubt they intended to have the entire question of slavery decided before the highest tribunal at the close of the war; and in the event that it was not restored everywhere, they confidently hoped that they, as loyal citizens, would be fully compensated for all losses, whether within or without the proclamation, or emancipation line. This faction, therefore, while agreeing with their fellow Unionists that the secession convention and its acts were illegal, and while ready to join hands in complete repudiation of the "folly and madness" of the "principal plotters of rebellion," strenuously opposed the calling of a constitutional convention. They alleged that the Constitution of 1852 was sufficient for all needs, and that it needed only to be *revived*.[29] In short, their theory of a dormant constitution seemed to coincide with Lincoln's theory that the state was never out of the Union, and that since the acts of secession were null and void, the state must be resuscitated by the original instrument of 1852, which provided for slavery, and for representation on a basis of total population, white and black.

Being obsessed with this theory of preserving the Union, this faction, which appeared to be in the minority, refused to abide by a report made by the Committee of the Union Association suggesting that Governor Shepley be requested to provide for an election of delegates to a constitutional convention.[30] It even adopted the policy of making a bid for Lincoln's support. In pursuance of this course, it now dispatched Thomas Cottman, E. C. Mathoit, and Brandish Johnston to Washington—that they might prevail upon the President to instruct the military authorities to allow the approaching November elections, which would be held as provided for under the Constitution of 1852. This committee presented its credentials and asked that Louisiana be permitted to return to its place in the Union "with its Constitution unimpaired, and with all its rights recognized as they have existed previous to the passage of the ordinance of secession, and to the full enjoyment of all rights and privileges exercised by other States under the Constitution."[31] Lincoln, who evidently refused to be embarrassed by the official reception of this committee of Unionist planters, received its petition in writing, and answered in like manner, clearly demonstrating that he was in sympathy with the radical leaders of his party, and with them was taking more advanced ground. The complete text follows:

MESSERS E. E. MATHOIT, BRANDISH JOHNSTON, AND THOMAS COTTMAN:

Gentlemen—Your letter which follows has been received and considered:

To HIS EXCELLENCY, ABRAHAM LINCOLN, PRESIDENT OF THE UNITED STATES,

The undersigned, a committee appointed by the planters of the State of Louisiana, respectfully represent that they have been delegated to seek of the General Government a full recognition of all the rights of the State as they existed previous to the passage of an act of secession, upon the principle of the existence of the State Constitution unimpaired, and no legal act having transpired that could in any way deprive them of the advantages conferred by the Constitution. Under this Constitution, the State wishes to return to its full allegiance in the enjoyment of all rights and privileges exercised by the other States under the Federal Constitution. With the view of accomplishing the desired object, we further request your Excellency will, as Commander-in-chief of the army of the United States, direct the military Governor of Louisiana to order an election, in conformity with the Constitution, and laws of the State, on the first Monday of November next, for all State Federal officers.

With high consideration and respect we have the honor to subscribe ourselves your obedient servants,

E. E. MATHOIT
BRANDISH JOHNSTON
THOMAS COTTMAN

Since the letter reliable information has reached me that a respectable portion of the Louisiana people desire to amend their State Constitution, and contemplate holding a Convention for that object. This fact alone, as it seems to me, is a sufficient reason why the general government should not give the Committee the authority you seek to act under the existing State Constitution. I may add, that while I do not perceive how such a Committee could facilitate our military operations in Louisiana, I really apprehend it might be so used as to embarrass them.

As to an election to be held next November, there is abundant time without any order or proclamation from me just now. The people of Louisiana shall not lack an opportunity for a fair election for both federal and state officers by want of anything within my power to give them.[32]

The other faction, which soon dominated the Union Association and the subsidiary Union Clubs, had, in the main, little or nothing at stake, and grew more radical with the changing course of events. It seems to have recognized that a social revolution was in the making and apparently advocated breaking with the past, and, whether or not it yet believed that the state had committed "political suicide," it now proceeded on the theory that it had. This "Free State Party," as it soon came to style itself, urged the formation of a new constitution. It contended that slavery was dead, and that a convention should frame a constitution that would meet the needs of the new conditions, and would at the same time provide for a "Free State," according to the stricter interpretation of the term. It was no longer willing to submit to the rule of the "Black God of the South," but was determined to have a constitution by which both the rights of "white men" and a "free soil State government" would be secured.[33] Accordingly its committee filed a complete report with Governor Shepley, recommending in detail the action that they hoped would be taken in response to their resolution for a convention. It urged upon him the desirability of a state convention to be held within the near future in New Orleans, and insisted that "every loyal free white male" citizen of the United States, twenty-one years of age, six months in the state, and one month in the parish, who met all the additional requirements, should vote for delegates. It suggested one delegate for every 2,500 of the free white people of each parish by the census of 1860, one for each fraction over 1,250, and at least one for each parish, regardless of population. The number of delegates under this "white basis" plan would be 148, of whom 60 would represent the city, where the previous arbitrary arrangement would now be eliminated, and where there was only a small colored population. The committee made further provision that a number of registrars should be appointed to register the people and administer an ironclad loyalty oath to all who wished to participate in the reorganization of a state government.[34]

Governor Shepley's response was prompt and unequivocal: "The suggestions you make," he wrote, "are deserving of the highest consideration. . . . In the Associations are numbered a very large majority of the loyal and patriotic citizens. . . . Had the basis of representation been such as to have given a fair and equal representation to all the voters of the State, it is well known that the secession ordinance could never have been passed." He promised to issue an order for an immediate registration of the loyal, and concluded his communication with the assurance that "no citizen of Louisiana desires more earnestly than I do to see a civil government re-established."[35] This important order was immediately issued, and Thomas J. Durant was appointed commissioner of registration with strict orders to proceed at once to make "a full and fair registration" as a "preliminary to the re-establishment of civil Government in the State."[36]

Thus the Free State movement grew under the fostering care of the military; and, but for the almost fatal schism that developed shortly thereafter, and the fact that the city was the only place secure from the raids of the Confederates, the Free State Government might soon have been instituted, instead of being forced to wait many months for a more opportune time.

With the fall of Vicksburg and Port Hudson, and the receipt of the Gettysburg news, the struggle between the two Unionist factions for political power began in earnest. These reverses were generally interpreted to mean that the cause of the Confederacy was becoming more hopeless, and that state restoration could now be speedily effected with every hope of ultimate success. All Unionists became more outspoken, and vied with each other openly in manifesting their loyalty.[37] They felt that they could now reorganize the state unhampered; but the paramount question was: Would the factions harmonize their differences? If not, which would predominate? It soon became apparent that their differences were irreconcilable, and the movement which had appeared to take on a new impetus in July began to lag in August. The parties were now characterized in the press as manifesting a spirit of "listlessness, indifference, and stolid insensibility."[38] The spirit of factionalism almost paralyzed the movement. Neither faction seemed to desire a reorganization unless it was assigned the task. Each group, furthermore, took the position that if it could not organize with the assurance of complete control, it would, if possible, defeat reorganization until such time as it felt reasonably confident that it could. It was also generally recognized that Banks held the key to the whole difficulty; and now that he seemed to have the time, he was urged to restore the State, at the earliest possible moment, to its proper place in the Union.[39] The Gordian knot that needed to be cut, however, was the recent oath that had been prescribed as an indispensable requisite to registration. It had been so framed that "scarcely a man who had lived in the State during Confederate domination could conscientiously take it." It was, therefore, urged that Banks be given "plenary powers" to frame such an oath, and to take such action as to enable "every citizen to come forward and assist in the organization of a civil government."[40]

But General Banks evidently preferred not to act with undue haste. He proceeded on the assumption that the factions must fight out the issues among themselves, so that the stronger would emerge. And this is precisely what happened, for they adopted the policy, not of trying to reconcile differences, but of inaugurating a campaign to discredit each other, if possible, in the esteem of the administration. In this contest the less numerous Conservative Unionists, whose leaders had in many instances been identified in some way at least with the secession movement, or with the Confederacy, naturally found themselves at an unfortunate disadvantage. Such "delegations" of this party, as, for instance, Dr. Cottman, Christian Roselius, and Cuthbert Bullitt, who made trips to Washington to report on the management of Federal affairs and to obtain the ear of the administration, were attacked by the opposition party as being " a self-constituted delegation,"

[79]

a "delegation" that had "no constituents," and a delegation that had been identified with the "secession movement," and were therefore tainted by the Confederacy.[41] This group of Union men was frequently referred to as "copperheads," who would continue the negroes in bondage, and who would prevent the seizure of "the property of the traitor."[42]

On the other hand, when Hahn and others from the more radical Free State party made trips to Washington and the North "to obtain the ears of authority," they were represented by their press as being "no parasites" and no "time servers," but "able, judicious, and deserving men."[43] Their slogan, that the "Union of these states is more important than State or Constitutions," and their speeches, in which they designated their political opponents as "rebels, and traitors," seem to have been well received in the North, and undoubtedly influenced public opinion in their favor and against the Conservative Unionists.[44]

On one of these trips to the North, Hahn was invited to speak at Cooper's Institute. His speech was both interesting and illuminating. He represented that he came from a state that produced good Union men; that it would never have seceded in fact had it been allowed to vote, instead of being dragged out by the conspirators and rebels. He assured his audience, however, that the Germans in Louisiana were supporting Banks and that it would not be long before Louisiana would be restored to the Union.[45] This statement was enthusiastically received. But, more important to him and to his party, he was apparently building up a strong public sentiment in the North in favor of his Free State party, that was almost certain to influence the policy of the administration in such measure as materially to assist this radical Louisiana party.

The definite break between the Unionists did not occur, however, until the November elections. After spending some time in the North, Dr. Cottman had returned to Louisiana and announced his intention to run for Congress. The entry of the "Ascension Nag, Butler's old candidate," was greeted with derision by the more radical Free State press;[46] in fact, he was not taken seriously. The next move on the political chessboard by the so-called

[80]

"ambitious patriots" was met by the Free State party with an outburst of denunciation and vituperation. The Conservative Unionists, or a faction of this right wing, had assumed the privilege of selecting a complete slate of state and Congressional candidates for the regular November elections,[47] although the military had ordered no election. Confirmation of such intentions had been published in some papers on October 28, when there remained only four days in which to hold an election. This address, which called upon the people to elect "the officers of the civil government," had not in fact been authorized. Banks had certainly not been consulted. For these reasons, the press considered that the "absurdity of this movement exceeded, if possible, its audacity."[48] What or who inspired this address, which was published by order of the Executive Central Committee of Louisiana, and signed by such prominent citizens as W. W. Pugh, president, E. Ames, vice-president, and J. Q. A. Fellows, secretary, will doubtless remain one of the unsolved mysteries of this phase of reconstruction. The pertinent parts of this document follow:

We address you as loyal citizens . . . who have duties to perform to your country, your State, and Republican institutions. These institutions are in danger . . . and your State is without a regular organized civil government. Those obligations resting on you are paramount, and . . . require energetic and immediate action.

The want of a civil government in our State can, by a proper effort on your part, soon be supplied, under laws and a Constitution formed and adopted by yourself. It is your duty, therefore, to vote for all officers in November.

The day fixed by law is November 2nd. You need no other call to fix the time. It will be legal. Select your agents to carry on the government. The military will not interfere . . . in the exercise of . . . rights, and we think we can assure you that your action in this respect will meet the approval of the National Government. Should you suffer the day to pass, the whole country will be in a state of anarchy, without any civil government of the people's own choosing, and subject to be thrown as "vacated" territory into the hands of Congress, where it is the wish of many that it be thrown. . . . We charge this design upon a certain faction here and at the North, the result of whose action, in our minds, threatens to destroy Republican liberties, and Republican institutions.

We urge upon you action in this important crisis. It will convince the world of our determination to return to . . . management of our civil affairs. It will . . . bring peace. It will set an example to all. . . . In short, the tendency of your course on the . . . day of election . . . will be for weal or woe . . . as you act the part of true citizens by voting, or by failing to vote.

On the 2nd, . . . then go to the polls, and cast your vote as usual. Your chosen Congressmen will take their seat. . . . Your chosen Legislature . . . will meet. . . . Your State officers will . . . be inaugurated and the wheels of civil government will be set in motion. Fail . . . and your last opportunity for renewal of civil State Government in accordance with . . . legal provisions . . . will pass with probable destruction of Republican institutions.

Louisiana has always been at heart loyal to the United States. She never seceded by majority vote. . . . She was forced into the rebellion. But she is still one of the United States "thanks to the gallant army and navy."

If . . . events . . . require changes in our domestic laws, and policy, we shall hereafter have leisure to effect these changes.

Let us arise, then . . . and perform the sacred, and imperative duty of electing officers of civil government in Louisiana . . . and if we fail it may be the last time we shall have the power of acting as freemen.[49]

These Conservative Unionists at the same time dispatched the following communication to the Free State party, urging co-operation by this party in this movement:

We cordially invite you to join us, on Monday next, the 2nd, of November, the day fixed by the laws of Louisiana in a general election. . . .

Copy of rules and regulations adopted by us for the conduct of the election, in which we believe you will see proper to concur, is enclosed.

Endorsed is a complete list of our nominations for Congressmen, State officers, and the Legislative Representatives from New Orleans.

We assent to take the voice of the people, through the ballot-box, on the propriety of calling a Convention. The election of Monday next will in no wise interfere with or delay the call for a Convention. . . .

We trust you will reciprocate our courtesy and co-operate with us in the election to be held on Monday next.[50]

The proposal was duly considered by the more radical faction,

[82]

and it was unanimously resolved by the General Committee not to co-operate in such election. The reasons for declining were given in the brief answer, which indicated that the two factions had definitely come to a parting of the ways:

You invite us to join you on Monday next, the 2nd, of November. . . . We respectfully decline the invitation you have tendered. No election for members of Congress can be held in Louisiana until the State shall have been divided into five Congressional Districts. . . . The State can be divided into Districts only by the Legislature thereof, or by Congress.

We consider your proposal as a violation of the Constitution, and the act of Congress. . . .

There is no law in existence, as stated by you, directing elections to be held on the first Monday of November.

The Constitution of 1852, as amended by the Convention of 1861, was overthrown and destroyed by the rebellion. . . .

But not only is your movement illegal, but unjust; you are only a part. . . . You undertake to appoint your own Commissioners of Election; hold the polls at such places as you may select; admit such electors as may seem proper. . . . Neither you nor we, nor both of us together, are the people of Louisiana. . . .

The registration when completed, will make provision. . . . This we consider the only just path to the restoration of Civil Government . . . and we would be most happy if you would tread it in our company.[51]

When the conservatives ascertained that the Free State party had other plans, and that the military authorities regarded their movement as "opposed to the Government of the United States," they took hurried counsel among themselves, and decided that the hostile move of the military authority "had so completely affected the popular mind in the Parish of Orleans as to render it absolutely impossible to bring out the voters to the polls on Monday next." And, while this committee was of the opinion "that four-fifths of the voters" would, if given a fair opportunity, express their utter condemnation of the destructive principles advocated, and secretly maintained by the Free State party, it did not dare to defy the military authorities. The committee therefore resolved "that it is inexpedient to hold the election in the Parish of Orleans on

SECESSION AND RESTORATION OF LOUISIANA

Monday next." This resolution was given due publicity on the eve of the election.[52]

If the conservatives contemplated calling off the election outside of Orleans it was now too late to relay the message any distance. This led to a strange chapter in the abortive efforts of the Conservative Unionists to obtain the control. This episode was caused by the fact that a small scattering vote was actually cast outside the city, and an election claimed. The first evidence of the election is contained in a "notice" published in the *Daily True Delta*,[53] calling on "all persons friendly to the Constitutional Union Party of Louisiana, and in favor of restoring the Civil Government under the Constitution and laws existing," to meet at the Masonic Hall, No. 83, St. Charles Street "this evening" at six o'clock on "important business." The notice, signed by the secretary, J. Q. A. Fellows, must have proved that the conservatives had in no wise given up the struggle.

The *Times* gave an account of this meeting under the following headline: "The Knights of the Round Table." There were thirteen present around the table, including the reporter. After the meeting had been called to order, a Mr. Field, a recent candidate for Congress, arose and stated that he had received only one hundred and twenty-five votes, with two boxes to hear from. He declared, however, that he intended to go to Washington and urge his claim. Field contended, according to the reporter, that Virginia had elected a Congressman by a few votes, and that his claim was quite as valid. At the close of his speech it seems that a committee was appointed to get the signature of the whites who would agree to support the cause of these conservatives.[54]

The meeting adjourned to reconvene on the ninth. But there is no record of any public meeting on this date. In fact, the election of November 2 was ridiculed by the opposition as "a farce" until it appeared that the conservative Louisiana Congressmen might actually be received and gain recognition. When such action seemed possible, the Free State party, which had continued to hold its regular "Union Association Meetings" at Lyceum Hall, filed a vigorous protest with Speaker Colfax against the reception of the so-called Congressmen, giving the history of the "pretended election" and submitting six reasons, as follows, for non-recognition of the representatives of the "Masonic Hall Clique":

First—Because the State of Louisiana has not been divided into five districts. . . .

Second—Because no legislature has been assembled since the passage of said act. . . .

Third—Because the persons have attempted to hold such an election . . . without any opportunity for the legal people to participate.

Fourth—Because the Military Governor and the Commanding General have not been consulted.

Fifth—Because no laws exist either authorizing an election, or prescribing the qualifications . . . or providing for a test of the loyalty.

Sixth—Because the Military Governor of the State has ordered a registration to be made of all loyal citizens who desire to reorganize civil government in our State, which order provides a test oath. . . .[55]

Although the November election was treated with contempt in Louisiana, it was not so treated outside the state. The *New York Herald* was quoted in the *New Orleans Times* as carrying the following:

We are reliably informed that an election was regularly held in Louisiana on the first Monday in November, as the State laws directed; and that Mr. J. L. Riddell of New Orleans was elected Governor of the State, and Messers A. P. Field, of New Orleans, Joshua Baker, of St. Marys Parish and Thomas Cottman, of Ascension, were elected Representatives to Congress. The Chase and Stanton faction in New Orleans tried to prevent this election in order to keep Louisiana out of the Union until slavery be abolished; and we understand that Stanton used the Military to interfere with the elections, but unsuccessfully.[56]

Congress, it appears, had also been "reliably informed" as to the regularity of the November election, for Messrs. Cottman and Field were temporarily admitted to seats in that body.[57] Joshua Baker seems to have remained at home on his plantation.[58] On motion of Mr. Stevens of Pennsylvania, the clerk read the credentials of the two who presented themselves. Stevens filed a protest, but withdrew his resolution "that the Louisiana names be striken from the list," and despite the protest of the Free State Committee of Louisiana, and the Attorney General from that state, they participated in the organization. Cottman actually nominated Blair of Missouri for speaker, and he and his colleague cast the only two votes that Blair received.[59] Cottman resigned shortly thereafter; but Field remained to contest for his seat.

The committee subsequently reported a resolution to the effect that "A. P. Field is not entitled to a seat." The evidence in his case revealed, first, that the United States Senate had failed to pass a bill apportioning Louisiana into five Congressional districts; second, his vote had been insufficient. He had, in fact, received only 156 votes in St. Bernard Parish, and a much smaller number in Plaquemines. His credentials were also declared to be irregular because the man claiming to be governor had never been regularly elected or inaugurated. Finally, it was urged that no one be allowed a seat until a state government had been established by Congress.[60] But Field made a spirited defense, speaking convincingly of his loyalty, and showing that the military authorities had exceeded their legal power. Nevertheless, by vote of eighty-five to forty-eight, he was denied a seat,[61] although he was allowed compensation of $1,500 by vote of eighty-five to sixty-three.[62] Thus were dashed the hopes of the Conservative Unionists (or Constitutional Union party, as it was now designated) for national recognition.

Just why the Constitutional Union party entertained hopes of recognition is difficult to comprehend. Toward the platform of the party the President had already shown a growing hostility that was being reflected in the opposition of the military authorities in Louisiana. Furthermore, when it is recalled that the membership in the House of this first session of the new Thirty-eighth Congress had largely changed, and that the members as a whole were more radical than their predecessors, the position of these conservative Louisiana planters, although avowed Unionists, became impossible. The party, it therefore seems, was seeking to preserve the dead institution of slavery.

Slavery was, in fact, dead and no one appreciated this fact more than the negroes themselves. Already they had met and resolved that they were "men," and as such were "entitled to the rights of being registered as voters."[63] Furthermore their political claims and credentials had been respected by the Union associa-

tions to the extent of admitting, seating, and allowing negro delegations the privilege of voting in their associations' deliberations.[64]

The problem of the status of the negro was one which Banks
had inherited from his predecessor, and one which he made earnest
and repeated efforts to solve. He recognized that the institution
of slavery had ceased to exist. In fact, the $163,000,000 of slave
property in Louisiana was doomed—Lincoln's exemption proclamation of Louisiana's thirteen parishes to the contrary notwithstanding—and Banks so stated in one of his earliest addresses
when he said, "The first gun at Fort Sumter proclaimed emancipation."[65] Furthermore, by virtue of the fact that there had been a
suspension of all civil law and that the military authorities were
forbidden to return any slaves, even in the exempted parishes, as
Banks explained, the treatment of the negro as a slave was clearly
out of the question.[66] Besides, the state courts under Banks had
definitely fixed the status of the negroes in October, 1863, by
handing down decisions to the effect that their masters could no
longer keep them in a state of bondage.[67]

But it was soon plainly evident that some effective police regulations must be improvised to replace the inoperative state laws,
in order to control the insubordinate, the lazy, and the vicious,[68]
who had quit work upon the advent of the Union armies, and were
deserting the plantations. This state of affairs caused the planters
in the more thickly populated negro parishes to feel the need of
police guards and patrols to protect their property and lives. They
therefore appealed to the Provost-Marshal for recognition of their
local organizations and for additional assistance.[69] As this request
met with a favorable response, the planters of the First and Second
Congressional districts next met to devise ways and means to
prevent the abandonment of their plantations, by compelling their
negroes to work, if possible. They formulated resolutions providing
for the return of discontented enlisted slaves, for the return of
their mules, and for the appointment of police juries with powers
to organize and control patrols. These and other resolutions duly
passed and presented to General Banks, urged suitable arrangements for the working of abandoned plantations, and for the
speedy restoration of their own civil authorities in order that their

[87]

agreements, as proposed by the Sequestration Committee, might be carried out.[70]

Banks had demonstrated that he understood the labor situation when he declared, ". . . under no circumstances whatever can they [negroes] be maintained in idlenesss, or allowed to wander through the parishes, and cities of the State without employment"; he added that "vagrancy and crime will be suppressed by an enforced and constant occupation, and employment."[71] The General now undertook to co-operate with the planters in solving a most serious problem by ordering that an attempt be made to induce the negroes to return to their accustomed plantations and that they must work for "a share of the crop they produce." This order was issued as a "war bulletin," and carried a penalty by providing that "those [negroes] who are not thus engaged will be employed upon the public works without pay."[72]

The net result of an order that had such compulsory features for enforcing contracts might have been foreseen. It was not difficult to get the negroes to return to their comfortable homes,[73] where clothes, food and compensation could be obtained. Most of them had in their wanderings "had glimpses at the elephant and did not desire a second sight of him." In fact, conditions improved so rapidly that in a short time enthusiasts began to report that free negro labor was a success; and that it took an interest in its work, being stimulated by the "judicious distribution of rewards, and held in restraint only by the fear of wholesome punishment in the shape of fines, and expulsion from the plantation."[74] These same reporters also declared that free labor was cheaper and better than slave labor, and that the negro was laboring "more cheerfully than he did under the lash."[75] But it was only a delusion, for it must be remembered that this labor system of Banks's contained certain stringent compulsory features that never existed under the old regime.

Banks, however, felt compelled to continue the policy of his predecessor in reference to the use of negro troops. The contiguity of such troops to white soldiers at Baton Rouge and Ship Island "led to the manifestation of such a spirit of hostility to the negro officers that such officers of at least one regiment felt compelled to resign."[76] When this attitude became apparent, an urgent appeal was made to the white soldiers and officers to consider the exigencies of the service, and the "absolute necessity of appropriating every element of power to the support of the Government." At the same time, however, a concession was made to the white troops in an order issued for the organization of a "Corps d'Armee." It was to be designated as the "Corps d'Afrique" and was to consist ultimately of eighteen regiments. Uniforms were provided, and Banks assigned his best officers to the duty of organizing and instructing the blacks.[77] It was urged in defense of this policy of employing negroes generally "to put down the rebellion at any cost," that "they were to benefit the most, so let them fight."[78] Furthermore it was contended that they were only following the "example" set by the Confederacy, by arming the negroes,[79] for Banks, just as did his predecessor, Butler, used a Confederate military precedent, dated January 27, 1862.[80]

Acting accordingly, Banks, by the offer of liberal bounties, had induced negroes between the ages of twenty and thirty to volunteer.[81] They were reported to have "felt the music" and "their brass buttons," and were said to have conducted themselves heroically in battle.[82] But in general they probably proved to be very unprofitable soldiers.[83] The army correspondent of the *Hartford Times* wrote from Camp Stevens, Louisiana, as follows: "We had 1,500 negroes here, but most of them have been sent away to work. When we first came here there were about 3,000 of these poor ignorant beings. They will do nothing but lie in the sun and sleep, unless they are driven to work."[84]

Not all the negroes were "poor ignorant beings," however, for as a whole the negroes of Louisiana were superior in intelligence to those of other states, especially in and around the city; they readily understood, and soon appeared ready to respond to, the teachings of the radicals who began to invite them to insurrection by such incendiary language as: "The negro will fight. . . . No insurrections have occurred; but he has spared the master where the master would not have spared him."[85] Neither was he slow to take advantage of the free colored schools that were opened in the autumn of 1863, and that were taught chiefly by white

[89]

women from the North. Hundreds of colored children, "eager to learn," were reported to have flocked into these schools in New Orleans.[86] Nor was it difficult for these negroes, having already received equal treatment in the army, to begin meeting regularly and to demand equal political rights.

Such a so-called "equal rights" meeting was interestingly described in detail on November 6, 1863, by a reporter of the *Times*. The decorated hall, he reported, was crowded on this occasion and contained "more white American blood than African." The first speech, that of J. Fish, a white, was an eloquent emancipation address. He, however, advised the negroes "not to ask for political rights until their freedom was secured, and the rebellion crushed out." Francis Coisdore, a negro, who was next on this program, was reported to have said: "When our fathers fought in 1815 they were told that they would be compensated. . . . We have waited long enough. . . . If we cannot succeed with the authorities here we will . . . go to President Lincoln." The negro added: "Go to the registration office and see the crosses there of Irishmen and Germans. . . . There are no such men here." Dr. Dostie, the white radical of extreme views, followed with an eloquent speech in which he also advised the negroes not to press the question; but he concluded that if they had "well considered the matter, and had decided to go on with it, to go with their might." Captain Pinchback, another negro who was soon to play a very prominent role in reconstruction, was quoted as having said, among other things, that they did "not ask for social equality . . ." but that they did "demand political equality." Prompted by this, Fish again obtained the floor, and stated that there was "no color qualification to register as voters"; and that he was further convinced that Governor Shepley would "not hesitate to order it if the Registrator should refuse."[87]

The outcome of this "equality meeting" was the forwarding of a petition to Governor Shepley by the negroes, asking that they be "allowed to register themselves as voters." Less than a month later the proceedings of the Union Association revealed that negro delegates had been admitted by majority vote to participation in its meetings, and that a colored delegate had delivered the invocation,[88] praying for the success of the cause for which they had united. Thus Banks and his predecessor, Butler, had apparently laid the foundations for the restoration of civil government in Louisiana.

CHAPTER V

RESTORATION UNDER LINCOLN'S
TEN PER CENT PLAN

The Free State party, which had gained the ascendency by the end of the year 1863, interpreted the rejection of the representatives of the Constitutional Union conservatives by Congress to mean that Louisiana could not be restored until she "drove out forever the master spirit of treason—slavery," and it continued reorganization upon this principle.[1] This party, in fact, had reasons to believe that it was in the good graces of both Lincoln and Congress, and that its efforts to effect restoration would be successful. The gentle rebuke administered to the conservative planter element in the earlier part of the summer, and the subsequent correspondence with Banks, seemed to reveal that this more radical party now reflected the real sentiments of the President, and that it would be chosen as his special agent for restoration. That he intended to work with it is indicated in a letter of August 5, 1863, to Banks, in which he said:

While I very well know what I would be glad for Louisiana to do, it is quite a different thing for me to assume direction of the matter. I would be glad for her to make a new Constitution, recognizing the emancipation proclamation, and adopting emancipation in these parts of the State to which the proclamation does not apply. And while she is at it, I think it would not be objectionable for her to adopt some practical system by which the two races could gradually live themselves out of their old relation to each other, and both come out better prepared for the new. Education for the young blacks should be included in the plan. After all, the power or element of "contract" may be sufficient for this probationary period, and by its simplicity and flexibility may be the better.

As an anti-slavery man, I have a motive to desire emancipation which pro-slavery men do not have; but even they have strong enough reason to thus place themselves again under the shield of the Union; and to thus perpetually hedge against the recurrence of the scenes through which we are now passing.

General Shepley has informed me that Mr. Durant is now taking a registry, with a view to the election of a Constitutional Convention in Louisiana. This, to me, appears proper. If such a convention were to ask my views, I could present little else than what I now say to you. I think the thing should be pushed forward, so that, if possible, its mature work may reach here by the meeting of Congress.

For my part, I think I shall not, in any event, retract the Emancipation Proclamation; nor, as Executive, even return to slavery any person who is free by the terms of that proclamation, or by any of the acts of Congress.

If Louisiana shall send members to Congress, their admission to seats will depend, as you know, upon the respective houses and not upon the President.[2]

But registration had lagged for months, and it gained little impetus even after it appeared that the radical Free State party would dominate. This apparent apathy can be attributed in part to internal discord, and partially to the radical tendencies of the Flanders faction of the Free State party, whose social equality moves had no doubt served to dampen the ardor of many Unionists. Lincoln had observed this delay, as well as the growing spirit of factionalism, and had expressed his disappointment to Durant, the radical leader, when he said that he would countenance and uphold any loyal civil government organized by any substantial loyal faction in Louisiana.[3] Becoming exasperated, Lincoln again wrote to Banks on August 5:

Three months ago today I wrote you about Louisiana affairs, stating on the word of Governor Shepley, as I understand him, that Mr. Durant was taking a registry of citizens preparatory to the election of a Constitutional Convention for that State. . . . Nothing has as yet been done. This disappoints me bitterly. . . . Without waiting for more territory . . . go to work, and give me a tangible nucleus which the remainder of the State may rally around as fast as it can, and which I can at once recognize and sustain. . . . Time is important. There is danger, even now, that the adverse element seeks insidiously to preoccupy the ground. If a few professedly loyal men shall draw the disloyal about them, and colorably set up a State government, repudiating the Emancipation Proclamation, and re-establish slavery, I cannot recognize, or sustain their work. . . . My word is out to be for and not against them on the question of . . . permanent freedom.[4]

But there was continued delay, due partially to the lack of harmony or a misunderstanding between Governor Shepley and

General N. P. Banks as to the proper authority or method of procedure, and due partially to the chronic complaint of slow registration. These handicaps, and another urgent letter, influenced Banks to write to Lincoln "that if Lincoln desired . . . a government organized, it could be done, and if he gave him directions he would do it immediately."[5] Lincoln's answer, which was written on December 24, gave Banks the necessary plenary powers:

I have always intended you to be master in regard to reorganizing a State government for Louisiana. . . . I now tell you that in every dispute, with whomsoever, you are master. Gov. Shepley was appointed to assist the Commander. Instructions have been given him to spare you detail labor. This . . . it now seems was an error in us. . . . I wish you to take the case as you find it, and give us a free State reorganization of Louisiana in the shortest possible time.[6]

Banks, now cloaked with complete powers, forthwith bestirred himself. He gave new orders to add the oath of December 8, 1863, which was contained in the proclamation of that date, to the requirements for registration.[7] He ignored the resolutions submitted by the Free State party which had requested an election for delegates to a constitutional convention,[8] and he now surprised all parties by issuing an order for the election of the governor and six other state officers,[9] instead of an order for a constitutional convention.

Banks based the qualification of voters upon the President's Proclamation of December 8. This document, which has been designated as the "Proclamation of Amnesty," gave, in a general way, the Presidential plan of reconstruction, and was based on his thesis that the state had never been out of the Union, although it was temporarily out of the proper relationship and needed only to be resuscitated and restored to its former status. This task Lincoln would entrust to the proved loyal, and in order to offer the proper inducements, he proclaimed the following terms:

Whereas it is now desired by some persons, heretofore engaged in said rebellion, to resume their allegiance . . . and to reinaugurate loyal State governments . . .

Therefore, I, Abraham Lincoln . . . do proclaim . . . to all persons

. . . except as hereinafter excepted, that a full pardon is granted . . . with restoration to rights of property, except as to slaves . . . upon the condition that every person shall take and subscribe to an oath . . . as follows: I, ———, do solemnly swear in the presence of Almighty God, that I will henceforth faithfully support, protect, and defend the Constitution of the United States and the Union of the States thereunder; and that I will, in like manner, abide by and faithfully support all acts of Congress, passed during the existing rebellion with reference to slaves, so long and so far as not repealed, modified or held void by Congress, or by decision of the Supreme Court; and that I will in like manner, abide by and faithfully support all proclamations of the President made during the existing rebellion having reference to slaves, so long and so far as not modified or declared void by decision of the Supreme Court. So help me God!

All persons who voluntarily took this oath were to be considered as having restored themselves to all the privileges of citizenship, and all were allowed to take it except six classes: (1) all who had been civil or diplomatic officers or agents of the Confederate States; (2) all who had left judicial stations under the United States to aid the "rebellion"; (3) all military or naval officers of the Confederacy above the ranks of colonel in the army, or lieutenant in the navy; (4) all who left seats in the United States Congress to aid in the rebellion; (5) all who had resigned their commissions in the army and navy, and afterwards aided the Confederacy; (6) all who had engaged in any way in treating colored persons or white persons "in charge of such, other than as prisoners of war . . ." The proclamation continued with an outline of the plan as follows:

And I do further proclaim . . . that whenever in any of the States of Arkansas, Texas, Louisiana, Mississippi, Tennessee, Alabama, Georgia, Florida, North Carolina, and South Carolina . . . a number of persons not less than one-tenth in number of the votes cast in each State at the Presidential election of . . . 1860, having taken the oath aforesaid, and not having since violated it, and being a qualified voter by the election law of the State . . . shall reestablish a State Government which shall be Republican, and in no wise contravening said oath, it shall be recognized as the true government of the State. . . . I do further proclaim, declare, and make known, that any provisions which may be adopted by each State Government in relation to the freed people of such State, which shall recognize, and declare, their permanent freedom, and provide for their education, . . . will not be objected to by the National Executive. . . . It may be proper to further say that whether members sent to Congress from any State shall be admitted to seats, constitutionally rests exclusively with the respective Houses, and not to any extent with the executive; . . . and while the mode presented is the best the Executive can suggest with his present impressions, it must not be understood that no other possible mode would not be accepted.[10]

A later order, issued a few days prior to the election, which had been appropriately set for February 22 in accordance with the President's wishes, gave final, and somewhat modified, instructions as to the qualifications and procedure of voting. In addition to the oath it was specified that "every free white male 21 years of age," who had been in the state twelve months and six months in the parish, could vote; that the Unionists who had previously been expelled and those in the army or navy could vote at the nearest precinct; that the commissioners of election could administer the oath up to the time the polls closed and that it was incumbent upon these officials to make all election returns.[11] Thus the negroes, who had been publicly clamoring for the vote, were, as yet, denied that privilege. Their exclusion was justified by Banks, it seems, on the grounds that he was being guided by the Louisiana Constitution of 1852 in all essentials, except as to slavery. This feature had, of course, practically been abolished by the Emancipation Proclamation and military orders.[12]

Lincoln's ten per cent provisions, which he made applicable on the basis of the vote of Louisiana in the presidential election of 1860, excluded the negro, but not the large body of soldiers who had been and were then serving in the Confederacy. This has usually been interpreted as a liberal gesture, at least towards the South. However it must be remembered that this was the year for another presidential election, and a loyal state restoration in Louisiana with its seven electoral votes controlled by Lincoln carried with it great possibilities. It is hardly possible that a man of Lincoln's political experience could have overlooked this. Besides it was already demonstrated from the slow registration, that it would be difficult to obtain the required ten per cent. The *Times,* a Free State organ, frankly admitted just three weeks before the date set for the election that only 1,500 voters had registered, and frantically urged that meetings be held to stimulate registration else the whole movement would be a failure.[13]

The vote in Louisiana in 1860 had been 50,510; 1,500 was, therefore, considerably short of the required ten per cent which was 5,051. The total vote in the city in 1860 had been only approximately 8,000.[14] And now, with guerilla warfare in all the parishes outside the city, and the great possibility of further inroads at this time by the Confederates, it would be highly desirable that the 5,051 loyal ten per cent be accounted for, if possible, within the city or its environs. As shall presently be seen, Banks devised a way to overcome this apparently insurmountable difficulty.

The important proclamation ordering the election had, in fact, been cleverly drawn up, and was calculated to appease all factions, which it doubtless did in a large measure. The laws of Louisiana based on the Constitution of 1852 were made applicable in the election, except in so far as they recognized slavery. This was done with the idea of conciliating both the conservatives, who still adhered to the 1852 document, and the Free State party by a suspension of that part which made slavery legal. Banks assured the loyal conservatives, however, that the fact that he had suspended slavery laws because of military necessity, despite Lincoln's proclamation, would in no wise stop these loyalists from claiming compensation for any losses sustained.[15] This proclamation also contained provisions for the election of members to Congress, and a repudiation of the conservative "Masonic Hall" election held in November, which was then under investigation in Washington. This action and his notice of an election for delegates to a constitutional convention, were, it seems, his trump cards to appease the Free State party, which had contended all along that the November election was illegal, and had also persisted in their demands that a constitutional convention be called at the earliest possible date. Banks further asserted that the "fundamental law of the state is still martial," but again reassured

[97]

all that it was temporary in that it was only preparing the way for restoration. And what he did not accomplish by promises to both parties he trusted, it seems, to accomplish by patriotic appeals to the past:

Louisiana [he proclaimed on one occasion], in the opening of her history, sealed the integrity of the Union by conferring upon its Government the Valley of Mississippi. In the war for independence upon the sea, she crowned a glorious struggle against the first maritime power of the world, by a victory unsurpassed in the annals of war. Let her people now announce to the world the coming restoration of the Union, in which the ages that follow us have a deeper interest than our own, by the organization of a Free Government, and her fame will be immortal.[16]

The presumption was that there would be two sets of candidates, one representative of the Free State, and the other representative of the conservative party. It also seems to have been generally conceded that the former party would have the endorsement of the military authorities. The conservatives were, however, dissatisfied with what they considered an arbitrary abolition of slavery by Banks, and the Free Staters were equally dissatisfied with his bold recognition of the detested document of 1852. Both factions were no doubt displeased by the expressed sentiments on the continuation of martial law;[17] and for all these reasons both parties were reluctant to register, and enter the contest. A late development, however, must have stimulated registration on the part of the conservatives, who now had reason to believe that they would profit by a new turn of fortune. The new development was the threatened break between the radical left wing of the Free State party, led by B. F. Flanders, which was hampered by their principles of "negro equality," and the more conservative wing of these radicals, headed by the other Louisiana congressman, Michael Hahn.[18] Observing this early possibility of a fatal schism and the prospect of three tickets,—two Free State and one conservative,—the *Times* began a campaign for a united front at the nominating convention or caucus which was to meet shortly. Using the slogan that "Faction is Treason," this journal made an appeal to the party to present a "solid front" in order not to "give comfort to the enemy,"[19] and to support the one man who would "unite all Unionists, and thereby strengthen the hands of the government."[20]

Hahn, indeed, appeared to be the logical choice. He had the solid backing of the German element and enjoyed the prestige of an overwhelming vote in his recent election to Congress, at which time, it will be recalled, he had run as the "people's candidate" to defeat the choice of the Union Association. He also enjoyed other elements of strength, for while his strongest rival in his own party for the nomination, B. F. Flanders, had indiscreetly admitted negroes into meetings over which he presided, Hahn had as yet been noncommittal on the question of slavery. There was even a strong possibility of his being nominated by the conservatives, if passed over by the Free State party. But in addition to being neither pro-slavery nor anti-slavery, he was "going to run, nomination or no nomination." Furthermore Hahn held another card— a trump card: "he was the candidate of the General commanding the department," and according to a rumor which the *Times* seemed to reject as false, it had been "gravely asserted by men who ought to know . . . that the Commanding General is mustering every unemployed laborer into the levee brigade, for the sole purpose of marching them up to the ballot-box to vote for Mr. Hahn." "General Banks," said the *Times*, "as a military officer is not supposed to have any preferences . . . and he has too much self-respect to use the military power entrusted to him, or the influence of his position to force his private opinion upon the people whose rights he was sent here to respect." "Such imputations," the editor concluded, "against the General's lofty character are infamous."[21]

The simon-pure Free Staters, despite all these qualifications, did not at first support Hahn, but preferred to drag a "skeleton out of the closet" in their efforts to prove that he had been a "rebel." And his record did appear to be vulnerable, for in raking up the sins "committed in the earlier and darker days of the rebellion," it was discovered that Hahn had in May, 1861, presented a flag to the Confederate Calhoun Guards, with the solemn injunction to "keep the beautiful flag from any taint of dishonor." Furthermore he had subsequently become notary public by appointment of Confederate Governor Moore and had so continued until the occupation by the Federal forces; in addition, it was now objected that he had at least twice sworn "a falsehood" when he swore that he "never sought nor attempted to exercise office under any authority, or pretended authority in hostility to the United States!"[22] In the light of this sensational evidence, which was produced to show that he was "a criminal and had perjured himself," and because he deliberately refused to come out against slavery at this time, it is not surprising that the administration paper, *The New Orleans Times,* openly opposed Hahn's nomination and candidacy, at least until it was convinced that he had the unqualified support of the military authorities. It was only on the eve of the election, when it became "patent to every observing mind that Mr. Flanders did not stand a ghost of a chance," that this journal endorsed Hahn on the ground that "a house divided against itself must fall."[23]

The proceedings of the nominating convention of the Free State party, which had assembled on February 1, reveal not only the clash of personal ambitions, but also the real issue—the future status of the negro—that was being bitterly fought out within the inner counsels of the party. The names of Judge Whitaker and Judge Howell had been submitted by the press, and were generally advocated as deserving of the highest esteem;[24] but they received scant consideration before this body of delegates.

The first motion, that the delegates be required to show their registration papers before being seated, was the signal, according to the unfriendly press, for "hours of indescribable confusion." When someone answered that registration papers were not required, everybody, it seemed, tried to speak, and "began roaring 'Mr. President' as loud as he could, while sonorous imprecations which would not look well in print, were heard in various parts of the hall." Among the numbers who secured the floor was a drunken man who "tried to speak," and who almost succeeded in breaking up the meeting. This first motion was finally defeated, as was the second, a motion "to let Dr. Dostie speak." The credentials committee next reported, but "such confusion" now arose that it was never possible to get a vote on its adoption.

When, because of this "pandemonium," it became evident that no nomination could be made in the hall, it was moved that the delegates adjourn to the Free State committee rooms. As soon as this was done, and the din had subsided, a Lieutenant Duane, who it seems had been appointed by police to keep order, blew his whistle and ordered "outsiders" out of the room, stating that there "would be trouble." Mr. Fish then "called himself" to the vacant chair, and his new "Committee on Credentials" reported favorably upon all the delegates excluded by the former committee. This was followed by speeches in one of which a Mr. C. Meade stated that he "had indubitable evidence that Mr. Lincoln endorsed General Banks, and that all who opposed Banks, the mouthpiece of the President, opposed the President himself." Dr. Dostie, the extreme radical, who had, however, remained with this Hahn faction, was now allowed to take the floor, and after expressing his satisfaction upon the withdrawal of the Free State nominating convention, concluded that "as sure as there is a God above, and Abraham Lincoln reigneth, the 22nd of February will witness the election of Michael Hahn." The following complete administration ticket was then nominated: Governor, Michael Hahn; Lieutenant Governor, J. M. Wells; Secretary of State, S. Wrotnowski; Treasurer, J. G. Belden; Attorney General, B. F. Lynch; Auditor, Judge Atocia; Superintendent of Education, Jno. McNair.[25]

In the meantime the radical "Flanders faction" continued its session within the committee rooms of the Free State party. This "simon-pure" wing presented what it asserted to be the "bonafide" ticket: Governor, B. F. Flanders; Lieutenant Governor, J. M. Wells; Secretary of State, Jona C. White; Treasurer, Dr. A. Shelley; Attorney General, Chas. W. Horner; Auditor, Judge Atocia; Superintendent of Education, B. L. Brown.[26] Its claim that it had "the duly qualified and legally elected" delegates did have some foundation for the report showed that all the parishes within the lines were entitled to only eighty-one. Of this number the Flanders faction now claimed a majority, although a number of the chosen delegates had refused to adjourn to the committee rooms. It openly charged that the Hahn faction had admitted fifteen delegates from the "rebel parishes," and that a number of the others were neither citizens nor even residents of the parishes or wards they purported to represent and to which they were credited.[27]

That the original nominating convention had degenerated into an "ungovernable mob," and that there had been irregularities in the choice and seating of delegates, especially on the part of the Hahn faction, can hardly be controverted. It would appear, furthermore, that the division was caused largely by personal strife over the spoils of office, and not over principle, for both Wells and Judge Atocia were nominated on both original tickets, and both platforms denounced slavery in no uncertain terms. It is also true that Flanders, from his past record, was generally regarded as leaning toward negro equality, a principle that Hahn had yet to reveal.

There is no gainsaying, however, which one of the two the administration favored. The Flanders faction had doubtless taken an advanced position on the negro question too rapidly to suit the purposes of Lincoln. It must have incurred his displeasure also through a recent publication in its Free State party organ severely criticizing the amnesty provisions of the President's proclamation, which had made reconstruction possible. This journal, which was openly supporting Flanders at this time, came out boldly against the exemption policy, stating that not over 1,200 would be excluded or punished for their great "crime" of rebellion. According to the editor's interpretation, too large a class was omitted. Among this exempted class it placed Governor Moore of Louisiana, and Morse Manning and Company; it objected to their being put upon the same footing with the unwilling conscript, "since it was they who had really engineered the treason and ruin of Louisiana, and it was their tyranny that had forced this unwilling conscript to fight against the Union."[28] For these reasons, and the additional reason that Hahn appeared to be a sure winner, Lincoln and the administration seem to have withheld their support from the Flanders ticket, and to have bestowed it upon the ticket that could defeat the conservatives.

The conservative party, which was constituted largely of native Louisianians, met on February 4 and declared through its chief spokesman, J. Ad. Rozier, that it would "stand on the platform of the Constitution of the United States."[29] The party appears to have accepted in good faith that part of Banks's proclamation which tentatively promised remuneration to all loyal slaveholders for any losses sustained as a result of the war. But it withheld, for the present, the announcement of its ticket, preferring, it seemed, to wait for a response to a communication forwarded direct to Lincoln by one of its influential members. This illuminating letter expressed grave doubt that a one-tenth vote would be cast, unless he made some changes in the oath required in his December 8 proclamation. The party therefore requested that Lincoln modify the oath, and that he give additional instruction.

I think [the writer concluded] you meant only to require the oath, which accompanies your proclamation, of those who had not previously taken the oath of allegiance to the United States. Those whose names were registered and who took the oath and voted at the last Congressional election, which election was recognized by Congress, think you did not intend by your proclamation to disfranchise them when they had all the qualifications required by the laws and Constitution of Louisiana. . . . If the President will so modify, or explain . . . or authorize General Banks to do so . . . he will greatly subserve the question to be decided by the approaching election. Citizens who have not sinned cannot honorably accept a pardon.[30]

A similar letter was addressed to General Banks on February 8, expressing the belief that unless there was a liberal ruling in this matter the vote would probably be so small as to defeat the proposed state organization. This letter, which requested a prompt reply, was not answered, for some unexplained reason, until the fourteenth; the answer was a polite but definite refusal to comply with the request. Banks, in fact, ruled that all, both loyal and disloyal, must take the oath of December 8. When the conservatives realized that further requests would in all probability be futile, they unanimously recommended their ticket as follows: Governor, J. Q. A. Fellows; Lieutenant Governor, J. M. Pelton; Secretary of State, George S. Lacey; Treasurer, John Gauche; Attorney General, J. Ad. Rozier; Auditor, Julian Neville; Superintendent of Education, Denis Cronan, Jr.[31]

Hahn, who it was said could speak three languages, made a

most aggressive campaign. His oratory was confined at first to a denunciation of the demagogues who had brought on the revolution, thereby paralyzing commerce, ruining thousands of the wealthy, making plantations desolate, and sending thousands of widows, orphans, and citizens into exile and beggary. But the revolution, he continued, had not been unmixed with blessings, for the coming of the Union army had resulted in a revival of trade and industry, and the establishment of a system of schools and free labor for the blacks; it had removed all fears of negro insurrection, and had inaugurated a rule of justice, peace, order, and prosperity.[32] He paid his respects to slavery and the negro question in his speech at Baton Rouge, in which he accepted the fact that the institution was dead, and declared that he was inflexibly opposed to any attempt to revive it. He also paid his respects to the candidate of the negro equality party by declaring that he was unalterably opposed to the fanatical doctrine of the political equality of the negroes. And he closed his campaign by charging his opponent, Flanders, with transporting arms for the rebel government, denying at the same time, in unequivocal language, that he had ever uttered a disloyal word, or that he had ever sworn allegiance to the rebel government.[33]

But Flanders, who had the support of the *Times* until it transferred its allegiance to Hahn on the eve of the election, also made a determined and spirited canvass. He favored giving slavery a decent burial instead of embalming it, as his conservative opponents appeared to advocate; and in answer to the frequently repeated charges that he was the negro equality candidate and that he and his faction were seeking to effect such a program, he asserted that negro suffrage was not an issue in this campaign, that he had never advocated it, and that he did not deem it practicable.[34]

But the question of negro suffrage had been injected into the canvass, and did become quite an issue. In fact, the subject was referred to or debated in practically every speech in this brief campaign. Some months previous, the intelligent negroes had made it a live issue. At that time [November 9, 1863], the free men of color who were the "intelligent, educated, enlightened, and wealthy class from Jamaica, Hayti, and Cuba," as opposed to the "ignorant" and "degraded" slave class "from the wilds of Africa,"[35] had assembled, and framed a strong petition, requesting that they be permitted to register and cast their votes at the impending elections. They had alleged in their petition to the military governor that General Jackson had availed himself of their services and had recognized them as citizens whose loyalty had been clearly demonstrated at the Battle of New Orleans, and that they had ever since been peaceable citizens and taxpayers on property that was valued at many millions.[36]

But this colored class either failed to make the proper impression on the military governor, or he deemed it inexpedient as yet to grant their request, for the records do not indicate that Shepley ever made any formal reply. But this colored Radical Union Association, determining not to be thus ignored, sent a special committee to him to urge again the claims of the free men of color to the suffrage. In reply Shepley merely referred them to the highest authority in command, General N. P. Banks, who in turn must have referred them to the President, for their committee now delegated several of its members to journey to Washington.[37] Lincoln seems to have been favorably impressed, for he at once sent a Mr. McKay to New Orleans as special commissioner to inquire into the condition of the colored people in Louisiana, and, as McKay stated in the great mass meeting on February 8, "to ascertain their wishes."

McKay visited their schools and expressed himself as being most "favorably impressed." He also suggested that they appoint a committee to confer with him, and to "draw up resolutions expressive of their wishes." This they now did by declaring that since they had contributed their wealth and labor to the prosperity of Louisiana, and had obeyed its laws, they wished to have ample school facilities. In addition, they wished to have the odious black code abolished; to have protection, by having a voice in the legislation; to have Frederick Douglas visit the city at his earliest convenience; and to express, in conclusion, their "unbounded and heartfelt thanks to the President."[38]

The Conservative Union party was greatly handicapped in the triangular race by being designated as "copperheads," and was frequently referred to as the party that refused to become reconciled to the loss of slavery. Its voice, it was charged, was continually heard in the land bewailing the untimely passing of the institution.[39] But in reality the Hahn faction appeared to be stealing its thunder by representing Hahn as being strenuously opposed to political and social equality for the blacks, and even as favoring compensation for loyal slaveholders.[40] In short, the Hahn faction represented itself as being "the true conservative party," or the party which "accepts facts as they exist," whereas the old Conservative Unionists, it charged, were still endeavoring to resurrect the corpse of slavery.

Despite its handicaps there is some evidence to warrant the assertion that this conservative faction, headed by Fellows, would have emerged as victor but for the campaign strategy that may have been designed by Lincoln, and which was ably executed by General Banks. Those conservative men who had been loyalists all along could see no necessity for taking Lincoln's December 8 oath. Most Unionists, it seems, had taken the original oath of allegiance. But many would not and did not subscribe to the Lincoln oath of December 8, which required them in advance to support all acts that Congress had passed, or might pass. The administration's refusal to excuse any loyalist from this oath, even though he had subscribed to the original oath of allegiance, must have caused a great number of conscientious objectors to refrain from registering and voting with the conservatives.

Another efficient piece of strategy on the part of the military authorities to bring out a one hundred per cent Hahn vote was the declaration by Banks that the qualified must vote. Such a proclamation could have been inspired partially by his desire to bring out the necessary one-tenth, or approximately 5,000 votes. The registration must have been in excess of this. But any abstention on the part of any considerable number would have operated to defeat the entire movement. Banks, who had promised Lincoln a state government, and who now had all the election machinery in his own hands, must have been confident also that he had a Hahn majority, provided he could get them to the polls, even though the conservatives, who had not as yet entered a ticket,

[106]

should decide to participate. For these obvious reasons, Banks felt justified in issuing his proclamation in which he asserted that it was the solemn duty of all persons claiming future protection to assist in the earliest possible restoration of civil government, and in which he called upon all "people not exempt by the law of nations" to take the oath. "Men who refuse to defend their country with the ballot-box or cartridge box," he declared, "have no just claim to the benefits of liberty regulated by law"; and in order that he might not be misunderstood, and that there might not be any "squaw men" among those who had so loudly proclaimed their allegiance, he added: "Indifference will be treated as a crime, and faction as treason."[41]

The results of such an election must have been gratifying to the military authorities.[42] The administration ticket won by huge majorities, Hahn receiving 6,171 votes out of a total of 11,355. J. Q. A. Fellows was second with 2,959 votes; Flanders received only 2,225,[43] due doubtless to the eleventh hour desertions to Hahn, who seemed to have united "all the elements of power at home" and to have satisfied "the demands of the radical masses of the North."[44] The total vote that Banks reported was really more than twenty per cent of the 1860 vote. In fact the 5,771 votes polled in Orleans parish was more than Lincoln's required ten per cent, and here, as almost everywhere else, Hahn received a decided majority over his two opponents. Baton Rouge, Carrollton, Donaldsonville, Franklin, Buras, and other places all reported heavy majorities, "through the military telegraph," for the Hahn-Wells ticket.[45] The election revealed a voting population of over 10,000—more than twice the required number; and more than four-fifths of these had expressed themselves in favor of organizing a free state government.[46] This first step appeared to be an auspicious beginning.

After the election, the press began a check-up on the manner of men who had been elected to the seven state offices. The Lieutenant Governor, James Madison Wells, was the only native-born citizen of Louisiana. He had been a slaveholder and prominent planter in his native parish of Rapides. But he had refused to join the secessionists, and it was reported that he had been forced to flee.[47] According to the New Orleans correspondent of the *New York Times* who sent biographical sketches to his paper, three of the other officers were born in foreign countries, and the other three had come from the state of New York.

The Governor-elect, Michael Hahn, was born in Bavaria in 1831, but had lived in New York and Texas before coming to Louisiana, where he received an excellent education in law in the Louisiana University, and where he had resided during the twenty-five years preceding the war. This brilliant young orator had always acted with the Democrats, but he actively campaigned for Douglas, and like some other Douglas supporters, he refused to support secession. Upon the arrival of the Federals, he displayed his love for the Union, which was said to be proverbial, by organizing the first Union Association.[48]

The scholarly Secretary of State, Stanislas Wrotnowski, a native of Poland, landed in New Orleans in 1849, and finally located near Baton Rouge, where he reared his accomplished sons and daughters, and where he became a man of considerable means. Bartholomew Leahy Lynch, the Attorney General, was a native of Ireland, who arrived in America in 1851. He had taught school for a number of years in and around Alexandria, Louisiana, while occupied in studying law. The State Treasurer, Dr. James G. Belden, from New York State, and a nephew of Noah Webster, had for seventeen years been practising his profession in New Orleans. Meanwhile he became a slaveholder; but the "rebellion" seems to have converted him to emancipation. The State Superintendent of Public Education, John McNair, had emigrated from western New York, but since 1845 had lived in New Orleans, where he had been engaged as a teacher. Dr. A. P. Dostie, the Auditor of Public Accounts, also from the state of New York, practised dentistry for a number of years in New Orleans before the outbreak of the war. He had, however, made, and was to make, many bitter enemies in New Orleans by his impulsive temperament and by his condemnation of the rebellion. He had found it to his interest to go North when Louisiana seceded. But when Federal authority had been restored, he, like others of Union sentiments, had returned[49] with fellow soldiers of fortune—but not, it seems, to practise dentistry.

[108]

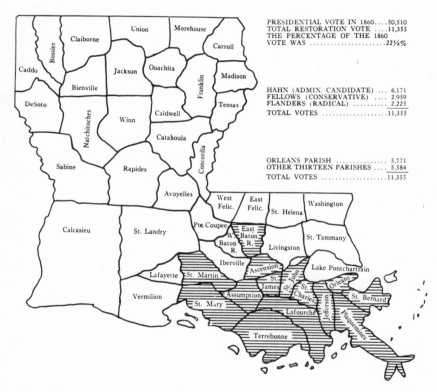

PRESIDENTIAL VOTE IN 1860....50,510
TOTAL RESTORATION VOTE 11,355
THE PERCENTAGE OF THE 1860
VOTE WAS 22½%

HAHN (ADMIN. CANDIDATE) ... 6,171
FELLOWS (CONSERVATIVE) 2,959
FLANDERS (RADICAL) 2,225
TOTAL VOTES 11,355

ORLEANS PARISH 5,771
OTHER THIRTEEN PARISHES 5,584
TOTAL VOTES 11,355

THE RESTORATION OF CIVIL GOVERNMENT UNDER THE "TEN PER CENT PLAN" (THE
FOURTEEN SHADED PARISHES PARTICIPATED)

The inauguration program on March 4 was conducted with much pomp and ceremony. A large platform, erected in the middle of Lafayette Square, was surrounded with rows of seats, decorations, flags, banners, and such inscriptions as: "Michael Hahn, First Free State Governor of Louisiana," "Major General Nathan P. Banks, the noble citizen and dutiful soldier," "General N. P. Banks, the Hero of Port Hudson and Freedom of Louisiana," "Admiral Farragut the Bravest of the Brave," and "Louisiana, first of the erring sisters, keeps step to the music of the Union." An immense throng of 30,000 is reported to have assembled at this place and joined with the thousands of school children in singing the national anthem and other patriotic songs, and participated in the elaborate program. It was of course featured by the carefully prepared inaugural address of Hahn, and the "eloquent speech" of General Banks.

The Governor in his inaugural expressed his usual sentiments on the state and nature of the Union. The State, he argued, was never out of the Union; and he showed that the proposed constitutional convention to revise the constitution, and its provisions for a legislature, would offer a solution of Louisiana's problems. He also continued to hold out the usual promise of compensation to loyal slaveholders for loss of slaves, and pictured the return of prosperity and revival of industrial life in this first Free State. His conclusion was reported to have electrified the vast throng:

Fellow-citizens, again from the bottom of my heart I thank you for the confidence you have reposed in me, and the honors you have now heretofore lavished upon me. My fondest and most cherished hope is that when my term of service shall have ended, you may enjoy the inestimable blessings of "a more perfect Union," with its accompanying justice, domestic tranquility and liberty, and that you may be able to assure me that I have not disappointed your expectations, or proved unworthy of the distinguished trust which I have this day assumed, and which as a true son of Louisiana, I shall feel more ambitious to discharge meritoriously than any other upon earth.[50]

It was also fitting that General N. P. Banks should be present at the inauguration of his youthful protégé, and should participate in these imposing ceremonies. This soldier-politician, who was now planning the 1864 Red River Campaign to redeem the entire state,

[109]

spoke with an optimism that must have inspired confidence in the cause when he said:

Of all human institutions, States are of the shortest growth. . . . Like a statute, they cannot be brought into existence by an edict, or decree, or Constitution. The Constitution that has this day been revived, and the State that is this day recreated, has then a permanent foundation. It is not called into life by a vote of the people. . . . It has a stronger and deeper basis . . . and that is in the changed habits of the people . . . and the demands of the new and great age upon which we are entering. . . . I say then that the day we celebrate has the basis of a century, for we have accomplished and achieved deeds of a century in the past two years; and so long as people are faithful and true to themselves, so long will stand Louisiana, the first returning State, in which every man is a free man, and the architect of his own fortunes with nothing between him and the Almighty God upon this auspicious day and occasion. I shall ask of Him in the plentitude of his power and wisdom to do no more and to do no less than to impress upon the people of Louisiana, a fitting idea of their responsibilities and their duties.[51]

This new state government, the legality of which was already being questioned, needed and now received the paternal blessings of Lincoln. This official recognition was at once bestowed in two important communications received by Governor Hahn shortly after the inaugural. The first of these recognized him as civil governor under the old constitution and laws; and, anticipating that circumstances might arise to which the 1852 constitution might not be applicable, a second communication invested him with all the powers then being exercised by Governor Shepley, the military governor.[52]

Lincoln no doubt intended that this military feature should last only until Louisiana had adopted a constitution harmonizing with the age. But his other communication to Hahn is significant because it is the first evidence that Lincoln had adopted a new and radical policy toward negro suffrage. Its contents suggest that the crusade for equal political rights launched in Louisiana some months before by the negroes was at last making its converts in high places.[53]

[110]

But despite the paternal blessings of Lincoln, and the auspicious beginnings under the military setup, the state government and its chief executive were soon beset with difficulties from within and from without. The first was the questioning of the legality of the whole proceedings by a number of Louisiana's Unionists who contended that Banks had totally disregarded the constitutional provisions of the state in his several orders, under which the "alleged election" was held. These Unionists emphatically declared that Banks had not only violated the Constitution by arbitrarily setting for the election a different time than that specified by the Constitution, but that his subsequent order defining the "qualifications for voters" had been drawn up and issued by him "without reference to any Constitutional provision or law of the State of Louisiana."[54] Thomas J. Durant, president of the Union Association, in his correspondence with Henry Winter Davis and others, openly denied the legality of such a state reorganization. In his letter, which was given wide publicity in the Northern press, he submitted statistics to prove that of a total population of 708,902 in 1860 only 233,185 were within the lines; and he added that in some of these parishes "in certain parts election polls could not be held." He stated furthermore, that the returns showed that votes were cast by soldiers at Pensacola, Florida; and that the election was certainly not decided by qualified voters as was plainly required by Lincoln's December 8 proclamation, since the sailors and soldiers—and there was known to be a large number of them—were "illegal" voters. The election, Durant further declared, was not a fair one, for the influence of Banks, of the whole police force of the city, and of all the civil employees, was exerted in favor of Hahn. He had previously written, he said, to Senator Boutwell, H. L. Dawes, Thad Stevens, and even to Lincoln showing in detail the extent of the corruption.[55] And now, for all his trouble in airing these grievances, this radical Unionist seems not only to have been ignored, but actually to have been accused of being "devoted to slavery, and, therefore, the rebellion."[56]

The prestige of the new government was not enhanced by facts connected with Governor Hahn's past, facts that were now brought to light and given wide publicity. Both defeated wings of Unionists had joined in producing documents to prove that this new "military governor" of Louisiana held and exercised the office of Notary Public in New Orleans under, and by the authority of the "rebels." They further called Mr. Lincoln's attention to the fact that by a statute of the United States,[57] it was provided that every person, before entering upon the discharge of the duties of an officer of the United States should take and subscribe to an oath, a material part of which was that "I have neither sought, nor accepted, nor attempted to exercise the functions of any office whatever, under any authority, or pretended authority in hostility or inimical to the United States." They also reminded Lincoln that the said act provided that if any person swore falsely under this same act, he should be deemed guilty of wilful and corrupt perjury, and liable to be punished accordingly. Finally, they quoted at length a certificate of the sale of a slave made on the eighth of April, 1862, to which Mr. Hahn certified in the following terms:

> This done and passed, in my notarial office at the city of New Orleans, in the presence of Charles Geo. Eckhart and W. H. Barremore, witnesses of lawful age and domiciled in this city, who hereunto sign their names with the parties, and me, the said Notary
>
> Original signed:
> CHAS. G. ECKHART
> W. H. BARREMORE
> O. ANFOUR
> THOMAS H. LEE
>
> MICHAEL HAHN, *Notary Public*
> (L.S.) a true copy
>
> MICHAEL HAHN, *Notary Public*

They added a certificate of Mr. Hahn's oath on accepting the office of Prize Commissioner, in July, 1863, which showed that he had falsely subscribed to the oath in the said act, and demanded that for this act of perjury, Mr. Hahn should forthwith be punished.[58] But Lincoln evidently made no reply.

This was not all, for other alleged evidence and other statistics were subsequently published in the conservative *Picayune,* which would tend to prove that an excessive amount had been spent to elect and inaugurate the seven state officers in Louisiana, and that this amount was actually paid by the state. These alleged irregularities were first brought to the attention of the public by a resolution adopted in July by the constitutional convention, which provided that $10,000 be appropriated out of the general funds to pay for the election and installation of state officers. Considerable opposition was manifested in the convention,[59] and this no doubt caused an investigation of the "Pay Roll Bill of Inauguration," with the result that an itemized statement was published on the first page of the *Times.*[60] This document was accompanied by other supporting evidence of a highly sensational nature, purporting to prove that the recently installed government was guilty of a more serious charge than mere "extravagance." It was to the effect that the Auditor's Reports showed that $10,000 was drawn from the state Treasury, whereas the pay roll totaled but $9,969.01. But the submitted evidence further showed that the supposed recipients of this $9,969.01 received only a portion of this amount. The alleged defrauders had devised the scheme of keeping the right hand column of figures in pencil on the "Pay Roll" in the column alloted for signatures, so that when paid as per pencil figures, these could be erased, and the signatures would thus operate as receipts in favor of the disbursing committee to the full amount of the bills. This report, which had been submitted by J. Q. A. Fellows and Benjamin F. Flanders, the two defeated candidates, claimed that many of the recipients received even less than the amount in pencil. It also conveyed the impression that the Pay Roll had been padded, for statements were submitted for men whose names appeared on the Pay Roll, but who said that they "never did any work for the inauguration ceremonies, never presented any bills, and never asked nor received any pay." And finally, in order to show the nature of the whole affair, and to prove their charge that this was "the first instance in political history, of the payment by the state of the

[113]

electioneering expenses of candidates for offices," Messrs. Fellows and Flanders appended the following typical bill:[61]

New Orleans, February 27th, 1864 Free State Executive Committee.
To S. D'Meza,

To services rendered electioneering for the Free State Ticket, headed by the Hon. Michael Hahn, and assisting parties in procuring naturalization papers, 8 days at $3.00......$24.00
Received payment.

A close examination of this "Bill of Inauguration," which had been approved by the State Auditing Committee as published, shows that there were one hundred and eighty-one separate items, and the total amount listed was $9,969.01, whereas only $8,343.98 had been signed for by the supposed recipients. Some of these items are descriptive of the services rendered, or the materials furnished, and others are not. Bill "Number One" was for fifty musicians, for which $250 had been appropriated, and only $225 signed for, or purported to have been disbursed. Several other bills were listed for advertising in the daily papers; the total amount for this was several hundred dollars. Yet some editors complained that they did not receive the full amount appropriated. *The Daily True Delta,* in fact, received nothing, although $164.50 was appropriated for this paper. Bills rendered for banners and evergreens totaled several hundreds of dollars. One item alone for evergreens was $550. Two hundred and fifty dollars was appropriated for fitting up Liberty Hall, although only $20.00 appears to have been actually disbursed. Refreshments, torches, ropes, burning fluid, lumber, flags, wagons, carriages, furniture, and similar items, and others just "For Services," were rendered and paid, increasing the sum total by hundreds of dollars. The most numerous items, however, were for "Canvassing," "Travelling Expenses," "Electioneering," "Election Returns," and "Refreshments." These items comprised at least some three or four thousands of dollars. For six barrels of alcohol $613.71 was appropriated, and $552.34 reported signed for. And, finally, among the many other various and sundry items, is one paid to a Mrs. J. Allen for "liquors."[62]

Thus the Free State government had completed the first step in the great task of restoring the state to the Union under the "ten per cent plan"; and it was now to undertake a task that required statesmanship of no mean order, the task of formulating the organic law of the "first Free State."

Chapter VI

THE CONSTITUTIONAL CONVENTION OF 1864

In his proclamation ordering the election of February 22, 1864, General Banks had given notice of a constitutional convention. Now, in fulfillment of that promise and to allay agitation, as well as to complete restoration, he issued an order for the election of delegates to such a convention. His order stated that an election would be held on Monday, the twenty-eighth day of March, to elect delegates for the purpose of revising and amending the Constitution of Louisiana. He assigned a total of one hundred and fifty delegates to the forty-eight parishes. These assignments were made to each parish upon the basis of the white population exhibited by the census of 1860, which gave Orleans sixty-three delegates. And in anticipation of success in the Red River campaign, upon which he was just now embarking, the order further provided that "any parish not now within the lines of the army shall be entitled to elect delegates of the convention, should at any time before the dissolution of the convention such parish be brought within the lines of the army." This order, which had been worked out largely by a committee appointed by Banks, provided further that only whites should vote, and their qualifications and procedure in voting should be the same as in the election held on January 22.[1] Such a basis was of course calculated to deprive the slaveholding conservatives of that control that had been guaranteed to them by the instrument of 1852, which based representation on total population; and it also gave New Orleans a much larger representation, which had been arbitrarily denied the city by the country parishes under the old regime.

Two tickets were presented throughout the city. One was the Free State ticket, composed of what was alleged by its official organ, the *Times,* to be the "earnest," the "sincere," the "Free State men." Their opponents, however, sneeringly spoke of them during the campaign as "men of no education," "men of no property," "men of no real standing," and "men of no professions."[2]

The other ticket, which is difficult to designate, may as well be called the opposition party. Thos. J. Durant, a leader of the radical

THE CONSTITUTIONAL CONVENTION OF 1864

Flanders faction, condemned the whole proceedings on the ground that only the Congress and the loyal people of Louisiana had the power to call or arrange for a convention. He thereby condemned the action of Lincoln and Banks, and the Constitution of 1852,[3] the greater portion of which Banks and the administration still seemed disposed to recognize. Nor did the "opposition ticket" have the endorsement of the Conservative Unionists. Honorable J. Ad. Rozier, who seemed at first to be the chief spokesman of this opposition, declined a nomination, and eventually refused to participate, giving as his reasons the statement that Banks had ignored the constitution and laws of Louisiana and had substituted other oaths.[4] This opposition ticket evidently contained some able candidates, as the Free Staters frankly admitted. However, their characterization of the ticket as a whole was anything but complimentary, for they alleged throughout the short canvass that this ticket was placed before the people by a few scheming politicians. They did admit that it contained a few names of honored and respected men; but the Free State official organ added that these few were in "bad company" since they were in the "motley crowd" of "thugs," "original secessionists," "political policemen," "returned rebel soldiers," "advocates for the admission of negroes into Union Leagues," and "the consorts of the colored people in processions."[5] If this be true, it was indeed a motley crowd, and if it must be judged by its success—or rather lack of successes at the polls—these observations must have contained an element of truth.

The election passed off quietly, and resulted in the choice of the Free State ticket with a few individual exceptions.[6] But the results of the voting must have been a great disappointment to the administration, for, whereas the vote cast in the January election for state officers was approximately 11,000, the March election returns, as promulgated by the Secretary of State, showed a total of only 6,355. It is interesting to note that 3,832 were cast in the city, and the remaining 2,723 were cast in the eighteen country parishes.[7] New Orleans and Orleans parish elected sixty-three delegates under the new apportionment and the eighteen country parishes of Avoyelles, East Baton Rouge, West Baton Rouge, Concordia, East Feliciana, Jefferson, Lafourche, Madison, Ra-

[117]

pides, St. Bernard, St. James, St. John the Baptist, St. Mary, St. Charles, Terrebonne, Ascension, Iberville, and Plaquemines, elected thirty-five delegates, making a grand total of ninety-eight, which was considerably more than the required quorum of seventy-six.[8] Delegates were also reported to have been elected in Natchitoches, St. Landry, Winn, and Catahoula, but they do not seem to have ever arrived or participated in any way. Only eighty-two answered to roll call on the first day, April 6, although the enrollment did at one time reach ninety-eight members.[9] But a full attendance was unusual, and the records would seem to indicate that it was often extremely difficult to obtain the necessary quorum of seventy-six.

Completely tabulated records of this election do not appear to have ever been received, doubtless because of the absence of Banks, who was occupied with the army in the interior, and because some election returns and delegates may have been intercepted by the Confederate troops. In New Orleans, where the majority of the votes were cast, few opposition votes were reported. The opposition may have cast more votes, which were not counted, since all the election machinery was under the control of the military authority. There is, however, a probability that a number of Unionists, who, because of a desire for office, had been stimulated to participate in the election on the twenty-second of February, now refused to participate. The more radical left wing, designated as the "Chase followers," seemed to be extremely lukewarm. The right wing, headed by J. Ad. Rozier, an influential conservative, gave to the press a full statement of their reasons for non-cooperation.[10] In voicing the apparent sentiments of the Conservative Unionists, Rozier alleged in defense of the course now pursued that in the recent election for state officers the authorities had not only disregarded the supreme law of the land, but had nullified certain clauses of the Louisiana constitution pertaining to elections, voting, the oath, and slavery; that the Constitution of Louisiana could be changed only by an explicit and authentic act of the whole people; and that the blind oath to support any future acts of Congress and any future proclamations of the President was unconstitutional because the government of the United States

MAP No. 7

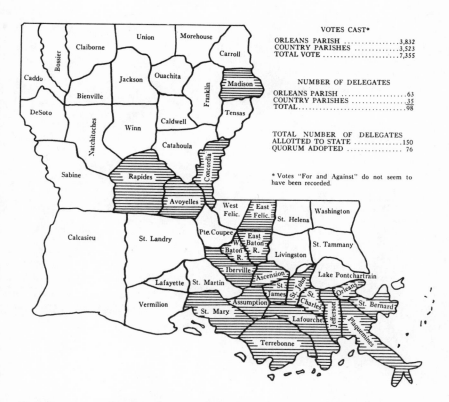

VOTES CAST*

ORLEANS PARISH	3,832
COUNTRY PARISHES	3,523
TOTAL VOTE	7,355

NUMBER OF DELEGATES

ORLEANS PARISH	63
COUNTRY PARISHES	35
TOTAL	98

TOTAL NUMBER OF DELEGATES ALLOTTED TO STATE	150
QUORUM ADOPTED	76

* Votes "For and Against" do not seem to have been recorded.

THE ELECTION OF DELEGATES TO THE CONSTITUTIONAL CONVENTION OF 1864 (THE SHADED PARISHES PARTICIPATED)

was a government of laws, and not of men. This conservative also lamented the fact that the Lincoln government was showing no discrimination between the loyal and the disloyal, and that it was, in fact, disqualifying many loyalists. He complained, furthermore, that the law of the state was nothing but martial law, and he strenuously protested against the voting and the controlling of elections by transient persons, or, as he designated them, "birds of passage," that had landed simply for lucre and gain during the war. In short, he urged that the government and constitution "should be the off-spring of our choice, uninfluenced, and un-awed."[11]

In pursuance of General Orders No. 35, issued by General Banks, the convention assembled on April 6 in Liberty Hall, the present City Hall, opposite Lafayette Square. This "fine body of men," as the enthusiastic and partisan *Times* expressed it, made "an impressive tableau," and "one upon which the pen of our future historian will delight to linger."[12]

But the convention had hardly organized before it learned of Banks's decisive defeats on the eighth and ninth at Mansfield and Pleasant Hill, south of Shreveport. When it was definitely ascertained that a great portion of Louisiana must be surrendered to the Confederates, the optimism that had pervaded the convention on assembling, now vanished overnight. It was plainly evident from this unexpected turn of events that the remaining parishes would not be represented in the convention, as had been confidently expected. In addition, Banks's retreat upon New Orleans following the victories of Richard Taylor placed the city under the constant menace of an attack.

The legality of this body had also been questioned by other Unionists, and now in order to give a shadow of authority to its acts, the convention unfortunately set its quorum at seventy-six, or a majority of the one hundred and fifty delegates assigned to the forty-eight parishes. The difficulty of obtaining a quorum, which was great in the early days of the session, increased as the weeks passed.[13] The convention adjourned at one time for several days because of lack of a quorum; at other times, in order to maintain a working quorum, the presiding officer had to order the door locked, and to dispatch the sergeant-at-arms and his assistants into the city for the absentees.[14] Toward the end of June the situation became so critical that it was feared the body would disintegrate. Their patron, Banks, had not made the state safe for the Republicans, nor the situation of a delegate any too comfortable.

To add to the woes of the convention, the working margin was constantly dwindling by the resignations of disgruntled delegates. The first to desert what appeared to be a bad cause were Christian Roselius and a Mr. Abbott. Both were conservatives, and both resigned as a protest against the "absurdity of so many oaths." The resignation of Roselius was indeed a great blow because this "Nestor of the Louisiana bar" had had the ripe experience of serving in other Louisiana constitutional conventions, and his assistance and the prestige of his name were now needed to bolster up the waning popularity of the convention. These resignations were soon followed by those of J. T. Payne, Edmund Goldman, and Baily, who became disgruntled over the passage of the police bill and over the proposed extension of the elective franchise. All this greatly incensed those who were endeavoring to carry on, and frequent punitive remedies were devised to check this exodus, and to restrain other apparently irresponsible delinquents who habitually absented themselves; but all to no avail.[15]

Nor were the character and ability of the delegates as a whole such as to command public esteem. There were, however, a few of proved ability. Judge Edward H. Durell, president of the body, was a lawyer of "pleasing personality" who had emigrated from New Hampshire a number of years before the war. An outstanding loyalist, he had been the head of the financial bureau under Butler, and now held a judgeship "of one of the District Courts in Louisiana by appointment under Banks."[16] His colleague, Judge R. K. Howell, also an immigrant to Louisiana, who had been on the bench for several years, was one of the only two who remained and retained their positions. He was recognized as an upright and highly qualified Union man whose restraining influence was needed in the convention.[17] Mr. Thomas, another "excellent young lawyer," and Mr. Shaw, a "talented" and industrious teacher, who spoke German, were both considered by the *Times* as valuable

[120]

assets to the convention.[18] But with the exception of these and a few others, such as Abell, Dr. Bonzano, and Bott, the delegates had little ability or standing.[19]

The first indiscreet acts of voting themselves the unusual amount of ten dollars per day, and of paying gratuities to printers, as well as giving other evidences of extravagance, alienated even the *Times,* heretofore a partisan sheet.[20] According to the press, most of the delegates early began to exhibit a notorious lack of experience and of respectability, and the frequent exhibitions of "bitter and vulgar prejudices" were such as to gain the contempt and downright hostility of the New Orleans populace.

Under these conditions, it is hardly surprising that friction developed between the citizens and these "creatures of Banks," as they were contemptuously called. The open feud, that was to last for many months, first flared when certain delegates charged on the convention floor that they had been assaulted and beaten by thugs in the streets of New Orleans.[21] The convention even authorized an investigating committee, whose report openly denounced the so-called thugs; this of course added fuel to the flames.

Lack of tact, however, appears to have been one of the lesser sins of the delegates, for if the press reports are to be credited, their conduct, their disorder, and confusion soon became notorious. In fact, on one occasion the convention was forced to adjourn in the wildest disorder.[22] Some members, including the president, so it was charged, developed the habit of coming into the convention in a drunken condition; a vote of censure, with threats of expulsion, failed to rectify this growing evil.[23] In truth, this so-called "deliberative body" tended to degenerate in proportion as the restraining influences of the ablest members were removed by their withdrawal.

The real situation seems to have been best expressed by the membership itself. Mr. Henderson feelingly voiced his disapproval on one occasion when he said: "I expected just this course would be pursued in this House today. When there is anything to do, you adjourn; when there is nothing to do you stay." He also complained that the delegates had been in session one month, and had accomplished nothing; that the time had been consumed by frequent "attempts to legislate," by "frivolous resolutions," and by efforts to set up an "inquisition to investigate." Another member asserted that "even now what little protection we have is due to the Federal armies. . . . I despise and hate this police."[24] A third member no doubt correctly diagnosed the real state of affairs when he said: "I thank God that we have General Banks, and General Canby to protect you and me. . . . The time has not come to restore civil government . . . for if you do the streets of this city will run red with blood. You will be the first victim of our enemies. I dont believe that we could sit here for two hours and a half, if the military were withdrawn."[25] And a fourth member, no doubt emboldened by the presence of the Federal soldiers in the square across the street, was given an ovation by his fellow members when he concluded an inflammatory address against the New Orleans citizens with these startling words: "My doctrine is to let the copperheads, rattlesnakes, and rebels go down to hell together."[26]

A membership so constituted could hardly long agree. The members were, of course, all opposed to secession, and all apparently favored emancipation. In fact, Judge Durell, when he accepted the chairmanship, reminded the delegates of their two great objectives, when he stated that they had assembled "to undo the work of folly . . . and remove that fatal curse of strife . . . forever."[27]

But strife was not removed, for it was at once introduced into the convention over the question of the degree of loyalty to the Union. It was charged that a number of the delegates were "copperheads," and that others were not even United States citizens; and with the idea of eliminating such questions, a resolution was introduced requiring all members to take the Lincoln oath of December 8 before the bar, or produce evidence that they had already taken this "iron-clad" oath. It provided further that the naturalization papers of members born in foreign countries should be produced. This resolution aroused a violent debate. Abell, as well as others, strenuously objected to the absurdity of four or five oaths, and Roselius protested that no discrimination was being shown between the loyal and disloyal. When this resolution passed by a vote of fifty-five to twenty-six, Roselius, as has been stated before, resigned and was followed by some other conservatives.[28]

This same controversial spirit was strangely and unexpectedly manifested over the solution of the first big objective, the repeal of the ordinance of secession. The resolution provided in part that:

> Now, we, the people of the State of Louisiana, loyal to the Constitution, and the government of the United States, do hereby, announce, declare, and ordain that the said pretended ordinance of secession, so passed by disloyal traitors, without the authority of the people . . . with all other ordinances, acts, and proceedings . . . and the State government instituted are utterly null and void.

This resolution, which would also have pledged the members to the suppression of "this most wicked rebellion," was tabled by a vote of forty-two to twenty-one.[29] Its defeat was at once attributed by its supporters to the fact that a quorum was not present, and that any action on a matter of such moment should be passed in such manner as to leave no doubt as to its legality.[30] Another less plausible explanation of the reverse vote was that the wording made this resolution too harsh in tone. But the fact remains that the required quorum was present on many subsequent days, and yet this most logical step of placing "first things first" was not taken until the closing days of the session, at which time an exact quorum was reported present, and the vote then stood sixty-eight to eight in favor of the following more moderate and dignified resolution:

> Whereas a Convention claiming to act in the name of the State . . . did . . . pass an ordinance to dissolve the Union between the State of Louisiana and other States, and
>
> Whereas such ordinance of secession was based upon an unfounded assumption of State sovereignty, Therefore,
>
> Be it resolved that we do solemnly denounce the doctrines of State rights and State sovereignty, and
>
> Be it resolved that the Ordinance of Secession is and always has been null and void.[31]

No satisfactory explanation was given for this apparently inconsistent vote in the early days of the session. The "lack of a quorum" argument does not seem to be valid, for forty-two members, more than half the regular attendance, were to all outward appearances opposed to its revocation. The fact that a quorum was present on following days, and yet no action was taken, would certainly discredit such statements. The sentiment was evidently not yet ripe enough to warrant favorable action, although the delegates seem to have been elected on this issue. Perhaps for financial reasons, the members may have desired a long-drawn-out session. Some were certainly desirous of compensation for slaves before voting in the affirmative, for the convention had not at this time been purged of this element. But possibly the great majority, who were said to be Banks–Lincoln followers, and would obey their command, were just waiting for the proper "pressure" from Banks.[32] The members may have been motivated by these and other reasons; but the fact remains that certain members reversed themselves on this question, as they did on other important measures.

Emancipation, with its many ramifications, was unquestionably the biggest problem that was offered for solution. It was brought to the attention of the convention shortly after the completion of organization, by Judge Howell, who offered the following resolution: "Resolved that a committee be appointed to whom shall be referred the subject of immediate and permanent abolition of slavery."[33] Needless to say, it opened a floodgate of oratory, debate, and discussion that ended only with adjournment. It also revealed the usual differences of opinion as to the methods to be employed, and even the expediency of such action. A substitute motion, offered by Abell, who had evidently remained in the convention for the purpose of protecting slave property of loyalists, was to the effect that no proposition should be entertained for the abolition of slavery until ways and means had been first provided for a full, fair, and equitable compensation to all lawful owners, and that all emancipated slaves must be removed from the state.[34]

The advocates of the original resolution tried at once to table this motion, not because of opposition to compensation, for they were apparently not deeply concerned about remuneration, but because they desired early action on the Durell resolution in

[124]

order to forestall any charges of "copperheadism." But the substitute measure had a capable and determined defender in the person and leadership of Abell. He opposed immediate emancipation without the consent of the owner, contending that slavery was a vested property right, guaranteed by the Constitution, and so recognized by all courts; that it was, after all, detrimental to the best interests of the slave because of his tendency to idleness, and because his ignorance and lack of skill would leave him a prey to his vices, to dissipation, to diseases, to death, and to the money-making speculator or sharper, who had already put in his appearance, and who must inevitably be substituted for the interested and humane master; and that 312,000 negroes would either be free to compete with the whites, or a system of peonage would result, which would, in either case, be a menace to the safety of the state. Gradual emancipation on the plan that had been used in some of the Northern states would, he reasoned, be preferable to the arbitrary method of ruthlessly dispossessing other men of their property, when they were not represented, since, as he explained, "only 2,000 votes out of a possible 40,000" had been cast in parishes where the principal slaveholders resided.

The conclusion and summary of this powerful appeal for fair play was that emancipation was unconstitutional, a violation of the first principles of right, and unjust to the loyal owners; that it would be ruinous, demoralizing, and destructive to the best interests of the slave, and dishonorable and dangerous to the safety of the state; that the state should now take over and hire out all unclaimed slaves; and that since their Northern brethren were philanthropists, "let them contribute both for compensation to all loyal owners, and for permanent removal of the emancipated slaves from the State."[35]

Other speakers agreed that it was manifestly unfair to destroy $150,000,000 worth of property at one stroke, without some compensation; and some favored emancipation after a number of years with compensation to loyal men only. But the majority, recognizing the fact that the institution no longer existed *de jure,* or *de facto,* appeared to accept Judge Durell's advocacy of immediate and unconditional emancipation, for the "purpose of crushing out this odious rebellion," and expressed themselves as entirely willing to leave the matter of compensation for loyal owners to the "fair sense of justice of the Washington government." They, therefore, gave a substantial majority in favor of tabling the substitute, and for referring the original resolution to the proper committee.[36] But subsequent events were to demonstrate that the "die-hards" had only begun their fight for "compensation before emancipation."

A study of the problem of making provision for the education of negro children, first discussed on the convention floor as a result of Banks's General Order No. 38, which was issued on March 22, gives some illuminating evidence on the attitude of these Unionists toward this much agitated question.[37] This military order had made provision for a board of education with extensive powers, which was to establish schools for freedmen in school districts to be defined by the military authorities. The board was to supervise the erection of school buildings, select teachers, and furnish books for negro children; the financing of this novel requirement was to be effected by a tax levied upon all real and personal property in the respective school districts.

The order had apparently aroused the hostility of most whites, and a resolution was accordingly introduced in the convention characterizing this order as unconstitutional and derogatory to the sovereignty of the people.[38] This resolution was defeated, doubtless because the members feared to defy the military authorities; but it did not indicate that these Unionists were yet ready to make provision for negro education. In fact, the first resolution required that free public schools be established for all white children only by a general tax, which must be distributed in proportion to the number of white children. In the debates that followed, the attitude of the convention seems to be best explained by a Mr. Sullivan, who said: "It leaves out colored children altogether, because I think white people have enough to do to attend to their own affairs, without attempting the education of the negro children."[39] Others urged in opposition that the negroes were not yet free, the proclamations to the contrary notwithstanding.[40] A substitute compromise resolution was at length adopted, specifying that a tax be

[126]

levied on whites for whites, and on the colored for separate colored schools.

But this compromise necessitated defining the degree of blood that constituted a colored person, and it must have required much courage and little discretion to introduce a resolution that would dispose of this "highly explosive" subject.[41] But one was introduced which defined all people above the quadroons as whites, because "they could not be distinguished from the whites by facial features or color." The proponents then cited many laws and authorities to substantiate their contention that a person was almost universally legally declared to be white after the quadroon, or fourth, degree. But all in vain, for attempts to solve this highly controversial problem in other days and by wiser heads had led to personal encounters and duels. This resolution was accordingly rejected by a vote of forty-seven to twenty-three.[42]

But the debates continued as to whether the word "may" or "shall" should be used in the article which was to provide negro education; in this connection the difficult problem of taxation was again debated. The opponents of negro education reasoned, with plausibility, that, whereas taxes had formerly been levied chiefly on slaves and real estate, now, with slaves free, this revenue would decrease by one-half at the very time that the number to be educated would be doubled; this meant that if the schools were to be maintained at the standards then existing, the tax rate would have to be increased four-fold. That the members of this convention were looking forward to happier days can be inferred from the fact that they believed this tax burden would fall chiefly on the loyal, for it was generally agreed that the confiscated property of the secessionists and disloyalists would shortly fall into the hands of the loyalists by purchase or otherwise.[43] These prospective owners now hesitated to assume such tremendous burdens without the aid of the national government.

But other influences were also at work. Governor Hahn; J. Madison Wells, who was soon to become governor; A. P. Dostie, an extreme radical; General Banks; and possibly others were objecting to incorporation in the organic law the words "white," "black," and "color," and were exerting their efforts to convert the opposition to their position.[44] They persisted, with the result that late in the session an article was reported from the committee, making provision for the establishment of free public schools for all the children, and for general taxation; and specifying that all moneys be distributed in proportion to the number of children, but that schools must be separate.[45] The opposition had at last been converted, or in some way silenced. It no longer expressed any fears of negro uprisings or race equality as a result of popular education, and the affirmative vote of fifty-three to twenty-seven for incorporating this article in the constitution is evidence that a number of the opponents had become proponents. In this manner, as one member interpreted the result, the convention had provided a common education for "every child of the soil."[46]

The history of the suffrage article that made possible its extensions to negroes likewise affords an interesting study of how the convention could reverse itself under what was generally believed to be pressure from the military authorities. The earliest debates, it will be recalled, in which emancipation was the subject, revealed a strong sentiment against negro franchise, and against even allowing the negro to come into the state. Such sentiment soon found expression in a resolution which provided that "the Legislature shall never pass any act authorizing free negroes to vote or to immigrate into this State." The passage of this resolution by the overwhelming vote of sixty-eight to fifteen[47] clearly revealed the attitude of practically the entire membership toward the negro race. One delegate remarked at this time that "the negro should never vote. Let them go into Yankeedom and die there. That is their business."[48] Another more extreme group advocated "pushing the African off the soil of the country." The moderates were willing to let them become citizens, enter the trades and professions, and acquire property, but they must "never vote." They were, in short, almost a unit in opposition to the extension of the suffrage to the black race.

But there was a determined and persisting minority which argued that the negro paid taxes on $130,000,000 worth of property, and that some of the "mixed members" even owned plantations, and a few actually voted by special act of the legislature.

However, the resolution that this group sponsored—to leave the matter of voting to the legislature—was likewise rejected. Still undaunted, the minority, approaching the matter from another apparently innocent angle, proposed the following article: "The Legislature shall have power to extend suffrage by laws to such persons, citizens of the United States, as by military service, by taxation to support the government, or by intellectual fitness may be deemed entitled thereto."[49] This article, which is almost the same phrasing as the secret Lincoln letter to Hahn, was soon discovered to be another "nigger resolution," and a motion to strike it out was carried by a vote of fifty-three to twenty-three.[50] The matter was by no means regarded as a lost cause, for the vote indicated that a few votes were being changed. The fact is, certain influences then at work were soon to change this adverse vote into an affirmative vote.

But the free colored people, becoming dissatisfied with Banks's policy of total exclusion, had ere this decided to appeal directly to Washington. Accordingly, a delegation had quietly slipped out of New Orleans during the last days of February, and had secured an interview with Lincoln. Their chairman had represented in substance that the old freedmen constituted about 30,000 of the entire population, and he produced evidence to show that all but about 1,000 of these could read and write. He represented further that they paid taxes on $15,000,000 worth of property, and that they were better educated and richer than any equal body in the state. Furthermore, they were the descendants of the original French and Spanish settlers; and he alleged that although they had paid taxes since the [Louisiana] Purchase they had been debarred from the public schools and forced to employ private teachers. The spokesman contended, therefore, that they had been discriminated against, which was a violation of their sacred treaty rights. He called Lincoln's attention to the fact that they were fairer than many so-called whites, and could also point to a better record than their loyal white brethren. It was they alone, he reminded Lincoln, who had responded almost to a man to repel what was believed to be an impending attack of General Magruder. And yet despite all these valid claims to the generosity of the

Washington government, he complained, they had been excluded from all participation in the re-establishment of a government in Louisiana.

This appeal for political and economic justice was evidently irresistible.[51] Besides, with factionalism developing in Louisiana, Lincoln may have felt that he needed the support of this "one-tenth of Louisiana's population." There is of course little direct evidence, but there is a strong supposition that he must have been deeply impressed, for shortly after the departure of this delegation, he wrote the letter which is the earliest evidence of a radical change in his reconstruction policy. The complete text of the letter follows:

HONORABLE MICHAEL HAHN,

My dear Sir: I congratulate you on having fixed your name in history as the first free-State governor of Louisiana. Now that you are about to have a convention, which among other things, will probably define the elective franchise, I hereby suggest for your private consideration whether some of the colored people may not be let in—as, for instance, the very intelligent, and especially in our ranks. They would probably help, in some trying time to come, to keep the jewels of liberty within the family of freedom. But this is only a suggestion, not to be public, but to you alone.[52]

The general tone and contents of this letter present certainly more than a striking coincidence when it is closely compared with the aforementioned appeal to Lincoln. This private letter was, of course, not made public for many months, but Banks and others within the inner circle must have been apprised of its contents, and this letter no doubt prompted the continual resurrection of the "nigger resolution." It also may have motivated Banks to conclude one of his characteristic orations before the convention at this time with the prophetic words:

. . . the Legislature that will succeed will be compelled to follow to completion in the work so honorably begun. . . . The act of emancipation is a great and parent act of wisdom. . . . The extension of the franchise hereafter will . . . attract the attention of the country.[53]

The oration and the presence of the military authorities seem to have impressed the delegates, for the "nigger resolution" was now resurrected and incorporated into the organic body of the law by a vote of forty-eight to thirty-two. The article made it possible for the legislature to "follow to completion" by making provision for that body to extend the suffrage to the black race. It must have been the unrelenting work—or pressure—of Banks and his immediate followers that had changed approximately forty votes[54] of these poor whites, who had been and were apparently still bitterly hostile to the negro and to negro suffrage.

Meanwhile the question of emancipation, which had slumbered in committee for several weeks, had been reported to that body as Articles One and Two of the proposed constitution, and had been adopted at once by a vote of seventy-nine to eleven. Number One provided that "slavery and involuntary servitude, except as a punishment for crime, whereof the party shall have been duly convicted, are hereby forever abolished and prohibited throughout the State"; the second simply declared that "the Legislature shall make no law recognizing the right of property in man."[55] The convention went even further and passed a resolution memorializing Congress to secure this object by submitting a Constitutional amendment to that effect. In so doing the majority did not violate any principles, for, although they had been unable to get prompt action, because of the determination of the minority to hold up final enactment until some definite assurance was given on the important question of compensation, they must have favored immediate and unconditional emancipation from the outset. But now on final passage the proposition to compensate owners was defeated by a vote of seventy-one to nineteen, and in addition the proposed amendment to compensate only loyal owners met a similar fate.[56]

The matter of compensation was, in fact, close to the hearts of a number of Unionists, and the debates revealed several schools of thought. Wells, a prominent slaveholder, suggested compensation only if it was paid with confiscated disloyalist property. But he was in favor of leaving it for future settlement.[57] In truth, the majority now realized the obvious fact that slavery nowhere existed, since thousands of the blacks were already enrolled in the ranks of the Unionists, and they argued that to continue to debate compensation might place the delegates in the false light of defending the rebellion. The emancipationists appear, in fact, to have arrived at the conclusion that this was no longer a state question but a national one that must be settled in a way consistent with national policy. For these reasons the majority had evidently favored emancipation first, and proposed afterwards to seek compensation for loyal owners, which they professed to believe would be granted by the Congress. And they felt that they had just cause for such compensation, for the disloyal slaveholders, as the loyalists now pointed out, still possessed their slaves and were still enjoying the fruits of their labors, whereas inside the Federal lines, the slaves of Unionists had everywhere been freed because of military necessity.

Thus it would appear that an additional handicap was being placed on loyalty. Recognizing the obvious injustice of such a policy and wishing to conciliate the loyalists who were demanding compensation, the convention now passed a resolution memorializing Congress to compensate loyal owners,[58] and in addition, appointed a committee to correspond with the leaders of that body. This memorial set forth the claims that emancipation had practically bankrupted the Louisiana Unionists, and in asking relief, called the attention of Congress to the fact that the body had adopted the policy of giving compensation in the District of Columbia. It pointed out finally that the British had adopted a similar measure in 1852. But no evidence has ever been produced to prove that this appeal was favorably considered by Congress.

When it became apparent that in the matter of compensation Congress was disposed to treat the loyalists and disloyalists alike, the members of the convention devised the plan of having state representatives in Congress at the next session, to look after their interests. They seem to have reasoned that if compensation was to be a matter beyond the jurisdiction of the state and was to be settled by Congress and the United States courts, it was incumbent upon Louisiana to be ably represented. Therefore, the ordinance for the purpose of having able men in Congress to look after the interests of the state and to have owners of slaves compensated received an almost unanimous support in the convention.[59]

The question of providing a judiciary was regarded by the delegates and the public as one of the most important subjects that would engage the attention of the convention. There appeared to be a lack of confidence on the part of the members, in the entire judicial system of the state. The debates over the respective merits of the appointed and elective judiciary were, therefore, exhaustive and illuminating. The conservatives urged the appointive system to prevent corruption and to secure a respectable, permanent, and highly qualified non-political judiciary[60] whereas the more radical were at first in favor of retaining the elective system. All appeared, however, to desire the retention of their present loyal Supreme Court judges. The majority of the delegates, therefore, took issue with Dr. Dostie, and other extremists, who were contending all along that the state had gone out of the Union, thereby terminating the Supreme Court. They passed a resolution declaring that the Supreme Court had never been terminated, and requested that the recently elevated Chief Justice, Judge Peabody, who held a dual judgeship as an appointee of Lincoln, be recalled, and that his military judgeship be abolished.[61] Nor did they desire to retain the so-called "rebel system" of courts in which, it was alleged, justice was sold to the highest bidder by the partisan judges, who had been elevated to the bench by the elective system.[62]

While the delegates were in this frame of mind it was not difficult to appeal to their prejudices. So, when the advocates of the appointive system represented that the "traitors Slidell and Benjamin" had worked for and effected popular election of judges in the Convention of 1852, and when they showed further that the appointive system would prevent "disloyal voters from placing disloyal traitors on the bench" who would make a nullity of emancipation and the election laws—then their representations were accepted without question. The acceptance, however, of such statements clearly demonstrated that the uninformed members were being misinformed, for John Slidell was not even a member of the 1852 convention, and Benjamin, who had served as a member of the 1844 and 1852 conventions, had strongly urged the appointment of judges for life.[63] But such arguments, whether for good or evil, were apparently decisive, and Article 79, which provided "that judges of all courts be appointed, with the advice, consent,

[133]

and approval of the Senate" was incorporated into the constitution.[64]

The convention now became involved in another matter pertaining to the legality of slavery. Banks had abolished it within the lines, *de facto* but not *de jure,* whereas Lincoln had abolished it beyond the lines possibly *de jure* but not *de facto.* The legal view was generally entertained that it could not be considered technically abolished until the act of emancipation of the convention had been ratified by vote of the people. Judge W. W. Hamlin, a strong Unionist, and judge of the Third District of Appeals, had evidently arrived at such a conclusion, for he ruled that a negro woman could not sue her master because she was a slave, and being a slave she was of course not a citizen and had no standing in court. This decision, which was rendered very shortly after the passage of the emancipation ordinance, so disturbed the equilibrium of the convention that it felt constrained to take summary action. It, therefore, entertained the resolution "that all decisions of the courts of the states that declare slavery exists in the State, are contrary to the fundamental laws of the State, and are contempts of the emancipation ordinance passed by this Convention."[65]

The more conservative members, on the contrary, reasoned that the resolution was both fanatical and destructive of the independence of the judiciary, for, said they, Banks could not have destroyed slavery within the lines, since this convention had been called for that specific purpose; and that such a resolution was not in order, for slavery technically existed until formal ratification of the emancipation, despite any ruling to the contrary. But the resolution carried by the close vote of forty to thirty-eight. To make the situation worse, Governor Hahn, acting in his military capacity, at once removed the offending judge, and caused Judge Howell, another devoted Unionist who entertained the same views, to resign.[66]

There were still other important features of this proposed constitution. It contained provisions that all able-bodied men, white and black, must be armed and disciplined for the defense of the state,[67] and that representation in the legislature would henceforth be based on "qualified voters." This meant that both the "population" basis and the recently employed "white population" basis had been rejected. It also contained an article stating that any person could vote at his nearest precinct if he was a citizen of the United States and had lived one year in the state.[68]

The membership also appeared to have the same attitude toward foreigners that they had manifested toward the negro. Responding to a memorial presented by several thousand mechanics and laboring men, setting forth their grievances and praying for redress, certain delegates proposed that none except United States citizens, or those having made legal declaration of becoming citizens, would be granted a license to practise any profession or business in the state. The illuminating debates now brought out the facts that thousands had lived as foreigners for twenty years or more with no idea of becoming naturalized and that this article was intended to protect the foreigner who came in good faith, but not the foreigner in Louisiana who had enlisted and "formed a battalion to fight for the Confederacy." Finally, in defense of this resolution, it was charged that the houses of these unnaturalized aliens "were the regular rendez-vous of all the secessionists," and that "nine out of ten were plotting openly and giving aid and comfort" to the Confederacy. They would, therefore, punish that foreigner who could brazenly declare: "We make a great deal more than any naturalized citizen, and do as we d—— please."

The sentiment was apparently overwhelmingly in favor of the passage of this resolution. It was postponed, however, from time to time by the parliamentarians, and was eventually defeated.[69]

The members of this convention, who have gone down in history because of their liberality in disposing of other men's slave property, were also liberal in disposing of the public funds. They first appropriated, out of general funds, the sum of $100,000, and then voted themselves the sum of $10 per day compensation. This amount, however, proved inadequate for a number of officers. It therefore became necessary to appropriate an additional $25,000.

It was, however, with apparent reluctance that this body could be induced to appropriate $10,000 for inauguration expenses. In

[135]

fact, this item evoked a discussion which brought to light many interesting sidelights on the late state election. When it was proposed that the recent election deficit and inauguration expenses be included in the one item of "Inauguration expenses," a substitute motion was offered to make it read "to pay the election expenses of the State officers." It was objected that the salaries of these officials had been greatly increased, and that if they wished to maintain their popularity, they should take care of the deficit from their own salaries. Furthermore, as it was contended, the defeated "Flanders-Chase party," and the conservative could, with equal propriety, ask for the payment of their election expenses out of the public treasury. Those who favored the appropriation rejoined with a charge that the defeated radicals had been liberally supplied with funds, and that their agents had collected in the North approximately $35,000, a portion of which they had spent corrupting the electorate in the recent election, and a greater portion of which they had retained. There were two items, however—one for a bill of $1,000 for "candles," and another for $150 for "repairing flags"—that all members seemed disposed to question. Nevertheless, on final passage the entire appropriation of $10,000 was approved by a vote of sixty-four to fourteen.[70]

This convention seems to have discredited itself in the eyes of the public. The Unionist press became openly hostile. Its attitude is best reflected by the exposure in both the *Times* and the *Picayune* of the contingent fund expenses. The *Times* supplemented an editorial on "Expenses and Accomplishments" with the following items of "contingent expenses":

Ice	$ 414.50
Liquors and cigars	9,421.55
Dinners Galpins	65.00
Fitting up Liberty Hall	9,150.25
Goblets, wine glasses	791.60
One pen case presented to General Banks	150.00
Daily papers	4,237.50
Police Duty	1,904.00
Stationery	8,111.55
Carriage hire, etc.	4,304.25
Sundry items	236.35

Bill for printing 7,000.00
Amts. for which no vouchers 608.70
_____
Total ....$46,393.25[71]

A special investigating committee of the legislature, meeting shortly after the adjournment of the convention, had discovered the above items. And further testimony of witnesses revealed additional evidence of extravagance.[72]

In addition to this contingent expense, the *per diem*, the mileage, and the salaries of the officials totaled $150,000 or approximately $1,600 per day. At this same time it seems, this body denied aid to certain charitable institutions giving as a reason that the people were groaning under taxation burdens. The official records also reveal that the convention distributed sums to the clergy who acted as chaplains. Apparently a precedent was set with the free bar.

An episode occurred on the eve of adjournment which illustrates the state into which the members of the convention as a whole had fallen. Thomas P. May, a loyalist officeholder under Chase and editor of the *Times,* had published an article headed "Great Times in Convention," in which he had described the proceedings of the Convention of July 21 as "sickening and disgusting."[73] This article, which purported to give a true picture of the actual happenings,[74] had declared that a certain member had had the "boot applied" to his rear extremities; it had further set forth, on apparently good authority, that the members were, as a whole, a set of drunken men, and that the President was also "drunk and a d—— fool." The charge of drunkenness, which affected the character of the members, had at once thrown the convention into an "uproar[i]ous debate." The charges and insinuations were denied *in toto,* and it was counter-charged by a member that he [May] was a "copper-head editor," who gave "aid and comfort" to the enemy. This member added: "the nearer the rebels get to the city the prouder these copper-heads become." Another member accused May of being in league with Salmon P. Chase. "I say," this member concluded, "that I believe we have an enemy among us in the person of Salmon P. Chase . . . a rival of the President."[75]

[137]

The outcome of the whole matter was a novel proceeding for a deliberative body. A resolution was hurriedly passed, summoning the editor to appear in person before the convention and purge himself of libel. He elected to ignore this mandate; but he did appear for trial in obedience to a command, as he alleged, from General N. P. Banks. He remained defiant, however, refusing to make any retractions whatsoever. Then the majority, asserting that the body was a sovereign body, passed, by a vote of forty-nine to thirty-one, another resolution, which imposed upon him a ten-day imprisonment term and the suppression of his paper, unless the body should adjourn sooner. The resolution also requested the President to remove the recalcitrant editor from the office of Assistant Treasurer of the United States. But General Canby, who had at this time replaced Banks because of the failure of his Red River campaign, ordered his release, and he was not punished.[76]

At the time of the adjournment a reconvoking resolution that was to have a far-reaching influence was passed. This apparently innocent resolution, which was to make possible the battle of July, 1866, which in turn helped to set in motion forces that were to make reconstruction legislation possible, was:

Resolved that when this Convention adjourns, it shall be at the call of the President, whose duty it shall be to reconvoke the Convention for any cause, for the purpose of taking such measures as may be necessary for the formation of a civil government. It shall also in that case, call upon the proper officers of the State to cause elections to be held to fill any vacancies that may exist in parishes where the same may be practicable.[77]

The legislature was also authorized in another clause to reconvoke this convention in case of "emergency"; the idea prevailed that this would prove a remedy should their enemies be successful in defeating the constitution at the polls.

This resolution did not pass, however, without some real opposition on the part of the legal-minded members. They reasoned that when the convention adjourned it could have no power to go further, for it would then have discharged the duties for which it had been elected, and that any attempt to continue its own existence would be a usurpation; that if the people should see fit to reject the works of the convention, the said people would have their own recourse in that they could elect other servants, who would "represent their views more faithfully." But such views did not prevail, and this reconvoking resolution was adopted by a vote of sixty-two to twenty-four.[78]

The final act, before adjournment on July 25, was the adoption of the constitution as a whole and the affixing of the signatures. Seventy-nine signed, and seventeen refused to sign this document, which was a revision of the 1852 constitution.[79] It was much briefer than is the present organic law of the state. The essential features, most of which have been discussed at some length, were the following: abolition of slavery, provisions for the extension by legislative action of the suffrage to the negroes, the establishment by public taxation of separate schools for blacks and whites, repudiation of all debts contracted in the interest of the Southern Confederacy, the provision that all able-bodied males should serve in the militia, and the appointment of representation on a basis of voting population instead of "population," which deprived the planters of their political power. Still other important features were the authorization of lotteries and gambling saloons, the location of the state capitol at New Orleans, the provision for a general assembly to be elected the first Monday in September, 1864, and the prohibition upon the legislature of passing laws requiring property qualification for officeholders. Finally an article was incorporated providing for the submission of the constitution for ratification or rejection by vote of the people on the first Monday in September, 1864.[80]

It was predicted that, because there was so little merit and respectability among the members, their work would not be ratified.[81] It is probably true that the convention had ceased to be a deliberative body; that there were delegates in the convention who had not been in the parishes they purported to represent; and that there were some members who had once enlisted in the United States army, as was charged, who now found it much safer and more profitable to serve as members of a convention that was protected by the United States army.[82] But the prophets had again reckoned without their host, for the same silent forces that had apparently been able on more than one occasion to change minorities into majorities were apparently still exerting their powerful backstage influences. This is attested by the following letter in which instructions as to methods of procedure are outlined:

EXECUTIVE MANSION

WASHINGTON, August 9th, 1864

MAJOR GENERAL BANKS,

I have just seen the new Constitution adopted by the Convention of Louisiana, and I am anxious that it shall be ratified by the people. I will thank you to let the civil officers in Louisiana, holding under me, know that this is my wish, and to let me know at once who of them openly declares for the Constitution, and who of them, if any, declines to so declare.

Yours truly

A. LINCOLN.[83]

In line with these instructions preparations were at once made to effect ratification on the first Monday in September; and, according to the press, several "monstrous" mass meetings and rallies were now arranged for the double purpose of adopting resolutions urging the ratification of the constitution and for ratifying the nomination of Lincoln and Johnson.[84] In fact, nothing seems to have been neglected. It was even charged that the Ward Union Leagues were manipulated by large sums of money. And finally on the eve of the election, all the government and quartermaster employees were called out in a final grand torchlight procession.[85]

The outcome of the voting might have been predicted, for the registration and election machinery were in the hands of the military authorities. There was an almost unanimous affirmative vote. It was larger, in fact, than the vote cast for the convention, although it was approximately thirty per cent smaller than had been the vote cast for the so-called civil government. The total vote in the twenty parishes that participated was 8,402, 1,566 being cast in the negative, which gave a clear majority of 5,270. Only 800 votes were recorded against it in the city, where a few "equal rights" tickets for members of the legislature had also been successful.[86] A few days later Governor Hahn gave the complete returns—which are tabulated on Map No. 8—and proclaimed the constitution in full effect in Louisiana.[87]

[140]

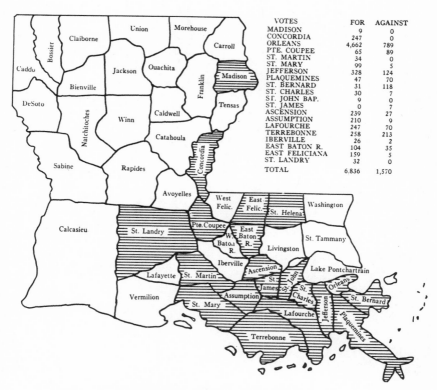

VOTES	FOR	AGAINST
MADISON	9	0
CONCORDIA	247	0
ORLEANS	4,662	789
PTE. COUPEE	65	89
ST. MARTIN	34	0
ST. MARY	99	5
JEFFERSON	328	124
PLAQUEMINES	47	70
ST. BERNARD	31	118
ST. CHARLES	30	7
ST. JOHN BAP.	9	0
ST. JAMES	0	7
ASCENSION	239	27
ASSUMPTION	210	9
LAFOURCHE	247	70
TERREBONNE	258	213
IBERVILLE	26	2
EAST BATON R.	104	35
EAST FELICIANA	159	5
ST. LANDRY	32	0
TOTAL	6,836	1,570

PARISHES THAT PARTICIPATED IN THE ADOPTION OF THE
CONSTITUTION OF 1864 (SHADED)

CHAPTER VII

THE PROBLEM OF CIVIL GOVERNMENT
DURING THE CIVIL WAR PERIOD

With the establishment of this so-called civil government in
New Orleans, Louisiana had two state governments and two state
capitals, for the Confederates, after the fall of New Orleans and
Baton Rouge, had first established their seat of government at
Opelousas, and subsequently at Shreveport. From the respective
capitols both made all possible efforts to administer an effective
government.[1] But we must concern ourselves with the Union-con-
trolled government under Banks.

Among the many problems that pressed for solution, perhaps
none caused greater concern to both governments than the regulation of the negroes.[2] Banks, who was actively sponsoring and supporting the newly created New Orleans government, had some
very definite ideas about the employment of the blacks. The demoralization of the multitudes of negroes who had flocked into the
city and within the Federal lines, and the growing menace of vice
and infectious diseases, were having a contaminating effect on his
Federal soldiers.[3] To correct these evils, and to put all idle negroes
to work, Banks had issued his famous General Order No. 23 as a
supplement to his labor system established January 30, 1863. The
essential features of these regulations were: the suspension of the
order enlisting negro soldiers from the plantations; a provision for
the establishment of public schools for the negroes; the fixing of
compensation at from $3.00 to $8.00 per month, or share cropping,
depending on the class and efficiency of such labor; the substitu-
tion of other punishments than flogging for the infraction of rules
or violation of contracts; the establishment of a Free Labor Bank
in connection with the Treasury Department; and the solemn injunction that while laborers would be permitted to choose their
employers, they would be held to their agreement and the universal
law of labor would be enforced.[4] As a further attempt to suppress
the alleged widespread indolence, crime, and disorder, it was directed that a certificate of employment be issued to all such laborers, and that all colored persons of either sex, who had no

[141]

visible means of support be taken in charge and put to work.[5]

A drastic enforcement policy, according to the report of the Superintendent of Free Labor, soon brought the desired relief. It showed that idleness and license had practically disappeared; that schools had been provided; that the negro status in all courts was exactly the same as that of white persons; and that more than 80,000 were happily and gainfully employed, whereas only 858 were being fed, excepting, of course, the 5,000 who had become recruits.[6] This report was substantiated in part by the planters,[7] who claimed, however, that there were defects in the new system, and recommended certain changes in the experiment. As a whole, they maintained that the laborer should work for a share of the crop, that capacity and not age should be the standard, and that some authority, preferably the military, should be in the vicinity to keep the labor from flocking to the cities—their heaven—and to force them to work, since moral suasion failed to accomplish this end.[8]

It was this condition of affairs that B. F. Flanders encountered when he took charge and control of the Freedmen in the Department of the Gulf on November 1, 1864, and became the first Supervising Special Agent of the newly created Freedmen's Bureau. New policies did not, however, go into effect because the same orders which transferred the authority, as well as old and new business, from the military to the new incumbent, made provision that "all orders issued heretofore from this Department in relation to the care and treatment of such freedmen will remain in force, and be executed until modified or revoked at the request of said Supervising Special Agent." The co-worker of Flanders was Thomas W. Conway, who was designated as "General Superintendent Freedmen Department of the Gulf."[9]

On January 1, 1865, this department, which was to play an increasingly important role, and which was to be backed by the military authorities, issued its first circular of instruction to planters and laborers, giving complete details concerning pay rolls and the payment of freedom. It forbade them from visiting the city of New Orleans, except under strict regulations, and specified that "laborers will be allowed to select their places of employment for the coming year, subject to such regulations as may be promulgated by the proper authorities."[10] The bureau officials, however, in a subsequent order elected to ignore the planters' recommendations relative to share cropping, but did continue in force the system of wage payments. This regulation, which was promulgated on April 25, 1865, provided for quarterly cash payments, and, in case of refusal or failure, a severe fine, which was to go for the benefit of the Freedmen's Orphan Asylum.[11]

Such a system, whereby the planters were deprived of control over wages and over the time of payment, could not be expected to work out satisfactorily with the negro, who had been accustomed to forced labor. As a natural consequence there developed a rather strong sentiment to import white labor. And yet it is significant to note that the first annual report of the Superintendent of this Bureau gave the old resident planters credit for dealing fairly with labor, in fact more fairly than the new lessees.[12] It is also significant that this "Bureau system" was inaugurated in Louisiana and had been in full force and effect almost one year before General O. O. Howard was designated as Chief of the Bureau of Refugees, Freedmen, and Abandoned Lands,[13] and before he issued his first important order that the freedmen should be allowed to retain possession of the abandoned lands until the crops were harvested.[14]

Another new element in respect to the solution of the negro question also grew out of the third article of this labor order. This article had made provision for a system of public education for the blacks; and now, under the auspices of General Banks, and in obedience to that inaugural suggestion of Governor Hahn that "the blessings of education ought not, as heretofore, to be excluded from the blacks," a commission of three had been charged with the responsibility of providing school facilities and competent teachers.[15]

In pursuance of its instructions the board was soon engaged in mapping out school districts, acquiring plots of land, erecting suitable school buildings, employing a corps of teachers, regulating the course of study, and last, but by no means least, in assessing, levying, and collecting taxes on personal and real property.[16] If early reports of these sponsors are to be accepted as authentic, its wards, the "former slaves, could, within a short period, read and write better than their old masters," and what was considered more remarkable, were evincing "something of Yankee tact in managing to keep their children in school."[17] The ten-page pamphlet, under the head of "The Progress Made," issued by Conway as superintendent of the bureau, was more detailed, and contained the information that illiteracy was fast disappearing. The number of schools, according to Conway, had been greatly increased until there were then sixty-nine in the Department, in addition to some thirty in the regiments—Corps d'Afrique—all of which were "in successful operation." An aggregate of 8,000 "scholars" of the 15,340 colored children within the Union lines had been enrolled. It was expected, however, that within the next three months the "remaining moiety" would also be placed under instruction. "About half of these children did not know their alphabet," continued this report, "but they are now reading in the First Readers, and solving with facility problems in the primary rules of arithmetic." The more advanced classes, it added, were reading with facility in the Third and Fourth Readers, and had acquired a knowledge of geography, and arithmetic as far as long division and fractions. All of this had come to pass within the brief period of eight weeks.

The result of this new chapter of human experience [this September report concluded] will be a general resurrection of buried minds. Our military expeditions do the pioneer work. Education follows a most glorious work. Freedmen are receiving instruction, counsel, and culture. The day of antagonism is over, and that of befriending begins. Behind the advancing lines of our forces follows the small pacific army of teachers and civilians; and the school house takes the place of the whipping-post and scourge.[18]

By March, 1865, the close of its first fiscal year, this Board of Education could report that there were over 11,000 in the colored schools, under the charge of 162 teachers, 130 of whom were of Southern birth, and who were said to have borne "the load of calumny, sneers, and social proscription." The attendance, it admitted, had been very irregular, and the tax was expected to yield only $150,000.

The general purport of the document, however, was that remarkable progress had been achieved under the energetic administration of the board. In fact, the progress reported had been too rapid, and was questioned by some of the Unionists themselves. Such tendency to exaggerate was condemned by the editor of the Unionist *Times,* who cautioned "that the tone of a considerable part of the document is hardly calculated to win that support" desired, and who dismissed the subject with the admonition:

The publication of this Report is, doubtless, intended to accomplish good at home, as well as to circulate in the North, and a greater degree of moderation in the expression of opinions, would, we believe, have rendered its influence more potent for beneficial results.[19]

Meanwhile the first free-state legislature, which had been elected on the same day that the Constitution had been ratified,[20] met in special session on October 3, 1864.[21] A communication from the Secretary of State gave the roster of the membership elected to both houses. Forty-four members represented the parish of Orleans, all of whom except two were elected from the city, and forty-two members had been elected from twenty-four other parishes.[22] New Orleans had elected nine to the Senate, a portion of the parish outside of the city being joined to Plaquemines and St. Bernard District. Twenty senators were reported to have been elected outside the city, making a total of twenty-nine in that body. But the status of two of these seems to have been of a doubtful nature.[23]

The lower body, with a quorum present, elected Simeon Belden of St. Martin, speaker;[24] the Senate organized with Lieutenant-Governor Wells in the chair, and twenty-three senators present.[25]

Upon completion of organization by the appointment of the proper committees and the election of a number of minor officers, the Governor's message was read. This document, with its recommendations, was calculated to supply the legislature with ample food for thought. He began with his usual claims that the state was, in every legal and constitutional requisite, on a par with any of the Northern states; he reviewed the events subsequent to the reassertion of the national authority, and epitomized the report of the State Treasurer, which showed that there was only $18,000 in currency in the general fund. In connection with this fund, which the salaries of the state officials would soon exhaust, the Governor reminded the legislature that the expenses of the late constitutional convention were very heavy, and added that it was highly incumbent that the legislators practise the most rigid economy.

The legislature was charged, however, with the task of devising some means of securing revenue, and cautioned, at the same time, that the people could not bear the weight of a reckless and heavy expenditure. The financial corporations, the governor believed, should be dealt with in such a way as would best secure the interests of the people. Some of them, he alleged, could become solvent by receiving possession of specie, or cotton, which, though belonging to them, was within the rebel lines. He paid a handsome compliment to the Louisiana Union soldiers, stating that the honor of the state demanded that positive provision he made for their families. He further recommended the enrollment of all able-bodied citizens, the condemnation of foreign residents who refused to aid in the local defense, the enactment of wise and careful laws governing compensated labor, the adjustment between capital and industry, a new city charter, a permanent police for New Orleans, and the appropriation of funds for public charities. Avowing, finally, that his only "ambition in accepting office" was to "aid the cause of the Union, and to give slavery its death blow," he dramatically concluded:

The rebellion everywhere is at its last gasp. . . . Everything portends a general collapse within the contracted lines of treason. . . . With hearts full of gratitude to Him who rules over nations . . . and with the wisdom, patriotism, and fortitude becoming the occasion, let us apply ourselves to the important duties assigned us by our fellow-citizens, and to the sacrifices demanded by the best interests of our Union.[26]

In view of the fact that the convention had prepared the way for negro suffrage, it is interesting to note what action, if any, the two houses took. A careful examination of the journals and debates of both houses indicate that there was practically no sentiment in the legislature for such a measure. T. G. Chamberlain, from the (then) tenth ward of New Orleans, did give notice of

[146]

his intention to introduce a bill to submit the question of negro suffrage to the people at the next general election. This occurred late in the session, and the proceedings do not show that it was ever mentioned again.[27] A bill providing "that every person having not more than one-fourth of negro blood, shall be considered and recognized as white" was, however, introduced in the Senate by Charles Smith.[28] His bill was at once objected to by several members, who maintained that the convention had already gone further than most states,[29] in making the negroes the equals of whites, and who cautioned delay, at least until the state was recognized by Congress. The debate, strangely enough, revealed that the negro organ, "The Tribune," was opposing such a law as being partial.[30] The matter was eventually tabled by a vote of twenty to four; whereupon Smith gave notice that he would at some future time introduce a bill to extend the right of suffrage to colored persons on a basis of military service, property qualification, and intellectual fitness.[31] He did introduce such a bill, but it was rejected by a vote of fifteen to five on the first reading.

But the negroes, especially those in the army, did not let the matter rest, for shortly thereafter a Mr. Hill stated on the floor that he held in his hand a petition from 5,000 negro soldiers, requesting the privilege of suffrage, and he urged that their request be granted.[32] However, the only response that he appears to have received in the legislature was from a Mr. Montant, who stated that he would not oppose its reading, but that it would "be time enough to grant the prayer of such petitions when all the other free States of the Union have set us the example." "I am," he concluded, "a native of Louisiana, and when this State extends to the negroes the right of suffrage, I shall leave it forthwith and go to China."[33] This attitude seems to have been the sentiment of the large majority, for this petition does not appear to have ever been received or presented. This indeed reflected the attitude of the Governor at this time although he reversed himself within the next few months. He had not mentioned negro suffrage in his message of October 7, but some time later did express himself as unequivocally opposed when he said: ". . . our Constitution . . . has provided for their complete equality before the law, including

[147]

the extension to them of the highest privilege of citizenship." He added:

I have no hesitation in saying that its terms will justify the adoption of Universal suffrage, whenever it shall be deemed wise and timely; and if the most devoted enthusiast shall complain that the doors have not been thrown open at once to all, he must admit, as we can claim, that our State had progressed further than three-fourths of the Northern States. . . .[34]

Sentiment, however, seemed to be ripe for affirmative action on the Thirteenth Amendment. A concurrent resolution, introduced shortly after convening, instructing and requesting Louisiana's Congressional delegation to vote for the Thirteenth Amendment, which prohibited slavery, did meet with some opposition in the House, the objection being that Congress and the President had no right to deprive citizens of a large amount of valuable property, especially without remuneration. But such objection was withdrawn when the opposition was convinced that affirmative action would be the most powerful argument in favor of the admission of the Louisiana delegation to Congress; it passed the House by a vote of sixty to five.[35] The Senate also voiced some slight objection; one member stated that "the authorities at Washington do not seem to regard Louisiana as in the Union, except when it is convenient for them to do so, or when they want us to perform some special act. In this matter they are willing to regard us as a State."[36] The opposition, however, decided that discretion would no doubt be the better part of valor, and the concurrent resolution received a unanimous vote on final passage,[37] thereby pledging the legislature to ratify such amendment if submitted.[38]

The Thirteenth Amendment was shortly submitted by Congress—an act which must have technically at least recognized Louisiana as a state in the Union—and passed both Houses.[39] The House this time recorded an affirmative vote of seventy-nine, and no votes against it—a vote that was reported to have been cast upon the urgent request of Governor Hahn.[40]

A deep interest was manifested in the presidential election by the Unionists in general, and the members of the constitutional convention and legislature in particular. A state convention for the purpose of electing delegates to the Republican National Convention at Baltimore on June 7 had been urged as early as April 23.[41] It was also suggested by the *Times* that men of character and standing should be selected, and that Louisiana should not send men "wedded to a single idea"; that is, wedded to Lincoln.[42] But despite such evident hostility to Lincoln, all fourteen delegates were instructed for him.[43]

It was felt, however, that there would be some opposition to the Louisiana delegation because of a rule of the National Executive Committee "that only members could be received, whose State was fully represented in the National Congress."[44] This apparently insurmountable handicap was to be overcome, as the *Times* prophesied, by the fact that "Lincoln will need the seven votes of Louisiana."[45]

Another delegation, the conservatives, headed by J. L. Riddell, and laboring under the same apprehension as the Lincoln delegates regarding admission, presented its petition at Chicago, praying to be united with the Northern Democracy. It was, however, given a rebuff when its petition to be admitted was referred to the Committee on Credentials.[46] These conservatives, nevertheless, upon their return to Louisiana, adopted the slogan of "McClellan and moderation," as opposed to what they designated as the "despotic, unconstitutional, and military rule of Lincoln."[47] The rallies that followed were reported in the press as containing the "largest audiences . . . since 1840."[48] Their resolutions were also both bold and expressive of confidence. They declared through their press that Louisiana would cast two-thirds of its votes for McClellan, provided a fair election and honest count could be obtained. They seemed disposed, however, not to enter the contest unless allowed to use only the oaths required by the United States Constitution, and the Louisiana Constitution of 1852.[49]

However, at the last moment the conservatives were denied the privilege of participating in any form, for the Lincoln supporters, who evidently feared the results of a popular vote, had laid other plans whereby, as the Conservative Unionists in desperation complained: "those men not agreeing with Mr. Lincoln's views are to be refused the right to deposit their ballots."[50] "The slimness" of the pre-election "Lincoln rallies," had in fact convinced the Lincoln supporters that their cause was hopeless, as the *Times* frankly stated. But the legislature, in sympathy with Lincoln, now found a way out of the difficulty by passing an act which provided that *it* would elect the seven electors from Louisiana because of "the present unsettled condition of the interior of the State."[51] The act provided, further, that such election in the future would be by popular vote. In accordance with this act, the legislature in joint ballot met on November 8, and elected seven electors to represent Louisiana in the electoral college.[52] Thus Louisiana's seven votes were made available to Lincoln. But, as subsequent events shortly proved, Lincoln obviously did not need the proffered aid of Louisiana; and, as will presently be shown, these electoral votes were rejected by Congress.[53]

In fact, the legislature is best remembered for what it failed to do, rather than for what it accomplished, for during the period of over six months that it was in session, which included the special fall session of 1864 and the three months' winter session, a great number of subjects were debated at length, and dropped altogether. One of the more important matters considered was a bill to permit marriages between whites and colored persons. It would have repealed Article 95 of the Constitution, as Mr. Mane, its sponsor, stated.[54] However, it was rejected by the vote of fifty-seven to five.[55] Another important resolution was passed, providing for a special committee to report a bill with a special code of laws for the emancipated.[56] The committee was appointed to "investigate and propose the necessary laws,"[57] but no such bill was ever reported.[58] Bills were proposed to prevent dual office holding,[59] the contention being that such was unconstitutional; but they apparently were dropped, for the reason that the legislature would have been "left without a quorum."[60] So-called internal improvement bills were introduced into both houses,[61] but were defeated after considerable debate because it was pointed out that their introduction had been motivated, and that their passage would lead to fraud.[62] Bills proposing the floating of loans to carry on the government were introduced from time to time, but no such bills ever became laws.[63] Several bills to levy taxes for the support of negro schools were introduced and debated at intervals for weeks, but failed of passage because of an apparently overwhelming sentiment against the education of the blacks.[64]

An act to abolish the "Black Code of 1855" passed the House,[65] and was placed on the calendar of the Senate, where it died at the end of the session.[66] An amnesty resolution, authorizing the seizure and sale of property of persons in rebellion, which also was calculated to extend pardon and amnesty, was rejected in the Senate on the third reading by a vote of twelve to nine;[67] and a similar bill, purporting to disfranchise a large number of Confederates, who would otherwise, as some of the legislators believed, soon "occupy these very seats," met a similar fate in the lower House by a vote of forty-six to fifteen.[68] Resolutions making provisions for a thorough investigation of the enormous expenditures of the late convention were introduced into both Houses, and the fraudulent character of the proceedings of that defunct and discredited body seems, from the mass of evidence produced in the thorough airings that it received over a period of weeks, to have been clearly established; but the only result was an attemped whitewashing.[69] In fact, condemnation of the convention by this legislature, as the debates disclosed, would have been like the "creature bringing the Creator to account." Besides, it now appeared that the legislature was living in "a glass house" and dared not cast any stones.

This offspring of the "glorious Constitutional Convention" did not prove untrue to its parentage, especially in the matter of expenditures. Its first appropriation of $100,000 had been exhausted before the special session ended,[70] and the deficit necessitated an additional appropriation at the beginning of the regular session. This second bill, which provided for an appropriation of $250,000, was speedily enacted,[71] and made it possible for the body to remain in session until it expired by the statute of limitation on April 4.[72] In addition, it made provision for the payment of a printing bill of the State Printers for approximately $40,000,[73] making a total for expenditures of almost $400,000.

But if this legislature passed little that was constructive, it must be said in its defense that it was compelled, almost from its convening, to act on the defensive; that is, to consume a considerable portion of its time in an attempt to defend its own legality. The legality of the September election had been seriously questioned,[74] because, it was alleged, of wholesale fraudulent registration. It was charged, furthermore, that many members "on this floor are not entitled to their seats," since for many months before the election they had been absent from the parishes they then pretended to represent.[75] Others were from parishes from beyond the lines,[76] one member having been elected to represent De Soto parish by a constituency of eight who had met and elected him, so it was charged, "that he may receive $8.00 a day, and divide that with its other spoils among these eight constituents."[77]

The decorum—or lack of it—was also a contributing factor to the apparent contempt with which the members of the legislature came to be regarded by the public. The frequent ridicule by the playhouses, especially the Academy of Music, reflected the low repute into which they had fallen.[78] The records reveal that members were in the habit of making the House ridiculous by causing confusion, disturbances, and disorders, and by "scaling the railing, breaking a quorum, and using insulting language."[79] This lack of dignity, together with the more serious charges of extravagance, "bribery, and corruption," that were being circulated,[80] eventually caused the *Times* to repudiate these "ignorant, pretentious, and selfish incapables," who were playing "such fantastic tricks before high heaven and the State as might make devils laugh, and angels weep."[81] This journal, which was supposedly the mouthpiece of the military authorities continued to characterize the attitude of both Houses as disgraceful in the extreme, and it even intimated that "some morning another Cromwell may visit our Legislature and thrust you forth. . . ."[82]

But the so-called "Legislative Farce" continued until the statute of limitations forced adjournment, an event that prompted the *Times* to remark, "They are leaving their records blazoned on the historic page printed at the expense of the taxpayers."[83] The *Picayune* seems to have been equally happy over the fact that adjournment *sine die* had at last come by limitation; and it was equally as caustic in its summary of the cost and valuable time consumed. Asking: "What has it done for this?" the editor abruptly concluded, "But let us not rake up its ashes."[84]

The legislature had, apparently under public pressure, passed an act to set up the Supreme Court, and thereby made possible the completion of the state system of courts. But in order to understand the need of such a court it is necessary to give a brief résumé of the judiciary during the interval between the passing of Confederate authority in New Orleans in 1862 and the restoration. The whole system had virtually collapsed with the fall of the city. Being faced with chaos and lawlessness, Butler had found it absolutely necessary to establish an improvised system of military courts. These tribunals were constituted of military officers, who must have had some knowledge of law.[85] This court, usually designated as a "provost court," assumed, evidently of necessity, jurisdiction in both criminal and civil cases, and proved to be highly unsatisfactory from its very inception.[86] It had, therefore, been supplemented by Lincoln's "Provisional Court," which had begun to function on December 31, 1862, with Judge Peabody presiding,[87] as a result of the following order:

By an executive order, dated the 20th day of October, A.D., 1862, Abraham Lincoln, President of the United States, has constituted a "United States provisional Court for the State of Louisiana" and appointed the Honorable Charles A. Peabody to be a provisional judge to hold said court.

By the terms of this order he is invested "with authority to hear, try, and determine all causes in law, equity, revenue and admiralty, and particularly to exercise all such powers and jurisdiction as belong to the District and Civil Courts, conforming his proceeds, as far as possible, to the cause of the Courts of the United States and Louisiana. His judgments are to be final and conclusive."[88]

The Executive order provided, further, that Judge Peabody was "empowered to make and establish such rules and regulations as may be necessary . . . and to appoint a prosecuting attorney marshall, and clerk. . . ." Such powers, it will be observed, were so broad that they were almost unlimited, and it was accordingly "trusted that the emergency which imposed this necessity will pass, and the regular judicial tribunals be reinstated."[89]

Judge Peabody, who was said to be an eminent jurist, asserted less authority than his commission vested in him. Otherwise much disorder might have resulted from a conflict of authority between the Peabody Court and the Butler system. Butler had previously prevailed upon the judge of the probate court to resume his position, and had also thereafter opened three of the six District Courts, with Judge Rufus K. Howell resuming his duties in the Sixth Disrict, Judge Hienstand being appointed to the First, Judge Handlin to the Third, and Judge Duplantier to the Sixth after Judge Durell had been transferred to the Second District Court. These three judges, who were old citizens well versed in the civil law of Louisiana, also took over the duties of the other three vacant District Courts.[90] In addition to these inferior courts, the United States District and Circuit courts had been opened on June 25, 1863, with solemn and impressive ceremonies. This event was hailed as an important step in the gradual restoration of the civil authority.[91] Judge Edward H. Durell, formerly of New Hampshire, but for many years a prominent lawyer and public-spirited citizen of New Orleans, had been appointed to preside over the United States District Court. He was assisted by Rufus Waples, District Attorney, and James Graham, United States Marshal. Waples was a native of Delaware, but had been identified with the educational and legal professions in New Orleans for many years. Graham was born in Ireland, but had also been in Louisiana for some time, where he was recognized as a printer and writer of ability.[92]

The Louisiana Supreme Court, despite an urgent demand on the part of the bar in the city, had not been re-established in 1862, nor in 1863 at the time these inferior courts had been re-established.[93] It is true that the "Provisional Court" was functioning as a kind of court of higher justice, but it was never recognized as a "desideratum," if the views expressed by the bar and by some members of the convention and legislature are to be given credence. The chief objection, it seems, was not that it had wide range of powers which made oppression possible—for it had self-imposed limitations and was never arbitrary—but that there were many cases on the docket of the old Supreme Court which could not—it was thought—be properly brought before the "Provisional Court" on account of the differences between the laws governing the United States Courts, and those of the Supreme Court of Louisiana.[94]

Thus the matter of filling the vacancies in the State Supreme Court and completing the organization of the judiciary system of the state, had been delayed until the convention, voicing its disapproval of Lincoln's arbitrary court in its debates, had made provision for a complete judiciary, including a new State Supreme Court.[95] The members had urged the early reorganization of this supreme tribunal in lieu of the "Provisional Court," that had, since April, 1863, purported to act in the dual capacity of the Louisiana Supreme Court and "Provisional Court";[96] but months passed before the legislature took cognizance of the important matter of creating a Supreme Court. In the meantime hundreds of cases had been appealed, and the law's delay in such appeals to a court that in reality did not exist, was giving a loophole to all dishonest men who sought to avoid discharging their obligations. This intolerable state of affairs now caused such a public demand upon the authorities[97] through the press that at last the desired relief was obtained by an act of the legislature, which created a Supreme Court of a Chief Justice and four associates. This court, which was to have appellate jurisdiction in disputes exceeding $300, and in most criminal and all constitutional matters,[98] was speedily organized with William B. Hyman as Chief Justice, and Rufus K. Howell, R. B. Jones, Zenon Lebauve, and John H. Ilsley as associates.[99]

A resolution had also been introduced into the lower house of the legislature requesting the President to "withdraw and abolish" the "Provisional Court." The reasons assigned were that it was supposed to be temporary; that civil government had been restored and recognized by the President; and that the President had recognized the regular constitutional courts, which were in active operation. It set forth, further, that many difficult cases had arisen, concerning which there was a conflict of jurisdiction; and finally that the best lawyers in the country had denied the constitutionality and legality of said court.[100]

The arguments must have had some weight with the administration for it now further restricted the powers and jurisdiction of this court. But it continued to exist, doubtless for the purpose for which Lincoln had created it; that is, not to render decisions in confiscation and similar cases, as had been commonly supposed, but primarily for the purpose of rendering decisions in disputes or

[155]

litigation in which foreign residents were involved or concerned. If such was its original purpose, it was eminently successful, for no longer did complaints continue to pour into Washington as had been the case under the Butler regime. In fact, such complaints almost ceased, and thus, in this limited capacity, this court continued to dispense justice until the end of the war, at which time Judge Peabody tendered his resignation.[101] The last chapter was written on this strange court in July, 1866, when Congress abolished it and transferred all pending cases to the proper Federal courts.[102]

Congressmen were also elected, it will be recalled, on the same day that the legislature had been elected and the constitution ratified. The contests had been animated in both the New Orleans districts. M. F. Bonzano, the author of the Article of Emancipation, opposed Edmund Abell in the First District, and in the Second District Dr. A. P. Dostie, "the Robespierre of the revolution," had been the opponent of A. P. Field, a supporter of the constitution and a former unsuccessful claimant of a seat in the House.[103] The "official returns" indicated that Bonzano defeated Abell by a vote of 1,607 to 1,511, and that A. P. Field defeated Dostie by a vote of 1,357 to 1,023. The returns also contained the information that three other members, who had no opponents, had also been declared elected. They were: Third District, W. D. Mann, 1,908 votes; Fourth District, T. M. Wells, 465 votes; Fifth District, R. M. Taliaferro, 211 votes.[104]

The credentials were duly signed and presented to the House. All five were allowed the privileges of the Hall until their credentials, and also a protest against them from a number of Louisiana citizens, could be passed upon by the Committee on Elections.[105]

The committee, after duly considering the credentials and the remonstrances, submitted a resolution on its first report that A. P. Field and W. D. Mann were entitled to seats from the Second and Third districts respectively;[106] and later submitted a similar resolution declaring that M. F. Bonzano was also entitled to a seat from the First Congressional District.[107] The report of the majority indicated, however, that the popular vote had not been sufficient in the case of the others—Wells and Taliaferro—to warrant their being seated.

But none was, as a matter of fact, to be accorded the honor of a seat, for the entire matter was deferred until near the close of the session, and a resolution was then adopted on the eve of adjournment that the five claimants each be allowed $2,000 for compensation, expenses, and mileage for the three months that they had spent in prosecuting their claims. They were, therefore, practically refused seats, since the financial remuneration had been given, as the debates revealed, because the gentlemen had been encouraged to come to Washington, and had had honest expectations of being seated.[108] No vote, in fact, was taken on the matter of seating the three, despite the favorable committee report. But they did receive some slight encouragement, for Mr. Stevens' motion that the words "claimants for seats" be struck out met with an adverse vote. He had not, it seems, wished to recognize the idea. Thus the matter had been left undecided, and the Louisiana congressmen had, at least for the present, been rejected.

The United States senators from Louisiana were equally unsuccessful in the prosecution of their claims. The first election by the legislature, on October 10, had resulted in the election of R. King Cutler to fill the unexpired term of Slidell, and Charles Smith in the place of J. P. Benjamin, whose term would expire March 4, 1865;[109] and in the second election, held in January, 1865, Governor Hahn had defeated Charles Smith for the six-year term by a vote of ninety-two to two.[110]

The first two elections were regarded among Unionists as not only unfortunate, but downright objectionable. It seems to have been the intention of Governor Hahn, according to Dennison, that Judge Durell and Cuthbert Bullitt should be elected,[111] while other sources would indicate that General Banks and Governor Hahn were the choices that had been contemplated in this first election. But the legislators had disregarded all such plans, and taking "the bits in their teeth" had elected Cutler and Smith; and it was the money of the former, combined with the shrewdness of the latter, so it was alleged, that had "hocussed" the legislature into electing two obscure men. Hahn's election in January, to begin March 4, 1865, was calculated to correct this mistake.[112]

Smith and Cutler had, in the meantime, obtained and presented their credentials and other supporting evidence to the United

States Senate. Benjamin Wade of Ohio had at the same time presented a three point memorial of Louisiana citizens, "numerously signed," remonstrating against their admission, and against the reception of the Louisiana electoral vote, and praying, at the same time, for the passage of an act guaranteeing a republican form of government. All of these papers were now referred to the Committee on the Judiciary.[113]

But the admission of the Louisiana senators was to be contingent upon the fate of another resolution recommended by this same Committee on the Judiciary. It had looked with favor upon the reception of the senators, and had so reported, but at the same time, it had reported a joint resolution to recognize first the Louisiana government, which would of course have made possible the admission of the two senators. This resolution was as follows:

Resolved, etc., That the United States do hereby recognize the government of the State of Louisiana, inaugurated under, and by the Convention which assembled on the 6th day of April, A.D. 1864, at the city of New Orleans, as the legitimate government of the said State, and entitled to the guarantees, and all other rights of a State government under the Constitution of the United States.[114]

A similar resolution, introduced earlier by Mr. Elliott, had been referred, by a close vote, to the Select Committee on the Rebellious States.[115] The aforementioned resolution of the Committee of the Judiciary, however, was the only resolution ever considered, and was designated thenceforth as Senate Resolution Number 117.

This resolution to admit Louisiana was at once bitterly assailed. Charles Sumner made an unsuccessful effort to strike out all matter after the enacting clause, and to insert in lieu thereof an amendment to the effect that no representatives be elected from any State "until the President by proclamation" had declared the insurrection at an end; nor until the Congress had passed an enabling act, and the state had "adopted a Constitution and laws of the United States."[116] But other senators objected to the admission resolution. One senator charged that the "chief object in recognizing the State Government . . . is to allow that State to vote for the proposed amendment. . . ." The chief objections, however, as the debates revealed, were that the President's oath which had been required in Louisiana was both humiliating and unconstitutional; that an insufficient vote had been cast; that Banks had threatened the people with punishment by his declarations that "indifference will be treated as a crime"; and that he had thus by his tyrannical and military force set up a "government of the bayonet."[117] Wade indulged freely in the use of invective. He believed that Lincoln's ten per cent state government was monarchical, and that it was a miserable mockery to undertake to recognize it.[118] Sumner added that it must be Republican in form, and that it could never be, until the loyal men, white and black, recognized it. Having opened the debate, this strong proponent of negro suffrage, who had been largely instrumental in filibustering the resolution to death, was now allowed to close it. This he did with the following sensational, but fairly descriptive metaphor:

The pretended State Government of Louisiana is utterly indefensible whether you look at its origin or its character. To describe it I must use plain language. It is a mere seven months' abortion, begotten by the bayonet in criminal conjunction with the spirit of chaste and born before its time, rickety, unformed, unfinished . . . whose continued existence will be a burden, a reproach, a wrong. . . .

The result of such filibustering was obvious. The matter of state recognition was necessarily postponed by a vote of thirty-four to twelve.[119] Thus the Louisiana senators were denied seats, and the Lincoln government in Louisiana stood condemned and repudiated for strictly political purposes, by both the conservative and radical Unionists factions in Louisiana, and by Congress.

[159]

CHAPTER VIII

PRESIDENT JOHNSON'S RECONSTRUCTION POLICY IN LOUISIANA

President Johnson, who now took up the "cause of Lincoln,"[1] encountered still greater difficulties. War did not cease nominally until he issued his official proclamation on April 6, 1866.[2] But upon the cessation of actual hostilities there was a reaction against the further exercise of the great "war powers" of his predecessor. This, however, could not properly be expressed by Congress until that body assembled in December. In the meantime the President, with the aid of the returned Confederates, was making rapid progress in his plans to complete the restoration of stable civil governments in the South.

Johnson, a former slaveholder and a Jacksonian Democrat, who had always lived in the South, was perhaps better qualified in some respects than Lincoln to solve these complicated problems of reconstruction. He was, furthermore, a man of incorruptible character, always zealous for popular rights, and endowed with an "abiding interest and faith in the masses." But he had experienced a meteoric rise from obscurity, in the course of which he had been consistently opposed by the so-called aristocrats, who had been accustomed to dominate the state and national politics in the South.[3] He had also grown to manhood in the mountainous part of East Tennessee, where aristocracy did not thrive. These facts caused him to dislike, and no doubt distrust, the aristocrats, who had guided the destinies of the South under the old regime. He was, therefore, the more easily led to the conclusion—and possible delusion—that the natural leaders of the South, the aristocrats, had been chiefly instrumental in carrying the South out of the Union —a Union to which unquestionably he was sincerely devoted. For this reason he believed that those who were the actual leaders at the time of secession had been guilty of treason, and—while the real fighting was still in progress—he had said that "he that is guilty of treason deserves a traitor's fate."[4] Again, with the account of Lincoln's assassination before him, he asked, referring to the murderer: "Is he alone guilty? The American people must be

[160]

taught—if they do not already feel—that treason is a crime and must be punished; that the government will not bear always with its enemies; that it is strong not only to protect, but to punish."[5] He was said to have entertained these sentiments for the leaders, including Louisiana's two former senators, Slidell and Benjamin, for some months after his inauguration.[6] But if Johnson thought no punishment too severe for these individual wrongdoers during the war and immediately after the assassination, the responsibility of the Presidency evidently had a sobering effect, for such statements were no longer attributed to him.

The Republicans, who had believed that the accession of Johnson to the Presidency would prove a "God-send to the country,"[7] were soon to have their minds disabused; for, although he may have favored meting out stern justice to the leaders, he could add: "I also say amnesty, conciliation, clemency, and mercy to thousands of our countrymen whom you and I know have been deceived or driven into this infernal rebellion. . . . I intend to bring back peace to our distracted country."[8] And if the Stevens–Wade–Sumner group believed that he would subscribe to their theory of "conquered provinces" they were to be further disillusioned by his utterances in response to an Indiana delegation during the last days of April, 1865. He said in this interview:

Upon this idea of destroying States, my position has been heretofore well known, and I see no cause to change it now. . . . Some are satisfied with the idea that the States are to be lost in territorial and other divisions; are to lose their character as States. But their life-breath has only been suspended, and it is a high Constitutional obligation we have to secure each of these States in the possession and enjoyment of a Republican form of government. In . . . putting the government on its legs again, I think the progress of this work must pass into the hands of its friends. If a State is to be nursed until it again gets strength, it must be nursed by its friends, not smothered by its enemies.[9]

Thus Johnson proclaimed his conception of the nature of reconstruction and the needs of the hour, and that he, as President, was determined to carry into effect the fundamental principles outlined by his predecessor.[10]

On the twenty-ninth of May, 1865, in his reconstruction proclamation relating to North Carolina, President Johnson "cast the die." It was a general amnesty based on recent acts of Congress and upon his Constitutional power to grant "reprieves and pardons."[11]

To the end [declared the proclamation] that the authority of the government of the United States may be restored, and that peace, order, and freedom be established, I, Andrew Johnson, President . . . do . . . hereby grant to all persons who have . . . participated in the existing rebellion, amnesty and pardon with restoration of all rights of property except as to slaves. . . .[12]

Subsequent clauses did except fourteen classes from this general amnesty, but the classes were the same as those excluded on December 8, 1863, except those who had "voluntarily participated in said rebellion and the estimated value of whose taxable property was over $20,000."[13] The proclamation promised, furthermore, for these fourteen classes thus excluded, "that special application may be made to the President for pardon by any persons, belonging to the excepted classes, and such clemency will be liberally extended as may be consistent with the facts of the case and the peace and dignity of the United States."[14] This promise Johnson was said to have fulfilled "sincerely, fully, and wisely," especially in his relationships with Louisiana.[15]

On the same day [May 29] Johnson issued a second proclamation authorizing those states that had not already done so "to organize a State government whereby justice may be established, domestic tranquillity insured and loyal citizens protected in all their rights of life, liberty, and property." It expressly declared, in reference to the franchise, that a person to be "qualified as a voter" for "choosing delegates to frame a Constitution," or "eligible as a member of such convention," must be "a voter qualified as prescribed by the Constitution and laws of the State in force immediately before the 20th day of May, A.D. 1861, the date of the so-called Ordinance of secession." An additional clause provided that such delegates and voters "shall have previously taken and subscribed to the oath of amnesty as set forth in the President's proclamation" of that same date; and it further embodied the complete principle of local self-government by providing that "The said Convention . . . or the legislature . . . will prescribe the qualification of electors and the eligibility of persons to hold office under the Constitution and laws of the State—a power the people of the several states composing the Federal Union have rightfully exercised from the origin of the government to the present time." Finally, "all officers and persons in the military and naval service" were directed to "aid and assist the provisional governor in carrying into effect this proclamation," and were commanded "to abstain from in any way hindering, impending or discouraging the loyal people from the organization of a State government as herein authorized."[16]

Such a clear-cut and unequivocal recognition of a state, as a state within the Union subject to all the duties and entitled to all the rights and privileges of a state, seems to have heartened the citizens of Louisiana. It meant that Johnson, who had already indicated his willingness to recognize the government, had now clearly defined its status.[17] Johnson had inspired confidence by these proclamations; and the belief soon obtained in Louisiana, according to the conservative press, that he was "eminently the man for the crisis," that he was possessed with a thorough knowledge of the affairs of the South, and that he had the statesmanship and the moral courage to support his convictions.[18]

Therefore, with the capitulation of Kirby Smith on May 26,[19] and the departure of Governor Allen for Mexico,[20] the state was ready to "accept the situation," and to co-operate with Johnson in completing the reorganization of the government.[21] This spirit was manifested by many of the returned Confederates, who now availed themselves of the privilege of Johnson's amnesty proclamation. The oath of December 8, 1863, and certificate, as Governor Wells explained, were absolutely necessary before they could exercise the right to vote.[22] For this reason, and for the further purpose of reclaiming and recovering their abandoned or confiscated property, many found it to their interest to have the clerks of the State District courts administer these oaths; the early published reports indicated that many in the city and out in the state were meeting this technical requirement.[23]

[163]

Even those Confederates in the exempted classes, induced by a desire to recover their property, made application for the special Presidential pardon. It is reported that by March, 1867, the President had issued three hundred and fifty such pardons to Louisianians, who were thereby restored to the privileges of citizenship.[24] Such oaths were, in fact, almost obligatory, for in this way only could they regain possession of their former property; even then it was often required that it be purchased.[25]

The civil government in Louisiana had, however, encountered difficulties, according to the conflicting reports that reached President Johnson. In fact, this struggling and discredited government —discredited by both Congress and the Congressional faction in Louisiana—appeared to be in dire straits, if dispatches from Governor Wells and others to Johnson are to be credited. Banks, according to a telegram from Wells, had recently returned from Washington and openly proclaimed his purpose of overthrowing the government, which he had so lately defended, and it was believed that the "military would aid him." This same dispatch conveyed the further intelligence that Dostie, the auditor, was also encouraging every kind of seditious tendency and was most industrious in disseminating treasonable counsels. For these reasons Wells urgently requested the support of the Washington government. He asked "to be clothed with the military, or the military be ordered to co-operate when requested, and not to interfere."[26]

Meanwhile there were a number of others, chiefly radical in tendency, who believed that the President was one of their number, or could be converted to their way of thinking. They now conceived it to be their duty to inform and advise the President. One who designated himself a "close observer of the progress of events" was of the opinion that it was not yet time to withdraw the military, since recent events had so disorganized the parties that there was nothing like a respectable organization in support of the government. This informant advocated the retention of Banks because of his long experience. He added that Louisiana also needed a strong executive, since Wells was too weak to come up to the requirements of the occasion.[27] A former congressman who believed that Louisiana by her popular vote was decidedly opposed to secession suggested that Johnson let "bygones be bygones," but advised that it was impracticable to free the slaves and give them citizenship.[28] Another less prominent informant who approved Johnson's avowed policy of "punishing the leading traitors and forgiving deluded followers" boldly suggested in a letter to the President that "if a single seceded State is again allowed a representative in Congress without allowing the colored citizens the full right of suffrage, we shall doubtless be cast out of power, as we should well deserve. We can ill afford to ignore justice in this respect."[29] Another still more prominent Unionist volunteered the information that Wells was a power-seeking conservative who had appointed a rebel sheriff.[30]

L. Christie, a consistent Louisiana Unionist, complained to Johnson that "traitors, copperheads, infidels," and "signers of secession" were being knowingly commissioned, and were getting back into power.[31] And a communication from a Mr. L. W. Graham conveyed the intelligence that Dr. Cottman, Hugh Kennedy, and J. Madison Wells, who were said to be on their way to Washington to see President Johnson, were not to be trusted. Graham asserted that "the first had signed the ordinance of secession and was openly disloyal," the second, who was the newly appointed city Mayor, had, as editor, "stirred up disaffection," and the third, the Governor, was one of "the traitors who had taken the oath to save their slave property." "All three," he concluded, "favored slave oligarchy, and opposed the reorganization of the society of the South on the basis of freedom and equal rights."[32]

A member of the first Free State legislature of Louisiana also assumed to speak for his constituency, "the poor downtrodden people" of his recently adopted state, and to advise the President upon matters of state. "Wells," he telegraphed, "who will be on his way to Washington tomorrow to ask for the military appointment, is a pliant tool of the treasonable rebels, who may all have taken the oath of allegiance"; but who, in his humble opinion, should have served an apprenticeship for disowning "the best government that God ever established on earth before they should again have been allowed political power and influence." He feared further, that Wells, like John Tyler, was betraying the party that elected him, and that under his present course Louisiana would again have slavery revived. His humble petition to the President closed like a number of others: "If we are to have a military governor, give us one of undoubted loyalty and one who has no favors for rebel leaders."[33]

It was Banks, however, who purported to "explain the real condition of affairs" and to recommend the proper remedy. He confided to friends in Washington, who seemed to have acted as his intermediaries with Johnson, that "we now encountered the copperhead forces in an organized form," who "were put into power during my absence." "Governor Wells," Banks stated, "was classed, when nominated, with the most violent of the anti-slavery men. He belonged to the party that advocated immediate negro suffrage." He had now, to Banks's disappointment, turned out to be a thorough rebel working with General Hurlburt. "Both of these officers had begun," Banks continued, "to remove every Union man" from the Mayor on down, and were filling the vacancies "from among Rebels, secessionists, returned officers and soldiers, and the worst sort of copperheads." Banks had, as he stated, already corrected "the evil" in part by the prompt removal of the Mayor, Dr. Kennedy, and had put in his place "Colonel Quincy, a son and grandson of the Quincys of Boston." This appointee, as Banks represented, was "a man of integrity, and capacity and entirely acceptable to the people."

Banks informed Washington in another communication that "Wells and Kennedy and Dr. Cottman had practically no following in Louisiana." On the contrary, he felt confident that the people were "so loyal to his [Banks's] cause that he could carry an election triumphantly at any time"; that "if they [he and his followers] were not disturbed," they could be depended on to settle every question in Louisiana connected with reconstruction, and could do it satisfactorily to the country, without involving the administration in any trouble. In order, finally, to leave no doubt as to what he meant when he proposed to "settle every question," he stated that it also included even the question of negro suffrage, which he proposed to "settle so satisfactorily that other Rebel States will follow the example of Louisiana as if it were a pillar of cloud by day and of fire by night."[34] Thus did citizens, both prominent and obscure, of many shades of belief, seek to inform, advise, and influence the President in formulating his policies for reconstructing Louisiana.

Nor had the Conservative Unionists, who also hoped to direct the destinies of the state government, been idle. As early as April 20 Cathburt Bullitt had in a communication expressed an abiding faith in the President, and unqualifiedly pledged loyalty to him.[35] Two days later he informed Johnson that a number of leaders, including Wells, had perfected the organization of the "Andrew Johnson Club of Louisiana," and had pledged themselves "to emulate the lofty patriotism of him whose honored name we inscribe upon our banner."[36] The response, which was instantaneous, must have dismayed and disarmed the radicals in Louisiana, who had until now had every reason to expect the early capitulation of all opposition. The new policies of Johnson, announced a few days later, gave impetus to the movement, and when the Confederates, who were returning home just at this time, began to join and give their wholehearted endorsement to the Johnson policies, the momentum became so irresistible that opposition seems to have found it greatly to its interest to go underground, and to wait for a more opportune season.[37]

Johnson mass meetings became the order of the day, and the patriotic speeches delivered, the resolutions adopted endorsing his policies, and the enthusiastic throngs that were reported to have flocked to such meetings in New Orleans and out in the State, bespoke the strong sentiments of almost all of the Louisianians for him.[38] The espousal of the Johnson cause by a number of staunch and influential citizens, original Union conservatives who now became "original Johnson" men, insured its early success. One of them, J. Q. A. Fellows, defeated candidate for governor, deplored "evidences of a revengeful purpose and the exhibition of that pharisaical feeling of—stand aside, I am holier than thou."[39] Dr. Cottman, another who had recently returned from a personal interview with the President, assured his audiences that the "courteous and affable" Johnson was "the man for the crisis," and that his "thorough familiarity with the state of affairs at the South," and great "moral courage," and statesmanship, "pre-eminently fitted" him "to be President of the United States at this critical moment in its existence."[40]

The Unionist editor of the *Times* reported that he had "learned enough" in his interview with the President "to honor him as the worthy successor of a line of Presidents, whose name will live forever in the annals of the world." He expressed himself as highly elated over the facts that the President "could recognize no difference between the North and South" and that "Johnson held that the freedom of the negro did not imply his right to vote." In short, the conviction deepened with all—except the unreconciled radicals, who seem never to have had more than a handful of so-called office-seeking followers in Louisiana until the negro was enfranchised—that the President would direct the present and future policy of the Government "wisely and well."

Nor were the ex-Confederates, according to their press, less profuse in voicing their gratitude to one who, had he been the demagogue that his enemies charged him with being, might so easily have allied himself with the radicals. He had, they alleged, saved the state from the bitterness of humiliation and the degradation of "becoming a subject province"; he had saved its citizens from becoming disfranchised and "subjected to the dominion of their enfranchised bondsmen"; and he had saved the state from "confiscations more ruthless than those of Alva," and "inquisitions more merciless than the inquisition of Philip." Thus, for the reasons that he had "stood up boldly and bravely against a domineering" and vindictive party "that clamored for blood," and was "relying for support and success only on the returning reason of the Masses," *The New Orleans Crescent,* one of the organs of the ex-Confederates, declared that he was entitled "to rank among the very first statesmen," and that his name would ever be stamped "with ineffaceable glory and renown."[41]

But, becoming alarmed at the attacks against the President and the alleged calumnies against the South on the part of the radicals in the North,[42] the Johnson supporters in Louisiana decided that the time had come when Louisiana must render moral support by both word and deed. Acting accordingly, the legislature that was in session in the early part of 1866 deemed it the part of wisdom to dispatch special commissioners to Washington to assure the President of its "warm sympathy and individual support in his impending controversy with the radicals," and to make the solemn pledge that it would "sustain the President with all its power and ability."[43]

The public, it appears, became aroused at the same time over the Freedmen Bill veto controversy and demanded through the press that aid of some kind be tendered "at once."[44] It was urged that the attitude of Louisiana should be made manifest to the country "first," and by the "grandest public demonstration ever seen on this continent."[45] The Andrew Johnson Club of Louisiana also took decisive action. It met in what was reported to be a full attendance and unanimously resolved to endorse the principles enunciated by the President, and pledged itself to support his policy for the rehabilitation of the government.[46]

The efforts of Governor Wells to secure complete recognition had been successful despite radical opposition. He returned from Washington, where he had been invested with the full and unrestricted functions of both the civil and military Governor,[47] and was accorded an enthusiastic reception in token of these achievements.[48] He responded at length, clearly indicating what his future policies would be. He bade the country parishes organize civil government, and requested that the people recommend good men, who would be appointed "for the present"; he urged that this be done with expediency in order, as he said, to eliminate the "leeches," who had through the convention and legislature bankrupted the state, and who were ready for a "renewed banquet," if given a chance. He told them, furthermore, that in the fall there would be an election for governor, state officers, legislators, and Congressmen.[49] His interview with Johnson, he said, had also been highly satisfactory. He predicted that "the Radical corrupt Republican party" would be overthrown by the conservatives, but that political adventurers in the South, by the extension of suffrage to negroes, would make a tremendous effort to prevent this; he closed with the prophecy that "President Johnson's administration" would "be one of the brightest pages in our history."[50]

Wells had received the endorsement and moral support of the President, as well as the support of a large element of ex-Confederates, who no doubt found it expedient to endorse him for the time. But he was in a difficult position, and misfortunes, due partially it would seem to his own indiscretions and lack of tact, continued to beset him. His first controversy arose with Dostie, who it will be recalled, had been elected auditor. Alleging that Dostie had failed to furnish a lawful bond, and as he was also "thrusting out the thieves and money-gamblers," Wells removed him and appointed Julian Neville to fill the place until the election. An open quarrel naturally ensued; but the Governor continued his indiscretions by "forcibly ejecting" some one from office nearly every day, and, *vi et armis,* injecting some one else."[51]

Negro suffrage also contributed to the difficulties of the Governor. The "friends of universal suffrage," a small but aggressive minority, raised this issue. The Central Executive Committee, speaking for this small faction, addressed a communication to Wells, stating that the "rebellion has overthrown the Constitution and Civil Government of Louisiana." They requested that in ordering a general state election for a "new State," the Governor use his "discretionary powers" to allow all the loyal citizens, without distinction of race or origin, to register and vote provided they had resided in the state twelve months. They represented further that by so ordering they could neutralize and overpower the rebel elements, which could not be "successfully excluded from the polls." In answer to this address, to which they respectfully asked a reply in writing, Wells denied that the constitution and civil government had been overthrown. Wells also refused—as Durant and the twenty others on the Central Executive Committee had probably expected—to comply with what he termed a "dictatorial and presumptive" request to register "ignorant, incapable and inexperienced" negroes; and in

addition, he charged that his opponents were exhibiting a "versa-
tility of opinion!" He reasoned further that, from his knowledge
of negro character, nine out of ten of the late slave population
would support their former masters, personally, politically, or
in any way, in preference to all strangers; and he concluded
with his usual unqualified and definite committal to the administration:

I have full faith [he said] in the National Administration. The
President of the Republic has enunciated his policy of reconstruction;
that policy has my cordial approval and support. . . .[52]

Wells had deferred the state election until the late fall. Meanwhile, economic problems pressed for solution. The most serious
was the question of rebuilding the levees, which had so deteri-
orated from neglect during the war that the state was threatened
with the permanent abandonment of vast areas. In fact, many
places that had been farmed for forty years were reported to
have become places of desolation—"the abode of only the alli-
gator and the reptile." Tax sources had almost completely dried
up, and it was generally believed that only the general Government, with its "giant power," could save the situation.[53] For
these reasons it was urged that the destroyed levees could be
rebuilt if the proper authorities would direct the surplus colored
laborers, the vagrants, and the idlers. This large labor surplus,
it was believed, might replace the many miles of levees washed
away, and thus reclaim hundreds of these plantations and entire
parishes that were inundated.[54]

Major General Canby, who seems to have had some conception of the seriousness of conditions, proposed to Governor
Wells that they seek a loan of $400,000 from Congress—a sum
equivalent, as he stated, to that which had been spent by the
convention.[55] But this plan never materialized, and in the spring
and summer of 1866 there was a repetition of the "terrible over-
flows" that brought heartrending loss and distress, and caused
a general exodus of citizens, who went in search of new homes.[56]
To add to the disasters, there were crop failures, caused by the
army worm, worthless seed, and frosts, and by the fact that the

[171]

negro had not as yet apparently understood President Johnson when he said that "freedom is freedom to work."[57]

Governor Wells, however, appeared to be more interested in the political situation as it affected him than in the economic rehabilitation of the state. Ex-Confederates, as has been indicated, had been returning during the spring and summer, and he had been engaged in currying favor with them by appointments and by recommending many of their cases to Johnson for pardon.[58] In addition, it seems that he had determined to fortify his new position by beginning a new registration. He had discovered that out of 9,995 voters inscribed between November 14, 1862, and March 6, 1865 (that is, chiefly during Banks's period of occupancy), 4,918 had been "imperfectly registered," or, as Thomas J. Durant expressed it, "registered against law and without any evidence of qualification."[59]

The alleged fraud that was said to have been perpetrated by the "bad elements" of the Free State party of reorganization in Louisiana while professing to be "the champion of liberty," had apparently first been exposed in a "letter of confession" to Governor Wells by the registrar of voters, J. Randall Terry.[60] The fraud, which up to now had been concealed, and which was to jeopardize the recognition of the Free State government by Congress, consisted in "imperfectly" registering, so it was charged, some five thousand, four thousand of whom had never been naturalized. Most of these voters had of course been registered in the city; and since only 5,451 votes had been cast in the city, this exposure meant that in substance the constitution had been illegally ratified, and that the first Free State legislature had been illegally elected. Hundreds of the names so registered were shown to have been in immediate succession, to have had nothing but the sign manual or cross to attest them, and the names themselves were said to have been in the same handwriting.[61]

Wells now felt, according to his statement, that it was his duty to publish all these facts, although he realized that he would be "denounced as a traitor" to the party that had elected him, and it might also mean that the "whole State government" would be cast overboard. But his "moral honesty," as his press

[172]

friends now put it, was such that he could not "connive at the frauds" that had been "perpetrated" by the "unscrupulous leaders."

And thus being motivated by his alleged ideal of restoring "the purity of the ballot-box as the only safeguard of popular rights," Wells now issued his official proclamation that "in order to prevent polling of illegal votes in the future" a new registration would be held "from and after the first of June,"[62] which meant that not only approximately five thousand voters must be rejected,[63] but that he was condemning the 1864 constitution, the legislature, and in fact, the entire state government. But such arguments now had little weight with the Governor, for, as will presently be shown, he had planned to elect new state officers and a new legislature; and a new state constitution was in the offing. Besides, he had aided in so shaping political events that he would be the only logical choice to direct the contemplated reforms.

There was need of a more stable state government, chiefly because the material interests of Louisiana at home demanded it. More than she required a congressional delegation, Louisiana needed money in the treasury in order to rebuild the levees and to provide aid for the charitable and educational institutions that had been sadly neglected. But more than all this there was a crying and growing need that ways and means be devised to reform the labor system.[64] The legislature, it was urged, should meet and apply some practical solution. But it was felt at the same time, that the entire state should now be represented, and that the "humbug" representatives, who had pretended to represent parishes beyond the lines and who really held no legal title, should be displaced. Besides, the general belief in the state that the acts of the convention and the recent legislature were not binding, because of the questionable title to seats that many of the so-called delegates and "representatives" and "senators" held, made the election of a new legislature imperative.[65]

In obedience to these general sentiments, which were expressed in public meetings throughout the state,[66] the Governor issued his proclamation on the twenty-first day of September, announcing that an election would be held in the forty-eight

[173]

parishes for the purpose of electing a governor, lieutenant governor, secretary of state, auditor of public accounts, treasurer, attorney general, superintendent of public education, senators to the lower house of the legislature, and Congressmen in the five congressional districts. It specified that all male whites twenty-one years of age who had resided in the state for twelve months prior to November 6, the day designated for the election, and had subscribed to the Lincoln and Johnson oaths of amnesty of December 8, 1863, and May 29, 1865, respectively, were qualified to vote. He could not, as he explained, include the fourteen exempted classes, except such as secured Johnson's special pardon. The election in all other respects was to be conducted in accordance with the law.[67]

Three parties, the National Democrats, the National Union Conservative party, and the National Republican, participated in this election.[68] The first-named party was urged by J. Ad. Rozier, the president of the State Executive Committee, to organize Democratic clubs, and to send delegates to a state convention. His suggested platform opposed the "territorial State of purgatory," opposed negro suffrage, which was being advocated by a "few beknighted fanatics," the "emissaries of the disturbing and fanatical elements of the North," and opposed "unconstitutional confiscations" and "unconstitutional test oaths." This platform had already been delivered to the public in a lengthy address on August 20.[69]

In response to this and subsequent calls, the Democratic State Convention, which was composed of delegates from all but a few parishes, met on October 2 for a two-day session.[70] Except for a faint indication of a disturbing element on the first day, "all was harmonious and the business was transacted in a decorous manner." Former Governor Wickliffe presided, and "representative men of high position and integrity" were nominated.[71] The resolutions that constituted the platform accepted the decision on the questions involved in the late struggle, gave "unqualified adhesion to the National Democracy," opposed radicalism and the radical Republican party and held that the negro "cannot be considered as a citizen, but this is a government exclusively of white people." It further recognized the existing state government as a *"de facto* government," despite the fact that the Constitution of 1864 was the creation of fraud, violence, and corruption. It also banned all religious controversies, recommended the calling of a state constitutional convention, asked "for compensation for all losses sustained by the emancipation policy," and "favored a return to the economical administration of the finances."[72]

The nominees, except the one for Governor, were largely ex-Confederates. The names of former Governor Robert C. Wickcliffe, who presided; former Governor Henry W. Allen, who was a fugitive in Mexico City; and Judge Voorhies, a former District and Supreme Court judge of distinct ability, had been prominently mentioned in the press for governor. The sentiment was strong for Voorhies in New Orleans, and stronger for the fugitive war-governor in the "Red River country," and there seems to be little doubt but that the delegates would have personally preferred either of these to Governor James Madison Wells.[73] But Wells, from a standpoint of practical politics and as a matter of expediency, was the logical choice. He was a native of Louisiana, a war Unionist, and last but by no means least, he had the unqualified support of the National administration. For these reasons the convention used discretion in tendering him the unanimous nomination. As was to be expected, he accepted with a written communication, in which he unqualifiedly agreed to run "on the platform of this respectable, intelligent and patriotic body of citizens." "My sole ambition in accepting office," he assured the delegates, "is to serve my native State, to strengthen his [Johnson's] hands in upholding the Constitution," and to prove "worthy of his wise, liberal, and conciliatory policy in our behalf."[74]

The National Conservative Union party began its organization in August, 1865, by subscribing to the Constitution of 1864 and appealing chiefly to that class of Conservatives who had never been Confederates.[75] The salient points of their platform, which was first published in the August "address," and was subsequently republished with slight modifications after the convention, pledged the party (1) to support the Union, and the administrations and policies of President Johnson and Governor Wells; (2) to maintain the *status quo* of suffrage, that is, to oppose its extension to the negro; (3) to claim all the rights and privileges of the State of Louisiana as before the war, with the exception of slavery; (4) to ban all religious questions and controversies from politics; (5) to oppose all secret political organizations; (6) to support full and complete amnesty. They did not ask for compensation; nor did they condemn secession, or repudiate the Confederate debt, although their platform did repudiate the debt of the Convention of 1864 and that of the legislature of that same year.[76]

This party, which was composed largely of those elements that had originally opposed secession, but which now differed from the Democrats only as to methods of attaining complete restoration, met shortly after the Democrats had adjourned. Twenty-two parishes were represented, although the status of some of the delegates was questionable, since they had participated in the recent Democratic Convention. Judge Taliaferro appears to have had considerable support for nomination for the governorship. But after much discussion, and some dissension, Wells was tendered the nomination, although the remainder of the ticket differed from that selected by the Democrats.[77]

Wells, who could see "no material difference between the two parties," answered that: "Both platforms are in unison with the principles, liberal measures, and harmonizing policy of the National Executive, whose lofty patriotism and efforts to uphold the Constitution are fully endorsed." Reasoning thus, he concluded: "I am, therefore, consistent to accept both."[78]

These two parties now began a spirited canvass;[79] and although they had decided as a matter of expediency, to fuse their tickets for the governorship an unexpected candidate was entered in the lists. A considerable minority had from the first advocated former Governor Allen's candidacy, and this group, said to be composed of many of Louisiana's "first citizens," now printed a document known as "The Allen Circular," and distributed it widely in the Red River and North Louisiana parishes.

It declared in substance that Allen was eligible to serve and gave strong reasons for his election.[80]

The absent ex-Governor was of course not cognizant of such a movement, and according to his biographer would doubtless have discouraged such a procedure.[81] A number of his close friends, who thought it extremely inexpedient, and who had possibly already committed themselves to Wells because he was known to be in the good graces of the President, did attempt to discourage this movement. They issued an address to the voters protesting "against unauthorized use of his name," alleging that he was absent and that Louisiana needed action *now*. They stated further that Allen was "liable to arrest and prosecution as the highest civil officer of Louisiana under Confederate authority," and that "his election would retard readmission and prolong military rule."[82]

Notwithstanding, big public meetings continued to be held in Allen's behalf, especially by the younger men, who organized a number of "Young Men's Allen Associations."[83] And having espoused the Allen cause, these "boys," as they were called, continued their demonstrations to stimulate enthusiasm. They answered their critics with the rejoinder that Wells had always been an "old line Whig" and a supporter of Banks, and pointed out that Allen had always been a Democrat. In addition, they advanced the plausible argument that in the event Allen should be elected, and could not return or qualify, the place could easily be filled by either of the candidates for Lieutenant Governor, Judge Albert Voorhies, or J. G. Taliaferro, both of whom, they claimed, were "capable, upright, and honest."[84]

These irreconcilables, therefore, remained faithful to the end, and cast for Allen a highly respectable vote; and, but for the determined efforts on the part of his friends to quash the movement, there is a strong supposition that Allen would have been elected and would possibly have returned and become reconciled to the new state of things as did Governor Humphries in Mississippi.[85]

The short campaign of rallies and speeches between the Democrats—chiefly returned Confederates—and the Conserva-

[177]

tives resulted in the usual charges and countercharges. The Democrats, who were in the majority, charged that their opponents, who had "not only stolen our thunder but our thunder bearer," were only "sowing dissention and seeking the division of the State under the false name of conservative when they are so manifestly Republican." The Democrats also paid their respects in no uncertain terms to the "Black Republican Party" and to the Radicals. This so-called "small party" of Republicans was referred to during the canvass as "those of that dark meeting held in the Custom House."[86] In fact, the parties vied with each other in denouncing the scheme of the Radicals to force the vote upon the negro, and to give him equality; and it was indeed a conservative, in a conservative meeting, who was given tremendous applause when he said: "God forbid the black man should be the equal of the white man. . . ."[87]

With such a common unity of purpose in all essentials, it is somewhat surprising that these two Louisiana groups did not reconcile their differences as to details and methods of procedure, especially in the face of what they termed the "radical menace." There seems, however, to have been few as yet in Louisiana who believed that the Radicals had any possibility of carrying out their avowed purpose. Both factions seem indeed to have still had implicit confidence in Johnson's ability to vanquish radicalism.

The last "grand Democrat mass meeting," to which there was reported to have been a "tremendous turnout of the whole city," was indicative of the outcome.[88] As the Democrats had repeatedly predicted, the voting resulted in a virtual "landslide" for the ex-Confederates in "the most orderly election ever held in New Orleans." The result was an overwhelming majority for "the Johnson policy as represented by Wells," and "for the entire Democratic State ticket, and Democratic legislature."[89] The official returns from the forty-eight parishes gave Wells 22,312 votes; the absent Allen, who was not cognizant of the fact that he was running, received 5,497. Map No. 9 shows that he received a substantial vote in the city, and in the Red River district, where, despite the efforts of his friends to prevent it, he carried a few parishes.

[178]

MAP No. 9

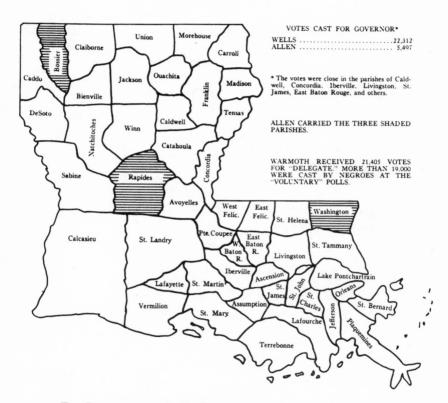

VOTES CAST FOR GOVERNOR*

WELLS 22,312
ALLEN 5,407

* The votes were close in the parishes of Cald-
well, Concordia, Iberville, Livingston, St.
James, East Baton Rouge, and others.

ALLEN CARRIED THE THREE SHADED
PARISHES.

WARMOTH RECEIVED 21,405 VOTES
FOR "DELEGATE." MORE THAN 19,000
WERE CAST BY NEGROES AT THE
"VOLUNTARY" POLLS.

THE RESTORATION OF STATE GOVERNMENT IN LOUISIANA UNDER
PRESIDENT JOHNSON'S ADMINISTRATION

The other candidates on the Democratic ticket defeated their Conservative Union friends by still greater majorities as follows: Lieutenant Governor, Albert Voorhies of St. Martin, 23,364; J. G. Taliaferro of Catahoula, 5,302; Secretary of State, J. H. Hardy of St. Landry, 20,869; T. J. Edwards of Avoyelles, 4,181; Auditor of Public Accounts, E. H. Peralta of East Baton Rouge, 22,339; Attorney General, A. S. Herron of East Baton Rouge, 22,966; George S. Lacey of Orleans, 4,384; Superintendent of Public Education, R. M. Lusher of Orleans, 22,006; R. C. Richardson of Livingston, 3,663.[90]

But the few white radicals, who constituted the national Republican party, and who were chiefly ex-officers and soldiers of the Union army and Northern citizens who had settled in Louisiana, did not propose to let this election go entirely by default. A number of these who had established themselves as lawyers and plantation owners or managers during the regime of Butler and Banks were, under this new order of things, faced with the alternative of giving up much of their gains from confiscations and other sources, and returning North, or of organizing and fighting for their "rights" to remain in the state.[91] They chose the latter course. As Henry Clay Warmoth, one of their leaders, so aptly put it: "We young men proposed to fight, and we accepted any and all legitimate allies."[92] But such a momentous decision could not, it seems, have been made without a promise of aid from the Radicals.[93]

Having made their decision shortly after Warmoth had returned from an "extended visit to Washington and the North" whence he had been "on important legal business,"[94] they met in a small room over the Carrollton Railway Depot on July 11, 1865, and launched the "National Republican Association." Warmoth, who became the first president of this revolutionary organization, as its platform reveals, presided at this initial meeting, and Banks, who still lingered in Louisiana, practicing law, and A. P. Dostie, a radical, were among those present and participating.

The platform that was adopted did not endorse the policy of President Johnson—it was openly hostile to the government that he had reorganized in Louisiana. It contained resolutions

[179]

that "the power of Government should be derived from the consent of the governed"; that "we stand pledged to the adoption of a system of universal education"; that "we stand pledged to support universal suffrage as the only true basis of a representative form of government, where all are equal . . ."; that "we will advocate the enactment of such laws as will dignify labor"; and that "we further advocate the distribution of the lands owned by the State into free homesteads to heads of families. . . ." In addition, it not only endorsed a proposition calling "for the removal of Governor Wells," but

resolved that the Civil Government of Louisiana, as administered by his Excellency, Acting Governor J. M. Wells, is subversive and destructive of the rights, and liberties of the loyal people of this State, and that we protest against the Government, and call upon the President of the United States to appoint a provisional Governor and organize the State upon the basis of universal freedom and suffrage.[95]

Thus it will be observed that this small group of radicals, who advocated negro suffrage, subscribed to the views of the more radical Congressmen, in condemning the existing state government that Johnson had recognized.

The next move of the National Republican party, however, was one that most probably astonished their Democratic and conservative opponents. They declared that the state had reverted to the status of a territory by virtue of secession, and proceeding on this assumption, they now proposed to elect a delegate to represent it in Congress. They therefore called a convention which "submitted to the people the name of H. C. Warmoth," adopted an official platform, the essential features of which have been given, and designated the sixth of November as their official election day.[96]

This movement was either ignored or regarded with contempt by the Democratic and conservative press. But to its dismay and the dismay of most whites, the negroes were registered by the officials of the bureau under "Article One, Section Five, of the Constitution of the United States," and under the auspices and encouragement of this bureau they actually voted in this election.[97] The ballots, on which they were instructed to write the name of Henry Clay Warmoth, were tendered to the "Commissioners in charge of the bureau," and deposited in special boxes.

Nor were the negroes "indifferent to their rights," for Warmoth was reported to have run far ahead of Wells in New Orleans.[98] In fact this total vote was reported on November 10 to be 16,512. This vote was compiled from the returns of the parishes of Orleans, Jefferson, St. John, St. Charles, Ascension, Pointe Coupee, St. Tammany, and Terrebonne.[99] But it was evidently incomplete, for some disorder, which happened despite Governor Wells's proclamation not to interfere with the negroes unless they tried to vote at the legal polls,[100] prevented complete returns at this time.[101]

Warmoth's credentials, however, which were verified by James Graham of New Orleans, a Notary Public, and by the oaths of Oscar Dunn and J. L. Montieu, negroes, gave him 19,105 votes at the voluntary polls, that is, at the negro polls. But he was reported to have received some white votes in addition at both the "Wells" and "voluntary" polls, making a grand total of 21,405, an analysis of which is given as follows in his official organ, the *Tribune:* White votes at Wells's polls, 2,300; white votes at voluntary polls, 2,500; colored free-born soldiers at voluntary polls, 1,000; other free-born at voluntary polls, 5,000; colored free soldiers at voluntary polls, 2,000; other colored freedmen at voluntary polls, 8,605.[102]

A mass meeting which was called by the Republican party at the Orleans Theatre on November 13 for the purpose of ratifying Warmoth's election with proper resolutions, reveals the progress of this revolutionary group. B. F. Flanders, the president, opened with an "incendiary speech," in which, according to the opposition press, he denounced the "rebels" for "denying their offices to Union men," and in which he counselled the negroes present to demand "equality before the law." Rufus Waples followed with a tribute to Warmoth, who, he said, would represent Louisiana, not as a state, for "the State had ceased to be," but "Louisiana as a territory." He believed that the work

[181]

of adopting a form of state government and petitioning Congress for admission belonged "to the people of the territory, to the whole people, and to them only"; but added that the temper of the "unrepentant traitors" was such that it would be "inexpedient to attempt the making of a new State by white voters."

After lengthy resolutions had been adopted, denouncing the "rebels," the "State government," the "proclamations of President Johnson," and, in fact almost every prominent person connected with the Confederacy, the delegate-elect, Judge Warmoth, arose and thanked his negro constituents for the confidence reposed in him. Among other things, he said that he wished to correct an impression that had gotten abroad that the "Yankee" did not understand the negro. He assured them that the Yankee did understand the negro; that, in fact, he knew everything—"all about this war and how it will end." Warmoth stated further that the Yankees were "inventing new machines every day"; and that when he went North, it was his intention to try to get one of them to invent a machine that would pump out the "black blood" of his listeners, and pump in "white blood." Finally, he urged that they send their delegates, both "white and black," to Washington; he concluded as follows:

Fellow-citizens, I thank you for your attention, and I feel happy to-night because I am going home; that is, I am going where I used to call home before I came down here—going to see my friends, and tell them in a plain, common sense way all about you, what kind of people you are, how clever to me; and I know that statement will go right straight to their hearts. I will tell them of your loyalty, and enthusiasm for the Government; that you are the only people who love the Republic, and sing the songs of the Union and wave the flag; that the rebels hate the flag, and do not love the Republic, and sing only one song, and that is Dixie. When I shall have come back I hope I shall be able to say that I did my duty, and succeeded in the great enterprise which we all have at heart.[103]

Such proceedings naturally tended—they may have been so calculated—to arouse bitter resentment on the part of the native Louisianians, especially the returned Confederates. The press, with the exception of *The Tribune,* the organ of the negroes and of these Republican radicals, generally reflected the indignation. "The negro people, black and white," as one editor expressed the feelings, "held a meeting last night. Some of the speakers will be taken in hand by the Grand Jury. As a matter of course, we do not report the proceedings; no decent paper would."[104] But the *Times* did report the proceedings and condemned them as "treason against the people and the laws." It charged further that "the pretended election of Mr. Warmoth" was "a ridiculous farce," and that such "incendiary addresses delivered at such meetings" were "certain to have the most mischievous effect"; and it concluded this denunciation of those who were now openly seeking "to undermine the political and social order," with words that were apparently the sentiments of an exasperated populace:

> The highest judicial power of the Government has pronounced upon the negro status . . . and the highest executive power of the Government has recognized all the States as in the Union. . . . Therefore, it is treason against our entire population, as well as against the law, to attempt to deceive the negro by a solemn electoral farce, to sow the seeds of increased bitterness between the two races in the South, and to oppose the Government in its holy work of reestablishing harmony to a long distracted land.[105]

But the young so-called "adventurer" was not dismayed, for, armed with his credentials and other supporting evidence, which he states "were signed by the Secretary of State, with the seal of the State attached," he repaired to Washington. Here, as a delegate representing the "territory" of Louisiana, he expected to "represent the views of the Union men of Louisiana."[106]

Warmoth seems in fact to have been well received, and was "accorded a seat on the floor of the House" while his certificate of election was being examined and considered by the Joint Committee on Reconstruction.[107] He spent several months in Washington on this mission, and although he was not officially received, he seems to have heartily enjoyed the predicament of his opponents, the Senators and Representatives elected by the Johnson–Wells State government, who "had to be contented," as he states, "with seats in the Gallaries" during the entire time that they remained in Washington.[108]

[183]

It is interesting to note that Warmoth was probably engaged in other activities while in Washington. The evidence tends to prove that he had entered into a working agreement with the radicals. His letter to Senator Williams, Chairman of the sub-Committee on Reconstruction of Louisiana, indicates such an alliance. He stated in this letter, in alluding to a recent October ordinance of the town of Opelousas—passed, so it was alleged, because the swarms of negroes had become a public menace—that: "If any man thinks slavery is dead in Louisiana, I advise him to go there and see for himself."

Such statements were given wide publicity in the North, and were interpreted by the Louisianians, and by Southerners, to mean, according to press reports, that Warmoth was "deliberately disregarding all honor and truth in his efforts to create prejudice against the South in the North." And, in fact, Warmoth had failed, it seems, to supplement his statement with the explanation that such regulations had been approved by the highest Federal military authority in Louisiana before they had been issued, and that the regulations had been passed more to frighten the blacks than to be used. He had also failed to explain to his Northern audiences that these rules and regulations had been adopted as "temporary" expedients. And these statements and omissions created the impression, if reports be true, that he was "trying to palm such regulations off on the country as productions of a rebel town and as a law still in force one year after the emergency had passed," so that by such "low artifices and dodges" he might "prevent the South from attaining its rights." That such "contemptible meanness," as the *True Delta* expressed it, had been inspired by his being in league with the radicals, seems to have been generally accepted in Louisiana.[109]

CHAPTER IX

THE LEGISLATURE COMPLETES RESTORATION

Meanwhile there had been considerable agitation to call the recently elected legislature into extraordinary session. The labor problem and the problem of regulating the conduct of the negroes of all classes were becoming more and more matters of urgent importance. The conduct of the negro troops, especially in their careless and reckless use of firearms in the parishes of the state and in the city, was daily becoming a matter of grave complaint.[1] An impression had also got abroad that the negro was to be the special object of the nation's care, and as such he was to receive a portion of the lands and all the necessary equipment for farming.[2] And despite the efforts of Conway, the Assistant Commissioner of Freedmen, to disabuse the minds of the blacks, the idea still persisted. His lengthy circular to his subordinates and to the negroes had contained one sentence that should have corrected this evil. It read: "Instructions will, therefore, be given to all officers, and agents of this Bureau to compell those of you who do not do so, to work, and fulfill your obligations, unless you have been unfairly dealt with by your employer."[3]

But this advice to go to work had gone unheeded. The negroes had continued to collect in the towns, and since there was no longer any master to feed and clothe them and give them proper medical attention, their condition became extremely pitiable. With the first cold snap death began to reap a harvest among them.[4] In these destitute circumstances, and with their minds thus unsettled over the false hopes of divisions of confiscated lands, it is not surprising, as the press reveals, that they began "to pillage, to steal, to drink, to gamble, to fight, to carouse, to quarrel, to prowl in squads, and to live in filth, idleness, debauchery, and lastly to die."[5]

To make bad matters worse, disgruntled and embittered freedmen were daily coming in contact with the negro troops, who were reported to have little discipline, and whose influence began to

[185]

cause great apprehension of an insurrection in those parts of the state outside the city where the blacks outnumbered the whites. Moreover the white population was "almost wholly unarmed," whereas the negro population was said to have been "generally provided with the best revolvers" and other arms, and to have gone constantly armed. Besides, the chief of the bureau and his subordinates, exponents of and participants in the "Universal Suffrage" party, were inculcating in the negroes' childlike minds a feeling of distrust and dislike toward their former masters. The spirit of hostility grew to such proportions that all signs pointed to a "contemplated insurrection" among the negroes.[6] Therefore, in order to relieve this general uneasiness and apprehension on the part of the whites, who would otherwise have been forced to congregate in the villages as a proper measure of security, and in order to serve the agricultural interests, which were being seriously imperiled by the abandonment of the fields, it was deemed highly expedient that the legislature meet in special session to organize speedily an efficient state militia to cope with the negro unrest, and to enact other needful laws and police regulations.[7]

Because of this "extraordinary emergency" the Governor, in deference to what was apparently a widespread and urgent demand, issued his proclamation convening the legislature in extraordinary session.[8] This body, which met on November 23, was the first in four years to represent the whole state, and was probably one of the most intelligent legislative bodies ever assembled in Louisiana.[9] The upper house had approximately fifty per cent new members, whereas the lower body was composed of an entirely new membership. The Constitution of 1864 had provided for overlapping terms for the state senators, and for a new delegation in the lower house every two years fresh from the people.[10] The Democrats, representatives of the returned Confederates, were practically unanimous in this lower house, and controlled the upper. The roster of the House included such distinguished citizens as John B. McEnery, Duncan S. Cage (speaker), J. B. Eustis, B. F. Jonas, W. E. Eagan, C. E. Fenner, and a number of others, who were now designated by their opponents as "rebels, who had participated in the rebellion."[11]

[186]

THE LEGISLATURE COMPLETES RESTORATION

Governor Wells's message was full of practical suggestions. The more important of these included: the election of two United States Senators, the restoration of the levees, and an issue of treasury warrants to the extent of $1,000,000. To the redemption of these warrants he would pledge six thousand bales of cotton, purchased by Governor Allen, and, as additional security, all swamp lands of the state. The Governor thought that the legislature should merely provide for the enforcement of labor contracts, and leave the terms of the contracts themselves to be adjusted by the persons concerned. "But under no circumstances," he advised, "should corporal punishment be administered in enforcing them."[12]

Other objects that, in the Governor's opinion, demanded attention were the suppression and extirpation of all secret organizations having dangerous political objects, the exclusive application to the education of colored persons of the taxes collected from them, the support of the neglected charitable institutions, and the building of the penitentiary and State House. The State Militia should also be organized and held in readiness, he urged, because the reorganization of the state would be followed by the withdrawal of the Federal troops. And, finally, the message closed with a eulogy of President Johnson, and an invocation to the people to stand by and sustain him in his policy.[13]

This "Black Code Legislature," as it has been designated, was in session less than one month,[14] and seems to have proceeded with extreme caution because of the unfriendly attitude of Congress.[15] This is evidenced by the history of two proposed measures. The first, which was passed during the opening days, provided that all agricultural laborers should be compelled to enter into annual contracts during the first ten days of January. It provided further that

wages due shall be a lien on the crop, one-half to be paid at the time agreed upon by the parties, the other half to be retained until the completion of the contract; but in case of sickness of the laborer, wages for the time shall be deducted, and where the sickness is supposed to be feigned for the purpose of idleness, double the amount shall be deducted; and should the refusal to work extend beyond three days, the negro shall be forced to labor on roads, levees, and public works without pay.

[187]

The laborer would have been required also to pay for "injuries done to animals or agricultural implements committed to his care, or for bad or negligent work," which would have been deducted from his wages. It carried other penal features which specified that "For act of disobedience a fine of one dollar shall be imposed upon the laborer," and "impudence, swearing or using indecent language in the presence of the employer, his family, or his agent, or quarreling or fighting among one another" would be considered as acts of disobedience.[16]

The other proposed bill, which apparently furnished Congress with material for its reconstruction program, provided that "every adult freedman or woman *shall furnish themselves with a comfortable home and visible means of support within twenty days after the passage of this Act.*" It also carried the stringent penal clauses that

any freedman or woman failing to obtain a home and support as thus provided shall be immediately arrested by any parish, or by the police officer in any city or town in said parish where said freedman may be, and by them delivered to the Recorder of the parish, and by him hired out, by public advertisement, to some citizen, being the highest bidder for the remainder of the year.

For leaving without the consent of the employer the laborer could be arrested and assigned to labor on some public works without compensation until his employer reclaimed him; absence without leave was to be deducted from his time at the rate of two dollars per day, or else worked out at the same rate.[17] Finally, another proviso would have denied him the privilege of keeping any livestock.

A close examination of the *"Acts of The General Assembly"* discloses that neither bill became a law. The first, however, usually designated as the "agricultural labor bill," did pass both houses, but there is no record of its subsequent history.[18] It may have been intentionally suppressed as a precautionary measure after the attacks upon it by Blaine and Wilson. The second bill does not appear ever to have been reported out of committee, possibly for the same reason.[19]

But another set of laws, designated as the "Black-Code," did

[188]

become the law of Louisiana, and although not so stringent as the proposed laws, they were severe enough to invoke the hostility of the radicals in Louisiana, and that of Congress and the North in general.[20] These were the vagrant laws, which were evidently modeled after those of Massachusetts and other Northern, as well as Southern, states. The one that probably incurred the most criticism amended and re-enacted the 121st section of an act entitled "An Act Relative to Crimes and Offenses," which had been approved March 14, 1855. Vagrants, according to this 1855 act, were

All idle persons, who not having visible means to maintain themselves, live without employment; all persons wandering abroad and lodging in groceries, taverns, beer-houses, market-places, sheds, barns, uninhabited buildings, or in the open air and not giving a good account of themselves; all persons wandering abroad, and begging, or who go from door to door, or place themselves in the streets, highways, passages, or other public places, or beg or receive alms; habitual drunkards who shall abandon, neglect or refuse to aid in the support of their families, and who may be complained of by their families. . . .[21]

The act provided further:

That upon complaint made on oath before a justice of the peace, mayor, or judge of the district court, or other proper officer, that any person is a vagrant within the description aforesaid, it shall be the duty of such justice, judge, mayor, or other officer, to issue his warrant to any sheriff, constable, policeman, or other peace officer, commanding him to arrest the party accused and bring him before such justice of the peace or other officer; and if the justice or other officer be satisfied by the confession of the offender, or by competent testimony, that he is a vagrant within the said description, he shall make a certificate of the same, which shall be filed with the clerk of the court of the parish, and in the city of New Orleans the certificate shall be filed in the office of one of the recorders; and the said justice or other officer shall require the party accused to enter into bond, payable to the Governor of Louisiana, or his successors in office, in such sums as said justice or other officer shall prescribe, with security to be approved by said officer, for his good behavior and future industry, for the period of one year; and upon his failing or refusing to give such bond and security, the justice or other officer shall issue his warrant to the sheriff or other officer, directing him to detain and to hire out such vagrant for a period not exceeding twelve months, or to cause him to labor on the public works, roads and levees, under such regulations as shall be made by the municipal authorities;

Provided, That if the accused be a person who has abandoned his employer, before his contract expired, the preference shall be given to such employer of hiring the accused; and provided further, that in the city of New Orleans the accused may be committed to the workhouse for a time not exceeding six months, there to be kept at hard labor, or to be made to labor upon the public works, roads or levees. The proceeds of hire in the cases herein provided for, to be paid into the parish treasury for the benefit of paupers; and provided further that the person hiring such vagrants shall be compelled to furnish such clothing, food and medical attention as they furnish their other laborers.[22]

Other acts were passed that have been classified as special features of this "Black Code." The carrying of firearms on the premises or plantations of any citizen without the consent of the owner was prohibited under penalty of the offender being "fined a sum not less than $1.00 nor more than $10.00, or imprisonment not less than one day nor more than ten days."[23] Trespassing was made a misdemeanor and carried a penalty of a fine "not exceeding $100.00 or imprisonment for a term not exceeding one month."[24] Act No. 16 provided for the punishment of persons tampering with, persuading, or enticing away, harboring, feeding, or secreting laborers, servants, or apprentices. Such offender was liable not only for damages but "subjected to pay a fine of not more than $500 nor less than $10.00, or imprisonment in the parish jail for not more than twelve months, nor less than ten days."[25] Act No. 19 was doubtless passed to take care of the orphans or children of the indigent. All such persons under eighteen, if females, and under twenty-one if males, were to be apprenticed as prescribed by the Civil Code, provided that orphans could "select said employers when they had arrived at the age of puberty," and such contracts became valid and binding.[26]

Neither were the employers of the laborers and apprentices immune from punishment, for Act No. 20 made them guilty of a misdemeanor if they hired any person already under contract, so as to deprive the first employer of such services. The offending employer was himself subjected to "a fine of not less than ten nor more than five hundred dollars," or "imprisonment" for a period "not exceeding thirty days." This act carried the same punishment if he refused to give such laborer or apprentice a written certificate of discharge upon the expiration of a term of service.[27]

It will be observed that although these laws were designed primarily to meet the immediate need of controlling the negro, they were in theory at least, equally applicable to the white race in that there was no discrimination because of "race, color, or previous condition of servitude." It will further be observed that, with the possible exception of Act No. 12, these vagrant laws hardly deserved the appellation of "Black Code." This statement, it appears, can be substantiated when a close comparison is made with similar laws enacted at the time in other Southern states. In Alabama two laws were passed at this time which made a distinction between the races. One "made it a misdemeanor, with a penalty of $100.00 fine and a ten days imprisonment, to purchase or receive from a free person of color any stolen goods, knowing the same to have been stolen"; and the other declared that the "freedmen" were "competent to testify only in open court, and in cases in which freedmen were concerned directly or indirectly."[28]

The Mississippi statutes were more severe than those of Alabama. One of these Mississippi acts which regulated the relations of master and apprentice as it "related to freedmen, free negroes, and mulattoes" declared that all of these classes "who were orphans, or were without means of support" must be bound out until they became of age, and "their former masters" were to be "given preference." This law also differed greatly from the Louisiana law in that the Mississippi master was empowered to "inflict moderate chastisement for misbehavior." Intermarriage between whites and negroes was also punishable by life imprisonment. Nor did the Mississippi code allow the negro to "rent or lease land except in incorporated towns and cities"; and it was also expressly provided that

all freedmen, free negroes, and mulattoes in the State over the age of 18 years, found on the second Monday of January, 1866, or thereafter, with no lawful employment or business, or found unlawfully assembling

[191]

themselves together either in the day or night time, together with all white persons so assembling with them on terms of equality, or living in adultery or fornication with negro women, should be deemed vagrants.[29]

In comparison with these codes the Louisiana statutes appeared to be moderate. In fact, the Louisiana code, as has been pointed out, was almost identical with those of a number of Northern states, notably those of Wisconsin, Massachusetts, Illinois, Rhode Island, and Connecticut, where the penal features were equally as severe.[30] Moreover, the demoralization of the negroes and the impression fostered among them by the agents of the Bureau that they would be maintained in their idleness, made some such regulation mandatory. The childlike negroes had misinterpreted liberty to mean license. They had consequently congregated in the more populous centers, awaiting that time when they could hold high carnival over the division of their masters' land; but meanwhile, they were forced to live by their wits or perish.[31]

One other act of this so-called "Black Code" legislature was generally overlooked during the days that followed. It was a joint resolution passed during the first days of the session which gave expression of the sentiment of that body in regard to "the situation." It declared "that there was no spirit of resistance to Federal authority," and "that the people of Louisiana are unreserved in their purpose of loyalty, and if permitted, that to the Constitution."[32]

As further evidence of its anxiety to restore Louisiana as speedily as possible to fellowship in the Union, the legislature elected Randell Hunt and Henry Boyce as United States Senators, and instructed them to repair to Washington to join the recently elected Congressional delegation that was already seeking admission.[33] It was felt that the highest interests of the state required their presence. Furthermore, their admission would mean, so they reasoned, that a complete restoration of the state had been effected. Besides, these Johnson supporters seem to have felt that the President would need the Louisiana votes to counteract the growing radical element which was obviously bent on passing a universal suffrage amendment.[34] All, however, as will presently be shown, were eventually rejected for the apparent reason that senators and congressmen from Louisiana did not as yet fit into the radical scheme of Congress.[35]

The Louisianians, and this legislature in particular, made no secret of the fact that they contemplated legislating the Freedmen's Bureau out of the state if possible.[36] But before treating this phase it becomes necessary to give a brief résumé of its origin in Louisiana. It will be recalled that Butler and Banks had attempted to make some satisfactory disposition of the blacks who swarmed about their camps. Butler had recruited his army from their numbers, aided their needy, organized some colonies of fugitives, and had made some effort to regulate their employment through his "sequestration commission."[37] Banks, who found "suffering, disease, and death everywhere" among the negroes, it will be recalled, had issued his general orders of January 30, 1863, and February 3, 1864, making the labor compulsory, and making special provisions for contracts. At the same time he had established a "Bureau of Free Labor" under the supervision of T. W. Conway, which attempted to provide schools, establish a free labor bank, fix the hours and terms of labor, and see that the negroes obtained justice.[38]

Thus the groundwork for the Freedmen's Bureau had already been laid in Louisiana before General O. O. Howard took charge of the "Bureau of Refugees, Freedmen, and Abandoned Lands." This institution was to be a temporary expedient, ostensibly for the purpose of (1) supervising the disposition of all abandoned, confiscated, or other lands that had come into the possession of the United States; (2) supervising and recording the acts relating to labor, negro schools, quartermaster's and commissary's supplies; (3) assuming control of the financial affairs; (4) dispensing hospital and medical service.[39]

Commissioner O. O. Howard continued Chaplain T. W. Conway as "Assistant Commissioner," and placed him in charge of the Louisiana district.[40] Conway, in the official organization of the bureau in Louisiana, appointed a superintendent to take charge of the schools of the state, and the proper officials to take over the commissary of subsistence, which was to distribute rations and

[193]

supplies. He also assigned a number of special officers and "assistant commissioners" to Shreveport, Alexandria, Clinton, Opelousas, the Home Colony in Lafourche parish, and other places, who were to constitute freedmen's courts, and who apparently conceived it to be their duty, rather than that of the legally constituted courts, to adjust all differences between the whites and the blacks. In addition, there were located in Louisiana a corps of provost marshals for freedmen, plantation inspectors, assistant quartermasters, bureau missionaries, counsellors, printers, storekeepers, district superintendents, superintendents of marriage relations, and a great number of "local agents."[41]

The organization had hardly been perfected before a number of complaints were registered. There were protests against the "Poll Tax" of one dollar, which was collected by the provost marshals from all planters and their hands.[42] The reluctance of the bureau, and in some cases the refusal, to release and return property to returning Confederates after they had received the pardon of the President, was reported as another source of "annoyance."[43] The levying and collecting of "back taxes" on property that had been used by the government during the past several years was considered as just another "millstone tied to the neck of the returned owners." One of the purposes in convening the legislature had been to secure a suspension of these "back taxes" and to secure the abolition of the colored school tax that Banks had begun to levy.[44] Still other complaints came from the Teche country to the effect that orders had been issued in August by the agents of the bureau that certain money payments must be made at that time. It was reasoned by the planting element that such instructions would prevent the gathering of the crops, since it would be impossible to make payments in money before harvest time.[45] And, finally, the restraint on the press caused the registering of other complaints.[46]

But it was the attempt of the bureau to set up a state within a state that seems to have caused most dissatisfaction. This tendency to encroach upon the state's jurisdiction is illustrated by a circular issued in December, 1865, by General Baird, Assistant Commissioner for Louisiana. It was declared by conservatives to be "vicious" in that it was an apparent attempt to nullify the recent acts of the legislature, and at the same time impose conditions that were considered ruinous for both planters and laborers. The legislature had only recently passed an act that gave the laborer a lien on the crop, as well as a free choice of his employer. Thus this circular of Baird's, issued at the same time that the laws were promulgated, instead of providing for aid in the enforcement of these laws, was to all intents and purposes a declaration that such laws were null and void, for it imposed such additional onerous conditions upon the employer as to make it practically impossible for him to enter into a contract. Issued ostensibly for the purpose of establishing "rules for the interpretation of contracts between employers and freedmen," it reimposed the burdensome "Poll Tax," prescribed that "corn meal, pork, and bacon" must be the food of the freedmen, required that the quarters of the laborers and his family must contain accommodations for cooking, and specified that "one-half acre of land contiguous to the houses will be set apart for each family for garden purposes." As many contracts had already been entered into for the next year under the bureau, this circular which prescribed separate culinary establishments, and other impracticable conditions, was generally considered a repudiation of all its own contracts.[47]

But perhaps the chief grievance against this "Pharasaical institution,"[48] as it was designated by the hostile press, was its attempt to assert exclusive legal jurisdiction over all cases wherein negroes were involved, instead of permitting them to be decided by the regularly constituted courts that were at this time in operation.[49] One instance, which occurred in Bossier parish, created such a sensation at the time as to bring the entire matter sharply to the attention of the authorities. It appears that a negro named John Gaines had been tried at Bellevue, in the court presided over by the venerable Judge James I. Weems, for the crime of horse stealing. All the forms of law had been observed, and the sentence of guilty had been pronounced by a jury of twelve men. Whereupon Mr. Callahan, an assistant commissioner of the bureau, intervened, and arrested and imprisoned the judge, the sheriff, and petit jurors who had been connected with the case. The commissioner had also intimated that, during the existing interruption of civil law, exclusive jurisdiction over the negro belonged to the bureau.[50] This procedure was denounced generally as an "outrage against the civil law of Louisiana which President Johnson had recognized," and against the courts over which the governor had recently appointed judges.[51] The result was that some relief was obtained by a temporary change in policy.[52]

In fact, the affairs of the bureau in Louisiana reached such a crisis that General Howard decided to make a personal investigation.[53] While in the city he spoke to a great throng of negroes in a tone of candor, urging them to work.

> They tell me constantly that the people [negroes] cannot support themselves and their families—cannot take care of the aged, poor, and sick. Now if they cannot, freedom is not to be a blessing but a curse. *They must!* In the providence of God they are set free, and they must!

Such sentiments, which tended to show that General Howard was becoming a convert to the coercion school, seems to have caused general disappointment among the negroes who had crowded the old Orleans Theatre with the expectation, so it was reported, that he would give special counsel concerning their votes in the approaching Congressional election.[54] Nor did his subsequent actions and orders bring aid and comfort to these blacks, for he removed Conway, a strong advocate of negro suffrage,[55] and, shortly after his visit, issued the following instructions to his agents relative to the expected division of the lands:

> It is said that lands will be taken from the present holders and be divided among them [negroes] next Christmas or New Year. This impression, wherever it exists, is wrong. . . . Take every possible means to remove so erroneous and injurious an impression. . . . It unsettles labor and gives rise to disorder and suffering. . . . It is for their best interests to look to property holders for employment. The commissioner deprecates hostile action and wishes every possible exertion made to produce kind feeling and mutual confidence between the blacks and whites.[56]

The earlier reports of these bureau officials are highly illuminating, for Howard and most of his subordinates appeared, as yet, to be in sympathy with the President's policies, and therefore, would naturally be expected to give a fair and unbiased account of conditions. General Howard, after giving a brief résumé of the activities of the bureau of Louisiana, arrived at the conclusion that the "restoration of property" was fast "depriving it [the bureau] of its sources of revenue," and that the four agricultural colonies were "not generally self-supporting." He believed, however, that the system of free labor was working fairly well, and the schools were reported to be in a "flourishing condition." The imposition of taxes had supplied the schools with a substantial sum; 141 schools and 256 teachers had been provided. The freedmen in Louisiana, he concluded, also "had the right to sue, and be sued," and to "give testimony in the courts."[57]

General Fullerton's report was considered an even stronger argument against the continuation of the bureau in Louisiana. It showed that there had been considerable fraud and bribery under the previous commissioner in connection with the recovery of abandoned and confiscated property, and that "extravagance" in the "administration of negro school funds by the Bureau would necessitate the closing of those schools." His closing sentences, which no doubt gave a correct estimate of the feelings and requirements of both whites and blacks, was a thrust at the radicals of Louisiana, who he alleged had been too prone to "magnify." Summing up, he said:

I do not believe that society, in this respect, is more demoralized at present in Louisiana, than in some States further North, as represented by the public press. By telling only the bad acts that have been committed, and giving these as an index of society, any large community could be pictured as barbarians.[58]

But perhaps the most enlightening and authentic information is gleaned from General P. H. Sheridan's testimony on Louisiana to the "Select Committee of Fifteen." He testified that the ex-Confederates accepted the situation and had an earnest desire for restoration; that "the feeling and sentiment of those within the limit of" his command, though not entirely satisfactory, was as good perhaps as could be expected; and that in Louisiana a majority of the people were on the side of the government and earnestly desired to be restored to a perfect Union with the other states.

He also most emphatically rejected the radical policy as fraught with mischief to the negro himself.

I believe [declared the General] that the best thing that Congress or the States can do, is to legislate as little as possible in reference to the colored man, beyond giving him security in his person and property. His social status will be worked out by the logic of the necessity for his labor.[59]

Such candid opinions of military officers and bureau officials were in most cases founded upon extended observation and experience, for all of these men had served in the South, and they all tended to substantiate President Johnson's sentiments expressed to the colored people some months previous, when he warned them against the barren philanthropy of those who were keeping up the hue and cry for negro suffrage for their own partisan advantage.[60] The state legislature reassembled in regular session on January 22, 1866; this time primarily for the purpose of passing the necessary enabling acts in order to resume, as soon as possible, the rights of local government.[61] There had been no disposition among the people to allow the Constitution of 1864 to be fastened upon them, and one of the first acts was the introduction of a resolution for the calling of a constitutional convention.[62] But the legislature was faced with a dilemma. There was considerable objection to such a call on the grounds that the status of Louisiana at Washington remained so unsettled. The 1864 constitution on the other hand might have been amended by simply convening the defunct convention as provided in a resolution of that body. But the advocates of a convention could hardly afford to agree that the legislature should in any way cause the amending of the 1864 constitution. Such recognition would have admitted that it was the legitimate organic law of the state. This resolution for a new convention was, therefore, almost immediately withdrawn by its friends who had apparently argued themselves into the belief that such a resolution was unwise and impolitic at this time.[63]

The convention resolution was, however, shortly reintroduced because of public sentiment and at once passed the first and second readings in the house by a vote of sixty-seven yeas to twenty-four nays.[64] But, upon the bill's being again called up, the house was informed that a dispatch had been received, stating that it was the desire of the President that it should not pass as it might interfere with his restoration policy.[65] It was therefore tabled in deference to the President's wishes, and in order not to prejudice the cause of Louisiana at Washington.[66]

Such enforced action, however, should have convinced the most optimistic—and most Louisianians apparently were optimists, at least up to this time—that the power of the radicals, the declared enemies of the President and the South, was not waning. But this action, so it was alleged, would be calculated to disarm them, for the Louisianians never seem to have doubted as yet that the radical power would be broken, and that Johnson's policy would eventually prevail.[67]

The history of other measures proposed by this legislature reveals that Wells was no longer in sympathy with the proposition to restore local self-government;[68] it was now becoming a matter of expediency for him to change again his political alignment. This difference of opinion between governor and legislature was first made manifest in December, 1865, by his veto[69] of a bill which provided for the suspension of the collection of taxes for the years 1861, 1862, 1863, and 1864.[70] This bill and a city election bill were introduced in the regular January session and passed both houses; both were vetoed by the Governor; and, in addition, he attempted to thwart further what seemed to be the public will by his veto of a bill providing for the election of parish and district officers throughout the state. The veto message on this last bill stated that it was unconstitutional because the time for giving notice was not sufficient under the law.[71] There was doubtless some constitutional justification for this veto, but the reasons for his veto of the "city election bill," that was next presented, were considered a poor defense. He declared that this bill was also unconstitutional for the reason that the "time was unusual," and there was "no necessity or demand for it." He thought, furthermore, that it would be best to devise some "methods for qualification" of voters, and provision of elections so that there might be "order in the future," and so that "transient" and "scum" would not control the proposed elections.

[199]

But these veto messages were not convincing. The citizens and members of the legislature considered them an attempt to show that they were entirely unfit to be trusted;[72] and, meeting his challenge, the legislature passed the two election bills over his veto by almost unanimous votes.[73] In addition, it passed the tax relief laws that he had formerly vetoed, which provided for the suspension of the taxes for the five years beginning with 1860.[74] The legislature was indeed no longer in a mood to submit. Nor does it appear to have intended any insult to Johnson's policy by its actions in attempting to restore local self-government, despite the fact that it was being accused in some quarters of "embarrassing and showing a spirit of hostility" to the national and state administrations.[75]

Several other acts of economic importance were passed. The most important—so it was considered at the time—was the bill that provided for a Bureau of Immigration, which was inspired by the fact that a great number of negroes had died, and by a deep-seated belief that the remainder would not work. The purpose was to attract white labor and to encourage immigration and capital, all of which was sadly needed in order to rehabilitate the state, and to assure the return of the old-time prosperity.[76] The Governor was also authorized to issue $1,000,000 in levee bonds, for the payment of which he was to pledge the public lands;[77] to issue $2,000,000 of certificates of indebtedness;[78] and to issue $1,500,000 in bonds for the payment of certain debts.[79] In addition, sufficient sums were appropriated for the maintenance of the charitable and other state institutions,[80] and for the general expenses of the state.[81] The sum appropriated for the total expenses of the General Assembly for this regular session was, however, only $75,000,[82] a modest sum when compared to the expenses of the first reconstruction body that had met a few months previous.[83]

The struggle between the Governor, who was apparently determined to maintain all his appointees in office, and his opponents, who appeared equally determined to restore local self-government in the city and state, did not end when the legislature passed the two election bills over his veto, for he now continued the struggle as an ally of the Radicals. His chief interest, and that of his opponents, was now manifested in the city election, which had been set by law for the second Monday in March.[84] There had been considerable complaint of corruption, extravagance, and misgovernment in the administration of the municipal government during the war; and it had been ardently hoped that the Wells appointee in 1865, Dr. Hugh Kennedy, a citizen, would be "the right man for the right times."[85] However, he had been in office but a comparatively short time before much opposition was being voiced through the press because of alleged misrule generally, enormous extravagance, and corruption. In fact, all his critics seemed to agree that he was a professional political spoilsman and partisan.[86] The press had therefore reflected considerable public disappointment and much dissatisfaction because Wells had not, in his proclamation in the fall of 1865, included a provision for the election of the city officials. And even now, despite the almost unanimous vote in both houses overriding his veto, he continued in his obstinacy. In fact, it was with the greatest reluctance that he finally issued his proclamation for the special election, and he acted then in obedience to what was virtually a command from the President, as the following letter reveals:

EXECUTIVE MANSION
WASHINGTON, D.C.
JANUARY 21, 1866

SIR: Your letter of the 19th ult. has been received by me, and in answer thereto, I would state that the military authorities will not interfere in any way with an election for the city offices in New Orleans which may take place in accordance with existing laws, or in conformity with regulations prescribed by the State Legislature, which will insure the election of loyal men to the offices referred to in your letter.

Respectfully yours

ANDREW JOHNSON

To Honorable John Perchell.[87]

The radical Republicans, a small minority until the negro was enfranchised, took no part in this election. But the National Democratic Union Conservatives did offer Joseph H. Moore, a native of Pennsylvania, for mayor, and presented a full opposition ticket.[88] However, their efforts were futile, for John T. Monroe, who was mayor at the outbreak of the war, and who had been imprisoned by Butler for protesting against his "woman order," was given a substantial majority vote. His ticket, with the exception of a few alderman, was also elected.[89]

The mayoralty election and that of J. O. Nixon, an alderman-elect, were at once contested by the incumbent and his constituents on the grounds that the newly elected came under the tenth and eleventh exception clauses of the amnesty, and, since they had never received the Presidential pardon, were not eligible to serve. Additional evidence was also submitted in a telegram to Stanton, which purported to prove that the mayor-elect had once attempted to secure the assassination of a Captain Baily, U.S.N.[90]

Meanwhile Mayor Monroe was not idle. He also sent telegrams to President Johnson stating that the "Union sentiment" was "unanimous against Mayor Hugh Kennedy," and that an effort was being made to keep him [Monroe] from his position, despite his loyalty to the Union and his support of the Johnson policy.[91]

Monroe had requested an answer, and evidently received it, for he and Nixon subsequently reported to Washington for an interview with the President.[92] They had, however, been prevented by Canby from being inaugurated on the seventeenth, as originally planned. General Canby appeared in fact to be defying the President in his orders[93] by which he actually appointed J. Ad. Rozier, and later George Clarke, to the mayoralty.[94] Clarke was suspended, however, when Monroe returned from Washington with the special pardon and was allowed to assume his duties as mayor.[95]

As provided for in the bill which the late legislature had passed over the Governor's veto, another election was held on the seventh of May, at which time all district and parish officials were elected in the forty-eight parishes. As usual, interest was centered in the city election.[96] The "Young Men's Democratic Association," an active organization that was affiliated with the National Democratic Party, had met and urged "harmony and unity" at "this critical moment."[97] But again there was no peace or harmony among the Democrats themselves, for some Democrats, who had not received the regular nomination, ran on what was called the "Workman's Democratic Ticket," and polled a highly respectable vote.[98]

The regular Democratic ticket was again successful in the city and state. The Democratic candidate for sheriff in Orleans parish, General Hays, who had only recently received the Presidential pardon, defeated the "Workman's" candidate by a vote of 5,035 to 2,280 in an election that was marked, so it was lamented, by a general apathy in voting.[99] Nevertheless it was now confidently believed that the final act had been consummated. The returned Confederates had at last effected a complete restoration of the state government; and, what was more to be desired, they apparently had it under their undisputed control.

CHAPTER X

THE OVERTHROW OF RESTORATION

The Revolution of July 30, 1866, commonly referred to by historians as the "New Orleans riot," was doubtless the most decisive event in the early struggle between the returned Confederates and those, chiefly newcomers, who had challenged their return to power. Because this event marked the end of the first phase of reconstruction, or more properly speaking, restoration in Louisiana, and because of its influence on the shaping of subsequent national reconstruction policies, it should be considered in its proper perspective. Its significance can hardly be understood without first treating the attitudes of the various conflicting forces, and most especially those that were national in scope.

As has been observed in the preceding chapter, the honeymoon period of the Confederates and the Unionist governor was soon terminated. It was, after all, an unnatural, or unholy, alliance. There could never have been much mutual respect or confidence in such a union. But at the time, the Democrats had felt compelled to endorse Wells as a matter of expediency, or more properly speaking, as an emergency governor and candidate to succeed himself. And on his part, he had been only too willing, it seems, to gratify his personal ambitions and maintain himself in power by a political alignment with what, he reasoned, would be the predominating party. He had sought, furthermore, to fortify himself politically by exercising his appointive power. And in so doing he had naturally filled the places in the forty-eight parishes, from the highest office to the lowly constable's office, with what he considered to be those of like faith and practice as himself. If they were not all good Unionists they were at least supposed to be loyal to him.

Wells, as a matter of fact, may have considered himself as an emergency governor. He had sought political entrenchment through the power of patronage he wielded; therefore, to acquiesce in the city election bill, and the bill for the election of all district and parish officers, would have meant, as he doubtless surmised, his exit from the political stage. For this reason he had vetoed these

[204]

and similar bills with the hope that his veto might be sustained. But as has already been shown, his veto had been overridden, leaving him but one possible recourse to continue himself in power. This recourse he now appeared willing to adopt in the early summer of 1866, for he had probably become convinced by this time that the cause with which he had allied himself some months before was becoming more and more hopeless; on the other hand, if it was not hopeless, he may have been convinced that he could make political capital by being instrumental in making it so. It is therefore easy to understand, especially in the light of the national situation, why Wells gravitated towards the radical camp. In so doing he was selecting, as he may have reasoned, another winner; but he was also seeking an alliance with a group who were as ambitious as he, and who were, as the event showed, to thwart his ambitions.[1]

In view of the fact that Louisiana's fate, and that of all the Confederate states, was being decided at Washington, and also in view of the fact that that decision was to be in some measure determined by the New Orleans battle of July 30, it now becomes necessary to consider the attitude of Congress, and also the nature of the feud that was rapidly developing between Johnson and the radical Congress as a result of this attitude. It will be recalled that Lincoln had in December, 1863, issued his plan of amnesty and reconstruction, whereby Louisiana and other states might effect their restoration to the Union. The oath of allegiance had been administered and pardons freely granted to all except six exempted classes, in order to allow the participation of at least the noncommissioned Confederate soldiers. He had, it will also be remembered, included a 10 per cent provision in order to facilitate the restitution of republican state governments.

Fearing that the South might regain her position of power certain members of Congress had resented the Lincoln proceedings; therefore, under the leadership of H. Winter Davis and Benjamin Wade, they had enacted a measure that would have annulled all restoration begun under the Executive authority, and had substituted a bill, the essential features of which provided for provisional governors who were to serve until a state government

[205]

could be recognized by the Government of the United States. The bill provided further that, after resistance had ceased, the male whites who took the proper oaths, excepting those who had been in the "rebel" service, were to be allowed to register and vote on the advisability of holding a constitutional convention. A majority of the whole number enrolled in the state was required for such proceedings. The convention, it specified, must forever prohibit slavery, repudiate all Confederate debts, and disqualify all civil or military officers who had held office under authority adverse to the United States. The constitution must then be ratified by the same state electors, and assented to by Congress, before the President could order, by proclamation, a reorganization. Finally it provided that the government so established, and none other, might have its senators and representatives admitted into Congress.[2]

This bill, which embodied the Congressional scheme of reconstruction, was fundamentally different from Lincoln's 10 per cent plan, which had been based on his Constitutional power to grant reprieves and pardons, and on the exercise of his war powers to guarantee a republican form of government. Lincoln, and later Johnson, adhered to the theory that the states still existed, whereas this bill would reduce them to mere territories subject to the will of Congress.

Since the bill would have jeopardized both the established Louisiana government and the work of the 1864 convention, Lincoln refused to sign it. At the same time he issued a proclamation in which he justified his intentions to persist in his recognition of the Louisiana and Arkansas governments.[3] He did not, however, speak disparagingly of the proposed plan. But this did not prevent the open rupture, occasioned by the "Wade-Davis manifesto," a virtual declaration of war upon the President over the issue of whether reconstruction would be effected by Congress, or whether restoration would be completed by the Executive.

This pronunciamento against the President declared it to be the duty of Congress to check the encroachment of the Executive on the authority of Congress, and warned the President to confine himself to his proper sphere. The Louisiana and Arkansas governments, it charged, were mere creatures of Lincoln's will, since he held their electoral votes at the dictation of his personal ambition. "It rests with Congress," the manifesto concluded, "to decide what government is the established one in a state"; and it made it plain that in the future Congress would decide.[4]

The military achievements of 1864, which contributed materially to the re-election of Lincoln, had given the radicals a setback. But it was only temporary, for Representative Ashley sponsored a substitute for the previous measure that was to be a forerunner of the carpetbag regime, a regime to be made possible by enfranchising the negro, and by disfranchising and degrading many of the leading whites.[5] Its introduction had been the signal for certain radicals to launch a preliminary attack upon Lincoln.[6] They did not believe that they could secure its passage at the moment. But they did expect to prepare the way for the passage of a better bill, as Ashley frankly stated, "at the next session when a new Congress fresh from the people, shall have assembled, with the nation and its representatives far in advance of the present Congress."[7]

But the radical leaders did not wait until the next Congress to renew their attacks upon Lincoln. They had ample opportunity during this session to continue the struggle over the admission of Louisiana as a state, over the admission of Louisiana's senators and congressmen, and over the counting of Louisiana's seven electoral votes. And the results of all these controversies indicated that they had begun to make considerable headway. Their first victory was recorded when they defeated the resolution recognizing the State of Louisiana.[8] Shortly thereafter they gained a second victory when the Louisiana electoral votes were rejected on February 6, 1865.[9] And finally, on the eve of adjournment, they scored their decisive victory against Lincoln when they refused to receive the two Louisiana Senators, who had only recently been elected by the Lincoln 10 per cent government.[10]

Lincoln had, in fact, been forced to yield almost everything to the Sumner–Wade–Stevens–Davis faction, and the apparent ease with which he seemed to have capitulated to his opponents prompted some critics to assert that "Mr. Lincoln has gone over to the radicals."[11] Whether he had or not, or what future course he might have pursued with the more radical Congress that fol-

[207]

lowed, can be only a matter of conjecture. But the fact that his policies, and the established state governments, had already been repudiated before his death cannot be controverted.

When Johnson inherited the Lincoln policies he also inherited the war that the radicals had declared upon those policies. And the circumstances that beset him on all sides made his position more difficult than that of his predecessor. A submission to his opponents would certainly have been more justifiable, it seems, than Lincoln's would have been. In the first place, as one recent authority concludes:

> The Radicals had been strengthened a thousand times by the hysteria resulting from the Presidential murder, they were organized as they had never been throughout the war, they were hindered by no obstacles, such as the victories in the field that had it seems saved Lincoln from Sumner's grasp.[12]

In the second place Johnson did not belong to the Republican party. Finally, the time was apparently ripe, politically, in the summer of 1865 for the Chase–Sumner–Phillips school to begin a campaign of stirring up agitation for negro suffrage.[13] Another factor that operated greatly in favor of the radicals was the fact that their leaders, Stevens in the House, and Sumner and Wade in the Senate, were enabled, by virtue of a well-planned and brilliantly executed program, to establish themselves as dictators,[14] to all intents and purposes.

The Black Codes, as they were labeled, which seem to have been necessitated by the exigencies of the situation, were also, unfortunately for Johnson and the South, interpreted by certain leaders in the North to mean the re-enslavement of the negro by the "rebels"; and the radicals appear to have exerted themselves to give color to such reports, and to raise a hue and cry against these codes.[15] The critics could also point to a number of brigadier generals, and other civil and military officers, who had only recently espoused the cause of the Confederacy, and who were now knocking at the doors of the capitol. They were, of course, adherents of the Democratic party, a party that the radicals now sought to make odious by labeling it the party of copperheadism and treason. As for their own party, it was represented as the

Grand Old Party that had saved the Union, and it was therefore a "symbol of patriotism."[16]

The radicals were also at this time effectively employing a number of so-called Southern scalawags and "Northern sojourners in the South," to prove that the late "rebel" states were in a "hopeless state of anarchy." In fact, a perusal of the report of the Joint Committee on Reconstruction discloses that the purpose of the committee was to manufacture a public opinion in the North hostile to the South, from scalawag and carpetbag Southern sources, in order to overthrow the Lincoln–Johnson policy of reconstruction. The radicals had not found to their liking the report of Grant, which declared that "the mass of thinking men of the South accept the present state of affairs in good faith." But they apparently hung on the words of Schurz when he said: "Treason does under existing circumstances not appear odious in the South." And when he concluded that the people of the South submitted only from "necessity and calculation"; that the Southerners were attempting to restore slavery in a modified form; and that no state should be readmitted until it had enfranchised its negroes, his report was characterized as "a very important document," and a "model report."[17]

This struggle between the President and his opponents had been intensified by Johnson's veto of the Freedmen's Bureau Bill. The purposes of this bill, so it was charged, were to abrogate the Southern laws, to set aside citizens' Constitutional rights, and virtually to reduce the states to "conquered territories." The proponents had, in fact, been making effective use of a number of reports and letters, such as the following, in order to create a Northern opinion favorable to the radicals' program of reconstruction:

The former masters exhibit a most cruel, remorseless and vindictive spirit towards the colored people. In parts where there are no Union soldiers I saw colored women treated in the most outrageous manner. They have no rights that are respected. They are killed and their bodies thrown into ponds or mud holes. They are mutilated by having ears and noses cut off.[18]

They were temporarily thwarted by Johnson because they

could not override his veto. But they lacked only two votes, and time and propaganda were on their side.[19] However, Johnson had won this first skirmish, and he now followed it up with his Lincoln Day speech in which he branded the three chief opponents of his policy as traitors. But he lost the next decision, for the radicals had now mustered enough strength to override his veto of the Civil Rights Bill, the first "force bill."[20] He won the next by defeating them on the Colorado Statehood bill;[21] but the opposition retaliated with the Fourteenth Amendment against which Johnson could only protest.[22] This he did, and in addition, he foiled them in their attempt to admit Nebraska; however, he was in turn forced to see his veto overridden in the passage of the Freedmen's Bureau measure by a bare two-thirds during the closing days of the session in July.[23]

But Congress did not as yet have a two-thirds majority that could be relied upon to complete its program of undoing the Lincoln–Johnson plan of restoration, and substituting therefor its own complete plan. Upon adjournment, the fight was, therefore, transferred from Congress to the country, and the campaign of propaganda which had been conducted for some months was now greatly intensified. The immediate objective of both sides was of course the control of the next Congress. The radicals needed at least a greater working margin, whereas Johnson desired at least to render them harmless, by depriving them of the bare two-thirds majority. Thus the Radicals now greatly augmented their forces and redoubled their efforts. They were apparently determined to prove to the North by the words of Southern men that their allegations against the South were true.

In this campaign Louisiana had been furnishing, and was now to furnish, a greater quota of agents. The late State Executive, former Governor Hahn, entering this campaign in Washington early in the fall of 1865, had represented that the reconstruction of the "rebels" was running very badly. "In one parish," he is reported to have told his Northern audience, "they had met in convention and re-established slavery by formal enactment and resolution."[24] This once "loud mouthed rebel," as his former associates dubbed him, now continued his speaking tour in the East

[210]

and West, and was reported to have rendered valuable service to the radical cause.[25]

Warmoth, who had also lived in Louisiana for a few months, made practically the same representations to a credulous Northern public. He proclaimed that there had been a virtual re-establishment of slavery in Louisiana. For this reason, it seems, his services were also in great demand in the Congressional elections. He continued his campaign for weeks "in the New England States, New York, Ohio, Indiana, ending at Springfield, Illinois, only a few days before the election."[26]

Other "turncoats," as the New Orleans press branded these orators who joined the radical ranks in the North before and after the "riot," were Judge Howell, who spoke "to the loyal people of the country" on the "massacres" in Louisiana,[27] and Governor Wells, who first addressed "The Loyal People of Louisiana,"[28] and later wrote letters for Northern publication in which he said of his associates, among other things, that they were "as good rebels at heart as they ever were."[29] B. F. Flanders, Parson T. W. Conway, A. P. Field, R. King Cutler, J. R. K. Pitkin, and others, some of whom had worn the gray, also found it to their interest, so it seems, to join the ranks of those whose favorite occupation was to speak disparagingly of their own native, or adopted, state.[30]

It was in the midst of this campaign, which was being carried on ostensibly for the purpose of arousing the North against the South, and at a time when the Congressional campaign of 1866 was just getting under way, that the riot, or more properly speaking, battle, of July 30 occurred to excite the country further. The revolution—for as will presently be shown, it should be classed as such—which culminated in this affair, had been brewing for several months. It will be recalled that the Convention of 1864 had, upon adjournment, passed a reconvoking resolution.[31] It must also be remembered that certain members of that body had, by their indiscreet language, provoked the citizens of New Orleans into open hostility.[32] And now, although that body had been adjourned for approximately two years, and although the contingency upon which it might have reasonably reconvened had passed at the time when the Constitution had been ratified, rumors became current in February of 1866 to the effect that certain members had petitioned Judge Durell, the president, to reconvene the body. They had based their petition, according to this rumor, upon the alleged "unsettled conditions of the State Government."[33]

The underlying motives for such a call on the part of those who opposed the established order seems to have been their hope of regaining control of the state government, which was being taken over by the pardoned Confederates. This could be accomplished, it was believed, by disfranchising a great number of the whites, and enfranchising the blacks, or, failing this, by precipitating a state of confusion or violence, which would help justify the radicals at Washington in overturning the President's government, both in Louisiana and elsewhere. This was, of course, the same program that the radicals at Washington were apparently propounding, and there is some evidence to warrant the assertion that this alleged conspiracy was instigated by the radicals in Congress, and that a few Louisianians were working in conjunction with them.[34]

There were two possible methods, as the Louisiana radicals must have reasoned, by which they might regain the power that was passing from them. They might possibly secure an election of a new body to draft a new constitution that would enfranchise the blacks and disfranchise the "rebels," or they might reconvoke their adjourned body and expedite their purpose by an amendment to the 1864 instrument. The possibilities of accomplishing the former appeared somewhat remote, for they were greatly in the minority and public sentiment in the state was against them.[35] Their only chance appeared to lie in the reconvoking clause. It at least meant that what they did could be done expeditiously; and speed was necessary, for the election bills recently passed over the Governor's veto meant that the ex-Confederates would shortly complete restoration, and there would be a return to normal conditions. They, therefore, adopted the program of reconvoking the convention.

These men had decided upon a revolutionary measure; but they must have felt that they could depend upon the aid and com-

[212]

fort of the radical Congressmen in Washington when they decided to make of themselves a self-perpetuating body. Without some such assurances their manoeuvers would either have been considered foolhardy, or would have been regarded by the citizens of Louisiana as so much harmless pleasantry.[36] But the fact that the national government appeared to be on the brink of a revolution, the object of which was apparently to pervert the organic law, and when it was further understood that the revolution to be inaugurated formed a part of the program of the radical revolutionists at Washington, it behooved those Louisianians who were interested in maintaining the supremacy of the white race not to treat this matter too lightly.

But the Louisiana radicals did not, on the face of things, appear at first to have the "aid and comfort" of their compatriots at Washington. The fact is that the report of the Reconstruction Committee, and the resolutions subsequently adopted by Congress, seem to have been interpreted as an effort to put an end to this revolutionary project in Louisiana. The pertinent part of this report, which was interpreted by the press to mean just this, follows:

The Governors appointed by the President could not exercise any but military power and authority. *They had no power to organize civil Governments, neither had the President any other than military power.* He might perhaps, permit the people to initiate local Governments and execute such local laws as they might choose to enact, and as soon as they could be left safely to themselves, he might withdraw military force altogether and leave the people to govern themselves without this interference.

Such conclusions as these were certainly an expressed declaration that the authority which had originally provided for the convention of 1864 had been powerless to reconstruct a state. There was, however, another passage in this report that the Democrats were wont to quote, which seemed to repudiate unequivocally the reconvoking of the body:

It has been shown by evidence that no proof has been given to Congress of a constituency in any of the so-called Confederate States, *excepting in Tennessee,* qualified to elect Representatives for Congress.

[213]

No State Constitution *has the sanction of the people*. All so-called Legislatures, Conventions, or otherwise, have been under military dictation. The conclusion of the Committee is that the power of Congress *is not so vested in the President,* that he can fix terms of settlement and confer Congressional representation on conquered rebels and traitors.[37]

Such construction did not mean that the Louisiana Democrats pretended to concur in the conclusions of the Reconstruction Committee, for they apparently did not. But it did mean that they approved of its estimate of the "Banks serio-comic political dramas," and could see in the report, or thought they could see, an end of the convention agitation. Some even felt justified in dismissing the whole subject in the early part of June, if press reports are to be accepted, with the conviction that "not only is the treasury safe from heavy drafts in the way of ten dollars per diem salaries, 'et ceteras,' but the members will remain in quiet seclusion for an indefinite and probably very lengthy period." The Democratic attitude was, in fine, that "it is an ill wind that blows no good."[38]

But the members did not "remain in quiet seclusion," for the rump of the 1864 convention called a caucus at the State House on June 26, from which the public was excluded. Seventy-six, a majority of the one hundred and fifty delegates assigned to the state, was a quorum; but this requisite number could not be induced to attend this or subsequent sessions, although it will be recalled that Orleans parish was represented by sixty-three delegates in the original convention. The number that actually attended, as the votes revealed, ranged from twenty-nine to about forty.[39]

The president, Judge Durell, who held that legal title when the convention adjourned, and who alone, so it seems, could have called the convention back into session before the adoption of the constitution in 1864, was one of those present at the caucus. He, however, expressed his disapprobation of the movement, and refused to issue the call for the reconvocation, or to participate in any way. He alleged that he feared he would not be sustained in so doing, and that he distrusted Governor Wells, who had apparently concurred in the proceedings. He also refused to resign since he considered himself *functus officio*. But he was deposed by

[214]

the caucus, and Judge R. K. Howell, who was no longer a member, but who now appeared to do the bidding of this "Jacobin Club," as it was now designated by the press, was elected president pro tem.[40]

It was contended by some few members then present, and by a number of the legal profession, that the most generous interpretation of the wording of the reconvocating resolutions did not give any authority for resurrecting "the remains." The preliminary words of that resolution had stated that it could be summoned "for any cause," but few authorities seem to have attached any force or importance to these introductory words.[41] Some have agreed that authority might have existed in one possible contingency—in case the constitution which they framed should be rejected, but this prescribed alternative ceased to exist when ratification was completed. In fact, the president's authority to "reconvoke" expired, so it was contended, when ratification was effected, since the convention had thereby accomplished the specific purpose for which it had been created.

The new legislature had also been empowered by a clause in this reconvoking resolution to exercise its discretion in calling the convention together at its first session. But it had met and adjourned twice since the 1864 convention had adjourned, and yet no steps had been taken toward seeking the advice of the convention. In truth, it would seem that not one of the conditions prescribed for its continuance existed. It was, therefore, supposedly defunct under the terms by which it undertook to prolong its own existence and was so recognized by several of the more intelligent of its members. To meet against the counsel and remonstrances of these same members, and to put itself into a course of active antagonism to the established order in the state, was regarded by its critics as little short of madness. In fact, it had become, in the opinion of its opponents, a public nuisance that needed to be abated; hence, the attempt to galvanize that body was to them a farce that might have been amusing had it not been so dangerous.[42]

When it was ascertained that the convention had really decided to meet, and that plans had been devised to send a delegation to

Washington to consult the radical managers and obtain their authority for this extraordinary action,[43] the Louisianians began to devise ways and means to prevent the reassembling of the convention. The *Times* suggested that there were laws in existence for dispersing riotous assemblies and for punishing disturbers of peace, and that these laws should now be invoked to prevent such "intolerable acts" and "petty rebellion as those now proposed."[44] The editor of the *Picayune* expressed his hope that, since the whole movement was "plainly part of the radical plan for defeating the President's policy and giving a triumph to his enemies" by subverting the government, a grand jury should at once be impaneled, and that the grand inquest should take cognizance of the plottings of this "Jacobin Club."[45] Other citizens believed that since this was "a traitorous war" that had been "declared against Johnson" and the established government, by "a caucus of irresponsible individuals," it would "be wiser to leave these conspirators to the disposition of the Federal Executive," and advised the people of Louisiana not to interfere with them.[46]

The Lieutenant Governor, Albert Voorhies, an ex-Confederate, also acted in behalf of the state government, which he now considered to be seriously threatened with dissolution. In the absence of Governor Wells, who was said to be on a tour of the Red River country, and who had not as yet publicly expressed his attitude, Voorhies called an informal meeting of the members of the legislature for the purpose of deliberating upon the proposed reconvocation, and to prepare for all possible emergencies. It was the "unanimous opinion" of the members present, who were reported to have "represented a more numerous and genuine constituency than did all the elect of the Convention together," that since the revolution which was "to be inaugurated" in Louisiana formed a "part of a program" of the "revolutionists at Washington," a commissioner should be sent to confer with the President. Honorable J. A. Rogers, a "distinguished citizen," was unanimously chosen "to fill this important mission."

The state authorities desired instructions, it seemed, as to whether the state government would "put down the conspiracy, which aimed at its overthrow." If left to their own resources and without interference, these authorities expressed themselves as entertaining no "serious apprehension." But, inasmuch as martial law had, technically, not been removed under the official interpretation given to the President's peace proclamation of April 6, 1865, the state authorities now desired that information be given to their commissioner relative "to the nature and extent of that interference should any trouble or collision ensue" in their midst.[47]

Meanwhile the "Rump Proclamation" to reconvoke appeared as an advertisement in the New Orleans papers.[48] The preamble and more pertinent provisions of this document, which was signed by Judge Howell, as president, and John E. Neelis, as the secretary were:

Whereas, the Constitutional Convention of the State of Louisiana, when it adjourned in 1864, adjourned subject to call in case of any emergency prior to the admission of this State into the Federal Union; and

Whereas, the *Civil Rights* bill has become a *law*, and certain amendments to the Constitution of the United States have *passed both Houses of Congress,* and now await the ratification of loyal Legislatures of the several States; and

Whereas, there is sufficient cause, and the emergency does *exist* for the reconvocation; and

Whereas, His Excellency, the Governor of the State of Louisiana, and a large number of the members of said Constitutional Convention, have personally and collectively, and at divers times within the past two months, waited upon, conversed with, and demanded of the Honorable E. H. Durell, President of said Convention, to issue his proclamation to reconvoke said Convention, or resign his position and office, and

Whereas the said E. H. Durell has repeatedly refused, therefore,

Be it resolved that the office of President be declared vacant. . . .

The proclamation further urged that the new president, Judge Howell, in conjunction with the Governor of the state, immediately issue their own respective proclamations, reconvoking the convention, and ordering elections to fill vacancies; also, it urged that the elections "be held within the shortest time possible."[49]

The hope had been freely expressed that the Governor would reject all "overtures" of the "Jacobins." But this proclamation and other testimony would indicate that the Governor had been connected with the so-called plot, and had himself been making the "overtures" for some months.[50] Moreover, his actions now demonstrated where his sympathies lay, for as soon as he had returned to the city, he recognized the reconvocation by ordering an election, not to fill the vacancies as they existed upon adjournment in 1864, but to bring in new members to the number of fifty-one from parishes not previously represented.[51]

Wells did not sign the official call for the convention to meet on July 30, but it would seem that he sanctioned it both by his election proclamation and by the fact that he had a son among the so-called revolutionists. The official call, it will be remembered, was signed by Judge E. K. Howell. This is why Wells could technically answer Johnson's inquiry truthfully when he said: "I have not issued a proclamation convening the Convention of 1864. My proclamation is in response to that call ordering an election on the 3rd of September."[52]

But neither Wells nor his associates, who had doubtless learned from these preliminary caucuses that they could not depend on more than a third of the required quorum, explained why the proposed meeting was not deferred until after his designated September 3 elections. Perhaps this date would have been too late to serve their purposes, or those of the Washington radicals. Furthermore, to have deferred action would in all probability have given the courts an opportunity to pass on the legality and to stop the entire proceedings of the revolutionists.

Other correspondence and interchange of telegrams during these critical days just prior to the proposed day of meeting are also highly illuminating. Mayor Monroe had addressed a communication to Baird, in temporary command during the absence of General Sheridan who was on a mission to Texas during this crisis. This letter, dated July 25, follows:

A body of men claiming to be members of the Convention of 1864, and whose object is to subvert the municipal, and state government, will, I learn, assemble in this City, Monday next.

The laws and ordinances of the City, which my oath of office makes obligatory upon me to see faithfully executed, declares all assemblies calculated to disturb public peace and tranquility, unlawful and as such to be dispersed by the mayor and the participants held responsible for violating the same.

It is my intention to disperse this unlawful assembly, if found within the corporate limits, holding them accountable to existing municipal law, provided they meet without the sanction of the military authorities.

I will esteem it a favor, General, if at your earliest convenience, you will inform me whether the projected meeting has your approbation, so that I may act accordingly.[53]

The next day Baird answered Monroe that "this projected meeting" did not have "the sanction or approbation of the military." He stated further that he would not furnish it with a guard, but that "the mayor of the City and the police will amply protect its sittings." This meant of course that the convention was to be allowed to meet, and that the city was expected to protect it. He added that they had a Constitutional right to meet, even though "the movement proposed might terminate in a change of existing institutions"; and that "no one ought to object" to such "harmless pleasantry." His conclusion further reveals his attitude:

As to your conception of the duty imposed by your oath of office, I regret to differ with you entirely. I cannot understand how you may or . . . can undertake to decide so important a question as the legal authority. . . . It doubtless will be decided upon in due time. . . . At all events, the Governor . . . would seem to be more directly called upon to take the initiative. What we want is . . . perfect order. . . . Lawlessness and violence must be suppressed, and in this connection the recent order of the Lieutenant-General . . . imposes high obligations for military interference.[54]

In desperation because of this answer, and as a result of a serious riot on the evening of the twenty-seventh, Voorhies, who was acting in conjunction with Monroe, telegraphed the President that "incendiary speeches" were being made; that he [Johnson] was "denounced bitterly," and that the radicals had called upon the "negroes to arm themselves." "The whole matter," he informed Johnson, "is before the Grand Jury, but impossible to execute civil processes without certainty of riot. Contemplated to have the members arrested under process from the criminal court of this District. Is the military to interfere or prevent process of court?"[55] The reply to him on the same day, as well as a similar dispatch to Wells, stated that "the military will be expected to sustain and not to obstruct or interfere with the proceedings of the courts."[56]

Baird also seems to have become apprehensive as a result of the speeches that were reported to be inflaming the negroes, and telegraphed Stanton on the evening of the twenty-eighth that he could not countenance or permit the state and city authorities to arrest the delegates without instructions to that effect from the President. He urged that he be instructed at once by telegraph.[57] But Stanton, for some reason that has not been explained, did not show this telegram to Johnson. Therefore, Stanton received no instructions and never replied to Baird. In fact, the President did not see this telegram until some time after the battle of July 30, when, at his suggestion, all the papers on the subject in possession of the War Department were sent to the executive mansion.[58]

Meanwhile the radicals, among whom there were reported to be fewer than five hundred whites, were endeavoring to make the freedmen believe that they were their friends, and that it was in their behalf and defense that the convention program was being carried out.[59] They had apparently been exciting and arousing the baser passions of the blacks for some time by their political views, but it was their sentiments uttered in the final rally of the negroes on July 27, that was said to have "alarmed the whole community."

Former Governor Hahn, who had recently returned from his sojourn in Washington and who was now taking a prominent, if not a leading, part in the proposed meeting, was the chairman and principal speaker on this occasion. Field, Hawkins, Henderson, Dostie, Heinstand, and others also spoke; all were reported by the press to have used vindictive and violent language. Dr. Dostie, according to some authorities, even went so far as to instruct the negroes to assemble armed at the Mechanics' Institute on the day specified for the meeting of the convention, and to resist by force of arms any authority that dared to interfere with the convention.[60] It would seem that the general understanding was that the negroes should march to the place of meeting on the thirtieth, and that they should act as a guard for the members of the convention. As subsequent events proved, the negroes so understood it, and apparently attempted to act accordingly.

Upon the adjournment of the meeting the excited negroes formed in procession and marched with torches through the principal thoroughfares, yelling and shouting. At one place, Lopez's Confectionery on Canal Street, several of them rushed in and struck some white men in attendance. This act almost precipitated a serious affair. It was, in fact, only through the "greatest vigilance of the large police force" that had been on duty throughout the meeting and on Canal Street during the marching, that the crowds were held in restraint, so that the negroes could reach their destination, the City Hall.

Before adjournment, Dostie and others delivered additional inflammatory addresses, whereupon most of the negroes armed themselves, chiefly with sticks and clubs. He advised them, however, to go to their homes, but that if they were molested by white men to "kill them."[61] Thus it would seem that he and the other leaders had set the stage, and all the elements were now present for the street battle that was to follow three days later.

At the appointed hour on the thirtieth the little "knot of revolutionists," as they were now designated, came together. Only twenty-five were present; and all but three of these were from New Orleans, the parish that had originally chosen sixty-three. The large majority had thus apparently either repudiated the program, or did not have the physical courage to come to the meeting. Nevertheless, those present began their deliberations.

The very boldness of their attempt to extemporize a state government would in itself have been madness had it not been that they were apparently depending on support from three sources. The first, or immediate source, was the armed negroes, whose presence they may have reasoned would overawe the citizens, and thus protect them while they accomplished their purpose of amending the 1864 document to enfranchise the negroes and disfranchise the whites. For their second support, they looked beyond the state, for the radical Congress must of course eventually approve their work. And, finally, they may have expected the support of the Federal troops.

The small band had one reason, at least, to depend on this essential support, for it seems that full expectation of the success of these revolutionists had already been entertained at Washington. This was evident when the date for adjournment was discussed at the caucus of the Republican members of Congress. At this meeting, Mr. Boutwell, a radical member from Massachusetts, had urged a delay for a few days, giving as his reason that the convention of Louisiana was about to meet, and a new constitution would come on in a few days for Congress to act upon.[62]

As was to be expected, when the negroes began to repair to the place of meeting, trouble ensued. It had been brewing all the morning, but the first outbreak occurred, according to the *Picayune*, at the corner of Canal and Dryades streets, where a procession of between one hundred and fifty and two hundred negroes was passing. "Every one of these colored gentlemen," the *Picayune* reported, "were armed, and showed their revolvers freely." One of the negroes "having run over a white man standing quietly at a curbstone, being remonstrated with, drew, *sans façon*, his revolver and fired." The negro was at once arrested by two policemen. Whereupon a number of negroes with revolvers in hand "shouted to the rescue and seemed determined to liberate their fellow." But upon being exhorted by their leaders they rejoined the procession, and only the one shot was fired in this first melee, which occurred about twenty minutes before the regular battle began.[63]

There were many attempts to give the "True Facts on the Riot," but almost all these seem to have been highly colored. These reports were apparently used largely for political purposes. However, a few significant facts stand out as highlights, and their significance can be understood when they are considered in logical sequence.

It was generally conceded, in the first place, that a revolutionary body was meeting. It was also a conceded fact that a feud of two years' duration existed between this body and the citizens, and that the aroused blacks were to be called in to act as a guard for this body. The municipal authorities, when denied the right to break up the convention by the aid of the military, had by proclamation asked the people to stay away. But when the negroes armed themselves and marched through the streets with fife and drum and iron clubs, it was hardly to be expected that excited white men, who were threatened with disfranchisement and black supremacy, could be prevailed upon to refrain from acts of hostility. As might be expected, the crowds did not obey the injunction to remain away, but followed the blacks, and, as might also have been expected, the inevitable collision occurred with fatal and fateful results.

It is impossible to determine who fired the first shot. But the battle proper began between the negro guards stationed around the building, and the white citizens, or "mob," that congregated in the immediate vicinity. Hearing the shots, the reserve police rushed to the scene in full force. While attempting to restore peace and order outside, they were, according to reports, fired upon from windows by the negroes within. Being thus attacked from the rear, the police and citizens, who had apparently become desperate, rushed the building, and when the police were met by another volley, after a white flag had been exhibited—so it was reported by the persons stationed inside the building—they committed excesses, and violent and blood-thirsty scenes ensued.[64]

When the smoke of this battle, which lasted from shortly after noon until approximately three o'clock, had cleared away, it revealed a scene that forms a sad chapter in the history of the city. In all, forty or fifty negroes had been killed and some two hundred wounded, and approximately forty police had been killed or wounded, some while protecting such men as Hahn, Shaw, Fish, and other members of the convention, from the "mob." A few of the whites, including Hahn, Henderson, Dostie, and others, who had so recently been delivering violent speeches, were listed among the casualties. That more were not killed in the battle was possibly due to the efforts of the police, who were said to have "performed their duty well." The small number of whites killed can also possibly be attributed to the poor marksmanship of the negroes, as most of their bullets either failed to reach a vital spot or went astray. It was not because the negroes did not show fight.[65]

But in drawing the curtain on the scene it must be concluded that it was the leaders who had counselled the negroes to go armed to the convention who were responsible for precipitating the "riot"; the most lamentable feature of the affair was that the negroes, who were largely of the humble class, suffered most as a consequence of their leaders' acts.[66]

As has already been indicated, there were other more remote factors that may have contributed to this so-called riot. Baird, as has been shown, manifested some hostility toward the authorities. He had at the same time shown a friendly attitude toward those who proposed to assemble. But, had not Stanton failed to answer the telegram, as Baird himself complained, it is highly probable that the whole deplorable affair could have been averted.[67] And had not Stanton withheld this dispatch from the President, Johnson would most probably have sent a personal telegram to Baird to "sustain the civil authority in suppressing all illegal or unlawful assemblies, who usurp or assume to exercise any power or authority without first having obtained the consent of the people of the State."[68] And Baird, after receiving such a telegram, would have been forced to act in conjunction with, and in a subordinate capacity to, the civil authorities.

But as events turned out, it appears that Baird proved somewhat derelict in his duty, and was apparently insurbordinate in his attitude toward the President. The fact that he received no reply from Stanton at such a critical time should have caused him to wire the President directly. This he did not do. There is a bare probability that he may have feared he would receive instructions from the President, and by adopting the course that he did he may have hoped that his conduct would be pardonable. But omitting this dereliction, Baird no doubt had sufficient instructions to carry out the wishes of the President for, as he stated, he was "in full consultation with the City Authorities" at all times, and there is some evidence to substantiate the statement that he was informed as to the President's attitude.[69]

A study of the relationships that existed between the civil and military authorities, and an analysis of the communications on the one hand, and the military on the other, on the eve of and on the day of the battle, will best serve to fasten upon the proper authorities the responsibility, if any, for the collision. The state and municipal authorities seemed bent on employing the usual remedy; that is, letting the law take its course. These authorities, therefore, had submitted the case of the proposed convention meeting to the grand jury. Meanwhile they called upon General Baird to ascertain whether the military would interfere if a warrant issued upon a regular indictment were placed in the hands of the sheriff for the arrest of the members of the convention. When Baird not only refused, but replied that the convention's meeting peaceably could not be interfered with by such officers of the law, and threatened the sheriff himself with arrest if he persisted in making such arrest,[70] the local authorities were forced to adopt another method of procedure. It was proposed to Baird that in case a warrant of arrest was placed in the hands of the sheriff, the latter, before attempting to use it, would call upon Baird, who would endorse his objections, and the matter would then be at once submitted to the President. Baird, according to the correspondence in the *Johnson Papers,* agreed to this.

On the same day, the Lieutenant Governor and the Attorney General telegraphed Johnson to ascertain whether the process of court for the arrest of the members could be thwarted by the military authorities. Johnson, as has been explained, answered that instead of obstructing, the military was expected to sustain such course. This communication was said to have been posted in the streets. Voorhies again called upon Baird and communicated this dispatch to him. In addition, he again urged Baird to station some troops in the vicinity of the Hall to preserve peace and order.[71] Baird answered that he had refused such an application from the members of the convention, and that he must likewise refuse the civil authorities. Still trying to keep their own record clear, the civil authorities then suggested to Baird that it might be construed as an intention to overawe the members, if too large a police force was stationed near the meeting place, and they urged that it would not be improper to have some troops to co-operate with a small body of police to preserve peace and prevent all possible attempt to bring about a collision. When they reminded him that, according to their agreement, they did not propose to arrest anyone until instructions were received from the President, he agreed to send the troops. But, as events proved, he actually took no steps to send this aid to assist the small police force that the mayor sent.[72]

About noon the Lieutenant Governor learned that large numbers of negroes were coming toward Canal Street, and he sent a message post haste urging Baird to send troops without delay.[73] But Baird did not send them. Jackson Barracks are only three miles away and it was yet an hour before hostilities began. In the meantime Baird had ample time to get a sufficient force to the danger zone, before the collision.

Thus it would appear from this résumé of events shortly before and on the day of the battle that the civil authorities took precautions to avert the outbreak; that they had also had an understanding for the military to act in conjunction with them; and that notwithstanding all this, they had been unsuccessful in their efforts to remove the cause of the "riot" by taking the proper measures to prevent the meeting of the convention.[74]

Therefore, it must be concluded from these facts that Baird did not discharge his duty, and that he was either incompetent, or was acting with "those who for sinister purposes had had in view this very result in order to reap a political harvest." His subsequent actions lend some color to such allegations. The fact that he and his military did not put in their appearance for at least two and one-half hours after the fighting had begun—and then he brought chiefly negro troops—and the fact that he imposed martial law after the police had apparently restored order, and the further fact that he was said to have "emptied the prisons of their rioters," without a hearing, would seem to indicate that if he was not in league with the revolutionists, he was in sympathy with their avowed purposes.[75]

A further study of the telegrams, especially those sent shortly after the battle, reveals other interesting sidelights. Sheridan returned a few days after the unfortunate occurrence, and at once sent a telegram to the War Department, which has usually been accepted as "about correct."[76] He seems at least to have placed the responsibility, if any, where it was due, when he said:

[226]

A political body styling itself the Convention of 1864 met. . . . The leaders were political agitators and revolutionary men, and the action of the Convention was liable to produce breaches of the peace. I had made up my mind to arrest the head men if the proceedings of the Convention were calculated to disturb the tranquility . . . but I had no cause . . . until they committed the overt act.

Sheridan concluded, however, that the action of the police and mayor was "murder," "cruel," and "atrocious."[77]

Johnson sent a long telegram to Sheridan on August 4 requesting a more complete report on the alleged "inflammatory and insurrectionary speeches" made by individuals urging the "mob to arm and equip" itself for "protecting and sustaining" an "illegal Convention" that was "calculated to upturn and supersede the regular constituted government."[78] To this inquiry relative to the difficulties at New Orleans, Sheridan, after some delay, sent an answer, "which was no answer," according to Welles, who "apprehended him badly prompted after his first telegram."[79] This telegram contained in substance the information that a very large number of colored people had marched in procession on July 27, and were addressed by a number of leaders. The speeches so far as he could learn, "were characterized by moderation," with the possible exception of that of Dostie. He did not enclose it, because "the version published was denied." Sheridan thought that "about twenty-six members were present in the Convention Hall, besides a number of colored men." There were, as he represented, "in front of the building some colored men, women and children, perhaps eighteen or twenty"; and he believed that there "might have been a pistol in the possession of every tenth man," among those outside and inside. "A procession," he represented further, "of say from sixty to one hundred and thirty colored men," that was "carrying an American flag," and "had about one pistol to every ten men, and canes and clubs in addition," while marching across Canal Street, became involved in a row. "A shot was fired," he believed, "by a policeman," and this led to other shots, and a rush after the procession. Sheridan learned, furthermore, "from the testimony of wounded men and others who were inside the building," that after this procession had entered the building "with the

[227]

flag" still flying, a row had occurred outside between the negro guards and the police, who were marched to this place, and who, "up to this time, had been held in hand." This had led to another row and "indiscriminate firing on the building through the windows by the policemen." Relying it seems on this same testimony, he stated that the police, ignoring a white flag on entering the building, "opened an indiscriminate fire upon the audience" and upon those who "escaped, or were passed out as prisoners." He concluded his version of the battle with the statement that "the wounded were stabbed while lying on the ground," their heads were beaten with brick-bats, and that "members of the Convention were wounded by the police while in their hands as prisoners."

Sheridan also attempted to place the responsibility. The immediate cause of the affair "was assemblage of the Convention." The remote cause "was the bitter and antagonistic feeling which had been growing in this community" since the advent of Mayor Monroe, who had in the organization of his police force he said "selected many desperate men, some of them known murderers." In addition, "Northern men" were no longer safe in life and property. They could not obtain "justice in the court"; and for "meting out justice to any parties" he could say "unequivocally that they [the civil authorities] cannot." Judge Abell, a Unionist judge in New Orleans, was represented as "one of the most dangerous men." Nor did Sheridan seem to hold any brief for the leading men of the convention. King Cutler, Hahn, and others were described as "political agitators" and "bad men," and Wells in his opinion had been "vacilating," and had "shown very little of the man."[80] And finally, he concluded by giving some suggestions to the effect that there must be "a thorough and determined prosecution" in order to avert similar scenes.

The radicals derived great advantage, it seems, from this and other reports, some of which have in the light of new evidence been partially discredited as political propaganda.[81] But reports emanating from the South were apparently taken seriously at this time in the North. No report seems to have had greater weight than that of Sheridan, who, as has been observed, did not in his last telegram describe the affair as a battle or "a riot," but (under the "inspiration" of the accomplished correspondent of the *New York Tribune,* so it was charged by those who opposed him), it was reported as a "massacre"; and it was caused, not by the culpability of the military authorities, but was, in his opinion, "perpetrated" by the state and municipal authorities, and executed by their agents, the police. It was they whose conduct had been "most reprehensible."[82] And because of Sheridan's military prestige, it was generally accepted as a genuine report. Furthermore this "answer" to Johnson, as it was designated during the campaign, was re-enforced and corroborated by similar reports that now came out of the South. Besides, the North had it from the mouths of "Louisianians" that such allegations were true.

The Unionist Southerners, as has been observed, had been doing yeoman's service prior to the battle; however, these men, who could supposedly speak with authority, now rendered most effective service in giving information to the radicals. And in addition to these so-called "Louisiana traducers," and the New York correspondents in New Orleans, who were said to have sent their reports direct from "headquarters,"[83] there were the reports of the "Special Military Board," the "New Orleans Riots Committee," and the "Republican State Central Committee of Louisiana." The Special Military Board, called by Baird upon orders from Stanton to "investigate the occurrence,"[84] made a report, without consulting or considering the civil authorities, so it was alleged, that was said to have been in line with the advanced reports of the New Orleans press. This report represented the convention as a "harmless pleasantry," reiterated the charge that the police were "thugs and assassins," and described the meeting of July 27 as "temperate." It was even alleged that "enemies" had "put words into his [Dostie's] mouth."[85] The Republican State Central Committee convened in special meetings and made up reports and passed resolutions that found their way into the Northern press. Perhaps their most significant document, published in the *New York Tribune* on August 31, purported to give both an authentic report on "conditions" and suggestions as to the proper method of procedure. Since it apparently served its purpose at the time it is quoted in full:

Whereas, on the 30th day of July, 1866, at New Orleans, Louisiana, an organized band of assassins did maliciously and brutally murder a large number of unarmed and unsuspecting Union citizens; and whereas in our opinion the same spirit which caused the late rebellion against the Government of the United States animated the perpetrators of the atrocious murders of July 30; and whereas under circumstances equally favorable other murders and outrages may be repeated from the same assassins, therefore,

Resolved, in the name of the loyal people of Louisiana, that we respectfully ask the Commander-in-Chief of the army and navy of the United States to maintain martial law over the city of New Orleans *at least* until the authors, aiders and abettors of the late massacre shall have been brought to such punishment as will secure the observance of law and order, and protect the lives of the Union citizens of New Orleans.

Resolved, That a copy of the above preamble and resolutions, which were unanimously adopted, be forwarded to Andrew Johnson, Commander-in-Chief of the army and navy of the United States.[86]

The net result was that the conspirators succeeded; and their revolution, which had aimed at the overthrow of the restored Lincoln–Johnson government, was immediate and complete. It is true that the Governor, the mayor, and other civil officers in Louisiana, including the police, were not officially suspended for some months,[87] because the public mind had doubtless to be prepared for such measures. But to all intents and purposes these officers had been rendered impotent from the time that martial law had been declared, a state of affairs that was continued by Sheridan, despite the protest that it was unnecessary and that the civil authorities were fully competent to enforce the law.[88]

Nor was this the only way in which the existing status had been changed. The courts had also ceased to function on the same day, and at the same time that the rioters were reported to have been set free by the military authorities.[89] The fact is, as the press charged —until it too was again censored—the civil laws were "silent," and "practically suspended whenever he [Sheridan] chose to speak officially."[90]

In fine, the statements that had reached the public following

[230]

the battle of July 30 had paralyzed the executive department and subverted the city and state governments. These facts were plainly recognized by the General Assembly, especially after the November elections had revealed that the congressional reconstruction views were in the ascendancy, when its Joint Committee on Federal Relations declared: "We have clearly no power to resist."[91]

NOTES

CHAPTER I

[1] *The Louisiana Democrat,* October 26, 1859; *The Opelousas Courier,* December 17, 1859; *The Daily Delta,* January 20, 1860.

[2] *The New Orleans Daily Crescent,* March 1, 31, 1860; *The Louisiana Democrat,* January 25, 1860; *The Sugar Planter,* December 31, 1859, and May 26, 1860. The course pursued by the Alabama Convention in its adoption of the Yancey Resolutions, which have been designated as the "Alabama Platform," and the "extreme doctrines" of South Carolina were denounced by a portion of the press as a "bad sign," and "tending to a dissolution of the Union." Dwight L. Dumond, *Southern Editorials on Secession* (New York: The Century Company, 1931), pp. 11-12, 517-18. This will be cited hereafter as Dumond, *Editorials.*

[3] *The New Orleans Daily Crescent,* March 21, 1860; *The Sugar Planter,* April 7, 1860; *The New Orleans Bee,* January 18, 1860; *The Daily True Delta,* February 1, 1860. The *True Delta* confidently asserted that Douglas would be elected, and that he would "satisfy the friends and foes. . . . "

[4] *The New Orleans Daily Crescent,* February 11, March 16 and 31, 1860; *The Daily Gazette and Comet,* February 21, 1860; *The Sugar Planter,* March 31, 1860. The *Crescent* was a strong advocate of Douglas, "the only man who has this essential popularity to defeat Black Republicanism."

[5] *The Daily Delta,* February 8, 14, 16, 28, 1860; *The Sugar Planter,* February 18, 25, and April 7, 14, 1860; *The New Orleans Daily Crescent,* February 13, 1860; *The Louisiana Democrat,* March 14, 1860.

[6] *The Daily Picayune,* March 6, 7, 1860; *The Sugar Planter,* March 3, 10, 1860; *The Opelousas Courier,* February 14, and March 3, 17, 1860; *The Louisiana Democrat,* March 21, 1860; *The Daily Delta,* March 7, 8, 9, 10, 1860;

The Weekly Gazette and Comet, March 11, 1860. Slidell was not present in this Convention, but his influence was felt. The opposition wing of Democracy hoped for Douglas's election in order that "King Slidell" might be dispossessed of his power as patronage dispenser in Louisiana.

[7] *The New Orleans Daily Crescent,* May 10, 1860; *The Sugar Planter,* June 9, 1860; *The Daily Picayune,* August 28, 1860; *The Daily True Delta,* May 10, 1860; *The Constitutional,* September 8, 1860; *The Daily Gazette and Comet,* March 7, 1860. Slidell, who was credited with being "the power behind the throne" for the Administration, became so apprehensive of Douglas's nomination that he attended the Charleston Convention and worked indefatigably against it. W. E. Dodd, *The Cotton Kingdom* (New Haven: Yale University Press, 1919), p. 139; *The Opelousas Courier,* May 19 and June 2, 1860. Lincoln carried California and Oregon. Louis Martin Sears, *John Slidell* (Durham: Duke University Press, 1925), p. 162-64.

[8] *The Sugar Planter,* May 12, 1860; *The New York Herald,* May 1, 1860; *The Opelousas Courier,* May 12, 1860; H. S. Foote, *War of the Rebellion* (New York: Harper and Brothers, 1866), p. 272; Dwight L. Dumond, *The Secession Movement, 1860-1861* (New York: The Macmillan Company, 1931), pp. 35, 52. The Louisiana delegation had accepted the "Alabama Resolutions," and "rallied behind Yancey." They had followed this lead, and when Alabama withdrew, the Louisianians also became "bolters." Richard Taylor, a former Whig, and a son of President Taylor, who was a member of the Louisiana delegation and who "made an earnest appeal for peace and harmony," stated that he might have succeeded but for Governor Winston's insistence on obeying instructions to the letter. It is interesting to note, as Taylor states,

that Yancey made an effort to get his delegation to disregard instructions, but failed. Taylor also states that Slidell came to the Convention, not as a delegate, "but under the impulse of hostility to the principles and candidacy of Mr. Douglas." Richard Taylor, *Destruction and Reconstruction: Personal Experiences of the Late War* (New York: D. Appleton and Company, 1879), pp. 10-12. Taylor's final rôle as a peacemaker—and he almost succeeded—is corroborated in full in John Witherspoon Dubose, *The Life and Times of William Lowndes Yancey* (Birmingham: Roberts and Son, 1892), p. 466.

⁹ *The Daily Gazette and Comet,* May 10, 1860; *The Daily Delta,* May 8, 10, 13, 1860; *The New Orleans Daily Crescent,* May 7, 1860; *The Opelousas Courier,* May 26, 1860; Dumond, *Editorials,* pp. 69-71. This editorial, which was taken from the *Daily Delta* of May 2, 1860, was entitled "The Attitude of the South." The withdrawing delegation addressed a communication to the Chairman, Honorable Caleb Cushing, which stated in effect that the delegation was being guided in its action by the principles enunciated in the "Louisiana Resolution." After quoting the full text of this resolution, this communication added by way of elaboration that: "The principles enumerated in the foregoing resolution are guaranteed to us by the Constitution of the United States and their unequivocal recognition by the Democracy of the Union, we regard as essential, not only to the integrity of the party, but to the safety of the States whose interests are directly involved. They have been embodied in both of the series of resolutions presented to the Convention by a majority of the States of the Union, and have been rejected by a numerical vote of the delegates.

"The Convention has, by this vote, refused to recognize the fundamental principles of the Democracy of the State we have the honor to represent, and we feel constrained in obedience to a high sense of duty, to withdraw from

its deliberations and unanimously to enter our protest against its action.

"We ask that the communication be spread upon the minutes of the Convention, and beg leave to express our appreciation of the justice and dignity which have characterized your action as its presiding officer."

[Signed]
A. Mouton
John Tarleton
Richard Taylor
Emile LaSere
F. H. Hatch
E. Lawrence
A. Talbot
E. W. Pearce
R. A. Hunter
D. D. Withers

"The undersigned, in explanation of their position, beg leave to annex the following statement, viz.:

"Whilst we took the same view with our colleagues, that the platform of principles, as adopted by this Convention was not what was expected by Louisiana and desired by ourselves, as sufficient to guard the rights of that State, and of the whole South, under the Constitution, we are now unwilling precipitately to retire from the Convention, until all hope of accommodation shall have been exhausted, and until the last moment had arrived, at which, in justice to our honor, and the interests and dignity of our own State, we would be forced to retire. We, therefore, were opposed to the retirement of the delegation at the time it was made; but believing that the other members of the delegation were actuated by the same motives which governed our own opinions, and desiring our State to present a firm undivided front, we being in the minority of the delegation, were willing to yield, and did yield our opinions to the judgment of the majority."

[Signed]
J. A. McHatton
Charles Jones

Charleston, S.C., May 1, 1860.
Quoted from Horace Greeley, *A Political Textbook for 1860,* p. 39.

[10] Dumond, *Secession Movement*, p. 66; *The Daily Delta*, May 2, 13, 1860. The delegates to the Democratic Convention that nominated Breckinridge and Lane published a long "Letter to the people of Louisiana," explaining their actions. *The Daily Delta*, August 9, 1860; *The Opelousas Courier*, August 26, 1860.

[11] *The Daily Delta*, May 11, 13, 1860; Dumond, *Secession Movement*, pp. 66-67. Such action by the commercial interests with whom Slidell was connected showed the identity of interests of New Orleans and the plantation South. Statistics reveal that the commerce of the city before 1860 had doubled during every decade. By 1860 approximately one-half of all the yearly exports from the United States passed through the New Orleans port alone. This included $25,000,000 in sugar, $100,000,000 in cotton, and $40,000,000 in other products. Dumond, *Secession Movement*, p. 126; Charles H. McCarthy, *Lincoln's Plan of Reconstruction* (New York; McClure, Phillips and Company, 1901), pp. 36-37; *The Daily Delta*, May 4, 15, 1860; *The New Orleans Price-Current*, June 16 and July 21, 1860; *The Daily Picayune*, September 1, 2, 14, 1860.

[12] Dumond, *Secession Movement*, pp. 67-68; *The Daily Gazette and Comet*, May 10, 1860; *The Daily Delta*, May 8, 15, 1860. The late state convention reassembled in Baton Rouge on June 4 for the purpose of determining the course to be pursued in reference to the proposed Baltimore Convention. It reappointed the same delegates and gave instructions as to their procedure at Baltimore. *The Sugar Planter*, June 9, 1860; *The Weekly Gazette and Comet*, June 4, 10, 1860; *The Daily Delta*, May 15 and June 8, 1860; *The Opelousas Courier*, May 26 and June 16, 1860. The Louisiana senators, Benjamin and Slidell, were two of the nineteen who signed the "Address to the National Democracy," urging the seceding delegates to return to Baltimore and work for reconciliation with the Douglas faction. Pierce Butler, *Judah P. Benjamin* (Philadelphia: Jacobs and Company, 1907), p. 192.

[13] *The New Orleans Bee*, May 13, 1860; *The Sugar Planter*, May 26, 1860; *The Daily Gazette and Comet*, May 30, 1860; Dumond, *Secession Movement*, p. 65. *The Daily Delta* called the disruption a "catastrophe!" and charged it to the "arrogant pretensions of the Northern delegations" who wished to "govern the Convention in its choice . . . and to impose upon it a platform of principles, which would be rejected by every Southern state." But more than twenty Louisiana journals had "spoken out" and approved the action of the delegates to Charleston by June 23. *The Opelousas Courier*, June 23, 1860.

[14] *The Daily Delta*, May 9, 1860; Dumond, *Secession Movement*, p. 65.

[15] Dumond, *Secession Movement*, pp. 65-66; *The Daily Delta*, May 12, 1860. Morse, the leader, had been an outspoken secessionist during the Kansas–Nebraska struggle, while a member of the lower house of Congress. It was asserted that he delivered the only disunion speech ever delivered in the city, and that he had been defeated for re-election to Congress as a result. Both speeches were published in *The Daily Delta* of May 12, 1860. A similar meeting was held in Baton Rouge, at which a resolution was "unanimously adopted" disapproving the "course pursued by the delegates from this state who withdrew from the National Democratic Convention held at Charleston." *The Daily Gazette and Comet*, May 30, 1860.

[16] *The Daily Delta*, May 20, 1860; *The New Orleans Daily Crescent*, June 2, 1860; *The Daily Delta*, May 20, 1860; Sears, *op. cit.*, p. 90. Soulé had been an "ultra" during the decade beginning with 1850. As a conservative, he and his followers now contended that the Charleston delegates had resigned, and they must now either fill the vacancies as requested by the resolution adopted at Charleston after the seven Southern states had withdrawn, or send the original delegation with new instructions.

A detailed account of the proceedings of this opposition meeting to the regular democracy is given in *The Daily Delta*, of May 20, 1860. Soulé seems to have been politically hostile to both Slidell and Benjamin, who had practically eliminated him from Louisiana politics. Pierce Butler, *op. cit.*, p. 186; Sears, *op. cit.*, pp. 155–56.

[17] *The Sugar Planter*, June 9, 1860; *The Daily Gazette and Comet*, June 9 and 10, 1860; *The Daily Delta*, June 8, 1860. A detailed account of what happened at Donaldsonville is given in this issue of the *Delta*. A brief résumé of the proceedings of this meeting is also given in Dumond, *Secession Movement*, pp. 68-70. As was to be expected, this contesting irregular delegation, headed by Soulé, was admitted by a committee vote of 16 to 9, and by a convention vote of 158 to 98, to the "exclusion of those reappointed" by the regular state democracy; and it participated in the Convention. Alabama was the only other Southern state that sent such a contesting delegation. Dumond, *Secession Movement*, pp. 65, 82-85; *The New York Herald*, June 21, 23, 1860.

[18] *The New Orleans Daily Crescent*, May 11, 1860; *The Sugar Planter*, May 12, 19, 26, 1860; *The Daily Gazette and Comet*, May 13, 27, 1860; Howard K. Beale (editor), "The Diary of Edward Bates 1859-1866," *American Historical Association Annual Report*, IV (1930), p. 375; *The Daily True Delta*, May 10, 1860. The *True Delta*, still supporting Douglas, opined that "the real cause for the secession was the certainty which confronted the bolters that the nomination of Stephen A. Douglas could not be defeated, or if nominated his election prevented."

[19] *The New Orleans Daily Crescent*, May 10, 31, 1860; *The Daily Gazette and Comet*, June 3, 1860; *The Constitutional*, August 31, 1860.

[20] *The New Orleans Daily Crescent*, May 14, 21, 1860; *The Sugar Planter*, June 30, 1860; *The Daily Delta*, May 29, 31, 1860.

[21] *The New Orleans Daily Crescent*, May 14 and July 6, 1860; *The Daily Delta*, May 29, 1860; *The Daily Gazette and Comet*, June 24, 30, 1860. The proposed state convention was subsequently held on July 4 at Baton Rouge for the purpose of ratification. Randell Hunt presided. A state-wide organization was effected and representative citizens were nominated electors. *The New Orleans Daily Crescent*, July 6, 1860; *The Sugar Planter*, June 30 and July 14, 1860; *The Daily Gazette and Comet*, July 4, 6, 1860; *The Daily Delta*, July 6, 1860; *The Weekly Gazette and Comet*, July 15, 1860. W. H. Hunt, *Randell Hunt* (New Orleans: F. F. Hansell and Brother, 1896), p. 39. Hunt and Roselius were former Whigs. Cf. Pierce Butler, *op. cit.*, pp. 103, 150; Hunt, *op. cit.*, p. 33.

[22] *The New Orleans Daily Crescent*, April 4, May 21, June 12, 21, 29, 1860; *The Weekly Gazette and Comet*, July 1, 1860; *The Opelousas Courier*, June 23, and July 7, 1860; *The Daily Gazette and Comet*, May 13, 24, and June 14, 17, 21, 1860; *The Daily Delta*, June 8, 12, 16, 20, 30, and July 6, 7, 1860. The *Delta* of June 30 gives a complete list of the Louisiana delegates who participated in the nomination of Breckinridge and Lane.

[23] *The New Orleans Daily Crescent*, May 18, 19, 28, 1860; *The New Orleans Bee*, May 21, 1860; *The Daily Delta*, May 19, 1860; *The Sugar Planter*, May 26, 1860; *The Opelousas Courier*, June 2, 1860; *The New York Herald*, May 18, 1860. The *Bee* expressed the opinion that the "nomination of Lincoln was a master stroke of political craft."

[24] *The New Orleans Daily Crescent*, June 25, 26, 1860; *The Sugar Planter*, May 26, 1860.

[25] *The New Orleans Daily Crescent*, June 23 and July 19, 1860; *The Daily Gazette and Comet*, June 21, 1860; *The New York Herald*, June 23, 1860; *The Weekly Gazette and Comet*, August 5, 1860; *The Daily Delta*, July 2, 1860; Dumond, *Secession Movement*, p. 65.

[26] *The New Orleans Daily Crescent*, July 7, 1860; *The Opelousas Courier*,

September 8, 15, 1860; *The Daily Delta,*
November 1, 1860; *The Sugar Planter,*
July 28 and September 1, 1860; *The
Weekly Gazette and Comet,* August
5, 12, 1860; *The Constitutional,* September 15, 1860; *The Daily Gazette
and Comet,* September 1, 1860. Taylor's
endorsement of the candidacy of Douglas
had been considered an "act of apostasy"
by many Democrats. *The Sugar Planter,*
February 11, 1860; *The Louisiana Democrat,* February 15, 1860. There was
manifested at this time some slight fear
of the formation of a "Black Republican" party in the state. According to
the press, Soulé was boldly preaching
"Douglasism" to the people, and declaring that "nobody but the slaveholder
has an interest in the preservation of
slavery."

²⁷ *The Daily Delta,* February 16, September 22, and October 6, 1860; *The
Opelousas Courier,* June 30 and September 15, 1860; Sears, *op. cit.,* pp.
171-72; John B. McMaster, *A History
of the People of the United States During Lincoln's Administration* (New York:
D. Appleton and Company, 1927), p.
32. This prophecy came true within
less than a year, for on May 1, 1861,
at Chicago, Douglas declared unequivocally for the Union. H. H. Flint, *Life
of Stephen A. Douglas* (Philadelphia:
John E. Potter and Company, 1863),
pp. 416-19; *The Daily Gazette and
Comet,* June 6, 1861.

²⁸ *The Daily Delta,* July 31, 1860.

²⁹ *The Daily Delta,* August 17, September 27, and October 6, 1860; *The Opelousas Courier,* July 28, August 11, September 1, 22, 29, and October 13, 1860;
The Constitutional, September 15 and
October 6, 1860; *The Weekly Gazette
and Comet,* September 15, 1860; *The
Daily Picayune,* August 16, 1860; *The
Daily Gazette and Comet,* September
11, 1860.

³⁰ *The Daily Delta,* October 6, 1860;
Sears, *op. cit.,* pp. 169-72; *The New Orleans Daily Crescent,* September 19,
1860; *The Sugar Planter,* September 29,
1860; *The Constitutional,* August 4,

1860. Slidell, "who was originally and
essentially a moderate," was forced by
circumstances to ally himself with the
extremists. He had been a lifelong Democrat and could not consistently ally
himself with the Bell–Everett Whig
group. Nor could he ally himself with
the "hated Douglas." His only recourse was to support the Breckinridge
ticket.

³¹ *The Louisiana Signal,* October 9,
1860; *The Daily Gazette and Comet,*
October 12, 1860; Clarence Phillips Denman, *The Secession Movement in Alabama* (Norwood, Mass.; J. S. Cushing Co., 1933), pp. 159-60; *The Daily
Picayune,* October 3, 1860; *The Sugar
Planter,* October 13, 1860; *The Opelousas Courier,* October 13, 1860; *The Constitutional,* September 22, 1860. One
Louisiana journal stated: "Mr. Yancey
proclaims that 'the pen is already nibbed
which is to write the story of revolution.' 'Tis more likely that the rope is
already twisted which is to be knotted
under the left ears of those who shall attempt to create a revolution." *The Daily
Gazette and Comet,* July 28, 1860.

³² *The Daily Delta,* October 31, 1860;
The Daily Picayune, October 30, 1860;
The New Orleans Daily Crescent, November 1, 1860; *The Daily Gazette and
Comet,* October 31, 1860; DuBose, *op.
cit.,* pp. 529-34; William G. Brown,
The Lower South in American History
(New York: The Macmillan Company,
1902), p. 144. Yancey was evidently well
received. A formal public holiday had
been declared in order that all might
hear him, and his visit aroused "intense interest." Several New Orleans
papers, and DuBose, gave Yancey's
speech in full, and a graphic description
of what happened from the time of his
entry until the time of his departure.
The *Picayune* stated that "Mr. Yancey
must have been gratified at the reception he received from the people of New
Orleans, whether or not of his party."
The Daily Picayune, October 30, 1860.

³³ *The Louisiana Signal,* August 29,
1860; *The Daily Delta,* August 15, 1860.

The *Delta* stated: "The Douglasites of this state have at last got an Electoral ticket."

[34] *The Louisiana Signal,* November 5, 1860; *The New Orleans Daily Crescent,* July 16, 26, September 26, and October 21, 1860; *The Daily Gazette and Comet,* August 1, 1860; *The Constitutional,* August 4, 1860; *The Weekly Gazette and Comet,* July 15, 1860; *The Daily Picayune,* August 15, 1860; *The Sugar Planter,* October 6, 1860. Some of these clubs shortly became Confederate military company units, and retained not only the name, but in many instances the personnel. The roster of the Bell–Everett Presidential electors, Rivere Gardere, G. De Ferriet, Christian Roselius, Duncan S. Cage, J. Q. Fuqua, H. M. Favrot, Thos. S. Lewis, Valein Fournet, John Ray, and B. L. Hodge, practically all business men of character and prominence, attests the popularity of the Bell–Everett ticket.

[35] *The Daily Delta,* July 25, 1860; *The Constitutional,* August 4, and September 1, 8, 29, 1860; *The Daily Picayune,* August 15, 1860; *The Sugar Planter,* September 1, 8, October 4, and November 3, 1860; *The New Orleans Daily Crescent,* October 9, 1860.

[36] *The Louisiana Signal,* October 23, 1860; *The Daily Picayune,* October 11, 13, 1860; *The Constitutional,* November 3, 1860. The *Constitutional* labelled the "Breckinridge ticket" as the "disunion ticket," and boldly advocated "death to the traitors." *The Constitutional,* September 8 and November 3, 1860.

[37] Hunt, *op. cit.,* p. 39; *The Daily Delta,* November 6, 1860. The other Louisiana journals also gave a detailed report of this meeting.

[38] *The Daily Picayune,* December 6, 1860; *The Daily Gazette and Comet,* November 8, 9, 1860; *The New Orleans Daily Crescent,* November 7, 8, 9, 1860; *The Sugar Planter,* November 10, 1860; Sears, *op. cit.,* p. 174.

[39] *The Daily Delta,* November 8, 1860; *The New Orleans Daily Crescent,* No-

vember 8, 9, 1860; *The Opelousas Courier,* November 10, 1860; *The Constitutional,* November 17, 24, 1860; Florence C. Tompkins, "Women of the Sixties," *The Louisiana Historical Quarterly,* I (1919), 281.

[40] *The Daily Gazette and Comet,* November 9, 1860; *The Sugar Planter,* November 17, 1860; *The Constitutional,* November 17, and December 8, 15, 1860; *The Opelousas Courier,* November 24, 1860.

[41] *The Daily Picayune,* November 4, 1860; *The New Orleans Daily Crescent,* October 15, November 5, and December 5, 1860; *The Daily Gazette and Comet,* July 29 and October 19, 1860; *The Opelousas Courier,* November 3, 1860; *The Constitutional,* September 29, and October 6, 29, 1860; *The Weekly Gazette and Comet,* September 2 and October 20, 1860.

[42] *The Daily Delta,* November 9, 1860; *The Daily Picayune,* September 27, and October 4, 11, 24, 1860; *The Opelousas Courier,* November 17 and December 1, 1860; *The Daily Gazette and Comet,* November 12, 22, 27, 28, 1860; *The New Orleans Daily Crescent,* November 23, 24, 1860; *The Sugar Planter,* December 15, 1860; *The Constitutional,* November 24, 1860.

[43] *The New Orleans Daily Crescent,* December 4, 1860; *The Daily Gazette and Comet,* December 5, 1860; Edward McPherson, *A Political History of the United States of America During the Great Rebellion* (Washington: Philp and Salmons, 1864), p. 1; "Louisiana," *Annual Cyclopaedia, 1861* (New York: D. Appleton and Company, 1869), p. 431; *The Daily Picayune,* December 6, 1860. This issue of the *Picayune* contains the complete tabulated parish by parish official returns.

[44] Sears, *op. cit.,* p. 174; *The New Orleans Daily Crescent,* December 4, 1860; *The Sugar Planter,* December 8, 1860; *The Constitutional,* December 15, 1860; *The Weekly Gazette and Comet,* November 9, 1860. Of this city vote Slidell said that "seven-eighths at least of the

votes for Douglas were cast by the Irish and Germans, who are at heart abolitionists."

⁴⁵ Henry Clay Warmoth, *War, Politics, and Reconstruction: Stormy Days in Louisiana* (New York: The Macmillan Company, 1930), p. 35; Henry E. Chambers, *A History of Louisiana* (New York: The American Historical Society, 1925), I, 626. This combined vote of

Bell and Douglas, which totaled approximately three-fifths of the state, has been repeatedly cited as so-called proof that a majority of the people of the State of Louisiana were not in favor of secession.

⁴⁶ *See* Henry T. Shanks, *The Secession Movement in Virginia* (Richmond: Garrett and Massie, 1934), *passim;* Denman, *op. cit., passim.*

CHAPTER II

¹ *The New Orleans Daily Crescent,* November 22, and December 4, 12, 1860; *The Opelousas Courier,* December 1, 1860; Emily Hazen Reed, *Life of A. P. Dostie* (New York: Wm. P. Tomlinson, 1868), p. 31; J. S. Kendall, *History of New Orleans* (New York: The Lewis Publishing Company, 1922), I, 232; L. C. Kendall, "The Interregnum in Louisiana in 1861," *The Louisiana Historical Quarterly,* XVI (1933), p. 184.

² *The New Orleans Daily Crescent,* November 10, 16, 1860; *The Weekly Gazette and Comet,* November 20, 1860; *The Opelousas Courier,* December 1, 1860; *The Daily Gazette and Comet,* December 8, 1860; *The Baton Rouge Advocate,* November 12, 1860.

³ *The New Orleans Daily Crescent,* November 9, 10, 15, 1860; *The Daily Gazette and Comet,* November 17, 1860; *The Constitutional,* November 17, 1860; *The Sugar Planter,* November 10, 1860; *The Weekly Gazette and Comet,* November 17, 1860. Douglas spoke briefly in New Orleans, and wrote a long letter for publication.

⁴ *The New Orleans Daily Crescent,* November 17, 1860; *The Weekly Gazette and Comet,* November 23, 1860; *The Constitutional,* December 1, 1860; *The Opelousas Courier,* December 1, 1860.

⁵ *The Daily Picayune,* November 17, 1860; *The Sugar Planter,* November 10, 16, 1860; *The Daily Gazette and Comet,* November 14, 22, 1860. Governor Moore was disposed at first to wait until after Louisiana's electoral vote had been counted. Public pressure no doubt caused him to decide to act earlier.

⁶ *The Daily Delta,* November 8, 1860;

The Sugar Planter, November 24, 1860; *Constitution of the State of Louisiana* (New Orleans: J. O. Nixon, Printer, 1861), p. 326; *The Daily Gazette and Comet,* November 21, 1860; *Report of the Secretary of State, May, 1902* (Baton Rouge: News Publishing Co., 1902), pp. 96-97, 106; *The New Orleans Daily Crescent,* November 16, 19, 20, 1860. These petitions, which were signed by thousands, seem to have been circulated largely by the Mount Vernon Club.

⁷ *The Daily Delta,* November 22, 1860; *The Opelousas Courier,* December 1, 1860; *The New Orleans Daily Crescent,* November 24, 1860; *The Daily Gazette and Comet,* November 23, 28, 1860; *The Constitutional,* December 1, 1860; *The Daily True Delta,* November 20, 1860; "Louisiana," *Annual Cyclopaedia, 1861,* p. 427. The *True Delta,* still cautioning a watchful waiting policy, denounced the Governor for "yielding before the pressure of Slidell and his rump retinue," and declared that this was the "first step in the march of disunion." The next regular session of the legislature would have met on January 21, 1861. Dumond, *Editorials,* p. 255.

⁸ *The Daily Delta,* November 24, 1860; "Louisiana," *Annual Cyclopaedia, 1861,* p. 428; *The New Orleans Daily Crescent,* January 1, 4, 5, 1861.

⁹ *The Daily True Delta,* November 21, 1860; *The New Orleans Bee,* November 23, 1860; *The New Orleans Daily Crescent,* November 22, 24, 1860; *The Daily Gazette and Comet,* December 21, 1860: M. L. Bonham, "Financial and Economic Disturbance in New Orleans on the Eve of Secession," *The Louisiana*

NOTES

Historical Quarterly, XIII (1930), p. 32.

[10] *The Daily Delta,* December 1, 1860;
Mabel Brasher, *Louisiana* (New York:
Johnson Publishing Company, 1929), p.
287; J. Barker, *The Rebellion* (New
Orleans: Commercial Print Company,
1865), p. 92; *The New Orleans Daily
Crescent,* December 3, 1860; *The New
Orleans Times,* April 30, 1864; *The
Baton Rouge Tri-weekly Gazette and
Comet,* August 17, 1865; *Private and
Official Correspondence of General Benjamin F. Butler During the Period of
the Civil War* (Norwood, Mass.: The
Plimpton Press, 1917), II, 407-09. This
will be cited hereafter as *Butler's Correspondence.* Leacock preached such a
sermon on November 29, 1860, "which
was published and run through four
editions of 30,000 copies."

[11] *The Daily Delta,* December 4, 1860;
The New Orleans Daily Crescent, December 4, 1860.

[12] *The Daily Delta,* December 8, 1860;
The Baton Rouge Advocate, November
12, 1860; *The New Orleans Daily Crescent,* November 14, 16, 1860; *The Opelousas Courier,* December 1; *The
Sugar Planter,* December 1, 8, 1860; *The
Constitutional,* December 8, 1860, and
January 12, 19, 1861; *The Daily Gazette
and Comet,* December 13, 1860.

[13] *The Daily Delta,* December 11, 1860;
Congressional Globe, 32 Cong., 2 sess.,
pp. 6, 22; *The New Orleans Daily
Crescent,* November 17, and December
3, 11, 13, 14, 24, 31, 1860; *The Daily
Gazette and Comet,* December 15, 1860;
The Sugar Planter, December 15, 1860;
The Constitutional, December 15, 1860.
The *Crescent* stated on January 4, 1861:
". . . it is not a compromise that we
want."

[14] *Acts of the Legislature of Louisiana,
Extra Session, 1860* (New Orleans: J. O.
Nixon, State Printer, 1861), pp. 5-7
(This will be cited hereafter as *Acts of
the Legislature, Extra Session, 1860);
"Louisiana,"* Annual Cyclopaedia, 1861,
pp. 427-28; Taylor, *op. cit.,* pp. 12-13.
Taylor, who was a member of the
upper branch, and chairman of its Committee on Federal Relations, assisted in

preparing and reporting the measure
providing for the Convention call. Writing almost twenty years later, he stated
that this special session met in January,
1861. He was mistaken. The special session met on December 10, 1860, and the
regular session met in January, 1861.

[15] *The Daily Delta,* December 15, 1860;
*Acts of the Legislature, Extra Session,
1860,* p. 16; Taylor, *op. cit.,* p. 12; *The
Daily Gazette and Comet,* December 12,
1860.

[16] *The Daily True Delta,* December
14, 1860; *Acts of the Legislature, Extra
Session, 1860,* p. 18; *The New Orleans
Daily Crescent,* December 15, 1860. *The
Crescent* of this date [December 15,
1860] states: "It is a significant fact that
the Convention, and appropriation bills
passed both houses of the Legislature
without a dissenting vote. . . ."

[17] *The Daily Delta,* December 22, 1860;
The Sugar Planter, December 15, 22,
1860; *The New Orleans Daily Crescent,*
December 17, 18, 19, 1860; *The Daily
Gazette and Comet,* December 22, 1860;
The Constitutional, December 22, 29,
1860; *The Weekly Gazette and Comet,*
December 18, 1860; "Louisiana," *Annual Cyclopaedia, 1861,* p. 428; Alcéi
Fortier, *A History of Louisiana* (New
York: Manzie, Joyant, and Company,
1904), IV, 3-4. The flag was not officially adopted until after the convention had acted.

[18] *The Daily Delta,* December 19, 1860;
The Daily Gazette and Comet, December
12, 1860; *The New Orleans Daily Crescent,* December 24, 1860; *The Weekly
Gazette and Comet,* December 22, 1860,
and January 5, 1861; *The Sugar Planter,*
January 5, 1861.

[19] *The Daily Picayune,* December 19,
1860; *The New Orleans Daily Crescent,*
December 5, 1860; *The Sugar Planter,*
December 1, 1860. *The Crescent* of
January 5, 1861, makes this statement:
"Here in New Orleans nobody knows
exactly what co-operation means. With
some it means delay, with some conference with other states, with some it
means submission."

[20] *The Daily Delta,* December 23, 1860;

The New Orleans Daily Crescent, October 30 and December 19, 1860; *The Daily Gazette and Comet,* November 17, 1860. Soulé evidently opposed secession, except as an extreme measure. But he followed his state and soon became an uncompromising Confederate. He was Confederate provost-marshal of New Orleans when Butler occupied the city. His continued support of the cause of the South caused his arrest and imprisonment. Amos Aschbach Ettinger, *The Mission to Spain of Pierre Soulé, 1853-1855* (New Haven: Yale University, 1932), p. 472.

[21] *The Daily Delta,* December 27, 1860; *The New Orleans Daily Crescent,* January 1, 1861.

[22] *The Daily Delta,* December 23, 1860; *The Daily Gazette and Comet,* December 20, 1860.

[23] *The Daily Delta,* December 23, 25, 1860; Pierce Butler, *op cit.,* pp. 203-05.

[24] *The New Orleans Daily Crescent,* November 30, December 8, 18, 1860, and January 2, 18, 29, 1861; *The Weekly Gazette and Comet,* December 29, 1860; *The Constitutional,* January 5, 1861; *The New York Daily Tribune,* March 2, 1861; *The New York Herald,* February 21, 1861; A. B. Bledsoe, *Is Davis a Traitor; or Was Secession a Constitutional Right Previous to the War of 1861?* (Baltimore: Innes and Company, 1866), p. 256.

[25] *The Daily Picayune,* January 8, 15, 1861; *The Sugar Planter,* January 12, 1861; Henry Rightor, *Standard History of New Orleans* (Chicago: The Lewis Publishing Company, 1900), p. 150; *The New Orleans Times,* January 15, 1864; J. K. Greer, "Louisiana Politics, 1845-1861," *The Louisiana Historical Quarterly,* XIII (1930), p. 642. The result will be understood from the official returns for the senatorial candidates. The names of the secession candidates are marked with a star (*). The more than eight thousand votes "counted up by the municipal districts" were as follows:

	1st Dist.	2nd Dist.	3rd Dist.	4th Dist.	Total
Durant	1654	937	746	581	3918
Hunt	1673	943	740	580	3936
Soule	1622	927	733	566	3848
Dufour	1662	968	756	577	3963
Jonas	1652	932	743	575	3902
*Bonford	1927	1185	563	646	4321
*Labutut	1904	1210	569	642	4325
*Adams	1903	1181	553	642	4279
*Kennedy	1916	1195	567	642	4320
*Michel	1894	1175	565	662	4296

Majority of the highest secession candidate over the highest co-operation candidate (Labutut over Dufour), 362. Majority of the lowest secession candidate over the lowest co-operation candidate (Adams over Soulé), 431. Majority of the middle secession candidate over the middle co-operation candidate (Kennedy over Durant), 402. Majority of the highest secession candidate over the lowest co-operation candidate (Labutut over Soulé), 477. Majority of the lowest secession candidate over the highest co-operation candidate (Adams over Dufour), 316. Average majority of the secession over the co-operation candidates, 397.

[26] *The New Orleans Crescent,* January 8, 15, 1861; *The Constitutional,* January 12, 1861; *The Sugar Planter,* January 12, 1861. In Madison, Lafourche, and Lafayette the immediate secession candidates, several in number, had no opposition. *The New Orleans Daily Crescent,* January 15, 1861. There were doubtless others. The Whig strength in many northern, western, and southern parishes had always been negligible.

[27] *The Daily Picayune,* January 9, 1861. The *Picayune,* strangely enough, attempted to show shortly afterwards that the co-operationists had won.

[28] "Louisiana," *Annual Cyclopaedia, 1861,* pp. 428, 431; *The Weekly Delta,* January 18, 1861.

[29] *The Daily Delta,* June 18, 1860; *The Daily Delta* listed six as "doubtful."

[30] *The New Orleans Daily Crescent,* January 18, 1864; *Report of the Secretary of State, May 1902, op. cit.,* pp. 110-11.

[31] *The Daily Delta,* January 18, 1860; *The New Orleans Daily Crescent,* Janu-

ary 15, 21, 1861. It is interesting to spec-
ulate how the state might have gone
had the delegates been distributed and
elected on a basis of white population
instead of total population, as was the
case, with the exception of New Orleans,
where an arbitrary arrangement existed.
In so far as the city would have been
affected, it would have at least increased
the immediate secessionist delegation.

[32] *The Daily Delta*, January 15, 1861;
Pierce Butler, *op. cit.*, pp. 209-11; *Congressional Globe*, 36 Cong., 2 sess.,
pp. 216-17.

[33] *The Daily Crescent*, January 16,
1861. Pierce Butler, *op. cit.*, pp. 212-
13.

[34] *The Daily Delta*, January 16, 1861;
Pierce Butler, *op. cit.*, pp. 210-11; *Congressional Globe*, 36 Cong., 2 sess., p.
217; Dumond, *The Secession Movement*, p. 147.

[35] *The New Orleans Daily Crescent*,
January 16, 1861; Alfred Roman, *Mili-
tary Operations of General Beauregard*
(New York: Harper and Brothers, 1884),
I, 16, 19; Pierce Butler, *op. cit.*, p. 213;
J. H. Greer, "Louisiana Politics, 1845-
1861," *The Louisiana Historical Quar-
terly*, XIII (1930), p. 645; *Congressional
Globe*, 36 Cong., 2 sess., p. 217; *The Daily
Picayune*, October 21, 1861. This speech,
and the comments on it, were given wide
publicity for some time in all the papers.

[36] M. L. Bonham, "Louisiana's Seizure
of the Federal Arsenal at Baton Rouge,
January 1861," *Proceedings of the Historical Society of East and West Baton
Rouge*, VII (1917-1918), pp. 47-49; *The
New Orleans Commercial Bulletin*, January 24, 1861; H. C. Clark, *Diary of the
War for Separation* (Augusta: Press of
the Chronicle and Sentinel, 1862), p.
158; *The Constitutional*, January 19 and
25, 1861. On February 22, 1861, in his
last public address in New Orleans,
Benjamin said: "I speak, gentlemen, in
the belief that our independence is not
to be maintained without the shedding
of blood. I know that the conviction is
not shared by others. Heaven grant
that I may prove mistaken. Yet fear-

ful as is the ordeal, and much as war
is to be deplored it is not the unmixed
evil which many consider it to be." *The
Daily True Delta*, February 24, 1861;
Pierce Butler, *op. cit.*, p. 226.

[37] *Acts of the Legislature of 1861*, pp.
10, 113, 129, 196. Harmony prevailed
again at this regular session, as it had
at the special three-day session that had
opened on December 10. If there was at
any time a spirit of Unionism in this
body, it did not manifest itself.

[38] *The New Orleans Times*, January
26, 1864. Taylor, who was a member
of this convention from St. Charles parish and chairman of the Military and
Defense Committee, makes the mistake
of stating that it met in March. He was,
of course, writing twenty years later,
doubtless from memory. He states furthermore that war was not contemplated
by that body, although he was certain
that war would come, and urged the
"necessity for preparation." Taylor, *op.
cit.*, pp. 12-13.

[39] *The New Orleans Commercial Bulletin*, January 24, 1861; The *New Orleans Daily Crescent*, January 24, 25,
26, 28, 1861; Chambers, *op. cit.*, I,
627; Taylor, *op. cit.*, p. 12; *Journal of
the Proceedings of the Convention of the
State of Louisiana* (New Orleans: J. O.
Nixon, State Printer, 1861), pp. 1, 5,
8. This will be cited hereafter as *Convention Journal*.

[40] Dumond, *The Secession Movement*,
p. 208; *The New Orleans Commercial
Bulletin*, January 26, 1861; *Convention
Journal*, pp. 5, 12, 20; Chambers, *op.
cit.*, I, 627; C. C. Wheaton, "The Secession Movement of Louisiana, January
26, 1861," *Proceedings of the Historical
Society of East and West Baton Rouge*,
VIII (1917-1918), p. 59. Both men were
received with marked enthusiasm.

[41] *The Daily Delta*, January 26, 1861;
Convention Journal, p. 15; *The New
Orleans Daily Crescent*, January 25, 26,
1861; Pierce Butler, *op. cit.*, p. 214.

[42] *Congressional Globe*, 36 Cong., 2
sess., pp. 720, 751; "Louisiana," *Annual
Cyclopaedia, 1861*, pp. 428-29; *Con-

vention *Journal*, p. 10; *The New Orleans Daily Crescent*, January 24, 1861; *The Constitutional*, January 25, 1861; *The Sugar Planter*, January 26, 1861; *The New Orleans Price Current*, February 6, 1861; E. A. Pollard, *Echoes from the South* (New York: E. B. Treat and Company, 1866), pp. 57-58.

[43] *Convention Journal*, pp. 10-11; *The New Orleans Commercial Bulletin*, January 26, 1861; *The New Orleans Daily Crescent*, January 25, 1861. L. C. Kendall, "The Interregnum in Louisiana in 1861," *The Louisiana Historical Quarterly*, XVI (1933), pp. 392-94.

[44] *Convention Journal*, pp. 15-16; *The New Orleans Daily Crescent*, January 25, 1861; C. C. Wheaton, "The Secession of Louisiana, January 26, 1861," *Proceedings of the Historical Society of East and West Baton Rouge*, VII (1917-1918), p. 58.

[45] *Convention Journal*, pp. 11, 16. *The New Orleans Daily Crescent*, January 25, 26, 1861; J. H. Greer, "Louisiana Politics, 1845-1861," *The Louisiana Historical Quarterly*, VIII (1930), p. 648.

[46] *The New Orleans Commercial Bulletin*, January 28, 1861; *Convention Journal*, p. 17; *The New Orleans Daily Crescent*, January 25, 26, 1861; *The Sugar Planter*, March 23, 1861; *The Constitutional*, February 2, 1861; *The Daily Gazette and Comet*, January 23, 1861. The *Constitutional* of March 30 commented on this vote as follows: "They will not submit the constitution to the people, because there are sufficient co-operationists to vote it down."

[47] "Louisiana," *Annual Cyclopaedia, 1861*, p. 428; *The New Orleans Daily Crescent*, January 28, and February 15, 1861; *Convention Journal*, p. 18; Chambers, *op. cit.*, I, 627. Five states had already seceded. Perkins said during the debate: "Why submit it to the people when it is known that it would be unanimously agreed to? Why refer it at a time when our sister states are calling for action! action! action!" *The New Orleans Daily Crescent*, February 16, 1861.

[48] *The New Orleans Daily Crescent*,

January 28 and February 16, 1861; *Convention Journal*, pp. 231-32. The following refused to sign: Garrett, R. C. Martin, Hough, Roselius, Pierson (of Winn), Stocker, Rozier, Taliaferro, Meredith, and Lewis (of Claiborne). Mr. Taliaferro protested vigorously against separate action, and insisted that his "reasons" be written into the records. *The New Orleans Daily Crescent*, January 31, 1861; *The Sugar Planter*, February 9, 1861; Barker, *op. cit.*, p. 93.

[49] *The New Orleans Daily Crescent*, January 31 and February 4, 1861; Kendall, *op. cit.*, I, 236; Rightor, *op. cit.*, p. 152; *The Weekly Gazette and Comet*, February 2, 1861; "Louisiana," *Annual Cyclopaedia, 1861*, p. 429; *Convention Journal*, pp. 22-24; *The Sugar Planter*, February 2, 9, 1861. The *Constitutional* stated that the defeat of "those two arch-tricksters and traitors, Slidell and Benjamin," as candidates for representatives to the Southern Convention at Montgomery "comes as a blessing." *The Constitutional*, February 9, 1861.

[50] *The New Orleans Commercial Bulletin*, February 6, 1861; *The Sugar Planter*, March 16, 1861; "Louisiana," *Annual Cyclopaedia, 1861*, p. 429.

[51] *The New Orleans Commercial Bulletin*, February 11, 1861.

[52] Milledge L. Bonham, Jr., "The Flags of Louisiana," *The Louisiana Historical Quarterly*, II (1919), pp. 443-44; *The Weekly Delta*, February 16, 1861; *The New Orleans Commercial Bulletin*, February 12, 1861; *The Constitutional*, February 16, 1861; *The New Orleans Daily Crescent*, January 28 and February 12, 1861; *The Sugar Planter*, February 2, 1861; Chambers, *op. cit.*, I, 627; Fortier, *op. cit.*, IV, 4; *Convention Journal*, p. 257; *Report of the Secretary of State*, May 1902, pp. 114-15. Louisiana was a free and independent nation from January 25 to March 21, 1861. L. C. Kendall, "The Interregnum in Louisiana in 1861," *The Louisiana Historical Quarterly*, XVI (1933), p. 175.

[53] *Congressional Globe*, 36 Cong., 2 sess., pp. 720-22, 754; *The Constitutional*, Feb-

ruary 5 and March 9, 1861; Pierce Butler, *op. cit.*, p. 218. Bouligny, who stated
that he had been "elected as an American
Union man," did not resign. On the contrary, he made a "Union speech" that
brought great applause in the galleries
and on the floor. *Congressional Globe,*
36 Cong., 2 sess., p. 754; *The New Orleans Daily Crescent,* February 11, 1861;
The Sugar Planter, February 16, 1861.

[54] *The Daily Delta,* February 12, 1861;
Pierce Butler, *op. cit.*, pp. 218-19; Sears,
op. cit., pp. 174-75; *Congressional Globe,*
36 Cong., 2 sess., pp. 720-21; *The Constitutional,* February 9, 1861; *The New
Orleans Daily Crescent,* February 11,
1861; *The Sugar Planter,* February 16
and March 9, 1861; James G. Blaine,
Twenty Years in Congress, 1861-1881
(Norwich, Conn.: The Henry Bill Publishing Co., 1886), I, 249.

[55] *Congressional Globe,* 36 Cong., 2
sess., pp. 721-22; *The Constitutional,*
February 9, 1861; *The New Orleans
Daily Crescent,* February 11, 1861; *The
Sugar Planter,* February 16 and March
9, 1861; Pierce Butler, *op. cit.*, pp. 220-
23; Sears, *op. cit.*, pp. 177-78. Italics
are Benjamin's. Sears states that "Slidell
had so completely identified himself with
Louisiana that there could be no question of his action when secession was
determined upon." But he did not regard
him "as a fire-eater, or, in any sense, a
rabid secessionist." In 1850 "his section
was decidedly in advance of him in this
respect." In 1853 he was mentioned as a
member of Pierce's cabinet because he
was a good "Union man," and he supported Buchanan because he desired "to
elect a moderate who should conciliate
antagonistic interests." This biographer
concludes that "all the outstanding features of his career, therefore, point to
Slidell as a follower rather than a leader
in secession." Furthermore he was both
old and rich, which alike must have
counseled conservatism. His expressions
certainly did not take on a menacing
character until after Lincoln's election.
Another biographer concludes that "Slidell was not a leader, but when secession
was decided upon" he "cast in his lot

with the South." Beckles Wilson, *John
Slidell and the Confederates in Paris,
1862-65* (New York: Minton, Balch,
and Company, 1932), p. 19.

[56] *The New Orleans Commercial Bulletin,* March 8, 1861; *The Sugar Planter,*
February 7, 1861.

[57] *The New Orleans Daily Crescent,*
January 18, 21, 1861; *The Daily Delta,*
January 18, 1861. Some scattering returns
were sent to the New Orleans papers
shortly after the election. Such returns
have been misinterpreted in many instances. For example St. James parish
cast seventy-three votes for immediate
secession, and five hundred and nine for
co-operation, which was, of course, only
another way to secede. One writer makes
the error of stating that this parish "cast
seventy-three for secession and five hundred and nine votes against it." Warmoth, *op. cit.*, p. 36. An eminent Louisiana historian makes the statement that
the "majority in favor of secession in
the State was only about 400." Fortier,
op. cit., IV, 3. The writer does not concur
in this conclusion. The issue was "immediate" or "co-operative" secession.

[58] *The Daily Picayune,* February 17,
1861; *The Daily Gazette and Comet,*
February 23, 1861.

[59] *The Daily Delta,* March 2, 1861;
The Daily Gazette and Comet, February
23, 1861.

[60] *The New Orleans Daily Crescent,*
March 18, 1861; *Convention Journal,* p.
16; *The Weekly Gazette and Comet,*
March 20, 1861.

[61] *The Daily Delta,* March 27, 1861.
The vote was given at this place, but
some one had clipped it from the copy
of the paper to which the author had
access. However, at least one other paper
[*The Weekly Delta* of January 18, 1861]
gave a parish by parish vote. It gave
the totals as follows: Secession, 20,448;
co-operationists, 17,296. This, and other
contemporary evidence, would seem to
warrant the substantial majority that
was claimed. The *Baton Rouge Advocate*
commented on the *Daily Delta's* figures,
and seems to have accepted its statistics
as correct. But the editor of the *Gazette*

and Comet said: "We refer to the figures of the *Delta* merely to set the Parish of East Baton Rouge right in the eyes of the people who love the truth for its own sake. The *Delta* sums up a majority in favor of secession—and against submission as it is pleased to call it—of 3,372 votes. Singularly enough it leaves East Baton Rouge out of the table. Eleven hundred and fifty-six votes were cast in this parish, of which eight hundred and sixty were cast for the co-operative ticket, giving the highest secessionist only two hundred and ninety-two votes. This is the fact from the official figures. In West Baton Rouge, where the *Delta* is pleased to say 227 votes were cast for secession and 550 for co-operation, the vote stood thus: Pope, co-operationist 263, Robertson, secessionist 57. There were other errors." *The Daily Gazette and Comet*, March 28, 1861. *The Sugar Planter* of March 30 corroborates this statement.

[62] *The Daily Delta*, April 4, 1861. This information was taken from the *Baton Rouge Advocate* by the *Delta*.

[63] Warmoth, *op. cit.*, p. 35; "Louisiana," *Annual Cyclopaedia, 1861*, p. 431.

[64] *The Daily Picayune*, March 29, 1861.

[65] *The Daily Delta*, March 30, 1861; *The Sugar Planter*, May 4, 1861.

[66] *The Daily Delta*, April 4, 1861. This paper made a specialty of copying editorials in the Northern press that were hostile to the action of the Louisiana convention.

[67] *Ibid.*, April 6, 1861. The New Orleans press, with the exception of the *Picayune*, carried full reports of these alleged "misrepresentations" by the press in the North. *The Constitutional* and *The Sugar Planter* also contended that the convention usurped powers never delegated to it directly or indirectly when it refused to submit the constitution to popular vote. *The Constitutional*, March 30, 1861; *The Sugar Planter*, March 31, 1861.

[68] *The New Orleans Daily Crescent*, April 11, 1861. It was even asserted among the Northern journals that the anti-secessionists had a majority of three

hundred. The co-operationists were unfortunately designated by immediate secessionists as "anti-secessionists," and this opinion naturally gained currency in the North.

[69] *The Daily Delta*, April 6, 1861. The *Delta* was a strong advocate of immediate secession.

[70] Denman, *op. cit., passim;* Shanks, *op. cit., passim; The Sugar Planter*, April 6, 1861; *The New Orleans Daily Crescent*, April 11, 1861; Walter L. Fleming, *Civil War and Reconstruction in Alabama* (New York: Columbia University Press, 1905), *passim.*

[71] *The Daily Delta*, April 4, 1861; *The Sugar Planter*, February 2, 1861; *The New Orleans Daily Crescent*, March 27, 1861. The day after the convention adjourned the editor of the *Crescent* commented: "The convention itself was composed of the leading citizens of the state—men eminent for their talents, their virtues and courage, and representative of the wealth of the state as well as its intelligence."

[72] *The Daily Delta*, June 16, 1861; *The New Orleans Daily Crescent*, March 5, 1861; *The Sugar Planter*, March 9, and May 4, 28, 1861; *The New Orleans Bee*, March 4, 1861; *The Constitutional*, March 9, 16, April 27, May 4, 25, and June 1, 1861; *The Daily Gazette and Comet*, April 18, 1861; *The Patriot*, June 15, September 7, 21, and October 5, 1861.

[73] A. B. Booth, "Louisiana Confederate Military Records," *The Louisiana Historical Quarterly*, IV (1921), pp. 379-411; *The New Orleans Daily Crescent*, July 20, 1861. The editor of the *Constitutional*, a co-operationist, reveals the predominating sentiment at this time in Louisiana and elsewhere in the South when he says: "The Southern states are united as a union of slave states. They are united, there is but one voice in the land, one purpose, one heart, and one destiny." *The Constitutional*, April 27, 1861.

[74] *Eighth Census of the United States:* "Population of the United States," p. 194; *The Constitutional*, March 2, 1861; *The New Orleans Price Current*, March

2, 1861; *The New Orleans Times,* January 31, 1865.

[75] *The Daily Delta,* July 14, 1861; *The Patriot,* August 31, 1861; *The Daily Gazette and Comet,* March 5, 1862; Chambers, *op. cit.,* I, 631; Grace King and John R. Ficklen, *A History of Louisiana* (New York: University Publishing Company, 1897), p. 214; Rightor, *op. cit.,* pp. 159-63; *Report of the Secretary of State,* May, 1902, *op. cit.,* pp. 674-75.

[76] *The Daily Delta,* April 30, 1861; Rightor, *op. cit.,* pp. 152-53; Fortier, *op. cit.,* IV, 7; *The Daily Gazette and Comet,* April 27 and May 11, 1861; *The New Orleans Daily Crescent,* April 29, 1861; *The Sugar Planter,* April 27, 1861; N. Bartlett, *A Soldier's Story of the War* (New Orleans: Clark and Hofeline, 1874), pp. 16-17. Even the negroes became infected with the military spirit, and "fifteen hundred colored men enrolled themselves in volunteer companies in New Orleans for active service." *The Sugar Planter,* April 27, 1861.

[77] *The Daily Delta,* November 24, 1861; *The Daily Picayune,* November 23, 1861; *The Sunday Delta,* November 24, 1861; Rightor, *op. cit.,* p. 154. Fortier states that "Louisiana responded with alacrity for troops." Fortier, *op. cit.,* IV, 6.

[78] *The Daily Delta,* April 17, October 16, November 9, 26, and December 15, 1861, and March 20, 1862; Fortier, *op. cit.,* IV, 10; *The New Orleans Daily Crescent,* February 12 and March 30, 1861; *The New York Daily Tribune,* January 29 and February 7, 8, 1862. A large Federal fleet soon appeared near the mouth of the river, and a large army was stationed on Ship Island, from which the commanding general issued a proclamation "to the loyal citizens of the Southwest." *The New Orleans Daily Crescent,* October 5 and November 25, 1861; *The Daily Picayune,* December 27, 1861.

[79] *The Daily Delta,* October 30, 1861; *The Daily Gazette and Comet,* July 27, 1861; *The New Orleans Daily Crescent,* April 11, 1861.

[80] *The New Orleans Daily Crescent,* February 14, 1862; Sarah A. Dorsey, *Recollections of Henry Watkins Allen* (New York: M. Doolady, 1866); *The Daily Gazette and Comet,* May 16, 1861; *The Daily Picayune,* September 20, 1861; *The Daily Delta,* April 12, 1862. Dorsey says that "the apparent negligence and indifference of the authorities at Richmond, in regard to New Orleans, was most culpable and most inexplicable."

[81] *The Daily Delta,* November 3, 29, 1861; Fortier, *op. cit.,* IV, 8; *The Daily Gazette and Comet,* April 27 and May 16, 1861; *The Daily Picayune,* September 18, 20, and November 29, 30, 1861; *The Sugar Planter,* October 5, 26, and November 2, 1861; Kendall, *op. cit.,* I, 248.

[82] *The New Orleans Daily Crescent,* January 10, 1862; *The Daily Delta,* February 28, and April 1, 2, 4, 27, 1862; T. A. Bland, *Life of Benjamin F. Butler* (Boston: Lee and Shepard, Publishers, 1879), p. 68; R. E. McHatton, *From Flag to Flag* (New York: D. Appleton and Company, 1889), p. 16; *The Sugar Planter* of April 27 had expressed its confidence in the city defenses as follows: "Let them come. If old Abe's followers are so demented as to attempt an invasion of the South by means of the Mississippi River, they will receive such a reception as will take kinks out of their conceit. But the joke is too good. We can't believe it."

[83] Grace King, *New Orleans, The Place and the People* (New York: The Macmillan Company, 1907), p. 300; *The Daily Picayune,* April 15, 26, 27, 29, 30, 1862; Julius Chambers, *The Mississippi River* (New York: G. P. Putnam's Sons, 1910), pp. 265-68; Fortier, *op. cit.,* IV, 19; Dorsey, *op. cit.,* pp. 109-13; *The New York Herald,* April 26 and 28, and May 2, 1862; *The Daily Delta,* May 2, 1862; G. G. Smith, *Leaves from a Soldier's Diary* (New York: G. P. Putnam's Sons, 1906), pp. 16-17; Chambers, *op. cit.,* I, 634; McMaster, *op. cit.,* pp. 206-07; Bland, *op. cit.,* pp. 67, 70, and 71; King and Ficklen, *op. cit.,* pp. 216-17. The official report of the capture of

New Orleans appeared some weeks later. *The Daily Picayune,* August 6, 1862; *The New York Herald,* July 28, 1862.

[84] *The Daily Delta,* May 1, 10, 14, and 15, 1862; Dorsey, *op. cit.,* pp. 104-05; *The Daily Picayune,* May 1, 2, 1862. General Lovell gave before a court of inquiry the reasons for the evacuation of New Orleans. *The New Orleans Times,* May 18, 23, 1864.

[85] G. W. Smith, *Confederate War Papers* (New York: Atlantic Publishing and Engraving Company, 1884), pp. 65-66, 87, 125, 135; Harriet Magruder, *History of Louisiana* (Boston: D. C. Heath and Company, 1909), p. 299; *The Daily Delta,* April 30, 1862; Dorsey, *op. cit.,* pp. 89-96; King and Ficklen, *op. cit.,* p. 215; R. B. Irwin, *History of the Nineteenth Army Corps* (New York: G. P. Putnam's Sons, 1892), pp. 10-11. The consensus in New Orleans seems to have been that Mr. Mallory's inattention was gross and inexcusable; criminations and recriminations followed between the press of New Orleans and that of Richmond when the latter intimated that the city had been surrendered because of the cowardice and infidelity of the citizens. The New Orleans press declared such charges to be false, calumnious, and infamous. *The Daily Delta,* May 15, 1862.

CHAPTER III

[1] *The New Orleans Daily Crescent,* May 2, 1862; *The Daily Delta,* May 2, 3, 16, 1862; *The Daily Picayune,* May 2, 3, 6, 1862; Bland, *op. cit.,* pp. 76, 80; McMaster, *op. cit.,* p. 207; Benjamin F. Butler, *Butler's Book: Autobiography and Personal Reminiscences* (Boston: A. M. Thayer and Co., 1892), p. 377. This will be referred to hereafter as *Butler's Book.* James Parton, *General Butler in New Orleans* (New York: Mason Brothers, 1864), pp. 283, 435. Parton states that the crowd did abuse the General, crying out: "Where is the d—d rascal?" "There he goes, G—d d—n him!" "I see the d—d old villain!" Parton, *op. cit.,* p. 281.

[2] *The Daily Delta,* June 5, 1862; *The Louisiana Democrat,* September 13, 1865; Chambers, *op. cit.,* I, 635; W. O. Hart, "The New Orleans Times and The New Orleans Democrat," *The Louisiana Historical Quarterly,* VIII (1925), p. 574; *Butler's Correspondence,* I, 476, 486.

[3] *The Daily Delta,* May 5, 6, 1862; Parton, *op. cit.,* p. 294; *The New York Herald,* June 4, 1864; McMaster, *op. cit.,* p. 207; Marion Southwood, *Beauty and Booty: The Watchword of New Orleans* (New York: M. Doolady, 1867), p. 56. Southwood kept a diary and scrapbook of this period.

[4] *The New Orleans Sunday Delta,* May 4, 1862; Parton, *op. cit.,* pp. 292-95; *Butler's Book,* p. 379-82; *The Daily Picayune,* May 4, 1862; *The New York Herald,* May 14, 1862; Bland, *op. cit.,* pp. 76-80; Barker, *op. cit.,* pp. 116-22; McMaster, *op. cit.,* p. 207; Kendall, *op. cit.,* I, 275; General B. F. Butler, *Department of the Gulf; General Orders, 1862* (New Orleans: E. R. Wagner, Publisher, 1862), pp. 4, 5. This will be cited hereafter as Butler, *General Orders.*

[5] *The Daily Delta,* May 3, 6, 7, 1862; *The Daily Picayune,* May 7, 1862; *The Weekly Gazette and Comet,* May 17, 1862; Parton, *op. cit.,* p. 295. The military governor, Major General George A. Shepley, was not appointed until several weeks later. *The Daily True Delta,* June 25, 26, 1862.

[6] Butler, *General Orders,* 7 and 8; Kendall, *op. cit.,* I, 277; *The Daily Delta,* May 3, 1862; Southwood, *op. cit.,* pp. 82-83; Parton, *op. cit.,* pp. 305-06; Bland, *op. cit.,* p. 87. Governor Moore, in his "Address to the People of New Orleans," said of this proclamation: "He basely attempts to state that the authorities have not done their duty. . . . General Butler's attempt to excite the poor against the more wealthy is characteristic of the man, and is as mean as it is contemptible. . . . As to the seizing of a lot of beef . . . a clever trick . . . and distributing it among those unable to get it . . . he would never have given it to them had he required it for his own troops, and not been afraid to use it."

Butler's Correspondence, II, 459-63.

[7] Southwood, *op. cit.*, pp. 78-79; *The New Orleans Daily Crescent*, May 14, 1862; *The Daily Delta*, May 13, 1862; *The Daily Picayune*, September 18, 1861; Kendall, *op. cit.*, I, 242; Rightor, *op. cit.*, pp. 153-54.

[8] *The Daily Delta*, May 31, 1862; Parton, *op. cit.*, p. 306; *The Daily Picayune*, July 2, 13, 16, 1862.

[9] *The Daily Delta*, August 1, 1862; *The New York Herald*, May 26, 1862.

[10] *The Daily Delta*, October 16, 1862; *Butler's Correspondence*, II, 448; Bland, *op. cit.*, p. 108; King and Ficklen, *op. cit.*, p. 219; *The Daily Picayune*, September 5, and October 15, 31, 1862; *The Daily True Delta*, October 5, 1862. This "relief" burden became so great that Butler was forced to issue an order that no relief would be granted to a family "that has a male member between eighteen and forty-five, who is either employed in daily regular employment, or is an enlisted soldier in the United States Army." *The Daily Picayune*, October 24, 1862.

[11] *The Daily Delta*, August 27, 1864; Parton, *op. cit.*, p. 599; G. W. Cable, *Creoles of Louisiana* (New York: Charles Scribner's Sons, 1901), pp. 305-06; *The Daily True Delta*, September 20, 1862; Chambers, *op. cit.*, I, 640; Bland, *op. cit.*, p. 88; Kendall, *op. cit.*, I, 286. Parton states that only one case was reported during 1862. Butler, who seems to have had grave apprehensions said: "I had learned that the rebels were actually relying upon yellow fever to clear out the Northern troops." *Butler's Book*, *op. cit.*, p. 396. It was generally expected that an epidemic would commence in August, and that at least 10 per cent of the army would die. "Diary and Correspondence of Salmon P. Chase" in *Annual Report of the American Historical Association, 1902* (Washington: Government Printing Office, 1903), II, 503. Cited hereafter as *Chase Correspondence*. Southwood states: "He (Butler) was the best scavenger we ever had among us." Southwood, *op. cit.*, p. 182.

[12] *The New Orleans Daily Crescent*, May 12, 1862; *The New Orleans Bee*, May 12, 1862; Parton, *op. cit.*, pp. 378-81; Bland, *op. cit.*, p. 107; Kendall, *op. cit.*, I, 387. The Holland government did make a vigorous protest. A complete investigation followed, which caused Butler's disavowal and restitution. *Butler's Correspondence*, II, 252-55.

[13] *The Daily Delta*, June 19, 1862; Parton, *op. cit.*, pp. 454-61; *The Daily True Delta*, June 20, 1862; *The New York Herald*, June 26, 1862; Butler, *General Orders*, p. 29.

[14] Butler to Mejan, August 14, 1862, in *The Daily Delta; The New York Daily Tribune*, June 30, 1862; *The Daily Picayune*, August 3, 16, 1862; *New York Herald*, August 25, 26, 1862; *The Daily True Delta*, August 12, 1862. Butler says himself, "We have danger here of a negro insurrection. I hardly know whether to wish it. . . . " And in the next sentence he adds: "I shall arm the free Blacks." This letter is addressed to his wife and dated August 12, just two days prior to the above date. In view of this fact, this letter, which was published in *The Daily Delta*, August 16, could hardly be considered in any other light than an invitation to the "Blacks," especially since he was demanding the arms of all the whites. Butler collected 25,000 arms of various kinds. *Chase Correspondence*, II, 311.

[15] *The Daily Delta*, October 24, 1862; Parton, *op. cit.*, p. 393; *The Daily Picayune*, July 13, 1862. Parton states that the conduct of the Spanish was "still more outrageous." Parton, *op. cit.*, p. 394.

[16] *The New Orleans Daily Crescent*, May 8, 1862; *Butler's Book*, p. 521; *Butler's Correspondence*, I, 630; Butler, *General Orders*, p. 7; Kendall, *op. cit.*, I, 284.

[17] Alcéi Fortier, *Louisiana Studies* (New Orleans: F. F. Hansell and Brother, 1894), p. 221; Lloyd Paul Stryker, *Andrew Johnson, A Study in Courage* (New York: The Macmillan Company, 1930), p. 379; *The Daily Delta*, May 16, 1862; Southwood, *op. cit.*, p. 109; *The*

Daily True Delta, May 21, 1862; Chambers, *op. cit.*, I, 636-37; Bland, *op. cit.*, pp. 96-97; McMaster, *op. cit.*, pp. 208-11; Hamilton Basso, *Beauregard, The Great Creole* (New York: Charles Scribner's Sons, 1933), p. 236; Parton, *op. cit.*, p. 327. Parton asked: "Why indeed should he permit his brave and virtuous New England soldiers to be insulted by those silly, vulgar creatures, spoiled by contact with slavery?" Butler said: "The order executed itself. . . . No arrests were ever made under it, or because of it. All the ladies in New Orleans forebore to insult our troops because they didn't want to be deemed common women, and all the common women forebore to insult our troops because they wanted to be deemed ladies." *Butler's Book*, p. 419. Butler defended this "Woman Order" in a letter which was published in Northern journals. *The Daily Picayune*, July 31, 1862.

[18] *The Daily Delta*, May 26, 1862; Parton, *op. cit.*, p. 335; *Butler's Correspondence*, I, 501; Bland, *op. cit.*, p. 98; Kendall, *op. cit.*, I, 275; Rightor, *op. cit.*, p. 159.

[19] *The Daily Delta*, July 9, 1862; Parton, *op. cit.*, p. 338; *Butler's Correspondence, op. cit.*, I, 431-32; Southwood, *op. cit.*, p. 54; *The New York Daily Tribune*, June 19, 1862; *The New York Herald*, June 17, 1862; *The Daily Picayune*, July 1, 3, 6, September 11, and December 9, 1862; Bland, *op. cit.*, p. 73. The first charge against Soulé was that he was the leader of a secret society known as the "Southern Independent Association," of which each member was solemnly sworn to oppose at the cost of his life, if necessary, the reconstruction of the union. The second charge was that Mr. Soulé was the author of the letter sent by the late mayor of New Orleans to Farragut, and that he was the principal supporter of the war in that city. *The Daily Picayune*, July 6, 1862.

[20] Dostie, *op. cit.*, p. 55; *The Daily Picayune*, December 18, 1862. This issue contains the correspondence between Butler and the ministers. *The New York Herald*, October 25, 1862; Parton, *op.*

cit., p. 484. They were permitted to return to New Orleans. Banks required the oath of them, and upon their refusal they were again committed to prison.

[21] *The Daily Delta*, August 17, 1862; Parton, *op. cit.*, p. 435. The "flag mania" offense was the most common, and many women were sentenced because they persisted in displaying Confederate flags. *The Daily Picayune*, July 19, 1862.

[22] *The Daily Delta*, November 29, 1862; Parton, *op. cit.*, p. 435.

[23] *The Daily Delta*, November 4, 1862; Parton, *op. cit.*, p. 436.

[24] *The Daily Delta*, August 6, 1862; *The Daily True Delta*, August 6, 1862; *The Daily Picayune*, August 15 and December 11, 1862; *The New Orleans Daily Crescent*, July 23, 1861; *The New Orleans Price Current*, August 17, 24, 1861; *The Daily Gazette and Comet*, July 24, 1861; *Butler's Book*, pp. 436-37. Butler was relieved by Banks six days after the second assessment, and as the assessment was to be paid on the seventh day, he alleges that "nobody paid it." He further states that Banks found himself under the necessity of renewing the order, but that "nobody paid anything." The evidence shows that Banks made a similar assessment in October, 1864, and it appears that it was paid. *The Daily True Delta* October 12, 1864; *The New Orleans Times*, October 12, 1864.

[25] Warmoth, *op. cit.*, p. 34; King and Ficklen, *op. cit.*, p. 319; *The Sunday Delta*, June 8, 1862; *Butler's Book*, pp. 438-43; Bland, *op. cit.*, p. 104; Stryker, *op. cit.*, p. 378. Butler contends that the flag had been placed on the mint by Farragut when he took possession of the city, and therefore, justified the hanging. *The Daily Delta*, July 31, 1862; Parton, *op. cit.*, p. 434.

[26] *The Daily Delta*, July 31, 1862; Parton, *op. cit.*, p. 434.

[27] *The Daily Delta*, June 5, 1862; Parton, *op. cit.*, p. 349; Bland, *op. cit.*, p. 103.

[28] *The Daily Delta*, July 11, 1862. This order was evidently repealed shortly afterwards as a matter of expediency.

[29] *The Sunday Delta*, June 8, 1862; *Butler's Book*, pp. 449-53. Butler had an efficient spy system. "The negroes all

[248]

came," he boasted, "and told me anything. . . . They received from my hands
some small compensation." Parton, *op.
cit.*, p. 423.

[30] *The Daily Delta,* June 14, 1862;
Parton, *op. cit.,* p. 423.

[31] James Schouler, *History of the
United States Under the Constitution*
(New York: Dodd Mead and Co., 1894-
99), VI, 259; Southwood, *op. cit.,* pp.
145-52.

[32] *The Daily Delta,* July 22, 1862; *The
Daily Picayune,* July 17, 24, and December 16, 1862; *The New York Herald,*
August 3, 1862; *The Daily True Delta,*
August 6, 1862; Parton, *op. cit.,* pp. 492-
95. Butler did not free all that came into
his possession, for he later published
lists of runaway slaves and those he had
for safekeeping, and called upon their
owners to pay charges, or they would be
released. He also advised that "safekeeping charges" must, in the future, be
prepaid. *The Daily Picayune,* July 15
and November 22, 1862; Butler, *General
Orders,* p. 33.

[33] *The Daily Delta,* July 30, 1862; *The
Daily Picayune,* July 26, 1862; Chambers, *op. cit.,* I, 636; McMaster, *op. cit.,*
pp. 244-45; Parton, *op cit.,* pp. 516-18.
Butler repeatedly called for re-enforce-
ments. When he received none, he "called
on Africa." He seems to have enrolled
free colored men at first.

[34] *The Daily Delta,* September 5, 1862;
Parton, *op. cit.,* p. 518. Public opinion
seems to have been divided in the city
in regard to arming the negroes. Dennison was enthusiastic. He wrote: "They
learn more quickly than white soldiers,
and will certainly fight." *Chase Correspondence,* II, 319.

[35] *The Daily Picayune,* July 30, August
27, and October 23, 1862; *The Daily
Delta,* August 27, 1862. There was friction in Butler's own camp between the
regulars and the negroes. His own
soldiers appeared to object to the rights
of the negroes to wear the Federal uniform.

[36] *The Daily Picayune,* August 27,
1862; *Butler's Book,* p. 489; *The New
York Herald,* August 13, 1862. Butler

reminded him that a recent act of Congress authorized a commander to employ
"the African to do the necessary work
about a camp or upon a fortification."

[37] *The Daily Delta,* September 12,
1862; Parton, *op. cit.,* p. 514; *Butler's
Correspondence,* II, 287; Barker, *op. cit.,*
p. 141.

[38] *The Daily Picayune,* July 17, and
September 4, 5, 8, 1862; *The New York
Herald,* August 13, 1862; Southwood, *op.
cit.,* p. 132.

[39] *The Daily Delta,* November 9, 1862.
The negroes regarded him as a deliverer
and friend, and he freely fraternized with
them. It is reported that a colored orator
on one of these occasions thought to
eulogize him by proposing the following
toast: "Here's to General Butler. He has
a white face, and a black heart." Samuel
S. Cox, *Three Decades of Federal Legislation, 1855-1885* (Washington, D.C.:
J. M. Stoddard and Company, 1885),
p. 425.

[40] *The Daily Delta,* September 24,
1862; *The Daily True Delta,* October
12, 1862; *The Daily Picayune,* September 24, 1862.

[41] *The Daily Picayune,* December 19,
1862; *Butler's Book,* p. 531. He said
that he turned over to Banks a sum
"amounting to nearly a million dollars."

[42] *The Daily Picayune,* May 27, 1863;
The Daily True Delta, August 23, 24,
and September 16, 1862. Butler was said
to have forced them to register, and
then freed their slaves by enforcing their
own laws.

[43] Parton, *op. cit.,* p. 449. A spirit of
defeatism evidently obtained at this time
because of so many reverses and disasters. This should have aided Butler in
effecting his restoration program. *The
Daily Delta,* March 7, 11, 1862; *The
Daily Picayune,* February 11, 12, March
25, and April 8, 18, 1862; *The Daily
Gazette and Comet,* April 11, 12, 1862.

[44] *The Daily Delta,* May 29, 1862;
Butler's Correspondence, pp. 136-38.

[45] *The Daily True Delta,* June 5, 7,
1862; *The Daily Delta,* June 7, 1862;
Parton, *op. cit.,* pp. 431-32; *The New
York Herald,* June 20, 1862.

[46] *The Daily Delta*, June 7, 1862; Parton, *op. cit.*, p. 432; *The Daily Delta*, June 7, 1862; *The Daily True Delta*, July 13, 1862.

[47] *The Daily Delta*, July 4, 31, 1862, and August 20, 1862; *The Daily Picayune*, August 22 and September 27, 1862; Dostie, *op. cit.*, p. 41.

[48] *The Daily Delta*, September 6, 1862; *The Daily Picayune*, September 19 and November 18, 1862; *The Daily True Delta*, November 16, 1862. There was a great similarity in all speeches.

[49] *The Daily Delta*, July 13, 1862. "Address of the Union Association of New Orleans," *The Daily Picayune*, November 18, 1862.

[50] *The Daily Delta*, October 23, 1862. According to the *Picayune*, the first "Union Meeting" of the colored people was held on September 2. This journal reported, on September 3, that "a union meeting was held last evening by colored men in a building on Roman Street, between Bienville and Customhouse streets, the manager having a permit from Col. Stafford."

[51] *The Daily Delta*, August 22, 1862.

[52] *Ibid.*, September 6, 1862. There was a considerable element of both Germans and Irish in New Orleans and its vicinity. The Germans printed a daily in their own language.

[53] *The Daily Picayune*, May 21, 1865; *Butler's Correspondence*, pp. 136-37; Abraham Lincoln, *Complete Works*, Edited by John J. Nicolay and John Hay (New York: The Century Company, 1907), I, 235. This will be cited hereafter as *Lincoln's Works*. The letter was not published until after the war ended.

[54] *The Sunday Delta*, June 15, 1862; Parton, *op. cit.*, p. 450; *The Daily True Delta*, June 17, 1862; Bland, *op. cit.*, p. 125; Butler, *General Orders*, pp. 13-15.

[55] *The Daily Delta*, July 29, 1862; Parton, *op. cit.*, p. 451; Bland, *op. cit.*, p. 125. According to a statement that was published in the *Picayune*, no one could secure the aid of the courts without taking the oath. *The Daily Picayune*, July 20, 1862.

[56] *The Daily Delta*, September 6, 1862; *The Daily Picayune*, September 23, 24, 25, and 30, 1862. Parton does not mention this, but possibly includes it in his statement that "60,000" of the inhabitants took the oath. Parton, *op. cit.* p. 474.

[57] *The Daily Delta*, August 7, 1862; Parton, *op. cit.*, p. 474; *The New York Herald*, October 2, 1862; *The New York Daily Tribune*, June 30, 1862.

[58] *The Daily Delta*, September 6, 1862; Parton, *op. cit.*, pp. 473-74.

[59] *The Daily Picayune*, September 24, 1862. Butler is silent on this. However, they must have subscribed to it before enrollment in the army.

[60] *The Daily Delta*, October 23, 1862; Parton gave 60,000; *op. cit.*, p. 474; *The Daily True Delta*, October 23, 1862.

[61] *The Daily Picayune*, October 5, 1862. Butler did not allow the clergy to remain neutral. He charged that they were industrious in disseminating secession sentiments. W. N. Mercer, a prominent citizen, who also requested that he be allowed to remain neutral, was directed to take it or register as an enemy. *The Daily Delta*, September 28 and October 5, 1862. Butler wrote him: "He that is not for us is against us." *Butler's Correspondence*, II, 332.

[62] Southwood, *op. cit.*, p. 136; *The Daily Picayune*, October 24, 1862. They took the oath in order to secure food and protection from violence, to save their property, and later to vote for a congressman.

[63] *The Daily Picayune*, June 28, 1862; *Butler's Correspondence*, II, 2, 3, 4.

[64] *The Daily Picayune*, July 17, 1862; Southwood, *op. cit.*, p. 183. According to the advertisements, there were extensive sales of household effects. The following is typical of what was taking place almost daily: "Complete furniture of thirteen well furnished houses, all to be sold." *The Daily Picayune*, August 23, 1862. Southwood says: "All property was confiscated. It was pitiable to see the most elegant houses stripped of their furniture and surroundings, given to the lowest sort of humanity. Some houses were taken as a 'military necessity,' and

such havoc and destruction never was seen; furniture broken; pianos taken to pieces, to look for concealed arms; bedsteads and other furniture packed up and sent North; large mirrors placed between beds and packed for colder climes; everything stolen." Another writer states that Butler robbed the homes. Caroline E. Merrick, *Old Times in Dixie Land* (New York: The Gafton Press, 1901), p. 31.

[65] *Butler's Book*, p. 518; *The New Orleans Daily Crescent*, August 7, 1861; *The New Orleans Price Current.* August 7, 17, 1861.

[66] *Butler's Book*, pp. 518-19, 520-21; Parton, *op. cit.*, p. 467; *The New Orleans Price Current*, June 22, 1861; *The Daily Delta*, February 22 and March 2, 1862.

[67] *The Daily Delta*, July 29, 1862; *Butler's Book*, p. 521; *The Daily True Delta*, July 31, 1862; Barker, *op. cit.*, pp. 128-31.

[68] *The Daily Delta*, July 2, 1862; *The Daily Picayune*, August 24, 1862; King, *op. cit.*, pp. 312-13. Butler's Order No. 87 later provided that "all persons sixteen years and up, coming within the lines will be held as spies, unless they take the oath of allegiance." *The Daily Delta*, November 5, 1862.

[69] *The Daily Delta*, September 26, 1862; *The Daily True Delta*, September 17, 26, 1862; *Butler's Correspondence*, II, 316; *The New York Herald*, October 4, 1862.

[70] *The Daily Delta*, December 6, 1862; Parton, *op. cit.*, pp. 473-74; *The Daily Picayune*, December 7, 16, 17, 1862; King, *op. cit.*, pp. 311-12.

[71] Southwood, *op. cit.*, p. 159; Parton, *op. cit.*, pp. 481-82; *The Daily True Delta*, September 21, 1862. When an Episcopal minister remonstrated with Butler, and sought its abandonment on the grounds that many were perjuring themselves, Butler refused.

[72] "Louisiana," *Annual Cyclopaedia, 1862*, p. 515; *The Daily Picayune*, August 9, 1862. The confiscated property was sold at auction, as the law provided, and, according to the advertisements in the *Picayune*, "household furniture of every description" was sold almost daily.

[73] *The Daily Delta*, October 26, 1862; *Butler's Correspondence*, II, 87, 315; Parton, *op. cit.*, p. 445. The robberies occurred when the homes were searched for arms. Butler did execute four of these "robbers." Parton, *op. cit.*, p. 448.

[74] *The Daily Delta*, November 11, 1862; *The Daily True Delta*, November 11, 1862; *The Daily Picayune*, November 13, and December 17, 18, 1862; *The New York Daily Tribune*, August 26, 1862. Butler had previously ordered that all arms of whatever description should be turned in. This was applicable to Unionists. Failure to do so made the offender liable to imprisonment and hard labor. *The Daily Delta*, August 31, 1862.

[75] *Butler's Book*, p. 522; Parton, *op. cit.*, p. 411. If Banks received this, he should have mentioned it in some of his reports. He never mentioned it. *Butler's Book*, p. 522; *Butler's Correspondence*, II, 318: It would seem to indicate that Butler had "caught the fever of speculation." His officers were speculating almost to the point of the demoralization of the army. Parton, *op. cit.*, p. 581.

[76] "Louisiana," *Annual Cyclopaedia, 1865*, p. 515.

[77] *Ibid.*, p. 516.

[78] *Chase Correspondence*, II, 297; *Lincoln's Works*, II, 217-18; Barker, *op. cit.*, p. 158. He wrote other letters at this time advocating restoration. McCarthy, *op. cit.*, p. 39.

[79] *The Daily Picayune*, May 27, 1863; *Butler's Book*, p. 532.

[80] *Lincoln's Works*, II, 172.

[81] *The Sunday Delta*, August 17, 1862. Bouligny had regarded his district as Union in tendency.

[82] *The Daily Delta*, November 4, 1862; *The Daily True Delta*, October 23, 31, 1862. Another argument is frankly stated by Parton: "For Union men, there were offices, employment, privileges, favors, honors, everything which a government can bestow." Parton, *op. cit.*, p. 596.

[83] *The Daily Picayune*, November 16, December 3, 1862, and May 27, 1863; *The Daily Delta*, November 16 and December 2, 1862. By General Order No. 22, of December 2, the only required

qualifications were a proper length of time as a citizen and a certificate of loyalty to the Government.

[84] *The Daily Delta*, November 30, 1862; Parton, *op. cit.*, p. 595; *The Daily Picayune*, December 2, 1862. Dennison wrote Chase that Flanders was "a thorough Union man" and "with the Republican party." *Chase Correspondence*, II, 396.

[85] *The Daily Delta*, December 2, 1862; *Chase Correspondence*, II, 337; *The Daily Picayune*, November 24, 1862. Dennison, United States Treasury Appointee in New Orleans, writes that Cottman withdrew "his name by request (order?) of General Butler."

[86] *The Daily Delta*, December 10, 1862; Parton, *op. cit.*, p. 395. No complete returns were published. Butler and Parton do not seem to have treated this election seriously. Both devoted only a short paragraph each to the whole proceedings. Warmoth made the error of stating that Banks held this election for congressman. Warmoth, *op. cit.*, p. 34.

[87] *The Daily Delta*, December 4, 1862; *The Daily Picayune*, December 10, 11, 1862; *The New Orleans Times*, January 15, 1864. Butler says: "The army did not vote." *Butler's Book*, p. 523. There is no record that the negroes voted although a "remarkable resolution" had recently been passed unanimously by a Union Association in the city endorsing suffrage for loyal negroes. *Chase Correspondence*, II, 335; The *Picayune* gave a complete parish tabulation of the two districts. *The Daily Picayune*, December 11, 1862.

[88] *The Daily Delta*, December 10, 1862; *The Daily Picayune* of May 27, 1863, quotes Butler's testimony before the committee on the conduct of the war as follows: "In the meantime I was informed from Washington that it would be very desirable to have Congressional elections held in that part of Louisiana which was under our control. . . . New Orleans was divided into two election districts. I therefore sent an expedition under General Weitzel to Donaldsonville, and swept down through that country.

I thus got under the control of the American soldiers, nearly the two districts now represented by Mr. Flanders and Mr. Hahn. I ordered that everybody in those districts be allowed to vote . . . and everybody did vote."

[89] *The Daily Delta*, December 10, 1862; Parton, *op. cit.*, p. 595; *The Daily Picayune*, December 11, 1862; Dostie, *op. cit.*, p. 62. Parton said that both were "unconditional Union men."

[90] *Congressional Globe*, 37 Cong., 3 sess., pp. 834, 861; *The Daily Picayune*, January 17, 1863.

[91] *Congressional Globe*, 37 Cong., 3 sess., p. 1936; *The New York Herald*, September 23, 1862; Stryker, *op. cit.*, p. 108.

[92] *The Daily Delta*, September 2, 1862; *The Daily Picayune*, September 4, 5, 1862; Parton, *op. cit.* pp. 595-96. Parton says he was popular in New Orleans. Butler, however, seems to have lived in dread of the hand of the assassin. Parton, *op. cit.*, p. 592.

[93] Parton, *op. cit.*, p. 597; *Butler's Book*, p. 504. Upon confirmation of his recall the editor of the conservative *Picayune* wrote: "We have seen more smiling faces in the streets within a day or two past than for months before." *The Daily Picayune*, December 19, 1862.

[94] *Butler's Book*, pp. 524-38; *The Daily Picayune*, December 19, 1862. He blamed Seward, who "sent that secession spy and agent, Reverdy Johnson, to New Orleans." He seems to think that the authorities were moved to act for two reasons: (1) because he, like McClellan, had been up to then "a very decided Democrat," (2) because of the pressure of foreign governments, which Seward must appease at all costs. *Butler's Book*, p. 536.

[95] *The Daily True Delta*, January 17, 1863; Parton, *op. cit.*, p. 599. Parton arrived at the conclusion that the French government caused his recall. Frank L. Owsley, *King Cotton Diplomacy* (Chicago: University of Chicago Press, 1931), p. 323.

[96] *The Daily Delta*, July 6, 1862. The order was never disavowed. It seems that

Lincoln and Stanton planned to return him to New Orleans, but were subsequently dissuaded. *Butler's Book,* p. 552.

[97] *The Daily Delta,* December 31, 1862. Dennison wrote Chase: "His removal gives great satisfaction to all classes." *Chase Correspondence,* II, 441.

[98] *The Daily Delta,* December 17, 18, 1862. Butler never became reconciled to "Reverdy Johnson, the Baltimore secessionist." *Butler's Book,* p. 522.

[99] Parton, *op. cit.,* p. 411; *The New Orleans Crescent,* May 17, 1868. Dennison wrote Chase: "Unionists and secessionists think he is interested in the speculations of his brother and others. . . . He is such a smart man, that it would, in any case, be difficult to discover what he wished to conceal." *Butler's Correspondence,* II, 270-71. He wrote again: "He (Butler's brother) does a heavy business, and by various practices has made between one and two million dollars since the capture of the city. . . . Butler knows everything, controls everything, and should be held responsible for everything." He added that General Butler had given permits to trade with the enemy, and concluded: "Many officers and soldiers want to go home, not wishing to risk their lives to make fortunes for others." *Butler's Correspondence,* pp. 355-60. Dennison gives a complete report of this trade. *Chase Correspondence,* II, 319-26.

[100] *The Daily Picayune,* May 27, 1863; *Butler's Correspondence,* published in 1917, proves that he did issue permits to trade within the "rebel lines." This was "expressly forbidden," and was, in fact, supposed to be treated as treason. *Butler's Correspondence,* II, 422-23. Letter of Chase to Butler. Much revealing and damaging information had been brought to light prior to this. *The New Orleans Daily Crescent,* May 17, 1868, contains the following item: "The Washington Correspondent of the *New York Herald* has had the privilege of inspecting the report made by Messrs. Baldy Smith and Jas. F. Brady on the administration of affairs in the Department of the Gulf while under command of B. F.

Butler." The substance of this report, which Butler seems ever after to have ignored, revealed that he not only supplied the Confederates with munitions— a fact that the Confederates attested to after the war—but that he also was deeply involved in speculation ventures. It showed that Butler was almost penniless when he arrived in New Orleans, and first borrowed $5,000; that shortly afterwards, from the same source, he obtained $100,000 more; that he traded with the "rebels," and in addition to other supplies, sold salt for $30 a sack, and took cotton in payment at 10 cents per pound; and that he made tremendous profits until Farragut broke up the trade by arresting his brother, Dr. A. J. Butler, who was paroled under a $30,000 bond, and who at once fled. Butler also, in addition, according to the testimony, had taken $320,000 out of the city treasury and passed it into the hands of this brother, who had been "engaged in removing crops from plantations" in government boats that were "guarded with from twenty-five to fifty soldiers." No port charges had been made, as General Butler allowed the boats to pass in and out with sugar as ballast, which he represented to be "sand." Much sugar was thus shipped as "sand" before the port was opened in June. In another transaction, according to the same report, he forced a sale of a steamer to himself, in "current funds," and sold or transferred it for $45,000 in greenbacks to another person. He then leased the steamer for the Government at $450 per day, although it could have been leased to the Government for $40 per day before he bought it.

[101] *The Daily Picayune,* December 23, 1862; *Butler's Book,* pp. 562-63; Parton, *op. cit.,* p. 612.

[102] *The Daily Picayune,* December 17, 18, 21, 1862; Parton, *op. cit.,* pp. 600-01; *The New York Daily Tribune,* December 29, 1862; Southwood, *op. cit.,* pp. 247-49.

[103] Parton, *op. cit.,* pp. 602-03; *The Daily Picayune,* December 25, 1862; Chambers, *op. cit.,* I, 640-41. Parton,

who had been working on a biography of Benjamin Franklin for three years, was so affected by "its perusal" that he at once abandoned this work, and wrote Butler that he wished to write a history of his administration in New Orleans. He added: "This I would do to honor one

who in this most difficult of wars, has shown a capacity equal to the occasion." He concluded: "Perhaps I should inform you in addition that I am a slavery loathing Democrat, and that you are my candidate for President." *Butler's Correspondence*, II, 282-83.

CHAPTER IV

[1] *The Daily Delta*, December 16, 1862; McMaster, *op. cit.*, p. 212. No general biography of Banks has been published.

[2] *Butler's Correspondence*, II, 564; *The Daily True Delta*, December 17, 1862; *The Daily Picayune*, December 16, 1862. Banks assumed command of the Department on December 16, 1862. *Chase Correspondence*, II, 239; Irwin, *op. cit.*, p. 55.

[3] *The Daily Picayune*, December 17, 18, 20, 1862; "New Orleans," *Annual Cyclopaedia, 1862*, pp. 653-54; *Butler's Correspondence*, II, 547. Practically all of Butler's and Banks's "orders" are found in *Butler's Correspondence*.

[4] *The Daily Delta*, December 24, 1862; Parton, *op. cit.*, p. 612; *The New York Herald*, January 3, 1863; "New Orleans," *Annual Cyclopaedia, 1862*, p. 654. The congressmen from Louisiana had not, as yet, been officially received.

[5] *The Daily Picayune*, December 3, 24, 1862, and January 29, 1863; *Butler's Correspondence*, II, 550; McMastser, *op. cit.*, p. 256; Howard K. Beale, *The Critical Year* (New York: Harcourt, Brace & Co., 1930), pp. 52, 53.

[6] *The Daily True Delta*, January 17, 1863; *The Daily Picayune*, October 24, 1862. The proclamation tended to divide the Unionists. Dostie, *op. cit.*, p. 81.

[7] Southwood, *op. cit.*, p. 267; *Butler's Book*, p. 522; *Chase Correspondence*, II, 340; *The Daily Picayune*, December 17, 1862.

[8] *The Daily Delta*, December 18, 1862; Southwood, *op. cit.*, p. 274.

[9] *The Daily Delta*, December 25, 1862; *The Daily Picayune*, December 25, 1862.

[10] *The Daily Delta*, January 12, 1863; *Butler's Correspondence*, III, 3; *The Daily Picayune*, December 25, 1862.

[11] *The Daily Picayune*, January 16,

1863; *The New York Daily Tribune*, December 29, 1862.

[12] *Chase Correspondence*, II, 572, 575; Warmoth, *op. cit.*, p. 3.

[13] *The Daily True Delta*, May 14, 1863; *The Daily Picayune*, January 8, 1863; *The New York Herald*, July 11, 1864; *The New York Daily Tribune*, May 23, 1863.

[14] Southwood, *op. cit.*, p. 278; *The Daily Picayune*, January 14, 1863.

[15] *The Daily Picayune*, May 1, 1863.

[16] *The Era*, May 13, 1863. The schools seem to have been searched frequently, and compositions were found in which the "Yankees" were "denounced in good set phrases."

[17] *The Daily True Delta*, February 18, 1863. The fact that Louisiana had not been reapportioned after the 1860 census does not seem to have been discussed. It was a reason given for the rejection of others sent at a later date.

[18] *Congressional Globe*, 37 Cong., 3 sess., p. 834; *The Daily Picayune*, February 28, 1863.

[19] *Congressional Globe*, 37 Cong., 3 sess., p. 861; *The Daily Picayune*, February 28, 1863.

[20] *Congressional Globe*, 37 Cong., 3 sess., pp. 1030-32; *The Daily Picayune*, March 3, 1863; *The Daily True Delta*, March 3, 1863.

[21] *Congressional Globe*, 37 Cong., 3 sess., p. 1036.

[22] *The Daily True Delta*, February 1, 1863.

[23] *Ibid.*, February 8, 1863; "Louisiana," *Annual Cyclopaedia, 1863*, p. 589.

[24] *The Daily Picayune*, March 8, 1863; Dostie, *op. cit.*, pp. 82, 83.

[25] *The Era*, March 20, 1863. Dennison wrote at this time that "Union sentiment has increased and improved· won-

NOTES

derfully." *Chase Correspondence,* II, 382.

²⁶ *The Era,* April 12, 1863; *The Daily True Delta,* March 22, 1863; Dostie, *op. cit.,* p. 83. Bills had been introduced into Congress, authorizing Louisiana and Tennessee to hold Congressional elections.

²⁷ *The Era,* April 26, 1863; Dostie, *op. cit.,* p. 83; *The Daily True Delta,* May 19, 1863.

²⁸ *The New Orleans Times,* October 21, 1864. It was eighteen months later. Dennison, a radical, wrote that "the whole matter was managed with entire secrecy"; and that they planned an election that would be "a kind of coup d'etat." *Chase Correspondence,* II, 417.

²⁹ *The Era,* June 9, 23, 1863; Kendall, *op. cit.,* pp. 289-90; *The New Orleans Times,* December 4, 10, 1863. They reasoned that: (1) The present constitution (1852) was sufficient and could, if necessary, be changed by the legislature; (2) the 141st article provided the mode of revising the constitution; (3) the present time was unpropitious; (4) it was unwise and unjust as all the loyal could not be represented; (5) political strife would cause a division of the loyal when unity was needed; (6) they should at least take a vote on it before calling a convention. It might be added that this faction evidently desired to retain political power within the state.

³⁰ *The Era,* June 23, 1863; "Louisiana," *Annual Cyclopaedia, 1863,* p. 590.

³¹ *The Daily True Delta,* July 4, 1863; *The New York Daily Tribune,* July 13, 1863; *Chase Correspondence,* II, 417-18; "Louisiana," *Annual Cyclopaedia, 1863,* pp. 590-91. These conservatives later adopted the seemingly strange policy of appealing to a radical Congress over the head of Lincoln.

³² *The Daily Picayune,* July 21, 1863; "Louisiana," *Annual Cyclopaedia, 1863,* p. 590; Lincoln to Committee, June 19, 1863, in *Lincoln's Works,* II, 356.

³³ *The Era,* June 3, 1863. This faction desired a new basis of representation.

³⁴ *Ibid.,* May 31, 1863; *The Daily True Delta,* June 14, 1863; "Louisiana," *Annual Cyclopaedia, 1863,* p. 589. This new

proportion was to defeat the purpose of the "Whig Constitution" of 1852. The 1852 convention, by giving New Orleans an arbitrary and reduced representation, where the whites were largely in the majority, and by arranging the balance of the state on a total population basis, had placed the power of the state in the hands of the slaveholders. It was not a "white man's State." Their aim was now to make it one. *The Era,* July 9, 1863.

³⁵ *The Daily True Delta,* June 2, 1863; "Louisiana," *Annual Cyclopaedia, 1863,* pp. 591-92; *The Weekly Gazette and Comet,* October 10, 17, 1863.

³⁶ *The Era,* June 2, 3, 1863; *The Weekly Gazette and Comet,* October 17, 1863. As registration was the only positive action required, he continued to register and administer the oath. In October, Shepley also appointed registrars of voters for the parishes. *The New Orleans Times,* October 13, 1863.

³⁷ *The Daily Picayune,* July 12, 1863; *The Daily True Delta,* July 11, 1863.

³⁸ *The Daily True Delta,* August 4, 1863.

³⁹ *Ibid.,* August 8, 1863; *The Weekly Gazette and Comet,* September 12, 1863.

⁴⁰ *The Daily True Delta,* September 9, 1863; "Louisiana," *Annual Cyclopaedia, 1863,* p. 589. The prescribed oath is given herein.

⁴¹ *The Daily Delta,* September 10, 1863. The Conservatives had the local and Northern press against them.

⁴² *The New Orleans Times,* September 20, 1863. This was the group that had been in correspondence with Lincoln for more than a year.

⁴³ *The Daily True Delta,* September 16, 1863.

⁴⁴ *The New Orleans Times,* September 20, 1863.

⁴⁵ *Ibid.,* October 12, 1863.

⁴⁶ *The Daily True Delta,* September 29, 1863.

⁴⁷ *The New Orleans Times,* October 26, 1863.

⁴⁸ *Ibid.,* October 28, 1863; *The Daily Picayune,* October 20, 1863.

⁴⁹ *The Daily Picayune,* October 28, 1863; *The Weekly Gazette and Comet,*

October 31, 1863. This address indicates that they understood the nature of the radical opposition to immediate reconstruction by presidential authority. These conservatives were, of course, making a bid for Lincoln's support. But they received little encouragement from him.

⁵⁰ Letter from Louisiana State Executive Committee to True State General Committee of the Union Associations of the Parishes of Orleans and Jefferson, October 27, 1863. It was signed by W. W. Pugh, president, Edward Ames, vice-president, J. Q. A. Fellows, secretary. *The New Orleans Times,* October 31, and November 1, 2, 1863; *Chase Correspondence,* II, 418-24; *The Daily Delta,* November 1, 1863.

⁵¹ Letter from the True State General Committee of the Union Association of the Parishes of Orleans and Jefferson to the Louisiana Executive Committee, October 28, 1863. It was signed by Thomas J. Durant, president. *The New Orleans Times,* October 28, 31, 1863; *Chase Correspondence,* II, 418-24.

⁵² *The Daily True Delta,* November 1, 1863; *Chase Correspondence,* II, 428-29; *The New York Daily Tribune,* November 14, 1863. Military Governor Shepley issued an order to stop this election on the day before the contemplated election. *Congressional Globe,* 38 Cong., 1 sess., p. 411.

⁵³ *The Daily True Delta,* November 6, 1863; *The New York Daily Tribune,* November 2, 1863.

⁵⁴ *The New Orleans Times,* November 7 and December 9, 1863. *The Times* continually ridiculed the movement. The free colored population had held a meeting November 5, and resolved to address Shepley for the right to be registered as voters. A lengthy "address" was submitted, but he did not grant the prayer of the petitioners. "Louisiana," *Annual Cyclopaedia, 1863,* pp. 591-92.

⁵⁵ *The New Orleans Times,* December 11, 24, 1863, and January 15, 1864.

⁵⁶ *Ibid.,* December 18, 1863; *Chase Correspondence,* II, 423. Dennison wrote: "Gov. Shepley, by two or three firm but mild letters, put a stop to the whole proceeding. Had they proceeded with an election he would probably have broken it up by arresting the whole gang. . . . The whole movement . . . was nothing but copperheadism and secessionism in disguise . . . and resolved itself into a ridiculous farce. . . . "

⁵⁷ *Congressional Globe,* 38 Cong., 1 sess., p. 5; *The New Orleans Times,* December 22, 1863.

⁵⁸ *The New Orleans Times,* December 18, 1863.

⁵⁹ *Congressional Globe,* 38 Cong., 1 sess., p. 17. Cottman seems to have quietly withdrawn when he learned that his pro-Confederate record was to be attacked. He had signed the ordinance of secession. *Butler's Correspondence,* p. 449; *Convention Journal,* p. 232.

⁶⁰ *Congressional Globe,* 38 Cong., 1 sess., p. 411.

⁶¹ *Ibid.,* p. 457.

⁶² *Ibid.,* pp. 595-97; *The New Orleans Times,* December 23, 1863; *The Weekly Gazette and Comet,* January 1, 1864. Stevens of Pennsylvania had apparently derived his information regarding Field's alleged disloyalty from B. F. Flanders, but he probably did not attempt to use it.

⁶³ *The New Orleans Times,* November 6, 1863; "Louisiana," *Annual Cyclopaedia, 1863,* p. 592.

⁶⁴ *The New Orleans Times,* December 22, 1863.

⁶⁵ *The Era,* March 3, 1863.

⁶⁶ *Ibid.,* April 14, 1863; *Chase Correspondence,* II, 378.

⁶⁷ *The Daily Picayune,* October 7, 1863. Judge A. A. Atochia, Banks's appointee, had rendered decisions declaring that slavery no longer existed. *The Weekly Gazette and Comet,* October 10, 1863; *The New Orleans Tribune,* November 5, 1863.

⁶⁸ *The Daily Picayune,* January 25, 1863; "Louisiana," *Annual Cyclopaedia, 1863,* p. 594.

⁶⁹ *The Era,* February 19, 1863; *The New York Herald,* March 4, 1863. St. Charles Parish was a danger zone.

⁷⁰ *The Era,* February 19, 1863; *The Daily Picayune,* February 20, 1863; *The New York Daily Tribune,* March 11, 1863.

[71] *The Daily Picayune*, June 21, 1863.

[72] *The Era*, February 19, 1863; "Louisiana," *Annual Cyclopaedia, 1863*, p. 594; *The New York Herald*, March 4, 1863; *The New Orleans Times*, November 17, 1863.

[73] *The Daily Picayune*, April 12, 1863; *Louisiana Annual Cyclopaedia, 1863*, p. 594; *Chase Correspondence*, II, 378-79.

[74] *The Era*, April 4, 1863. Corporal punishment was prohibited under this new system.

[75] *Ibid.*, April 11, 1863; *The New Orleans Times*, December 5, 1863. They were paid a wage, and subject to certain punishments other than whippings. They were subject to fines of from one to five dollars, and to expulsion and forfeiture of wages under certain conditions. "Louisiana," *Annual Cyclopaedia, 1863*, p. 594.

[76] *The Daily Picayune*, March 21, 1863; *Butler's Book*, p. 495; *The New York Herald*, January 3, 1863. Butler complained of the injustice of Banks after his departure. He says Banks did not allow them to be on an "equality with the white soldiers."

[77] *The Era*, May 9, 1863; *Chase Correspondence*, II, 347, 352. Dennison continued to write Chase: "The government can finish this war in twelve months, in one way, and in only one way. Arm the negroes. . . . It must be done. Why delay it? He [Banks] might have 50,000 in the service in three months—yes, 100,000 by energetically adopting proper means. . . . An army of negroes could be made most formidable. They could be inspired with a religious enthusiasm as terrible and persistent as that of the followers of Mahomet."

[78] *The Era*, June 14, 1863.

[79] *Ibid.*, May 22, 1863; *Chase Correspondence*, II, 377. In this letter to Chase, Dennison says: "By accepting a regiment which had already been in Confederate service he left no room for complaint [by the Rebels] that the Government was arming negroes."

[80] *The Era*, May 21, 1863. Butler had said that he enlisted free men of color in these three regiments. Dennison says that they were "mostly from the lately slaves." *Chase Correspondence*, II, 377.

[81] *The Daily Picayune*, September 30, 1863; *The New Orleans Times*, September 30, 1863; *The Daily True Delta*, October 1, 1863; *The Weekly Gazette and Comet*, October 24, 1863.

[82] *The Era*, June 21, 1863; *The Daily True Delta*, June 24, 1863; *The New Orleans Times*, December 5, 1863.

[83] *The New Orleans Times*, September 27, 1863. Much of this official information relative to the efficiency of the negro must have been propaganda for a Northern public.

[84] *The Daily Picayune*, December 23, 1863; Dennison wrote Chase: "There had been some trouble . . . the New England soldier could not consent to present arms to a colored officer, and treat him with necessary respect." This trouble occurred under Butler. *Chase Correspondence*, II, 361.

[85] *The New Orleans Times*, October 18, 1863. The radical *Times* appeared to be trying to stir up an insurrection. It had stated previously: "Would you have a negro who would not fight for his freedom?" *Times*, October 1, 1863. Dennison wrote Chase: "The free negroes of Louisiana are certainly superior, as a class, to the Creole descendants of French and Spanish settlers. They are intelligent, energetic and industrious. . . . They own one-seventh of the real estate of this city." *Chase Correspondence*, II, 311.

[86] *The New Orleans Times*, October 9, 1863.

[87] *Ibid.*, November 6, 1863. Dostie seems to have been continually inflaming the negro. Governor Warmoth told the writer that Pinchback was the son of a white Georgia planter, and that he was a negro of considerable ability.

[88] *Ibid.*, December 16, 22, 1863; *The New York Daily Tribune*, December 28, 1863. The *Times* of December 16 gives the information that "a number of free men of color were among the delegates, much the larger portion of them occupying seats in a body on the right of the chair, but several were scattered through the chairs on the other side, promiscuously with the white delegates."

CHAPTER V

[1] *The New Orleans Times,* December 29, 1863. The *Times* was the official organ of the Free State party during this period.

[2] McCarthy, *op. cit.,* pp. 39, 51; Dostie, *op. cit.,* pp. 83-84; *The New Orleans Times,* May 7, 1865; *Lincoln's Works,* II, 380-81. Copies were also sent to Flanders, Hahn, and Durant. Lincoln had cautioned them not to "make the letter generally public." It, therefore, did not appear in print until some months later.

[3] "Louisiana," *Annual Cyclopaedia, 1863,* p. 591; McCarthy, *op. cit.,* p. 52.

[4] *Lincoln's Works,* II, 435-36; McCarthy, *op. cit.,* pp. 52-53. Lincoln apparently feared that the conservatives would organize the state government in Louisiana.

[5] *Louisiana Election Case,* 38 Cong., 2 sess., H. Rept. No. 13, p. 17; McCarthy, *op. cit.,* p. 66.

[6] *Lincoln's Works,* II, 465-66; McCarthy, *op. cit.,* p. 65; *The New Orleans Times,* January 17, 1864; Chambers, *op. cit.,* I, 653.

[7] *The New Orleans Times,* December 29, 1863; "Louisiana," *Annual Cyclopaedia, 1863,* p. 592; *The Weekly Gazette and Comet,* January 16, 1864.

[8] Dostie, *op. cit.,* p. 85; *The New Orleans Times,* January 10, 1864; "Louisiana," *Annual Cyclopaedia, 1863,* p. 592. The Free State party had held several "Union Association" meetings of Unconditional Union men, at which they had attempted to stimulate interest in registration, and had worked out their program for the calling of a constitutional convention. *The New Orleans Times,* November 5, 9, 23, 26, and December 6, 8, 10, 13, 20, 30, 1863, and January 8, 10, 1864.

[9] *The New Orleans Times,* January 12, 1864; "Louisiana," *Annual Cyclopaedia, 1863,* pp. 592-93; McCarthy, *op. cit.,* pp. 67-69; Cox, *op. cit.,* p. 427; *The Weekly Gazette and Comet,* January 16, 1864.

[10] Dostie, *op. cit.,* pp. 86-89; *Lincoln's Works,* II, 442-44; *The Weekly Gazette and Comet,* January 16, 1864; *The New York Daily Tribune,* January 21, 1864; *The New York Herald,* January 21, 1864; McMaster, *op. cit.,* p. 511; *The New Orleans Times,* January 1, 27, 1864; Stryker, *op. cit.,* pp. 112-13; Cox, *op. cit.,* p. 427; McCarthy, *op. cit.,* p. 68-69; Walter L. Fleming, *Documentary History of Reconstruction* (Cleveland: The Arthur H. Clark Company, 1906), I, 109-12. This is cited hereafter as Fleming, *Documentary History.* This is Lincoln's "Proclamation of Amnesty and Reconstruction" of December 8, 1863.

[11] *The Daily Picayune,* February 14, 1864; McCarthy, *op. cit.,* p. 68; *The New Orleans Times,* February 14, 15, 1864; *The New York Herald,* February 27, 1864.

[12] "Louisiana," *Annual Cyclopaedia, 1863,* p. 592; *The New Orleans Times,* January 12, 1864.

[13] *The New Orleans Times,* January 27, 1864. The *Times* had given the following information on the twenty-seventh: "There are not more than 1500 duly qualified voters yet to participate. Every institution is now at stake! We appeal, then, to every man to exert himself for the common interest if Louisiana is to go back to her place in the Union and to go back free. . . ."

[14] *Ibid.,* January 15, 1864; "Louisiana," *Annual Cyclopaedia, 1863,* p. 431.

[15] *The New Orleans Era,* January 31, 1864; "Louisiana," *Annual Cyclopaedia, 1863,* p. 592.

[16] *The New Orleans Times,* January 12, 1864; "Louisiana," *Annual Cyclopaedia, 1864,* pp. 592-93.

[17] "Louisiana," *Annual Cyclopaedia, 1864,* pp. 593-94; McCarthy, *op. cit.,* pp. 69-70.

[18] *The New Orleans Times,* February 1, 1864; "Louisiana," *Annual Cyclopaedia, 1864,* p. 476. Hahn was said to have had strong leanings towards the so-called "copperheads" at this time.

[19] *The New Orleans Times,* January 16, 17, and February 1, 1864.

[20] *Ibid.,* January 17, 24, 1864.

[21] *Ibid.,* January 31 and February 1,

1864; "Louisiana," *Annual Cyclopaedia, 1864,* p. 476.

[22] *The New Orleans Times,* February 1, 1864. Other evidence, as shall presently be shown, was produced by his opponents later; but it was not presented until after the election.

[23] *Ibid.,* February 1, 17, 1864.

[24] *The New Orleans Times,* February 1, 1864; *The New York Daily Tribune,* February 1, 1864.

[25] *The New Orleans Times,* February 1, 2, 1864; *The Weekly Gazette and Comet,* February 6, 1864; *The New York Daily Tribune,* February 11, 1864; *The New York Herald,* February 15, 1864; Dostie, *op. cit.,* pp. 89-93. The reporter of the *Times* gave a complete report. Judge Atocia, who, it will be observed, was on both Free State tickets, declined to run, and Dr. Dostie was substituted. *The New Orleans Times,* February 3, 1864; Dostie, *op. cit.,* pp. 92, 93.

[26] *The New Orleans Times,* February 2, 1864; McCarthy, *op. cit.,* p. 69; *The New York Herald,* February 18, 1864.

[27] *The New Orleans Times,* February 3, 1864.

[28] *Ibid.,* January 7, 1864; *Chase Correspondence,* II, 430. Dennison made the observation that "the only distinction I feel able to make is that one is a Banks, and the other an anti-Banks party." He added: "One is as radical as the other." *Chase Correspondence,* II, 433.

[29] *The New Orleans Times,* February 3, 5, 1864; McCarthy, *op. cit.,* p. 69; *The Weekly Gazette and Comet,* February 6, 20, 1864.

[30] *The Daily Picayune,* February 16, 1864; *The New Orleans Times,* February 16, 1864; Barker, *op. cit.,* p. 163. The conservatives were now evidently convinced that they could carry the election. All the correspondence pertaining to the oath is in this issue of the sixteenth.

[31] *The Daily Picayune,* February 17, 1864; *The New Orleans Times,* February 14, 16, 1864; *The New York Daily Tribune,* February 22, 1864; Barker, *op. cit.,* pp. 164, 165-67. Banks issued an-

other proclamation in which he stated that the oath was to be required of all who participated. He "must have most solemn and explicit guarantees." *The New Orleans Times,* February 15, 1864; Barker, *op. cit.,* pp. 167-70.

[32] *The Daily Picayune,* February 6, 11, 1864.

[33] *Ibid.,* February 9, 20, 1864. Evidence was submitted after the election to prove that he had falsified. *The New Orleans Times,* August 20, 1864.

[34] *The New Orleans Times,* February 12, 21, 1864.

[35] *Ibid.,* February 9, 1864; *Chase Correspondence,* II, 432.

[36] "Louisiana," *Annual Cyclopaedia, 1863,* p. 591; McCarthy, *op. cit.,* p. 55; *The New Orleans Times,* February 9, 1864.

[37] *The New Orleans Times,* January 6, 17, 20, 1864.

[38] *Ibid.,* February 6, 9, 17, 1864. Some negroes had even expressed their hopes that such sentiments as "all should be equalized and fraternized" might be embodied in the resolutions. They were not included, although all signs indicated that they were in the offing.

[39] *Ibid.,* February 10, 1864.

[40] *Ibid.,* February 17, 1864.

[41] *Ibid.,* February 5, 1864; *The New York Times,* February 4, 1864; *Chase Correspondence,* II, 431. Dennison made this significant statement: "Fellows would probably have been elected had not General Banks issued an order requiring voters to take the proclamation oath. . . . "

[42] *The New Orleans Picayune,* February 23, 1864.

[43] "Louisiana," *Annual Cyclopaedia, 1864,* p. 476; *The New Orleans Times,* February 23, 24, 26, 1864. General Banks's letter to Senator Lane is published in pamphlet form under title: "The Reconstruction of States," New York, 1865. A copy will be found in the Howard Memorial Library, New Orleans.

[44] *The New Orleans Times,* February 21, 1864; Chambers, *op. cit.,* I, 653; Barker, *op. cit.,* p. 172.

[45] *The New Orleans Daily Picayune,*

February 23, 1864; *The New Orleans Times*, February 23, 1864; Stryker, *op. cit.*, p. 159.

[46] *The New Orleans Times*, February 23, 24, 25, 1864; James Ford Rhodes, *History of the United States from the Compromise of 1850 to the End of the Roosevelt Administration* (New York: The Macmillan Company, 1928), V, 52; *The New York Daily Tribune*, March 4, 7, 1864; *The New York Herald*, March 4, 1864. A complete parish-by-parish tabulation was not reported.

[47] *The New Orleans Times*, May 17, 1864; C. J. Barrow, *Biographical Sketches of Louisiana's Governors* (Baton Rouge: The Advocate *Book and Job Office*, 1893), p. 47.

[48] *Barrow, op. cit.*, pp. 45-46.

[49] *The New Orleans Times*, March 2 and May 15, 1864. Short biographical sketches of all but Wells had been printed in the *New York Times*, and copied by the *New Orleans Times*, on May 15, 1864. Cox, who served in a subsequent Congress with Hahn, described Hahn as a "short and lame" man with "dark curly hair, and a brown complexion." He states further that "he had a fervid love for his state," and that "the House was moved by his eloquence" in defense of Louisiana. Cox, *op. cit.*, pp. 427-28.

[50] *The New Orleans Daily Picayune*, March 5, 1864; *The New York Daily Tribune*, March 14, 1864; *The New York Herald*, March 14, 1864; Chambers, *op. cit.*, I, 653; McCarthy, *op. cit.*, p. 72; Warmoth, *op. cit.*, p. 35; Dostie, *op. cit.*, pp. 95-99; *The New Orleans Times*, March 3, 5, 6, 1864; "Louisiana," *Annual Cyclopaedia, 1864*, pp. 476-77. A detailed account of these elaborate ceremonies is given in the *Annual Cyclopaedia, 1864*, and in all the New Orleans dailies. The program, which had been given due publicity, was as follows: (1) 100 guns fired on levee; (2) ringing of all bells in the city for 30 minutes, morning, noon, and night; (3) instrumental music by bands of 300 musicians; also vocal performances; (4)

chorus by 5,000 school children; (5) artillery discharges at regular intervals; (6) anvil chorus [a novelty] by full band of forty beaters. *The New Orleans Times*, March 2, 1864.

[51] *The New Orleans Times*, March 5, 6, 1864; *The Daily Picayune*, March 5, 1864; Cox, *op. cit.*, p. 427; Dostie, *op. cit.*, p. 93. According to press reports, there was "prolonged applause," which would indicate that the speech had touched a responsive chord. It was evidently beautiful and eloquent, and must have been delivered in such an earnest and energetic tone as to carry a tremendous appeal. But a closer examination of "this literary production" leads the writer to the conclusion that it exhibited · more eloquence than sound logic. To speak of "The State that is this day recreated" must have conveyed the impression that Louisiana was not a state; that she had committed political suicide, and therefore, had no constitution. And if the state had no constitution, as was prescribed for a republican form of government, how was it possible to "recreate" the state? The Unionists must have asked themselves this question. Also they must have pondered over that part of his speech which seems clearly to indicate that the state needed no re-creation, because the Constitution had only been held in abeyance by the war, and was now resurrected and was in as full force and effect as ever. There indeed appeared to be many contradictory and irreconcilable statements in this high-sounding but meaningless address. *The Weekly Gazette and Comet*, March 12, also gives a full account of this elaborate inauguration.

[52] *Lincoln's Works*, II, 498; McCarthy, *op. cit.*, p. 73; Dostie, *op. cit.*, p. 112; *The New Orleans Times*, March 31, 1864; "Louisiana," *Annual Cyclopaedia, 1864*, p. 477. The letter follows:

EXECUTIVE MANSION, WASHINGTON, March 15, 1864.

HIS EXCELLENCY MICHAEL HAHN, GOVERNOR OF LOUISIANA: Until further order, you are hereby invested with the powers exercised hitherto by the military governor of Louisiana.

Yours truly,
ABRAHAM LINCOLN.

[53] *Lincoln's Works*, II, 496; *The New Orleans Times*, March 31, 1864, and July 6, 1865. The complete text of this highly significant letter is given in the next chapter.

[54] *The New Orleans Times*, February 25, 27, and March 1, 1864; McCarthy, *op. cit.*, pp. 70-71; Cox, *op. cit.*, p. 427.

[55] *The New Orleans Times*, May 3, 6, 1864; Dostie, *op. cit.*, pp. 111-13. This letter, and others by Durant to the same effect, were published in the New York dailies and were copied by the New Orleans journals. *The New Orleans Times*, August 18, 1864; *The Daily True Delta*, August 19, 1864.

[56] *The New Orleans Times*, May 2, 1864. Congressmen Boutwell, Stevens, Davis, Sumner, and other members of Congress were already opposing Lincoln's proposed plan of restoration.

[57] McCarthy, *op. cit.*, pp. 72-73; Dostie, *op. cit.*, p. 36.

[58] *The New Orleans Times*, August 20, 1864; *The New York Evening Post*, August 8, 1864. This revelation, which was given wide publicity, was intended to prove that Hahn had falsified during the election. It also weakened Lincoln's Louisiana government in the eyes of the country, and seems to have greatly strengthened the hands of Congress in its struggle with the President for power.

[59] *The Daily Picayune*, July 15, 1864.

[60] *The New Orleans Times*, November 15, 1864. These charges of corruption were never answered.

[61] *Ibid.*, November 15, 1864. The *Times* of this date gives a completely itemized statement of all the expenditures. This publicity tended to discredit the Lincoln government.

[62] *Ibid.*, November 15, 1864. This great scandal was made public as a result of a coalition that was formed between the two defeated factions, the conservatives under Fellows, and the radical Flanders faction. Dennison states that he had attempted a reconciliation of the two Free State factions, but had failed. *Chase Correspondence*, II, 434.

CHAPTER VI

[1] *The New Orleans Daily Picayune*, March 16, 1864; McCarthy, *op. cit.*, p. 74; *The New Orleans Times*, March 12, 17, 26, 1864; Hunt, *op. cit.*, p. 283. The desirability of holding a convention had been debated for months. In fact, a plan of representation had been submitted to Governor Shepley as early as May 29, 1863. *The Era*, May 31, 1863. Banks had appointed a local committee to draft a desirable plan. *The Daily Picayune*, March 12, 1864; *The New Orleans Times*, March 12, 1864; *The New York Daily Tribune*, March 17, 1864.

[2] *The New Orleans Times*, March 14, 16, 21, 1864. Warmoth made an error when he stated that "Hahn's Legislature" ordered this election "on March 28." As a matter of fact this legislature did not meet until October 3, 1864. Warmoth, *op. cit.*, p. 36. *The Daily Picayune*, October 4, 1864.

[3] *The New Orleans Times*, March 19, 1864.

[4] *Ibid.*, March 17, 1864.

[5] *The Daily Picayune*, March 27, 1864. Dennison wrote Chase: "The election for delegates to the State Convention passed off quietly, and the same party succeeded as before. I regret to say that the character, ability, and standing of the Delegates, is not such as could be wished. There are a few excellent men elected like Judge Durell, Judge Howell, Dr. Bonzana; but the majority of them are of little account. . . . It was of no use however. The combination of patronage and influence was too strong to allow us any chance of success." *Chase Correspondence*, II, 435-36.

[6] *The Daily Picayune*, March 29, 1864; *The New Orleans Times*, March 29, 1864; *The New York Daily Tribune*, April 8, 1864; Kendall, *op. cit.*, I, 290.

[7] *The New Orleans Times*, March 29, 1864; *Louisiana Constitutional Debates in the Convention* (New Orleans: W. R. Fish, Printer, 1864), p. 408. This will be cited hereafter as *Debates;* Mc-Pherson, *op. cit.*, pp. 74-75; Rhodes, *op. cit.*, V, 52.

[8] *Journal of the Convention for Revision and Amendment of the Constitution of Louisiana* (New Orleans: W. R. Fish, Printer, 1864), p. 5. This will be cited hereafter as *Journal;* Cox, *op. cit.*, p. 428; *The New York Daily Tribune*, April 11, 1864; Dostie, *op. cit.*, p. 123.

[9] *Debates*, p. 370; *The New Orleans Times*, April 7, 1864. This number actually attended on June 14.

[10] *The New Orleans Times*, March 17, 1864; McCarthy, *op. cit.*, p. 75.

[11] *The New Orleans Times*, March 17, 1864. This lengthy letter is published in this issue of the *Times*. Banks informed a committee of Congress that all the southeast section of Louisiana voted as the Parish of Pointe Coupee voted. He added, however, that "The City of New Orleans is really the State of Louisiana." McCarthy, *op. cit.*, p. 75.

[12] *Debates*, p. 2; *The New Orleans Times*, April 4, 7, 1864; *Journal*, p. 3. The *Times* soon reversed its position relative to the members of the convention.

[13] *Journal*, p. 14; *The New Orleans Times*, May 19, 1864; *The Daily True Delta*, May 21, 1864; King and Ficklen, *op. cit.*, p. 230.

[14] *Journal*, p. 52; *The Daily True Delta*, June 22, 24, 1864.

[15] *Debates*, p. 19; *The New Orleans Times*, April 10, 16. 1864; *Journal*, p. 12.

[16] *The New Orleans Times*, April 14, 1864.

[17] *Ibid.*, April 15, 1864.

[18] *Ibid.*, April 24, 1864.

[19] *Chase Correspondence*, II, 436.

[20] *The New Orleans Times*, April 17, 1864.

[21] *Debates*, p. 8; *The Daily Picayune*, April 22, 1864; *Journal*, p. 8. Dennison reported that "the Convention is composed mostly of persons who would do whatever he (Banks) should request." *Chase Correspondence*, II, 436-37.

[22] *Debates*, p. 697; *The New Orleans Times*, July 22, 1864.

[23] *Debates*, p. 116.

[24] *Ibid.*, p. 359. Under the heading "Shortcomings of the Constitutional Convention" the *Times* makes the following comment: "Mr. Hill defends the brandy drinking going on in that body, and he is one of the most indefatigable customers. One hundred dollars per day is the cost of the brandy in the Convention. Would Northern society and Northern States tolerate such immortal [sic] waste?" *The New Orleans Times*, July 2, 1864.

[25] *Debates*, p. 414. It will be observed that such statements mark the beginning of that feud between this body, and the citizens and police of New Orleans.

[26] *Ibid.*, p. 600. Such expressions were of course crystallizing a bitter spirit of hostility that was to result in the battle of July 30, 1866.

[27] *Journal*, pp. 7, 8; McCarthy, *op. cit.*, p. 75.

[28] *Journal*, p. 11; *Debates*, pp. 13-17.

[29] *Journal*, p. 22; *Debates*, p. 32.

[30] *Journal*, p. 22.

[31] *Ibid.*, p. 20.

[32] *Chase Correspondence*, II, 435.

[33] *Journal*, p. 12; Dostie, *op. cit.*, p. 102; *Debates*, p. 96.

[34] *Journal*, p. 25; *The Daily Picayune*, April 28, 1864; *Debates*, pp. 97-98. Dennison observes: "Prejudice against the colored people is exhibited continually—prejudice bitter and vulgar. The attempt to induce such a Convention to grant to colored men a limited right of suffrage, or any other right, would be futile." *Chase Correspondence*, II, 439.

[35] *Debates*, p. 97; Dostie, *op. cit.*, pp.

[262]

102-03; *The New Orleans Times,* May 6, 7, 1864; *The Daily True Delta,* June 4, 1864. Abell resigned on the eve of adjournment for the reason that he could not vote for the constitution. *The New Orleans Times,* June 28, 1864.

[36] *Debates,* pp. 158, 175; *The Daily True Delta,* June 1, 1864; *Journal,* p. 58.

[37] *The New Orleans Times,* March 23, 1864; *The Daily True Delta,* May 19, 1864; *Debates,* p. 34; *Journal,* pp. 23-24.

[38] *Journal,* p. 24. *The New Orleans Times,* April 25, 1864; *Debates,* p. 34.

[39] *Journal,* p. 139; *The New Orleans Times,* May 3, 4, 1864.

[40] *Journal,* p. 141; *The Daily True Delta,* June 1, 1864.

[41] *Journal,* p. 155; *The Daily True Delta,* July 16, 1864; *The New Orleans Times,* July 16, 1864.

[42] *Debates,* p. 547; *The Daily True Delta,* July 16, 1864; *The New Orleans Times,* July 19, 1864.

[43] *Debates,* p. 161.

[44] *Journal,* p. 157; *The New Orleans Times,* June 28 and July 2, 1864; *The Daily True Delta,* July 1, 1864; *Dostie, op. cit.,* p. 104.

[45] *Debates,* p. 479; *The Daily True Delta,* July 1, 2, 1864; *Report of the Secretary of State, May, 1902, op. cit.,* pp. 135-36. It will be recalled that Governor Hahn was a strong advocate of education for the freedmen. *The New Orleans Times,* March 13, 1864; *The Daily Picayune,* March 5, 1864.

[46] *Journal,* p. 143; *Debates,* p. 627; *The New Orleans Times,* June 19, 1864; *The Daily True Delta,* July 9, 1864. The records reveal that Sickles, Banks, and Canby visited the convention and made "eloquent speeches." *The New Orleans Times,* May 28, 1864; *The Daily True Delta,* May 28 and June 23, 1864.

[47] *Journal,* p. 71; *The New Orleans Times,* May 11, 13, 1864.

[48] *Debates,* p. 211; *Journal,* p. 119.

[49] *Journal,* p. 134; *Chambers, op. cit.,* I, 659.

[50] *Debates,* p. 250.

[51] *The New Orleans Times,* March 17, 1864.

[52] *Lincoln's Works,* II, 496; Warmoth, *op. cit.,* p. 36; Dostie, *op. cit.,* p. 160; McCarthy, *op. cit.,* p. 73; *The Daily Picayune,* July 6, 1864; *The New Orleans Times,* March 31, 1865; *The Baton Rouge Tri-Weekly Gazette and Comet,* July 8, 1865; Chambers, *op. cit.,* I, 659; Blaine, *op. cit.,* II, 40. Mr. Blaine says of this personal note: "It was perhaps the earliest proposition from any authentic source to endow the negro with the right of suffrage, and was an indirect but most effective answer to those who subsequently attempted to use Mr. Lincoln's name in support of policies which his intimate friends instinctively knew would be abhorrent to his unerring sense of justice."

[53] *Debates,* p. 301; *The New Orleans Times,* May 28, 1864.

[54] *Chase Correspondence,* II, 452; *The Daily True Delta,* June 25, 1864; Warmoth, *op. cit.,* p. 36; *Journal,* p. 130.

[55] *Journal,* p. 174; McPherson, *op. cit.,* p. 332; *The New Orleans Times,* May 10, 1864; *The Daily True Delta,* May 18, 1864; *The New York Daily Tribune,* May 19, 1864; *The New York Herald,* May 27, 1864; Kendall, *op. cit.,* I, 291; *Reports of the Secretary of State, May 1902,* p. 117.

[56] *Debates,* pp. 620, 623; McPherson, *op. cit.,* p. 332; *The New Orleans Times,* April 19, 1864.

[57] *Debates,* p. 214.

[58] *Journal,* p. 96. Most of these members did not appear to be interested in compensation *per se.*

[59] *Debates,* p. 558.

[60] *Ibid.,* p. 283.

[61] *Ibid.,* p. 512; *The New Orleans Times,* June 6, 26, 1864; *Journal,* p. 134.

[62] *The New Orleans Times,* March 9, 1864; *Journal,* pp. 107-08, 110-14.

[63] *Debates,* p. 294; *The Daily True Delta,* May 31, and June 3, 6, 16, 1864; *The New Orleans Times,* May 27, 31, and June 4, 16, 17, 1864; Pierce Butler, *op. cit.,* pp. 74, 77, 104; *Report*

of the Secretary of State, May, 1902, pp. 108-09.

[64] *Debates,* p. 296; Pierce Butler, *op. cit.,* pp. 74, 104-06; *The Daily True Delta,* June 4, 16, 17, 1864; *The New Orleans Times,* June 16, 20, 1864; *Report of the Secretary of State, May, 1902,* pp. 127-29.

[65] *Debates,* p. 540; *The Daily True Delta,* July 15, 16, 1864; *The New Orleans Times,* June 23, 25, and July 25, 1864.

[66] *Debates,* p. 546; *The New Orleans Times,* July 19, 1864; *The Daily True Delta,* July 22, 1864. All of these decisions and actions seem to have alienated a number of Unionists, and at the same time convinced them that the state government was only a shadow or creature of the military authorities, and that martial law was still in full force and effect.

[67] *Debates,* p. 262.

[68] *Ibid.,* p. 561; *Journal,* p. 174. This new apportionment gave New Orleans 44 of the 118 members in the House, but only 9 of the 36 members in the Senate.

[69] *Debates,* p. 449; *The New Orleans Times,* April 30 and June 24, 1864. The administration may have intervened in order not to become involved in any foreign complications.

[70] *Debates,* p. 536; Barker, *op. cit.,* p. 159; *The Daily True Delta,* July 15, 1864; *The New Orleans Times,* July 15, 1864. On a subsequent resolution endorsing Lincoln and Johnson as standard bearers, the vote was sixty to twenty.

[71] *The New Orleans Times,* July 2 and November 4, 5, 1864; *The Era,* July 1, 1864.

[72] *The Daily Picayune,* December 21, 1864; *The Daily True Delta,* December 14, 1864. According to the evidence published in the *Picayune* of this date (December 21, 1864), Mr. Markey, a witness, stated that he had sold De Coursey, Sergeant-at-arms of the adjourned convention, 76 gallons of brandy at $8 per gallon, making a total of $608, whereas the vouchers showed 81 gallons at $23 per gallon,

making a total of $1,863. A Mr. Pray testified that he sold the same Sergeant-at-arms 240 gallons of liquors at $8 per gallon, and 4 baskets of champagne at $44 per basket, making a grand total of $2,090, whereas the vouchers for these items showed 360 gallons purchased, and $3,480 drawn from the treasury, of which the said Pray received $1,920. Other evidence was published to substantiate statements that there had been similar transactions in stationery purchases, and that vouchers had been raised and records destroyed to prevent investigations.

[73] *The New Orleans Times,* July 22, 1864; *Journal,* p. 165. The record of this convention must be kept in mind in order to partially explain the battle of July 30, 1866, which resulted when it attempted to reassemble on that date.

[74] *Debates,* pp. 598-600; *The New Orlean Times,* July 22, 1864. An examination of the *Debates* discloses that there was so much confusion and disorder that the President had ordered the Sergeant-at-arms to arrest Mr. Pursell, an obstreperous member; when the Sergeant-at-arms hesitated to do so, the President declared: "I will arrest you, too, sir, if you do not keep order." But order was not restored; the President was compelled to leave the chair and to declare an adjournment amid the wildest confusion.

[75] *Debates,* pp. 600-01; *The New Orleans Times,* July 22, 23, 1864; *The Daily True Delta,* July 24, 1864.

[76] *Chase Correspondence,* II, 443; *The Daily True Delta,* July 23, 24, 1864; *The New Orleans Times,* July 24, 1864; *Journal,* pp. 166-67.

[77] *Debates,* p. 623; *The Daily True Delta,* July 26, 1864; Kendall, *op. cit.,* I, 291-92; *Journal,* pp. 170-71.

[78] *Debates,* p. 625; *The New Orleans Times,* July 26, 1864; *The Daily True Delta,* July 25, 1864; *Journal,* p. 171.

[79] *Journal,* p. 170; *The Daily True Delta,* July 23, 25, 1864; *The New Orleans Times,* July 23, 28, 1864; *The New York Herald,* August 2, 4, 1864.

[80] *Debates,* p. 631-42; *Journal,* p. 190; *The Daily True Delta,* July 27, 1864;

Cox, *op. cit.,* p. 428; Kendall, *op. cit.,* I, 291; *The New Orleans Times,* July 9, 1864; *The Daily True Delta,* July 9, 26, 1864; *Report of the Secretary of State, May, 1902;* pp. 117-38. As will presently be shown congressmen and members of the legislature were also elected on this same date.

[81] *Chase Correspondence,* II, 443.

[82] *Debates,* p. 550.

[83] *Chase Correspondence,* II, 447; *Lincoln's Works,* II, 561; Dostie, *op. cit.,* p. 132.

[84] *The Daily Picayune,* August 16, 1864; *The Daily True Delta,* August 10, 14, 1864; *The New Orleans Times,* August 14, 1864; Dostie, *op. cit.,* p. 125. The Governor's proclamation, which included complete instructions, was issued some time before. *The New Orleans Times,* July 27, 1864; *The Daily True Delta,* July 31, 1864.

[85] *Chase Correspondence,* II, 444; *The Daily True Delta,* August 11, 14, 21, 1864. Even the *Picayune* and *Times* eventually advocated its adoption on the grounds that it was at least an improvement over the 1852 document, and that it would make peace possible. *The Daily Picayune,* September 3, 1864; *The New Orleans Times,* September 5, 1864.

[86] *The Daily Picayune,* September 6, 1864; Hunt, *op. cit.,* p. 283; McCarthy, *op. cit.,* p. 75; *The Daily True Delta,* September 6, 7, 12, 1864; *The New Orleans Times,* September 6, 7, 23, 1864; Rhodes, *op. cit.,* V, 53. Records will be produced in a later chapter to show that a large majority of the votes were fraudulent. Rhodes makes the statement that the work was that "of a fair set of men," and that the "proceedings were orderly." But he seems to have relied chiefly on the *Debates.* General Banks also pronounced the works of the convention highly satisfactory. The full text follows:

"In a State which held 331,726 slaves, one-half of its entire population in 1800, more than three-fourths of whom had been specially excepted from the Proclamation of Emancipation, and were still held *de jure* in bondage, the convention declared by a majority of all the votes to which the State would have been entitled if every delegate had been present from every district in the State:—

"Instantaneous, universal, uncompensated, unconditional emancipation of slaves!

"It prohibited forever the recognition of property in men!

"It decreed the education of all children, without distinction of race or color!

"It directs all men, white or black, to be enrolled as soldiers for the public defence!

"It makes all men equal before the law!

"It compels, by its regenerating spirit, the ultimate recognition of all the rights which national authority can confer upon an oppressed race!

"It wisely recognizes, for the first time in constitutional history, the interest of daily labor as an element of power entitled to the protection of the State." McCarthy, *op. cit.,* pp. 75-76; *The New York Tribune,* October 14, 1864.

[87] *Lincoln's Works,* II, 597-98; *The New Orleans Times,* September 22, 23, 1864; *The Daily True Delta,* September 12, 30, 1864. Lincoln also expressed his satisfaction when he said: "A very fair proportion of the people of Louisiana have inaugurated a new State government, making an excellent new constitution—better for the poor black man than we have in Illinois. This was done under military protection, directed by me, in the belief, still sincerely entertained, that with such a nucleus around which to build we could get the State into position again sooner than otherwise." *Lincoln's Works,* II, 597.

CHAPTER VII

[1] *The Daily Picayune,* February 13, 1863; *Acts Passed by the Twenty-seventh Legislature, Extra Session.* December, 1862, and January, 1863 (Natchitoches: *Natchitoches Times,* 1864), pp. 1, 30, 32. This will be cited hereafter as *Acts,*

1862-1863; Dorsey, *op. cit.,* p. 241; *The Weekly Gazette and Comet,* November 21, 1864; *The Daily True Delta,* June 1, 1864. Colonel H. W. Allen, a gallant and popular Confederate soldier, had been elected governor on November 2, 1863. *The Weekly Gazette and Comet,* November 21, 1865; Barrow, *op. cit.,* pp. 42-45.

² The Confederate legislature, at the behest of its governor, passed an act which provided that slaves lost while impressed on the public works be paid for, and that all slaves who should engage in insurrection or rebellion or should bear arms against the Confederacy should be put to death. Dorsey, *op. cit.,* pp. 235-36. The acts of this Shreveport Legislature do not seem to have been published. The Confederate governor had also arrived at the conclusion that the slaves could be used to aid the cause of the Confederacy, as the subjoined extract from a dispatch to the Confederate Secretary of War reveals:

"The time has come for us to put into the army every able bodied negro man as a soldier. This should be done immediately. Congress should, at the coming session, take action on this most important question. The negro knows that he cannot escape conscription if he goes to the enemy. He must play an important part in the war. He caused the fight, and he will have his portion of the burden to bear.

"We have learned from dear bought experience that negroes can be taught to fight, and that all who leave us are made to fight against us. I would free all able to bear arms, and put them into the field at once. They will make much better soldiers with us than against us, and swell the now depleted ranks of our armies. I beg you to give this your earnest attention." This advice was not followed by the Confederates. But it did inspire the Federal authorities in New Orleans to retaliate with the following General Order No. 58.

"The class of persons to whom it refers, will not be conscripted into the armies of the United States. If they come within our lines all will be freed, and they will be received and treated as refugees. They will be accepted as volunteers, or will be employed in the public service, their families will be cared for until they are in a condition to care for them. If a draft again should become necessary, no discrimination against them will be made in the enrollment of draft." *The New Orleans Times,* October 14, 1864; Dorsey, *op. cit.,* p. 382. The full text of the Allen letter was given together with and included in General Order No. 58. They did draft great numbers of them in 1865. Long lists of those drafted were published almost daily for about three months. "Louisiana," *Annual Cyclopaedia, 1865,* p. 508; *The Daily True Delta,* February 16 to May 9, 1865. The *True Delta* stated on May 4: "Seven thousand whites and 20,000 blacks have been furnished. All ex-rebels were let off. Only union men suffer. Yet the draft goes on, and the war is over."

³ *The Daily Picayune,* April 7, 1864; "Louisiana," *Annual Cyclopaedia, 1865,* pp. 594-96. The full text is given.

⁴ *The New Orleans Times,* February 18, 1864; Pierce, *op. cit.,* pp. 16-18; *The Weekly Gazette and Comet,* February 13, 1864.

⁵ *The Daily Picayune,* April 7, 1864; *The New Orleans Times,* April 9, 1864. This order is significant. It was really the first of the so-called "Reconstruction Black Codes."

⁶ *The New Orleans Times,* September 21, 1864.

⁷ *Ibid.,* October 13, 15, 21, 26, and November 2, 22, 1864.

⁸ *Ibid.,* November 22, and December 16, 1864; Pierce, *op. cit.,* p. 19. Pierce gives a full treatment of negro labor in Louisiana in his first chapter, entitled: "Antecedents."

⁹ *The New Orleans Times,* November 1, 1864; "Louisiana," *Annual Cyclopaedia, 1864,* p. 480.

¹⁰ *The New Orleans Times,* December 28, 1864; "Louisiana," *Annual Cyclopaedia,* 1865, p. 515.

[11] *The New Orleans Times,* May 1, 1865.

[12] *Ibid.,* May 30, 1865. The Bureau reports were published in most of the New Orleans papers.

[13] *Ibid.,* June 1, 1865.

[14] *Ibid.,* June 8, 1865; Pierce, *op. cit.,* p. 44.

[15] *The New Orleans Times,* March 13, 1864.

[16] *The Daily Picayune,* March 23, 1864; Pierce, *op. cit.,* pp. 75, 131.

[17] *The New Orleans Times,* March 23, 1864.

[18] *Ibid.,* September 2, 21, and October 24, 30, 1864; *The Daily True Delta,* September 16, 21, 25, and November 30, 1864. The Federal lines had been retreating during 1864, not "advancing."

[19] *The New Orleans Times,* March 21, 22, 1864.

[20] *Ibid.,* July 14, 22, 27, 30, and September 6, 7, 1864; *The Daily True Delta,* August 30, and September 1, 2, 6, 7, 12, 1864.

[21] *The Daily Picayune,* October 4, 1864; *Journal of the House of the State of Louisiana for 1864-1865* (New Orleans: W. R. Fish, State Printer, 1865), p. 1. This will be cited hereafter as *House Journal, 1864-1865.* According to the official election notice of the governor, members were elected to both branches of the state legislature and to the Thirty-Eighth Congress. There were two boxes at each voting precinct: one for votes for and against the constitution, and the other for the votes for the candidates for the state legislature and for Congress. The Free State candidates had been nominated at a convention. They opposed the "equal rights" candidates. During the short but "lively" campaign there was much "excitement," and some "confusion," especially at the public meetings. But, as has been stated, only a few "equal rights" candidates were elected to the state legislature. *The Daily True Delta,* July 31, August 2, 27, and September 1, 2, 4, 6, 7, 1864; *The New Orleans Times,* August 22, 30, and September 2, 6, 23, 1864.

[22] *House Journal, 1864-1865,* p. 4;

The New Orleans Times, August 22, 30, and September 6, 7, 1864.

[23] *The Daily True Delta,* September 1, 2, 6, 7, 12, 1864; *Journal of the Senate of the State of Louisiana for 1864-1865* (New Orleans: W. R. Fish, State Printer, 1865), pp. 3-4. This will be cited hereafter as *Senate Journal, 1864-1865.* It will be observed that the representation was different from what it had been in the convention. Whereas the convention representation had been on the basis of total white population, this new representation was based on the total white voting population, according to provision in the new constitution. *Journal of the Convention of 1864,* p. 174.

[24] *House Journal, 1864-1865,* p. 6; *The Daily Picayune,* October 5, 1864; *The Daily True Delta,* October 4, 1864.

[25] *Senate Journal, 1864-1865,* p. 14; *The Daily Picayune,* October 4, 1864; *The Daily True Delta,* October 4, 1864; *The New Orleans Times,* October 4, 5, 1864. A complete roster of the state legislature is also given by *The Daily True Delta,* September 12, 1864.

[26] *Senate Journal, 1864-1865,* pp. 9-13; *House Journal, 1864-1865,* pp. 10-14; *The Daily True Delta,* October 6, 7, 8, 1864; *The New Orleans Times,* October 6, 8, 1864.

[27] *Debates in the House of Representatives of the State of Louisiana, Sessions of 1864-1865* (New Orleans: W. R. Fish, State Printer, 1865), p. 400. This will be cited hereafter as *House Debates, 1864-1865.*

[28] *Debates in the Senate of the State of Louisiana, Session of 1864-1865* (New Orleans: W. R. Fish, State Printer, 1865), p. 45; *The Daily True Delta,* November 11, 13, 15, 1864. The *Delta* commented on this bill as follows: "Perhaps the most exciting and delicate question that has ever been agitated in this community is that which has been brought before the Senate of the State by Mr. Smith of St. Mary." *The Daily True Delta,* November 13, 1864.

[29] *Senate Debates, 1864-1865,* p. 47;

The Daily True Delta, November 11, 1864.

[30] *Senate Debates, 1864-1865,* p. 48. It, of course, favored the extension of suffrage to all the male blacks.

[31] *Ibid.,* p. 51; *Senate Journal, 1864-1865,* p. 58. This had been Lincoln's suggestion. *The Daily True Delta,* November 16, 1864.

[32] *Senate Journal, 1864-1865,* p. 59; *The Daily True Delta,* January 15, 18, and February 18, 1865.

[33] *Senate Journal, 1864-1865,* p. 158.

[34] *House Debates, 1864-1865,* p. 371.

[35] *Ibid.,* pp. 292-93; *House Journal, 1864-1865,* p. 142.

[36] *Senate Debates,* p. 157.

[37] *House Debates, 1864-1865,* p. 293; *The Daily True Delta,* January 21 and April 4, 1865.

[38] *Acts Passed by the General Assembly at the First and Second Session, 1864-1865* (New Orleans: W. R. Fish, State Printer, 1865), p. 40. This will be cited hereafter as *Acts, 1864-1865; The Daily True Delta,* January 21, 1865.

[39] *Acts, 1864-1865,* p. 42; McPherson, *op. cit.,* p. 598; *The Daily True Delta,* February 18, 1865; *House Journal, 1864-1865,* pp. 173-74.

[40] *House Journal, 1864-1865,* pp. 173-74; *The New York Herald,* February 27, 1865; *The Daily True Delta,* February 18 and April 4, 1865.

[41] *The New Orleans Times,* April 23, 1864.

[42] *Ibid.,* May 7, 11, 1864. The *Times* was hostile to Lincoln, and, although it did not dare boldly to advocate Chase, it did say that "Mr. Chase has high claims on the public confidence."

[43] *The Daily Picayune,* May 18, 1864; *The New Orleans Times,* May 24, 1864; *House Journal, 1864-1865,* pp. 49-50.

[44] *The New Orleans Times,* May 16, 1864; *The Daily True Delta,* June 10, 1864.

[45] *The New Orleans Times,* May 25, 1864. The delegates were admitted to seats by a vote of 307 to 167. *The New Orleans Times,* June 16, 1864; *The Daily True Delta,* June 19, 1864.

[46] *The Daily True Delta,* September 9, 10, 11, 1864; *The New Orleans Times,* September 9, 1864.

[47] *The New Orleans Times,* October 7, 1864; *The Daily True Delta,* October 8, 1864.

[48] *The Daily Picayune,* October 14, 1864; *The New Orleans Times,* October, 10, 14, 16, 1864; *The Daily True Delta,* October 14, 1864.

[49] *The New Orleans Times,* October 14, 1864; *The Daily Picayune,* October 14, 1864; *The Daily True Delta,* October 8, 15, 1864.

[50] *The New Orleans Times,* October 21, 24, 1864.

[51] *Acts, 1864-1865,* pp. 4-6; *The Daily True Delta,* October 15, 16, 1864.

[52] *House Journal, 1864-1865,* p. 26; *Senate Journal, 1864-1865,* p. 49; *House Debates, 1864-1865,* p. 85; *The New Orleans Times,* November 8, 9, 1864; *The Daily True Delta,* November 9, 1864.

[53] *Congressional Globe,* 38 Cong., 2 sess., pp. 668-69, 711; McCarthy, *op. cit.,* pp. 382-83. Among the other minor acts passed were: An act to divide the state into five congressional districts; two bills in reference to the Charity Hospital; an act to amend the city charter; and a bill to provide for the reorganization of several district courts throughout the state. *The Daily True Delta,* March 25, 1865.

[54] *House Journal, 1864-1865,* p. 64; *The New Orleans Times,* November 22, 1864.

[55] *House Debates, 1864-1865,* p. 440.

[56] *House Debates, 1864-1865,* p. 141.

[57] *Ibid.,* p. 144.

[58] *Ibid.,* p. 171; *The New Orleans Times,* October 16, 1864.

[59] *Senate Debates, 1864-1865,* p. 116; *House Debates, 1864-1865,* p. 81.

[60] *House Debates, 1864-1865,* p. 101.

[61] *Senate Debates, 1864-1865,* p. 189; *House Debates, 1864-1865,* pp. 215-18; *House Journal, 1864-1865,* p. 102; *The New Orleans Times,* November 22, 1864; *The Daily True Delta,* November 29 and December 21, 1864.

[62] *House Debates, 1864-1865,* p. 227, 276; *House Journal, 1864-1865,* p. 138.

[63] *Senate Debates, 1864-1865,* pp. 15,

NOTES

26; *House Debates, 1864-1865*, pp. 143, 339, 427; *The New Orleans Times*, November 9, 1864.

[64] *Senate Debates, 1864-1865*, pp. 192-95; *House Journal, 1864-1865*, pp. 62, 76-81; *The New Orleans Times*, December 21, 1864; *The Daily True Delta*, December 22, 1864.

[65] *House Journal, 1864-1865*, pp. 34, 83, 186.

[66] *Senate Journal, 1864-1865*, p. 90; *The Daily True Delta*, December 15, 1864.

[67] *Senate Debates, 1864-1865*, pp. 70-73; *The Daily True Delta*, November 29, 1864; *The New York Herald*, December 9, 1864.

[68] *House Debates, 1864-1865*, pp. 375-94; *The New Orleans Times*, October 13, 1864.

[69] *Senate Debates, 1864-1865*, pp. 21, 29, 79-82; *House Journal, 1864-1865*, pp. 59, 99; *Senate Journal, 1864-1865*, pp. 37, 88-90; *The New Orleans Times*, November 1, 3, 4, 5, 10, 15, 1864; *The Daily True Delta*, December 14, 1864.

[70] *Senate Debates, 1864-1865*, p. 104; *House Journal, 1864-1865*, p. 22; *The New Orleans Times*, October 12, 14, 1864.

[71] *Acts, 1864-1865*, p. 170; *House Journal, 1864-1865*, p. 112.

[72] *House Journal, 1864-1865*, p. 225; *The New Orleans Times*, April 5, 1865.

[73] *Acts, 1864-1865*, pp. 32-39.

[74] *House Debates, 1864-1865*, pp. 3-13, 102-03; *Senate Debates, 1864-1865*, pp. 158-89; *The Daily True Delta*, March 21 and April 4, 1865.

[75] *House Debates, 1864-1865*, pp. 80, 313.

[76] *Ibid.*, p. 263; *The New Orleans Times*, January 28, 1865.

[77] *House Debates, 1864-1865*, pp. 313-14; *The New Orleans Times*, January 28 and February 8, 1865.

[78] *House Journal, 1864-1865*, p. 133; *The New Orleans Times*, January 14, 1865; *House Debates, 1864-1865*, pp. 282-90; *The Daily True Delta*, December 10, 1864. Vituperation and sneers were "showered on the legislature." It was styled variously as: "a rump parliament," "a mob," and "a beer garden." *The Daily True Delta*, December 10, 1864.

[79] *House Journal, 1864-1865*, pp. 138, 223; *The New Orleans Times*, December 28, 1864; *Senate Debates, 1864-1865*, pp. 189, 192.

[80] *House Journal, 1864-1865*, p. 211; *House Debates, 1864-1865*, p. 426.

[81] *The New Orleans Times*, February 14, 1865.

[82] *Ibid.*, February 17, 1865.

[83] *Ibid.*, April 5, 1865.

[84] *The Daily Picayune*, April 6, 1865.

[85] *Butler's Correspondence*, II, 27, 28-29, 48, 506-07; McCarthy, *op. cit.*, pp. 41-42; *The Daily Picayune*, May 9, 1864.

[86] "Louisiana," *Annual Cyclopaedia, 1863*, p. 586; *The Daily True Delta*, May 8, and June 10, 17, 1862.

[87] *The Daily Picayune*, December 30, 1862; McCarthy, *op. cit.*, p. 43; Kendall, *op. cit.*, I, 293.

[88] *The Daily Delta*, January 4, 1863; McCarthy, *op. cit.*, pp. 42-43; *The Daily Picayune*, December 31, 1863.

[89] *Ibid.*, December 31, 1863, and January 14, 1864; *The New Orleans Times*, June 6, 1864.

[90] McCarthy, *op. cit.*, p. 42; *The Daily Picayune*, September 23, 1864; *The Daily True Delta*, September 23, 1864; *The New Orleans Times*, July 9, 1864. This article gave a "Review of the Courts of Louisiana from 1861-1864."

[91] *The Era*, June 26, 1863; *The Daily Picayune*, October 16, 1862; *The Daily True Delta*, June 16 and 25, 1864.

[92] *The Era*, June 16, 1863; *The Daily True Delta*, June 25, 1864.

[93] *The New Orleans Times*, July 9, 1864; *The Daily Picayune*, April 12 and October 16, 1864.

[94] *The Daily Picayune*, April 12, 1863; *The New Orleans Times*, June 6, 1864. It seems to have been the consensus among the legal fraternity that in case of a conflict between the laws, the state laws should have been made applicable.

[95] *Debates in the Constitutional Convention, 1864*, p. 519.

[269]

[96] "Louisiana," *Annual Cyclopaedia, 1864,* pp. 480-85.

[97] *The New Orleans Times,* February 21, 1865.

[98] *Acts, 1864-1865,* pp. 18-20; *The Daily True Delta,* November 5 and December 8, 12, 1864, and March 17, 1865; *The New Orleans Times,* November 29, 1864, and March 16, 1865.

[99] *The Daily True Delta,* April 2, 1865; *The New Orleans Daily Crescent,* April 21, 1866; *The Daily Picayune,* April 1, 1865; W. K. Dart, "The Justices of the Supreme Court," *The Louisiana Historical Quarterly,* IV (1921), p. 120. The Chief Justiceship had at first been conferred upon Christian Roselius, an able jurist, by Governor Wells, who had succeeded Hahn as governor after Hahn's election to the United States Senate. But Roselius had felt compelled to decline the honor when, upon inquiry from General Hurlburt, Commanding General, he learned that the "whole machinery of the present State is subject to the military law." In his letter of refusal, he concluded: "From this it is clear that there . . . is in reality no civil government . . . of the people . . . and no Supreme Court, and consequently no office of Chief Justice, created by the Constitution of Louisiana." *The Daily Picayune,* March 16, 22, 1865; *The Daily True Delta,* March 25, 26, 1865; *The New Orleans Times,* March 16, 1865.

[100] *House Journal, 1864-1865,* p. 110; *The New Orleans Times,* June 26, 1864. Judge Peabody had felt compelled to defend the legality of his court the year before. He contended at that time that it was sanctioned by international law, since the State of Louisiana was "conquered territory," and Lincoln could, by this law, as Commander-in-Chief, establish such a court in such territory. The inconsistency of this "conquered territory" theory with that advocated by Lincoln at this time must have been apparent. With those critics who stated that civil government had displaced it, Peabody agreed, but declared that it must continue to function until abolished by Congress. As a matter of fact,

there was a precedent for this court in California; and the United States Supreme Court did sustain its legality in a subsequent decision. "Louisiana," *Annual Cyclopaedia, 1864,* pp. 480-85; *The New Orleans Times,* February 8, 1865.

[101] "Louisiana," *Annual Cyclopaedia, 1865,* pp. 480-85.

[102] *Congressional Globe,* 39 Cong., 1 sess., p. 4236.

[103] *The Daily Picayune,* September 3, 1864; *The New Orleans Times,* August 22, 30, and September 6, 8, 21, 23, 1864; *The Daily True Delta,* September 1, 2, 6, 7, 1864; *The New York Herald,* August 8, 1864; Dostie, *op. cit.,* p. 126.

[104] *The Daily Picayune,* September 21, 1864; *The Daily True Delta,* September 6, 7, 29, 1864; *The New Orleans Times,* September 6, 7, 8, 23, 1864.

[105] *The New Orleans Times,* December 11, 1864; *Congressional Globe,* 38 Cong., 2 sess., p. 23; *The Daily True Delta,* December 29, 30, 1864.

[106] *Congressional Globe,* 38 Cong., 2 sess., p. 870; *The New Orleans Times,* January 19, 29, and February 7, 1865; *The New York Herald,* January 22, 1865.

[107] *Congressional Globe,* 38 Cong., 2 sess., p. 1395; *The New Orleans Times,* March 7, 8, 1865. Lincoln took a lively interest in the admission of the Louisiana delegation, and often alluded to the subject when congressmen were visiting him. *The New Orleans Times,* January 28, 1865.

[108] *Congressional Globe,* 38 Cong., 2 sess., p. 1395; Dostie, *op. cit.,* pp. 126, 134.

[109] *House Journal, 1864-1865,* p. 21; *Senate Journal, 1864-1865,* p. 15; *The Daily True Delta,* October 11 and November 6, 1864; *The New Orleans Times,* October 11, 1864. The legislature erred in this. Slidell's term had expired March 4, 1861. He had not been previously re-elected. Benjamin's time would have expired March 4, 1865. The January election of 1865, in which Hahn was chosen, specified a six-year term, beginning March 4, 1865. Pierce Butler, *op. cit.,* pp. 170-72; *The Daily True*

Delta, January 15, 23, 25, 26, 1859; *The Daily Picayune,* January 26, 1859; Sears, *op. cit.,* p. 115.

[110] *Senate Journal, 1864-1865,* p. 119; *The New Orleans Times,* January 10, 15, 31, and February 28, 1865; *House Journal, 1864-1865,* p. 185; *The Daily True Delta,* January 5, 11, and February 28, 1865.

[111] *Chase Correspondence,* II, 453. Hahn, who probably was sent to Washington largely to plead the cause for re-admission, was succeeded by Lieutenant-Governor Wells. *The Daily True Delta,* March 4, 1865; *The New Orleans Times,* January 31, 1865; Dostie, *op. cit.,* p. 159.

[112] *The New Orleans Times,* December 9, 1864. The *Times* had copied this information from *The Little Rock National Democrat* of November 11.

[113] *Congressional Globe,* 38 Cong., 2 sess., pp. 5, 8; *The Daily True Delta,* December 29, 30, 1864. Durant presented this memorial. A. P. Dostie criticized Durant's course in a long letter addressed to the Chairman of the Committee on Elections in the House. This correspondence reveals a growing bitterness between the Unionist factions in Louisiana. *The Daily True Delta,* December 30, 1864.

[114] *Congressional Globe,* 38 Cong., 2 sess., p. 903; *The New Orleans Times,* January 10 and March 10, 17, 1865.

[115] *Congressional Globe,* 38 Cong., 2 sess., p. 26.

[116] *Ibid.,* p. 1011; Rhodes, *op. cit.,* V, 54. The debates revealed that there were two distinct classes of opposition to the recognition by Congress of the state government of Louisiana. One was under the leadership of Senator Powell of Kentucky whose aim seems to have been to demoralize, or "to clog the wheels of government," since he was "always at it." This class also contended that the State should represent a majority. The second class, under the leadership of Senator Sumner, objected to recognition on the ground that the "revolting states" had by act of secession forfeited their rights and constitutional guarantees as states, and were not entitled to representation in the "National Council" until they were re-admitted under such restrictions and regulations as Congress might impose on them. This class also made freedom of the slave and universal suffrage a prerequisite. *The Daily True Delta,* March 5, 1865.

[117] *Congressional Globe,* 38 Cong., 2 sess., pp. 1063-64; *The Daily True Delta,* March 7, 1865; McPherson, *op. cit.,* pp. 577-86. McPherson gives a full treatment of "The Louisiana Question."

[118] *Congressional Globe,* 38 Cong., 2 sess., pp. 1127-28; McCarthy, *op. cit.,* p. 333; Rhodes, *op. cit.,* V, 54. General Banks came to Washington, and lobbied indefatigably for weeks for recognition. He made out a very strong case for the vindication of the President's "one-tenth policy." *The New Orleans Times,* September 24, 1864, January 10, 21, 25, and March 7, 1865; *The Daily True Delta,* October 25, December 24, 1865, and January 27, 1866.

[119] *Congressional Globe,* 38 Cong., 2 sess., p. 1129; "Louisiana," *Annual Cyclopaedia, 1865,* p. 787; *The New Orleans Times,* March 7, 8, 1865; Rhodes, *op. cit.,* V, 54-55. It might also be added that this metaphor was fairly descriptive of the radical's bitter and uncompromising attack upon the executive policies of any form of reconstruction at this time; Sumner's partisan attack was directed against all such reconstruction, and was just as consciously political as Lincoln's "pretended State Government."

CHAPTER VIII

[1] Frank Moore (comp.), *Speeches of Andrew Johnson* (New York: Little Brown, and Company, 1866), p. 475. This will be cited hereafter as *Johnson's Speeches. The Daily Picayune,* May 21, 1865; Chambers, *op. cit.,* I, 660; Stryker, *op. cit.,* p. 220.

[2] James D. Richardson (comp.), *A Compilation of the Messages and Papers of the Presidents 1789-1897.* 10 vols.

(Washington: Government Printing Office, 1906), VI, 475. *The New Orleans Daily Crescent*, April 4, 1866; *The Southern Sentinel*, April 7, 1866; *The Sugar Planter*, April 7, 1866; *The Opelousas Courier*, April 14, 1866; Beale, *op. cit.*, p. 93. Four days earlier he had declared the "insurrection" at an end. Texas had been excepted. As a matter of fact, war did not cease officially until August, 1866, at which time the President declared by proclamation that the state of insurrection and war proclaimed by Lincoln was ended, and "that peace, order, tranquility, and civil authority" existed in and through the whole of the United States of America. This meant, technically, that martial law still obtained, at least until August, 1866. Richardson, *op. cit.*, VI, 438; McMaster, *op. cit.*, p. 651.

³ W. M. Caskey, "The Second Administration of Governor Andrew Johnson," *The East Tennessee Historical Society's Publications*, II (1930), p. 54.

⁴ *Johnson's Speeches*, p. 205. The writer believes that there is little justification, and little evidence, for the statement that "Johnson, like all persons of his social class in the South, disliked the negro and had no desire to give him political or social equality." He owned a few slaves, and does not seem to have been prejudiced. He did not, of course, wish for the negro to vote or have social equality. His telegram to Governor Sharkey of Mississippi, suggesting the vote for the negro, was apparently motivated by his wish to defeat the radicals. Beale, *op. cit.*, p. 8; Clifton R. Hall, *Andrew Johnson, Military Governor of Tennessee* (Princeton University Press, 1916), p. 182; Fleming, *Documentary History*, I, 117.

⁵ *Johnson's Speeches*, p. 470; McMaster, *op. cit.*, p. 63; Beale, *op. cit.*, pp. 29, 32, 85.

⁶ Thornton K. Lothrop, *William Henry Seward* (New York: Houghton, Mifflin and Company, 1896), p. 415; Blaine, *op. cit.*, II, 3-9; Sears, *op. cit.*, pp. 229-31. He seems to have ignored Slidell's letter in 1866, applying for permission to visit New Orleans. Sears, *op. cit.*, p. 230.

⁷ George W. Julian, *Political Recollections, 1840-1872* (Chicago: Jansen McClurg and Company, 1884), p. 255.

⁸ *Johnson's Speeches*, p. 480; *The Daily True Delta*, April 19, 25, 1865.

⁹ *Johnson's Speeches*, pp. 483-84; *The Daily True Delta*, April 19, 30, 1865; *The New York Herald*, April 21, 1865; Stryker, *op. cit.*, p. 208; Fleming, *Documentary History*, I, 116, 117.

¹⁰ *Johnson's Speeches*, pp. 481, 483, 484; Stryker, *op. cit.*, p. 208; *The Daily True Delta*, April 25, 1865; *The Weekly Gazette and Comet*, May 27, 1865. Blaine said that the "persuasive tongue of Seward" and the "flattery of Southern leaders" caused Johnson to reverse his policy. Blaine, *op. cit.*, II, 67-70. The writer does not concur in this conclusion. Johnson had not yet, to any appreciable extent, come into contact with the leaders, and Seward was still seriously ill and unable to speak.

¹¹ *Constitution of the United States*, Article II, Section II; *The New York Herald*, May 30, 1865; *The Baton Rouge Tri-weekly Gazette and Comet*, June 17 and July 22, 1865.

¹² Richardson, *op. cit.*, VI, 3, 10; Fleming, *Documentary History*, I, 168; McMaster, *op. cit.*, pp. 631-32.

¹³ Fleming, *Documentary History*, I, 168; McMaster, *op. cit.*, p. 632; Richardson, *op. cit.*, VI, 311; Beale, *op. cit.*, pp. 30-31.

¹⁴ Richardson, *op. cit.*, VI, 312; McMaster, *op. cit.*, p. 632.

¹⁵ *Journal of the Senate of the State of Louisiana*, 1866 (New Orleans: J. O. Nixon, State Printer, 1866), p. 144. Several legislative bodies of Louisiana passed resolutions expressive of their appreciation of Johnson's attitude.

¹⁶ Richardson, *op. cit.*, VI, 312-15; *The New York Herald*, May 30, 1865; *The Weekly Gazette and Comet*, June 17, 1865; Fanny Z. Lovell Bone, "Louisiana in the Disputed Election of 1876," *The Louisiana Historical Quarterly*, XIV (1931), 410. This proclamation referred only to North Carolina; but it was interpreted to be applicable to all states.

[17] *The New Orleans Times*, April 10, 1865; *The Weekly Gazette and Comet*, June 17, 1865.

[18] *The Daily Picayune*, June 21, 1865; *The Baton Rouge Tri-weekly Gazette and Comet*, August 24, 1865.

[19] *The Daily Picayune*, May 28, 1865; *The Louisiana Democrat*, June 14, 1865; McMaster, *op. cit.*, p. 626; J. P. Blessington, *Campaigns of Walker's Texas Division* (New York: Lange, Little and Company, 1875), p. 310.

[20] Dorsey, *op. cit.*, p. 307; *The Louisiana Democrat*, June 14, 1865; *The Weekly Gazette and Comet*, June 17 and July 25, 1865; *The New York Herald*, July 22, 1865. Governor Allen gave a touching "farewell address," which was printed in full in most of the Louisiana papers. Ex-Governor Moore and other civil officers had also emigrated. Moore had, however, returned in November. *The New Orleans Daily Crescent*, December 1, 1865.

[21] *The New Orleans Times*, June 8, 1865.

[22] *Ibid.*, July 21, 1865; *The Baton Rouge Tri-weekly Gazette and Comet*, October 21, 1865; *The Louisiana Democrat*, July 26, 1865. A special, stringent oath was prescribed for all attorneys before they could continue their practice at the bar of the United States Courts. The Confederate was virtually required to commit perjury, so it was alleged, if he took it, and if he refused he was practically deprived of a subsistence. The constitutionality of this act was called into question. Judge Durell announced that he thought it was unconstitutional, but he submitted to it, requiring the four or five hundred lawyers of New Orleans to take it before practicing in his court. Many refused; but the newcomers took it and obtained a lucrative practice. In fact this is how a number like Warmoth gained a foothold. *The New Orleans Times*, January 28, 1865; *The New Orleans Daily Crescent*, October 19, 1865.

[23] *The Daily True Delta*, September 21, 1865; *The New Orleans Times*, October 14, 1865; *The Daily Picayune*, July 8, 1865; *The Baton Rouge Tri-weekly Gazette and Comet*, July 8, 1865.

[24] "Louisiana," *Annual Cyclopaedia, 1867*, p. 476; *The Baton Rouge Tri-weekly Gazette and Comet*, October 26, 31, 1865; *The Daily Picayune*, July 8, 1865; *The New Orleans Daily Crescent*, June 4, 1866.

[25] Cox, *op. cit.*, pp. 434-35; McPherson, *op. cit.*, pp. 196-97; *The New Orleans Times*, April 16, 1866. The purchaser of confiscated property could hold it only during the lifetime of the offender. For this reason it could often be repurchased for a nominal sum.

[26] *Johnson Papers*, LX, 2981. Wells to Johnson April 28, 1865. This communication also carried the information that "some here bent on enriching themselves while serving, had bankrupt the State." The inference seems to be that Banks was one of those who had been "enriching themselves."

[27] *Johnson Papers*, LXII, 3321. J. T. Whitaker to Johnson, May 10, 1865.

[28] *Ibid.*, LIX, 2873. I. E. Moore to Johnson, April 21, 1865.

[29] *Ibid.*, LIX, 2869. D. S. Strait to Johnson, April 21, 1865.

[30] *Ibid.*, LXII, 3384. Fernandez to Johnson, May 7, 1865.

[31] *Ibid.*, LXII, 3384-85. Christie to Johnson, May 7, 1865.

[32] *Ibid.*, LXII, 3445. Graham to William Dennison, May 10, 1865.

[33] *Ibid.*, LXII, 3352-54. Brooks to Johnson, May 5, 1865.

[34] *Ibid.*, LXII, 3361-74. Banks to Preston King, May 6, and to Honorable George Ashman on May 7, 1865. These letters and telegrams appear typical of the many that the writer found among the *Johnson Papers* in the Library of Congress.

[35] *Ibid.*, LIX, 2824. April 20, 1865.

[36] *Ibid.*, LIX, 2826. Bullitt to Johnson, April 22, 1865. Governor Wells had evidently decided to cast his lot with those who appeared to be winners.

[37] *The New Orleans Times*, August 5, 1865. Banks had probably returned to New Orleans at Lincoln's request. He was now displaced upon representation,

so it was alleged, of Governor Wells and his delegation, and relieved by General Canby in June. *The New Orleans Times,* May 25 and June 4, 1865; Dostie, *op. cit.,* p. 188. After being mustered out of service, he practiced law for a short time in New Orleans, and was reported to have aspired to represent the State of Louisiana in the United States Senate. However, he decided to return to Massachusetts, and was subsequently elected to Congress. *New Orleans Daily Crescent,* November 3, 1865; *The Opelousas Courier,* July 22, 1865; *The Daily Picayune,* July 14, 1865.

³⁸ Dostie, *op. cit.,* pp. 175, 176, 179-81, 200; *The New Orleans Times,* May 18 and August 5, 1865; *The Daily True Delta,* May 17, 18, 1865; *The New York Herald,* May 28, 1865; *The Baton Rouge Tri-weekly Gazette and Comet,* September 23 and October 14, 1865.

³⁹ *The New Orleans Times,* May 19, 1865; *The Daily Picayune,* August 17, 1865.

⁴⁰ *The New Orleans Picayune,* June 24, 1865. Johnson's policy was also heartily endorsed at first by a number of radicals. Dostie, *op. cit.,* pp. 175, 176.

⁴¹ *The New Orleans Daily Crescent,* February 21, 1866.

⁴² *The New Orleans Daily True Delta,* February 20, 1866.

⁴³ *The New Orleans Daily Crescent,* February 23, 1866. This commission made a hurried trip to Washington, and Mr. Eagan, upon his return, made the report to the two Houses. He said that the President expressed himself as peculiarly gratified to receive the resolutions of endorsement from Louisiana; that he was willing to trust them in common with all the people in the South; and that he had no idea of yielding to the radicals. The President had, however, advised the postponement of the convention, lest the enemies of the South use it against him and thereby tend to embarrass his administration. Eagan stated further that they had been well received by the cabinet, which had encouraged them to believe that Congress would eventually yield in the struggle.

The *Journal* gives a complete report.

⁴⁴ *Ibid.,* February 24, 1866.

⁴⁵ *The Daily True Delta,* March 8, 1866.

⁴⁶ *The New Orleans Times,* April 10, 1866. These friends of President Johnson continued to uphold him and the Constitution by words and deeds. The Democratic State Executive Committee met in 1866 and selected a full quota of Louisiana's foremost and most influential citizens as delegates to the National Union Convention in Philadelphia. These delegates and Johnson's policy were endorsed in a big enthusiastic ratification mass meeting in Lafayette Square, at which twenty thousand were reported to have been present. *The Daily Picayune,* July 8, 12, 19, 24, 1866; *The New Orleans Times,* July 12, 15, 23, 25, and August 2, 25, 1866; *The New Orleans Daily Crescent,* July 12, 24, 25, and August 17, 1866; *The Southern Sentinel,* July 28 and August 18, 1866; *The Louisiana Democrat,* July 11, 1866.

⁴⁷ *The Daily Picayune,* June 7, 1865; *The Weekly Gazette and Comet,* June 17, 1865.

⁴⁸ *The Daily Picayune,* June 9, 1865; *The Weekly Gazette and Comet,* June 17, 1865; *The Louisiana Democrat,* June 28, 1865.

⁴⁹ *The Daily Picayune,* June 11, 1865; *The Baton Rouge Tri-weekly Gazette and Comet,* July 1, 1865. The Governor had been appointing officers of all grades in the city and out in the parishes. This practice he now continued. A list of such appointments was published almost every day. He had replaced Mayor Hoyt, a friend of Banks, with Hugh Kennedy, a supposedly pro-slavery man. It was thought that he did this in order to fortify himself politically, for the Mayor through his patronage and appointive power dominated the New Orleans elections, and therefore, had a controlling voice in the state elections. This act had brought on a crisis that had resulted in the trip to Washington. *The Daily Picayune,* June 20, 1865; *Chase Correspondence,* II, 456; Dostie, *op. cit.,* p. 188.

[50] *The Daily Picayune,* June 18, 1865. Wells seems to have been popular at this time, but his popularity was short-lived. *The Daily Picayune,* July 20, 1865; *Le Louisianais,* September 6, 1865.

[51] *The Daily Picayune,* June 14 and July 1, 2, 1865; *The New Orleans Times,* June 14, 1865; Dostie, *op. cit.,* pp. 190-98; *The Daily True Delta,* June 14, 1865. Lieutenant Governor Gastinel had been arrested and tried before a "Military Commission" on a charge of perjury; it was alleged that he was at one time in "rebel" service. Although this episode did not involve Wells, it did tend to keep things in a ferment.

[52] *The New Orleans Times,* July 12, 1865; *The Daily Picayune,* July 12, 1865; *The Louisiana Democrat,* July 19, 1865; *The Opelousas Courier,* July 22, 1865; *The Baton Rouge Tri-weekly Gazette and Comet,* July 13, 1865, January 13, and April 5, 1866.

[53] *The New Orleans Times,* January 5, February 6, and May 25, 1866; *The Baton Rouge Tri-weekly Gazette and Comet,* August 8, 15, September 5, and October 17, 28, 1865; *The Daily Picayune,* September 19 and October 15, 1865; *The New Orleans Daily Crescent,* February 1, 14, 1866.

[54] *The Daily Picayune,* June 22 and October 5, 22, 1865; *The New Orleans Daily Crescent,* October 14, 1865.

[55] *The New Orleans Times,* September 1, 1865. A levee convention was held on October 4, with many parishes represented. The convention gave a complete report of levee conditions in every parish, and made certain recommendations to Governor Wells and General Canby. The recommendations concluded: "If the levees are not reconstructed this season the next high water will make the evil almost irreparable." *The Daily Picayune,* October 5, 1865; *The Baton Rouge Tri-weekly Gazette and Comet,* October 17, 1865.

[56] *The New Orleans Times,* May 16, 25, 1865, April 16, 23, 26, June 2, 9, 24, 27, July 1, and September 17, 1866; *The Sugar Planter,* February 9, April 7, May 12, 19, June 9, 30, and July 30, 1866; *The New Orleans Daily Crescent,* April 7, 9, 10, 16, May 12, 18, 21, 26, July 26, and August 3, 1866; *The Southern Sentinel,* June 2, 9, 1866. An effort was made in 1866 to secure an appropriation of $4,000,000. After considerable debate the proposition was defeated by the lower house of Congress, due so it was alleged, to the hostility of the North. The Board of Levee Commissioners failed at the same time to sell one million dollars' worth of state levee bonds. *The New Orleans Times,* June 24, 27, and July 1, 1866; *The New Orleans Daily Crescent,* May 26, July 26, and August 3, 1866.

[57] *The New Orleans Times,* June 1, 1865, and April 21, 23, 1866. The *Tribune* attributed all these disasters to "disloyalty." It admitted, however, that some changes should be effected in order to make labor steady, reliable, and efficient.

[58] *The Daily Picayune,* July 1, 2, 4, 1865; *The Baton Rouge Tri-weekly Gazette and Comet,* July 4 and August 26, 1865. Almost daily over a period of weeks, a number of the papers printed long lists of appointees.

[59] *The New Orleans Times,* April 15, 1865; *The Daily True Delta,* May 14, 1865; *The New Orleans Tribune,* April 14, 1865. This was in an open letter published in the *New Orleans Tribune,* a negro organ, that seems to have been founded by radical Republican whites for the purpose of advocating and furthering the doctrine of equal suffrage. The purport of the letter was to condemn the method of organizing the Free State government, and also to protest against the registration of "four thousand," who had "not been naturalized," to the exclusion of "several thousand men of African descent who possessed every qualification," and who "had furnished regiment after regiment to defend the flag." This letter closed with a "solemn appeal" to "Congress and America to do away with the system so clearly wrong." Each member of Congress and other interested parties were reported to

have received copies of the *Tribune* daily.

⁶⁰ *The New Orleans Times*, May 23, 1865; *The New Orleans Daily Crescent*, June 27, 1866.

⁶¹ *The Daily Picayune*, June 17 and May 27, 1865. Terry attempted to justify his action in a letter published as an advertisement in *The Daily True Delta* of May 14, 1865.

⁶² *The Daily Picayune*, May 4, July 4, 11, and November 1, 1865; Dostie, *op. cit.*, pp. 203-04. He had apparently indignantly removed the offending registrar of voters, who had refused to resign. General E. R. S. Canby had refused to interfere, declaring that "It is within the legal discretion of the Governor." Besides, the question of the legality of the removal had been appealed to the Louisiana Supreme Court. *The New Orleans Times*, June 12, 1865.

⁶³ *The Daily Picayune*, October 15 and November 1, 1865; "Louisiana," *Annual Cyclopaedia, 1865*, p. 510. It is stated herein that many negroes had been registered. The writer finds no evidence of such registration.

⁶⁴ *The New Orleans Times*, June 29, 1865.

⁶⁵ *Ibid.*, June 13, 1865. The questionable status of the state had caused Wells to return to Washington in August, ostensibly for further instructions and to secure an appointment as Provisional governor. *The Daily Picayune*, August 10 and September 10, 1865; *The Louisiana Democrat*, August 16, 1865.

⁶⁶ *The Daily True Delta*, July 19 and August 17, 18, 21, 1865; *The New Orleans Times*, August 17, 1865; *The Louisiana Democrat*, September 6, 27, 1865. Sentiment favored the calling of a convention, in order to define the status of Louisiana. *The Daily Picayune* presented a complete program of reorganization for the state. *The Daily Picayune*, September 29, 30, 1865.

⁶⁷ *The Daily Picayune*, September 22, 1865; *The New Orleans Times*, September 22, 1865; *The Opelousas Courier*, September 30, 1865; *Le Louisianais*, September 23, 1865; *The Baton Rouge*

Tri-weekly Gazette and Comet, September 26, 1865; *The New York Herald*, September 30, 1865; *The New York Daily Tribune*, September 25, 1865. This meant that he was recognizing laws that were based on the Constitution of 1852. He was, however, calling this election according to articles contained in the Constitution of 1864.

⁶⁸ *The New Orleans Times*, August 23, 1865; *The Opelousas Courier*, August 26, 1865.

⁶⁹ *The New Orleans Times*, August 20, 1865; *The Daily Picayune*, August 17, 20, 1865; *The Louisiana Democrat*, August 30, 1865.

⁷⁰ *The Daily True Delta*, October 3, 1865. There is some uncertainty as to the number of representatives because some parishes were represented by proxies, and some delegates seem to have arrived late.

⁷¹ *The New Orleans Times*, October 4, 1865; *The Daily Picayune*, October 3, 4, 1865; *The Louisiana Democrat*, October 11, 1865; *The Daily True Delta*, October 3, 1865. Dr. J. L. Riddell, who called this convention to order, created a sensation when he said that "the secession of Louisiana was a crime involving treason and bloodshed." When asked to explain, he said on the platform: "The secession of Louisiana was worse than a crime. It was a blunder." This explanation was, of course, highly unsatisfactory; but when he promised to publish a satisfactory apology, the matter was dropped. *The Daily True Delta*, October 3, 1865; *The Times Picayune*, October 3, 1865.

⁷² *The New Orleans Times*, October 3, 1865; *The Louisiana Democrat*, October 11, 1865; *The Baton Rouge Tri-weekly Gazette and Comet*, October 7, 1865. This body also nominated a congressional and legislative ticket, and adopted by a unanimous vote a resolution requesting President Johnson to release and restore Jefferson Davis to citizenship.

⁷³ *The Daily True Delta*, September 30 and October 1, 1865; *The New Orleans Times*, August 10, 1865; *The Baton Rouge Tri-weekly Gazette and Comet*,

October 5, 7, 1865; *The Louisiana Democrat,* October 7, 11, 1865; *The New York Herald,* October 5, 1865.

[74] *The New Orleans Times,* October 6, 1865; *The Louisiana Democrat,* October 11, 1865; *The Daily Picayune,* October 4, 1865; *The New York Daily Tribune,* October 9, 1865; *The Opelousas Courier,* October 14, 1865.

[75] *The Daily True Delta,* August 8, 1865; *The New Orleans Times,* August 8, 1865; *The Daily Picayune,* August 8, 17, 1865.

[76] *The Daily True Delta,* August 8, 10, 20, and September 10, 1865; *The New Orleans Times,* September 10, 16, and October 16, 1865; *The Baton Rouge Tri-weekly Gazette and Comet,* August 12, 24, 1865; *The Daily Picayune,* September 12, 14, 1865.

[77] *The Daily True Delta,* October 10, 1865; *The New Orleans Times,* October 17, 1865; *The Daily Picayune,* October 10, 1865; *The Baton Rouge Tri-weekly Gazette and Comet,* October 14, 17, 1865.

[78] *The New Orleans Daily Crescent,* October 13, 1865; Chambers, *op. cit.,* I, 661; *Le Louisianais,* October 14, 1865. Governor Wells, who had been solicited to become the candidate of the conservatives, had answered: "I will not decline. . . ." *The Daily Picayune, September* 14, 1865.

[79] *The New Orleans Daily Crescent,* October 18, 1865; *The Daily Picayune,* October 10, 17, 18, 24, 31, 1865; *The New Orleans Daily Crescent,* October 17, 21, 31, and November 2, 1865. The National Republicans, accepting the "Province" theory, did not enter any state candidates; but, as will presently be shown, they did enter the Congressional race with one candidate. Ex-Governor Allen's friends also persisted in running him, although he never received an official nomination. In fact, when Allen learned about it, he wrote and thanked his friends for "putting down the movement." Dorsey, *op. cit.,* p. 346.

[80] *The New Orleans Times,* October 19, 1865; Dorsey, *op. cit.,* pp. 346-48; *The New Orleans Daily Crescent,* October 16, 24, 28, 1865; *The Daily Picayune,* October 18, 29, 1865; *The Louisiana Democrat,* October 25, 1865; *The Baton Rouge Tri-weekly Gazette and Comet,* October 26, 1865; *La Sentinelle Du Sud,* October 28, 1865. One paragraph of this "Address of Ex-Governor Allen's Friends" was so beautifully and touchingly written that it is quoted in full: "Fellow-citizens! Governor Allen is now an exile from home, kindred and friends —from the State he has served so long and faithfully, and loved so well—although his return is anticipated within a few weeks. Ruined in his private fortunes, crippled in his limbs, but with a heart as proud, as noble, as unsullied as ever beat within the breast of a human being, *what a compliment, what a testimonial of gratitude it would be to elect him to the first office in the commonwealth!* The people of Louisiana owe this to themselves, to him, to the country. The debt of gratitude they are under could not be as well discharged in any other way." *The Daily True Delta,* October 22, 1865; Dorsey, *op. cit.,* p. 347.

[81] Dorsey, *op. cit.,* pp. 346-47. It was argued, however, in his behalf that he was in the same class as Governor Humphries of Mississippi, and that he could be pardoned. He had also indicated in his "farewell" on June 2 his readiness to comply with the Constitution and laws of the General government, and had turned over all records to it. Dorsey, *op. cit.,* p. 346; "Louisiana," *Annual Cyclopaedia, 1865,* p. 510; Fortier, *Louisiana Studies,* pp. 229-30.

[82] *The New Orleans Daily Crescent,* October 24, 28, and November 4, 1865; Dorsey, *op. cit.,* pp. 346, 348-50; *The New York Herald,* October 29, 1865; *The New York Daily Tribune,* October 30, 1865; *The Daily Picayune,* October 28, 1865; *The Baton Rouge Tri-weekly Gazette and Comet,* October 26, 1865.

[83] *The Daily True Delta,* October 24, 26, 1865; Dorsey, *op. cit.,* pp. 348-57; *The Daily Picayune,* October 10, 15, 29, 1865; *The Louisiana Democrat,* October 25 and November 1, 4, 1865.

[84] *The Daily True Delta,* October 26,

28, 1865; *The Louisiana Democrat,* October 21, 1865; *The Baton Rouge Tri-weekly Gazette and Comet,* October 31, 1865; *The Southern Sentinel,* October 28, 1865.

[85] Dorsey, *op. cit.,* p. 346. Map No. 9 gives some idea of the vote for each. Allen died during the spring of 1866 from the effect of his Civil War wounds. Some months later his remains were exhumed by friends, and returned to Louisiana, where they were reinterred on the old State Capitol grounds, and a suitable monument erected to the memory of the "war governor." Dorsey, *op. cit.,* p. 362; *The Louisiana Democrat,* May 22, July 4, 14, 1866, and January 23, 1867; *The Sugar Planter,* May 19 and June 9, 1866; *The New Orleans Daily Crescent,* May 15, 16, 23, 1866; *The Baton Rouge Tri-weekly Gazette and Comet,* May 15, 1866; Fortier, *Louisiana Studies,* p. 230; *The Morning Advocate,* November 1, 1937.

[86] *The New Orleans Times,* October 15, 1865; *The New Orleans Daily Crescent,* October 16, 17, 25 and November 2, 1865. The leaders and orators were Fred N. Ogden, Mr. Tanner, B. F. Jonas, A. J. Herron, Albert Voorhies, Jacob Barker, Rozier, and others.

[87] *The Daily Picayune,* October 17, 1865; *The New Orleans Times,* October 17, 1865; *The New Orleans Daily Crescent,* October 17, 21, 1865.

[88] *The New Orleans Daily Crescent,* November 3, 1865; *The Daily Picayune,* October 25, 28, 1865; *The Southern Sentinel,* October 28, 1865; *Le Louisianais,* November 4, 1865.

[89] *Johnson Telegrams,* I, 127; *Le Louisianais,* November 11, 1865; *The Baton Rouge Tri-weekly Gazette and Comet,* November 7, 9, 11, 18, 1865; *The New Orleans Daily Crescent,* November 7, 8, 11, 1865; *The Daily Picayune,* November 7, 9, 10, 1865. Cathburt Bullitt to President Johnson, November 7, 1865. This telegram also included a statement that: "The Congressional delegation is not of the best material." The writer examined the three volumes of *Telegrams* in the Manuscript Division of the Library of Congress.

[90] *The New Orleans Daily Crescent,* December 4, 6, 11, 12, 1865; *The Louisiana Democrat,* November 15, 18, 1865; *The New York Herald,* November 10, 1865; *The Opelousas Courier,* November 11, 18, and December 2, 1865; *The Southern Sentinel,* November 18, 1865. These officers were installed on Monday, December 6, 1865. The total vote had been approximately 28,000, or more than 20,000 less than the last state-wide vote of 1860. This loss may be attributed in part to indifference, since the result had been a foregone conclusion. Many, of course, were not qualified, and thousands who had served outside of Louisiana never returned. "Louisiana," *Annual Cyclopaedia, 1865,* pp. 513, 516.

[91] *The New Orleans Times,* July 6, 1865. It had been rumored "that these newcomers would be compelled to leave." They, therefore, held a gathering at the Custom House and, after taking counsel among themselves, decided to remain.

[92] Warmoth, *op. cit.,* p. 25. This young man had served for a short time as Judge of the Provost Court for the Department of the Gulf at New Orleans. When this service ended, he, and many others, including Banks, remained to practise law. He soon "had a lucrative practise before court-martials, military commissions, Government Departments, and in the United States Courts," where Confederates could not practise without perjuring themselves. Warmoth, *op. cit.,* pp. 24, 25; Barrow, *op. cit.,* pp. 49-50.

[93] *The Daily True Delta,* July 12, 1865. At no time could they have numbered more than five hundred. Their movements were secretive at first, but the Democrats do not seem to have been deceived by the manoeuvers of the leaders, "the sanity of whom," as the Democratic press remarked, "might have been doubted had it not been that they exhibited some little method in their madness."

[94] Warmoth, *op. cit.,* p. 25.

[95] *The New Orleans Times,* July 12, 20,

[278]

1865; "Louisiana," *Annual Cyclopaedia, 1865,* pp. 513-14.

[96] *The New Orleans Tribune,* September 23 and November 5, 1865. This negro journal, which had begun publication during the year with three negroes as editors, according to Warmoth, may have been sponsored by the radicals. It was at least their official journal at this time. It was devoted to the cause of negro suffrage, and, in fact, to negro equality. The sixth of November was the same date as that fixed by the other two parties for their regular election of state officials and Congressmen.

[97] *Ibid.,* November, 1865; *The Southern Sentinel,* November 18, 1865; *The Daily Picayune,* November 7, 9, 1865.

[98] *The New Orleans Tribune,* November 7, 8, 9, 10, 1865.

[99] *Ibid.,* November 10, 1865. Negroes polled heavy votes in all eight parishes. There seems to have been some negro voting in East Baton Rouge parish also. The negroes, so it was alleged, had been organized in the vicinity of Baton Rouge by certain "low whites." *The Baton Rouge Tri-weekly Gazette and Comet,* September 16 and November 4, 1865.

[100] *The Daily True Delta,* November 7, 1865. The *Picayune* reported: "The negroes were enticed away from work and compelled to pay a dollar per vote at the polls for the privilege of going through the motion. . . . They lost a day's wages too. . . . We would invite the attention of the Freedmen's Bureau to this wrong and oppression of the freedmen. Suffrage in their case meant literally to suffer. . . ." *The Daily Picayune,* November 9, 1865.

[101] *The Daily True Delta,* November 8, 9, 1865. A ballot box was reported broken, and eighty dollars, "the amount of the contribution by the voters collected during the voting, was carried away." Other polls were reported closed. The eighty dollars indicates that negroes were contributing to the expenses of Warmoth.

[102] *The New Orleans Tribune,* December 13, 1865. *The New Orleans Daily Crescent* on December 1, 1865, denied

that whites and blacks voted at the same polls. It stated: "No black man voted at the legal polls, and no white man voted at the illegal." Warmoth says he received 19,396 votes from thirteen parishes. Warmoth, *op. cit.,* p. 45.

[103] *The New Orleans Times,* November 14, 1865. At the conclusion of this speech, Judge Warmoth was presented with a handsome bouquet by the Reverend Mr. Taylor, a negro clergyman. Warmoth does not mention this meeting in his recent publication.

[104] *The Southern Star,* November 14, 1865.

[105] *The New Orleans Times,* November 11, 15, 1865.

[106] Warmoth, *op. cit.,* p. 45. Other evidence would tend to prove that his credentials were not signed by the Secretary of State.

[107] *Congressional Globe,* 39 Cong., 1 sess., p. 101. Stevens was in charge of Warmoth's case. It was reported that "the gravity of the House was upset" when Mr. Stevens introduced the credentials of Mr. Warmoth as a "delegate from the territory of Louisiana." *The Baton Rouge Tri-weekly Gazette and Comet,* January 9, 1866; *The New Orleans Tribune,* December 13, 1865.

[108] Warmoth, *op. cit.,* p. 45. When the roll for United States House of Representatives was made up, "the other Southern states were excluded." A committee was then appointed to investigate and determine whether the Southern states were entitled to representation. The matter was debated at intervals for some time, but no Congressman or Senator was ever received until after the new congressional plan had been put into full force and effect. *The Daily Picayune,* December 10, 1865; *The New Orleans Daily Crescent,* October 31, and December 4, 1865; *The New Orleans Times,* January 3, 26, February 20, and March 8, 1866; J. Barker, *The Rebellion: Its Consequences and the Congressional Committee* (New Orleans: Commercial Print Shop, 1866), p. 31.

[109] *The Daily True Delta,* February 24, 1866; Dostie, *op. cit.,* p. 229.

CHAPTER IX

[1] *The New Orleans Times,* August 12, 18, 1865; *The Southern Sentinel,* November 18, 1865; *The Baton Rouge Tri-weekly Gazette and Comet,* November 21, 1865. There was a growing demand that the negro troops be removed, since they incited the freedmen to hostility. The whites also complained that if troops must be placed over them, white soldiers should be sent. The whites were, of course, never willing to accept "the bayonet in the hands of the negro." *The New Orleans Daily Crescent,* October 21, 1865.

[2] *The New Orleans Daily Crescent,* October 17, 1865; *The Daily True Delta,* December 28, 1865. The Bureau now claimed exclusive jurisdiction over the negroes.

[3] *The New Orleans Times,* October 21, 1865; *The New Orleans Daily Crescent,* October 17, 1865; *The Daily Picayune,* July 8, 1865.

[4] *The New Orleans Daily Crescent,* November 18, 1865; *The Baton Rouge Tri-weekly Gazette and Comet,* January 9, 1866.

[5] *The New Orleans Daily Crescent,* November 14, 24, 1865; *The Opelousas Courier,* August 19, 1865; *The Louisiana Democrat,* June 28, 1865; *The Daily Picayune,* July 18, 1865; *The Sugar Planter,* January 27 and February 24, 1866. It was observed in a communication entitled, "Negroes Fading Away," that "negro women are rarely troubled with infants," and when they were, the newly-born "soon returns to the dust as it was." This article also cast some additional light upon conditions by concluding as follows: "Where are the Louisiana negroes? Nearly half of them are in their graves." *The New Orleans Crescent,* December 20, 1865.

[6] *The New Orleans Daily Crescent,* October 20, 21, 1865; *The Daily Picayune,* December 23, 1865; *The Baton Rouge Tri-weekly Gazette and Comet,* October 28, 1865; *The Louisiana Democrat,* January 10 and July 11, 1866. It came to be generally believed that as soon as the negroes were disabused of the idea of a division of the land, in their disappointment, there would be a general uprising, such as had taken place in Jamaica; and, as a matter of fact, negro troubles did shortly break out in the parishes of Ascension, St. Bernard, St. Helena, Morehouse, and in Carrollton and other places. As soon as the negroes were relieved of their hallucination, some riots occurred, and a few "terrible outrages" were perpetrated. It was believed that the patrols, which had been organized by consent of the military, prevented a general uprising. *The Daily True Delta,* December 28, 1865, February 7, 25, and March 27, 1866. There was said to be one-half million vagrant negroes who needed "vagrant laws." Some system had to be devised for these paupers and vagrants, or else it would be necessary to continue to support them in their idleness. *The New Orleans Daily Crescent,* November 23, 1865.

[7] *The New Orleans Daily Crescent,* October 21 and November 18, 23, 1865; *The Louisiana Democrat,* October 18 and November 15, 1865; *Le Louisianais,* November 18 and December 2, 1865. A letter from the negro, Frederick Douglas, which stated that ". . . it seems plain to me that Johnson has sold us," and in which he urged the negro to "demand suffrage for the colored," was given considerable publicity by the negro-Republican organ at this time, and doubtless contributed to the general unrest. *The New Orleans Tribuné,* October 27, 1865. *The New Orleans Tribune* of December 6, 1865, did contain an article on "The Right of Insurrection" in which it advocated it as "properly to be considered at this moment."

[8] *The New Orleans Daily Crescent,* November 13, 1865; *The Daily Picayune,* November 12, 1865; *The New York Herald,* November 4, 1865; *The Sugar Planter,* February 3, 1866. The call of course embraced other objectives, including the working out of a levee sys-

tem and the election of a Senatorial delegation.

⁹ *The New Orleans Daily Crescent,* November 23, 1865; *The Daily Picayune,* November 24, 1865; *The Southern Sentinel,* November 18, 1865; *Journal of the House of the State of Louisiana, Extra Session* (New Orleans: J. O. Nixon, State Printer, 1865), p. 1. This will be cited hereafter as *House Journal, 1865; The Louisiana Democrat,* November 14, 1865. The negro-Republican organ was openly hostile and repeatedly denounced this legislature. It declared that this was a "white conspiracy"; and added: "Let those legislators go to work and enact their black code, for nothing short of a black code is contemplated." *The New Orleans Tribune,* November 28, 29, 1865. It continued its denunciation of the "secret sessions" of the legislature, and found fault because the legislature had been dilatory about "hoisting a flag outside." It must be recalled that every congressman, and possibly many others, received copies of this paper regularly.

¹⁰ *Journal of the Convention, 1864,* pp. 173, 175; *The Baton Rouge Tri-weekly Gazette and Comet,* November 9, 28, 1865.

¹¹ *The New Orleans Tribune,* December 13, 1865; *The Baton Rouge Tri-weekly Gazette and Comet,* November 28, 1865.

¹² *Johnson Telegrams,* I, 202. C. Bullitt to Johnson, December 1, 1865; *The New Orleans Daily Crescent,* November 29, 1865; *The New York Herald,* November 30, 1865.

¹³ *The New Orleans Daily Crescent,* November 30, 1865; *The Southern Sentinel,* December 9, 1865; *The Louisiana Democrat,* December 13, 1865. His allusion to the secret organizations seems to have been the first intimation that they existed. Public curiosity was evidently aroused to a high pitch; but when the legislature passed a resolution requesting him to give a fuller explanation, he replied that the ends of public justice would be defeated by so doing. *The Daily True Delta,* December 13, 1865; *House Journal,* p. 38; *The Ope-*

lousas Courier, December 9, 23, 1865; *The New Orleans Daily Crescent,* December 1, 1865. He had also strangely omitted to recommend the calling of a state convention, although the verdict of the people seems to have been emphatically in favor of such action. *The New Orleans Daily Crescent,* December 16, 1865.

¹⁴ *The New Orleans Times,* December 23, 1865; *Dostie,* op. cit., pp. 72-73. It adjourned on December 22. No records of its proceedings, other than the *"Acts of the General Assembly,"* seem to have been published, except fragments in the daily press.

¹⁵ *The Daily True Delta,* December 14, 1865. It was even proposed that it "might be sound policy to adjourn for a month or two, and await developments at Washington." It was contended by some members that the acts of the convention and legislature would be declared null and void.

¹⁶ J. T. Trowbridge, *The South: A Tour of Its Battle Fields and Ruined Cities* (Hartford: L. Stebbins, 1866), pp. 497-98; Blaine, *op. cit.,* II, 101-03.

¹⁷ *Congressional Globe,* 39 Cong., 1 sess., p. 39; Blaine, *op. cit.,* II, 102-03.

¹⁸ Blaine, *op. cit.,* II, 102; *The New Orleans Daily Crescent,* June 8, 1866; *House Journal, 1865,* p. 58.

¹⁹ *The New Orleans Tribune,* December 13, 1865; *The New Orleans Daily Crescent,* June 8, 1866. The *Tribune* published this proposed bill and commented upon it as follows: "Laborers are subjected to the same discipline they were under the old slave regime." The bill was continually designated as the "white conspiracy." *The New Orleans Tribune,* December 13, 1865. No journals of either house seem to have been kept of this short session. The "Acts" only are available.

²⁰ *The New Orleans Tribune,* December 21, 1865; *The Southern Star,* December 11, 1865; *The Southern Sentinel,* December 23, 1865; *The Louisiana Democrat,* December 27, 1865; Dostie, *op. cit.,* pp. 73-75.

²¹ *Acts of the General Assembly, 1865*

(New Orleans: J. O. Nixon, State Printer, 1866), pp. 16-17. This will be cited hereafter as *Acts, 1865; The New Orleans Daily Crescent*, June 8, 1866; Trowbridge, *op. cit.*, p. 403.

[22] *Acts, 1865*, pp. 16-21; *The New Orleans Daily Crescent*, June .8, 1866; Elizabeth Wisner, *Public Welfare Administration in Louisiana* (Chicago: The University of Chicago Press, 1930), pp. 137, 138, 141.

[23] *The Acts, 1865*, pp. 14, 15; *The Baton Rouge Tri-weekly Gazette and Comet*, December 9, 1865.

[24] *The Acts, 1865*, p. 16; *House Journal, 1865*, p. 58.

[25] *The Acts, 1865*, p. 24; *The New Orleans Daily Crescent*, June 8, 1866.

[26] *The Acts, 1865*, pp. 28-31; *The New Orleans Daily Crescent*, June 8, 1866; *House Journal, 1865*, p. 58.

[27] *The Acts, 1865*, pp. 32-37; *The Daily Picayune*, December 16, 1865.

[28] Walter L. Fleming, *Civil War and Reconstruction in Alabama* (New York: The Columbia University Press, 1905), p. 380.

[29] James W. Garner, *Reconstruction in Mississippi* (New York: The Macmillan Co., 1901), pp. 113-14; McMaster, *op. cit.*, p. 650; Stryker, *op. cit.*, pp. 250-51; Rhodes, *op. cit.*, V, 53; Fleming, *Documentary History*, I, 282. The laws in South Carolina were almost equally discriminatory. Francis Butler Simkins and Robert Hilliard Woody, *South Carolina During Reconstruction* (Chapel Hill: The University of North Carolina Press, 1932), pp. 48-50.

[30] Garner, *op. cit.*, p. 119; *The New Orleans Times*, June 25, 1866; Beale, *op. cit.*, pp. 194, 252.

[31] *The Daily True Delta*, September 24, 28, 1865; *The New Orleans Times*, September 23, 1865; *The New Orleans Daily Crescent*, February 14, 1866; Beale, *op. cit.*, pp. 194-95. These laws were calculated to eradicate such conditions, and, in addition, they were no doubt enacted in part to eradicate the Freedmen's Bureau.

[32] *Acts, 1865*, pp. 6-8; *The New York Daily Tribune*, December 5, 1865; *The Louisiana Democrat*, February 14, 1866; *The Baton Rouge Tri-weekly Gazette and Comet*, February 22, 1866.

[33] *Acts, 1865*, pp. 10-12; Hunt, *op. cit.*, pp. 52-54; *The Louisiana Democrat*, December 13, 1865; *The Daily Picayune*, December 3, 9, 1865; *House Journal, 1865*, pp. 32, 34, 35, 53; *The New Orleans Daily Crescent*, December 16, 1865. It will be recalled that Messrs. Michael Hahn and R. King Cutler had previously been elected United States Senators. But they were both now repudiated by this legislature by a joint resolution, which solemnly protested against their reception upon the ground that they had been "elected by a legislature representing but a small minority." *Acts, 1865*, pp. 8-9; *The Sugar Planter*, February 10, 1866; *House Journal, 1865*, pp. 24, 30; *Documents of the First Session of the Second Legislature of the State of Louisiana* (New Orleans: J. O. Nixon, State Printer, 1866), pp. 3-35. This legislature also presented evidence later to prove that only 9,995 of the 50,000 voters were registered, and of this number only 966 were legally qualified. Many soldiers unquestionably had voted. The acceptance of this evidence meant that Hahn and Cutler had been elected by an illegal body, and were therefore, ineligible. *The New Orleans Daily Crescent*, July 13 and December 15, 1865; *The New Orleans Times*, September 3, 1864.

[34] *The New Orleans Times*, January 28, 1866; *The Louisiana Democrat*, December 20, 1865; *The Opelousas Courier*, December 16, 23, 1865.

[35] *The Daily Picayune*, May 27, 1866; *The New Orleans Daily Crescent*, February 13, 1866; James A. Renshaw, "The Hunt Family," *The Louisiana Historical Quarterly*, V (1922), p. 343; Hunt, *op. cit.*, p. 55. When Randell Hunt returned the latter part of May, he stated publicly that he believed the Johnson policy would prevail. Most Louisianians seem to have been still laboring under this delusion. *The Daily Picayune*, May 21, 1866.

[36] *The New Orleans Daily Delta*, Sep-

tember 12, 1865; *The Baton Rouge Tri-weekly Gazette and Comet,* September 16, 1865; *The Louisiana Democrat,* September 27, 1865; *The New Orleans Times,* January 13, 1866. The National Conservative Union party had inserted in this official organ the following address to the voters: "Representatives of the General Assembly should be selected who favor the enactment of such laws for the regulation of labor as would induce the general government to relieve the State of that terrible incubus, the Freedmen's Bureau." *The New Orleans Daily Delta,* September 8, 10, 1865.

[37] Paul Skeels Pierce, *The Freedmen's Bureau* (Iowa City: Iowa, Published by the University, 1904), pp. 16-17.

[38] *Ibid.,* pp. 18-19; *The New Orleans Times,* January 5 and February 5, 1865; *The Daily True Delta,* February 11, 1865. Conway's February report for 1865 gave a complete résumé of the activities of the Free Labor Bureau. It not only praised the planters, but stated that "the free labor system has been successful." *The Daily True Delta,* February 23, 1865; *The New Orleans Times,* February 25, 1865.

[39] Pierce, *op. cit.,* pp. 44, 48-49; McMaster, *op. cit.,* p. 643.

[40] Pierce, *op. cit.,* p. 49; *The New Orleans Times,* June 30, 1865.

[41] Pierce, *op. cit.,* p. 49. *The New Orleans Tribune,* July 19, 1865; *The Daily True Delta,* July 23, 1865; *The Baton Rouge Tri-weekly Gazette and Comet,* July 20, 1865; *The Baton Rouge Weekly Gazette and Comet,* July 22, 1865; *The Daily Picayune,* July 16, 1865. Before this organization had been effected, General Herron had issued orders on June 11 from Shreveport that all freedmen remain with their former masters and make binding contracts for the year 1865. It was necessary, he said, "to prevent loss of the crops," and to prevent "untold suffering, starvation, and misery among the blacks." This was evidently in obedience to a circular of General Howard issued shortly before. *The New Orleans Times,* June 1, 20, 1865.

[42] *The New Orleans Times,* June 30,

1865. The entire burden had to be assumed by the employer himself.

[43] *Ibid.,* August 12, 1865; *The New Orleans Daily Crescent,* October 12, 1865; *The Baton Rouge Tri-weekly Gazette and Comet,* August 10 and October 17, 28, 31, 1865. Much property was said to be unlawfully withheld in October, and it was charged that T. W. Conway, State Commissioner, was responsible for such "arbitrary and unconstitutional acts." The bureau in Louisiana had leased fifty-eight plantations to negroes and fifty-seven to whites in 1865. *The New Orleans Times,* October 30, 1865; *The Daily Picayune,* August 11, 19, 1865.

[44] *The New Orleans Times,* September 26, 1865; *The Daily True Delta,* March 24, 1866; *The Baton Rouge Tri-weekly Gazette and Comet,* October 10, 1865. The legislature had appealed to President Johnson to suspend this tax. Howard issued instructions to proceed with the collection.

[45] *The Daily True Delta,* August 11, 1865; *The Baton Rouge Tri-weekly Gazette and Comet,* September 5, 7, 1865; *The Daily Picayune,* July 8, 1865; *The Sugar Planter,* July 7, 1866.

[46] *The Daily True Delta,* October 5, 1865. The editor of a paper in an inland town had been arrested and imprisoned by a provost marshal for denouncing the acts of that official as arbitrary, illegal, and unconstitutional. *The Daily True Delta,* October 5, 1865.

[47] *The New Orleans Daily Crescent,* December 19, 1865; *The Louisiana Democrat,* December 27, 1865; *The Southern Sentinel,* January 3, 1866.

[48] *The New Orleans Times,* January 13, 1866. This supposedly Republican journal complained: "We have had our Conways and Callahans here, with the smaller fry of missionary adventurers, and as the locusts were to Egypt, even so were they to us."

[49] *The Daily True Delta,* August 19 and September 24, 1865.

[50] *The New Orleans Times,* September 23, 1865; *The Daily True Delta,* September 24, 1865; *The Daily Picayune.*

August 20, September 23, and October 11, 1865; *The Louisiana Democrat,* September 27, 1865; *The New Orleans Daily Crescent,* October 12, 1865.

[51] *The New Orleans Daily Crescent,* October 12, 1865; *The Daily Picayune,* September 23, 1865; *The Baton Rouge Tri-weekly Gazette and Comet,* September 30, 1865; *Le Louisianais,* October 28, 1865; *The Louisiana Democrat,* September 27, 1865. A legal effort was made to have some of these transferred. In a rule to show cause why a case, in which certain colored men were accused of burglary, should not be transferred to the United States District Court under the provisions of the Civil Rights bill, Judge Abell, a devout Louisiana Unionist, followed the decisions of the judiciary in Tennessee and North Carolina, and pronounced that bill unconstitutional. He used, to some extent, the arguments of President Johnson in his veto message; that is, the bureau bill was not passed over the vote of the President by a legally constituted Congress representing all the states of the Union. The Louisiana judiciary and the Executive were in harmony on this question. But this judge decided that, even though the bill was unconstitutional, it had in no wise been violated by these proceedings, and that he had no right to transfer this case from the bureau to the United States District Court. The rule was thereupon dismissed. *The New Orleans Times,* May 11, 12, 1866; *The Daily Picayune,* July 3, 1866.

[52] *The New Orleans Times,* September 27, 1865; *The New York Daily Tribune,* October 3, 1865; *The Baton Rouge Tri-weekly Gazette and Comet,* September 30 and October 10, 1865. Conway evidently sought to correct such judicial proceedings by a circular issued to all his subordinates, which stated that: "Whenever any judicial officer of the State arraigns and tries freedmen for alleged faults, and shows by his proceedings that he is disposed to deal as justly with this class of persons as with white persons, no interference by any of the agents of this Bureau will be allowed.

The co-operation of such officers assists rather than retards the work of this Bureau."

[53] *The Daily True Delta,* September 28, 1865; *The Baton Rouge Tri-weekly Gazette and Comet,* October 3, 1865. *The True Delta* urged that all grievances should be laid before him; "and God knows," it concluded, "they are numerous and grievous."

[54] *The New Orleans Times,* November 6, 1865; *The New Orleans Daily Crescent,* November 8, 1865. They were at this very time being registered by the bureau.

[55] Pierce, *op cit.,* p. 173; *The Daily Picayune,* October 18, 1865; *The New Orleans Daily Crescent,* October 18, 21, 1865; *The Baton Rouge Tri-weekly Gazette and Comet,* October 26, 1865. Conway had published a long "report," which was characterized by the *Picayune* as "one of the most one-sided, inaccurate, unreliable, and grossly partisan documents we have ever known to emanate from a public official." *The Daily Picayune,* October 8, 11, 1865; *The Southern Sentinel,* October 11, 1865. This bureau agent, who was sowing the seeds of dissension between the whites and blacks, according to *The New Orleans Daily Crescent* of November 14, 1865, was succeeded September, 1865, by General J. S. Fullerton. Fullerton was shortly afterward [October, 1865] succeeded by General A. P. Baird. Baird remained in charge until October, 1866, when he was succeeded by General P. H. Sheridan, who remained until November 27 of this same year.

[56] *The New Orleans Times,* December 10, 1865. *The New Orleans Tribune* of December 17, 1865, advocated an eight-hour day, and appeared to be discouraging contracts. Congress did afford some relief later by opening all the public lands in Louisiana for entry by the negroes, and some were reported to have availed themselves of this opportunity. They were handicapped, however, by a lack of proper agricultural equipment. *House Reports, 40th Cong., 2 sess.,* No. 30, p. 16; *Statutes at Large,* XIV, 66.

[57] *The New Orleans Daily Crescent,*
January 3, 6, 1866; *The New Orleans
Tribune,* negro organ, had reported on
November 3, 1865, that 230 negro schools
were to be closed, and 15,000 children
deprived of education, "because of color."
The white schools, especially those outside the city, were in worse condition.
They had generally been closed during
the four years of war. In fact, the public
school system in the rural portions, in
particular in the plantation sections, and
to some extent in the city, had never been
general during antebellum days. The
"pauper institution" had "proved a failure in all the country parishes." But
the prejudice of caste was now reported
to be wearing away, due to the fact that
all citizens had been "reduced to a very
democratic state of poverty." *The New
Orleans Times,* September 29 and December 5, 1865.

[58] *The Daily True Delta,* January 11,
1866; *The New Orleans Times,* January
11, 1866; *The New Orleans Daily Crescent,* May 25, 1866. A condensation of
his report appeared in the *True Delta.* It
will be recalled that Fullerton was allowed to remain in Louisiana less than
one month. Pierce, *op. cit.,* p. 173. The
radicals were reported to have begun a
campaign of denunciation and vilifica-
tion against him for exposing this corruption, for turning the negro over to
the state courts, for refusing to participate in political meetings of negroes,
and for telling the negroes that they
must go to work. *The Baton Rouge Tri-
weekly Gazette and Comet,* October 26
and November 2, 1865; *The Daily Picayune,* October 21, 29, and November 8,
1865; *The New Orleans Daily Crescent,*
November 1, 14, 1865; *The New York
Daily Tribune,* October 30, 1865; *The
Southern Sentinel,* November 11, 1865;
The New Orleans Times, January 11,
1866.

[59] *The New Orleans Times,* May 11,
1866; *The New Orleans Daily Crescent,*
May 8, 1866; *The Southern Sentinel,*
May 19, 1866. It is interesting to com-
pare these and other similar statements
with those he made some time later,

that is, after it became apparent that
the radicals would predominate.

[60] McPherson, *op. cit,* p. 55; *The New
Orleans Times,* April 21, 23, 1866. There
was a noticeable improvement in labor
conditions in the spring and summer of
1866. It appeared that most of those
who had survived had decided to go to
work, and signs pointed to a satisfactory solution of all the problems. *The
Daily Delta,* March 2, 1866; *The New
Orleans Daily Crescent,* February 4,
1866.

[61] *The New Orleans Daily Crescent,*
January 22, 1866. The Governor did not
send any message at this time. *The Louisiana Democrat,* January 31, 1866.

[62] *The Daily True Delta,* January 24,
26, 1866; *The New Orleans Daily Crescent,* January 22, 1866; *Journal of the
Senate of the State of Louisiana, 1866*
(New Orleans: J. O. Nixon, State Printer, 1866), pp. 43-44.

[63] *The New Orleans Daily Crescent,*
February 20, 1866; *The Daily Picayune,*
December 1, 9, 1865; *The Louisiana
Democrat,* November 29 and December
6, 20, 1865. Public sentiment seems to
have condemned "a compromising and
temporizing policy, in order to propitiate
the authorities," as "needless humiliation" and "unavailing servility."

[64] *The New Orleans Times,* March 10,
1866; *Journal of the Senate, 1866,* p. 19;
The New Orleans Daily Crescent, March
9, 12, 1866; *The Louisiana Democrat,*
January 24, 31, 1866. This resolution
had declared that the Constitution of
1864 was "the creature of fraud, violence, and corruption, and did not in
any manner represent the people of the
State." Warmoth, *op. cit.,* p. 46; *Journal of the Senate, 1866,* pp. 43-44.

[65] *The Daily True Delta,* March 10,
1866; *The Southern Star,* March 6, 1866;
Le Louisianais, March 10, 1866; *The
New Orleans Daily Crescent,* March 10,
12, 1866. It appears that when this resolution was introduced Governor Wells
had telegraphed the fact to the President, who at once urged a delegation to
come to Washington. Messrs. Cage
[speaker], Eagan, and Eustis were hur-

riedly dispatched. As soon as he advised these delegates that the calling of a convention might do harm by putting weapons in the hands of the enemy, they at once telegraphed these facts to the legislature. *The Daily True Delta*, March 10, 1866; *The New Orleans Times*, March 10, 1866; *Journal of the Senate, 1866*, p. 107; *The Baton Rouge Tri-weekly Gazette and Comet*, February 22, 1866; *The Louisiana Democrat*, March 14, 1866.

⁶⁶ Warmoth, *op. cit.*, p. 47; *Journal of the Senate, 1866*, pp. 67-72, 107; *The New Orleans Times*, March 10, 1866; *The Southern Sentinel*, March 17, 1866; *The New Orleans Daily Crescent*, February 13, 1866; *The Louisiana Democrat*, March 28, 1866. Honorable W. B. Eagan was elected as a commissioner from the Senate. These commissioners also delivered a joint resolution to President Johnson, expressing strong approbation of his policies, especially his veto of the Freedmen's Bureau Bill. *Louisiana Session Laws, 1866* (New Orleans: J. O. Nixon, State Printer, 1866), p. 84.

⁶⁷ *Journal of the Senate, 1866*, pp. 144-45; *The Louisiana Democrat*, January 10, 1866; *The Southern Sentinel*, January 20, 1866; *The Sugar Planter*, February 17, 1866; *The Daily Southern Star*, March 7, 1866.

⁶⁸ *The Daily True Delta*, February 15, 1866; *The New Orleans Daily Crescent*, February 16, 1866. Wells never enjoyed anything more than a superficial popularity; he was an "expediency candidate."

⁶⁹ *The Daily True Delta*, December 17, 1865. This was evidently a "pocket veto," as it was reintroduced in the regular session.

⁷⁰ *The New Orleans Times*, December 23, 1865; *The New Orleans Daily Crescent*, December 9, 1865; *The Baton Rouge Tri-weekly Gazette and Comet*, December 26, 1865; *The New York Daily Tribune*, December 25, 1865; *The Louisiana Democrat*, January 3, 1866. The taxes had been paid to the *de facto* government, and he had, on the eve of the November election, ordered the sus-

pension of the collection of these taxes, alleging that "some thought it illegal"; and that further collection was "impossible without seizing property by military force." *Johnson Telegrams*, I, 136-37, November 9, 1865; *The Daily True Delta*, December 23, 1865. It was estimated by the *True Delta* that his reversal was due to some "Satanic prompter," and that his "prompters" were none other than "the radical element at Washington," with whom he was "anxious to make capital." His action, which would have meant "confiscation," was denounced by the *Crescent* as "so ungenerous, so undeserved, so unnecessary, that we can scarcely believe the Governor." *The New Orleans Daily Crescent*, December 25, 28, 1865; *The Daily True Delta*, December 23, 1865.

⁷¹ *Journal of the Senate, 1866*, pp. 49, 50; *The New Orleans Daily Crescent*, February 15, 17, 1866; *The Baton Rouge Tri-weekly Gazette and Comet*, February 6, 8, 1866; *The Louisiana Democrat*, January 3, 1866; *The New Orleans Times*, February 15, 1866; *The Sugar Planter*, February 16, 1866. The *Crescent* stated that his action had been "inspired by the determination of the actual officials to hold on to their comfortable places, in utter defiance of public opinion."

⁷² *Journal of the Senate, 1866*, pp. 44-46; *The Daily True Delta*, February 15, 1866; *The New Orleans Daily Crescent*, February 13, 16, 17, 1866; *The New Orleans Times*, February 6, 1866; *The Sugar Planter*, February 17, 1866; *Le Louisianais*, February 17, 1866; *The Opelousas Courier*, February 24, 1866. In these messages he referred to his constituents as "rebels." It was a source of deep regret, especially to the Democratic press, that he had "yielded to the influence of counsellors," and "defied the wishes and opinions of the public." He was also reminded that some 20,000 of the 23,000 votes that he had received for Governor were "Rebel votes." Wells had telegraphed President Johnson that the Legislature has passed this bill, and added: "I shall veto it, unless you direct

to the contrary." There is no record to show that Johnson answered. *Johnson Telegrams*, II, 18. Wells to Johnson, January 28, 1866.

[73] *Acts, 1866*, pp. 30, 32, 108; *The Daily True Delta*, February 15, 1866; *The New Orleans Daily Crescent*, February 14, 16, 17, 1866; *The Baton Rouge Tri-weekly Gazette and Comet*, February 8, 1866; *The Southern Sentinel*, February 11, 1866; *The New York Herald*, February 18, 1866; *The Louisiana Democrat*, February 21, 1866; *The Opelousas Courier*, March 17, 1866. The municipal election was ordered for the second Monday in March; the constitutional objection to the district and parish elections was overcome by deferring the date of election to the first Monday in May.

[74] *Acts, 1866*, p. 44; *The Daily Picayune*, June 8, 1866; *The New Orleans Daily Crescent*, March 22, 1866.

[75] *The New Orleans Daily Crescent*, December 5, 1865, February 17 and March 22, 1866. According to the *Crescent*, the legislature was being censured by the *Star*, a daily that had begun publication in the late fall of 1865. This regular session had passed another joint resolution expressive of its strong endorsement of the official course of the President. *Acts, 1866*, p. 84.

[76] *Acts, 1866*, pp. 198, 246; *The Southern Sentinel*, March 31, 1866; *Journal of the Senate, 1866*, pp. 78-79; *The New Orleans Daily Crescent*, December 20, 1865; *The Opelousas Courier*, December 23, 1865, and March 10, 1866. The Governor, who advocated immigration, had stated in his message that "due to the great mortality of negroes by sword and disease, and their unwillingness to work," only "one-third" of the hands formerly employed were available, and "only one-fourth" of the land could be cultivated. The *Times* and *Crescent* were advocates of immigration, including "coolies," who were thought to be specially adapted to the climate and cultivation of Louisiana soil. There was much agitation for their introduction during 1865. The *Picayune* and other papers opposed the plan because of the political and social prob-

lems that might arise. *The New Orleans Times*, July 1, 1865, and January 7, 11, February 22, and April 25, 1866; *The New Orleans Daily Crescent*, January 5, 1866; *The Daily Picayune*, October 22 and November 7, 8, 23, 1865; *The Baton Rouge Tri-weekly Gazette and Comet*, August 22, September 23, and November 11, 1865; *Johnson Telegrams*, I, 137. Fullerton to Johnson, November 9, 1865. He had stated that "additional laborers are needed."

[77] *Acts of the Legislature, 1865* (Extra Sess.), p. 56; *The Baton Rouge Tri-weekly Gazette and Comet*, December 21, 1865.

[78] *Acts, 1866*, pp. 4-5; *The New Orleans Daily Crescent*, March 1, 22, 1866.

[79] *Acts, 1866*, p. 26; *The New Orleans Daily Crescent*, March 1, 22, 1866.

[80] *Acts, 1866*, pp. 194, 204, 254; *The New Orleans Daily Crescent*, March 1, 22, 1866.

[81] *Acts, 1866*, pp. 225-33; *The New Orleans Daily Crescent*, March 1, 22, 1866.

[82] *Acts, 1866*, pp. 4, 96; *The New Orleans Daily Crescent*, March 22, 1866; *The Southern Star*, March 25, 1866. The expenses of these so-called reconstruction bodies have been discussed. It seems that the extra session of 1865, in session less than one month, spent only a few thousand dollars.

[83] *The New Orleans Times*, November 5, 1864, and February 23, 1864; *The Daily Picayune*, December 22, 23, 1864. Wells had now completely broken with the legislature. *Journal of the Senate, 1866*, pp. 149-50. He had refused to see a joint committee on the day before he sent President Johnson the following telegram: "Nine-tenths of members of Legislature show daily by acts that they are unrepentant if pardoned rebels. Madam Jefferson Davis was yesterday admitted to the honors of the House. They want a Convention for reactionary objects. Any bill they pass for the object will be vetoed." *Johnson Telegrams*, II, 87. Wells to Johnson, March 15, 1866.

[84] *Acts, 1866*, p. 30; *The New Orleans*

Daily Crescent, February 14, 1866; *The New York Herald,* March 9, 1866.

[85] *The Daily Picayune,* May 19 and June 23, 1865; *The Daily True Delta,* May 6, 10, 11, 17, 1865. The Fourteenth Amendment was received by Wells some time after the Legislature had adjourned. *The Sugar Planter,* June 30, 1866; *Le Louisianais,* June 30, 1866. During the six years beginning with 1860, the following served as mayors of the city: John T. Monroe, George F. Shepley, Godfrey Weitzel, John H. French, Captain Miller, Captain Hoyt, Hugh Kennedy, S. Quincey, Hugh Kennedy again, and John T. Monroe again. *The New Orleans Times,* March 29, 1866.

[86] *The Daily Picayune,* June 23 and August 5, 1865; *The Daily True Delta,* August 4 and December 1, 1865. One serious objection seems to have been that he had gained possession of the Jackson Railroad, and was running it through a board of directors elected by himself. *The Daily Picayune,* August 5, 1865.

[87] *The New Orleans Times,* February 11 and January 31, 1866; *The New Orleans Daily Crescent,* February 12, 1866; *The New York Herald,* March 9, 1866; *The Daily Southern Star,* March 7, 1866. *First Session,* pp. 5-6. Wells telegraphed Johnson as follows: "Although I do not approve, I will order the election for the 12th instant." *Johnson Telegrams,* II, 78. Wells to Johnson, March 6, 1866.

[88] *The Daily True Delta,* March 9, 11 1866; *The New Orleans Times,* March 9, 11, 13, 1866; *The Baton Rouge Tri-Weekly Gazette and Comet,* March 13, 1866.

[89] *The Daily True Delta,* March 13, 1866; *The New Orleans Times,* March 13, 1866; *The Daily Picayune,* March 13, 1866; *The Baton Rouge Tri-weekly Gazette and Comet,* March 15, 1866; *The New Orleans Times,* March 13, 17, 1866; *The Sugar Planter,* March 17, 1866; *The Southern Sentinel,* March 17, 1866; *The Southern Star,* March 13, 1866. The *Picayune* and other papers reported that there were no disturbances, and that with the exception of two

recorders, two aldermen, and four assistant aldermen, the entire national Democratic ticket prevailed. The vote for mayor was: Monroe, 3,469; Moore, 3,158.

[90] *The New Orleans Times,* March 19, 1866; *The Daily Southern Star,* March 9, 27, 1866; *The Louisiana Democrat,* March 28, 1866; *The New Orleans Daily Crescent,* March 12, 1866; *The Sugar Planter,* March 24, 1866; *Johnson Telegrams,* II, 98. Major General E. R. Canby to Stanton, March 23, 1866. He also sent another telegram on April 19, 1866, to the same person, and to the same effect.

[91] *Johnson Telegrams,* II, 89, 90. Both telegrams were sent on March 17; *The Southern Star,* March 21 1866; *The Sugar Planter,* March 24, 1866.

[92] *The Daily Picayune,* May 15, 1866; *The New Orleans Daily Crescent,* April 25, 1866; *The New Orleans Times,* April 25, 1866. The President had wired Monroe in return that the "presumption" was that the "persons elected can take the oath of allegiance and loyalty required." *The New Orleans Times,* March 20, 1866; *The Louisiana Democrat,* April 18, 1866.

[93] *The Daily True Delta,* March 20, 23, 1866; *The New Orleans Times,* March 19, 1866; Beale, *op. cit.,* p. 345; *The Opelousas Courier,* April 14, 1866; *The New Orleans Daily Crescent,* May 4, 1866; Kendall, *op. cit.,* I, 304.

[94] *The Daily True Delta,* March 21, 1866; *The Louisiana Democrat,* April 18, 1866.

[95] *The Daily Picayune,* May 15, 1866; *The New Orleans Times,* April 28 and May 15, 1866; *The New Orleans Daily Crescent,* May 4, 15, 1866. This act was displeasing to the Governor as he had hoped to retain his own appointee as mayor. Nor was he pleased with other appointments of President Johnson. Johnson had appointed A. P. Dostie, a radical, to serve as surveyor of the port of New Orleans. Wells wired him at the time that such an appointment was "incredible," and that it would "disgrace" his administration. *Johnson Telegrams,*

II, 26. This telegram was sent on January 20, 1866; *The New Orleans Times,* January 17, 1866.

⁹⁶ *The Daily Picayune,* May 8, 1866; *The New Orleans Daily Crescent,* March 21, 1866; *The New Orleans Times,* May 8, 1866; *The Baton Rouge Tri-weekly Gazette and Comet,* March 22, 1866; *The Sugar Planter,* March 17, 1866; *The Southern Sentinel,* March 24, 1866.

⁹⁷ *The Daily Picayune,* April 27, 1866; *The New Orleans Daily Crescent,* March 26 and April 24, 1866; *The New Orleans Times,* April 25, 1866.

⁹⁸ *The New Orleans Times,* April 15 and May 6, 8, 1866; *The Daily Picayune,* April 27 and May 8, 1866; *The New Orleans Daily Crescent,* April 23 and May 5, 1866; *The Louisiana Democrat,* April 25, 1866; *The Baton Rouge Tri-weekly Gazette and Comet,* March 17 and May 10, 1866. Their platform was: (1) Are you in favor of Andrew Johnson's policy? (2) Will you use your influence for eight hour laws?

⁹⁹ *The Daily Picayune,* May 8, 1866; *The New Orleans Times,* May 8, 1866; *The New Orleans Daily Crescent,* May 7, 8, 9, 1866; *The Sugar Planter,* May 5, 12, 1866. The *Crescent* of June 1 gives a complete list of all the important officers elected in every parish of the state. The Hays supporters had held several "enthusiastic meetings," at which the bands had played "Dixie" while Hays and his followers had pledged themselves to "rally around the Johnson standard." *The Daily Picayune,* May 6, 1866.

CHAPTER X

¹ Warmoth, *op. cit.,* p. 47. Governor Warmoth told the writer that, after this bitter feud had developed between Governor Wells and his Democratic friends, Wells, after denouncing them and ruing the day he had helped to bring them into power, came to him personally and solicited his co-operation in overthrowing them. But he seems to have received little aid and comfort from these radical Republicans, who must already have had designs on his office. Wells, according to Governor Warmoth, sought to overthrow the Democrats by asking the aid of the radicals in calling together the defunct Convention of 1864, and enfranchising the negro and disfranchising the "rebels." They naturally refused co-operation because they had already adopted the "province" theory. Warmoth, *op. cit.,* pp. 47-48. Warmoth became the next governor under the Congressional plan of reconstruction.

² *The New Orleans Times,* May 17, 1864; McMaster, *op. cit.,* p. 512; *The Daily Picayune,* April 13, 1864; "Congress of the United States," *Annual Cyclopaedia, 1864,* pp. 293-94; Edward Stanwood, *A History of the Presidency from 1785 to 1897* (New York: Houghton Mifflin Company, 1898), I, 279. An amendment had been added by the Senate which prohibited electors for President. "Congress of the United States," *Annual Cyclopaedia, 1865,* p. 310.

³ "Congress of the United States," *Annual Cyclopaedia, 1864,* p. 307; Beale, *op. cit.,* p. 53.

⁴ "Congress of the United States," *Annual Cyclopaedia, 1864,* p. 309; *The New Orleans Times,* July 22 and August 17, 1864; *The Daily True Delta,* September 11, 1864; McMaster, *op. cit.,* p. 513; Beale, *op. cit.,* p. 140. Michael Hahn, who had recently been invested with the military power by Lincoln, was referred to as "no officer of the United States," since the "President on his own initiative had made him dictator."

⁵ *Congressional Globe,* 38 Cong., 2 sess., pp. 969-70; Stryker, *op. cit.,* pp. 151-52; *The New Orleans Times,* March 12, 1866. The radicals had no choice but to support Lincoln in 1864.

⁶ *Congressional Globe,* 38 Cong., 2 sess., pp. 967-70; Stryker, *op. cit.,* pp. 151-52.

⁷ *Congressional Globe,* 38 Cong., 2 sess., pp. 967-70; Stryker, *op. cit.,* pp. 152-53.

⁸ *Congressional Globe,* 38 Cong., 2 sess., p. 1128; Stryker, *op. cit.,* p. 161.

⁹ Rhodes, *op. cit.*, V, 51; Stryker, *op. cit.*, p. 161.

¹⁰ McPherson, *op. cit.*, pp. 577-86; Stryker, *op. cit.*, p. 161. All of these events have been discussed in a preceding chapter.

¹¹ *The New Orleans Times*, January 6, 1865. The opinion obtained generally in Louisiana by the first of January, 1865, that Lincoln had capitulated to the radicals. It was asserted that he made little effort to save the Louisiana and Arkansas governments.

¹² Stryker, *op. cit.*, p. 219.

¹³ *Ibid.*, pp. 223-24. This was true of conditions in Louisiana, where they had been consistently cultivated and fraternized with for months by such Republican radicals as Warmoth, Chase, Durant, and Lincoln's emissaries. Chase had been enthusiastically received and lavishly entertained by the negroes of New Orleans in the summer of 1865. The Negro Union Ministerial Association had at this time expressed their appreciation for him "for his views on the question of human rights"; and, as a result of his visit, the negroes had resolved that "American citizens of African descent . . . should have equal access with all other loyal citizens to the ballot-box." *The New Orleans Times*, May 21 and June 5, 9, 1865.

¹⁴ Rhodes, *op. cit.*, V, 544; *The Louisiana Democrat*, April 11, 1866. A Congressional caucus had decided upon a "Joint Committee of Reconstruction," composed of fifteen, to whom all questions of admission must be referred. Stevens became chairman. This movement was regarded as "revolutionary," as it deprived each house of the Constitutional right to accept representatives.

¹⁵ McPherson, *op. cit.*, pp. 28-32; Rhodes, *op. cit.*, V, 558; Beale, *op. cit.*, pp. 143, 193-95. Louisiana's "Black Code" has been discussed in detail in the preceding chapter.

¹⁶ McPherson, *op. cit.*, p. 24.

¹⁷ McMaster, *op. cit.*, p. 636; Rhodes, *op. cit.*, V, 552-53; *The Daily Picayune*, September 29, 1865; *The Baton Rouge Tri-weekly Gazette and Comet*, October 3, 1865; *The New Orleans Times*, January 15, 1866; Beale, *op. cit.*, pp. 65-73; *The Louisiana Democrat*, September 13, 1865; *The New Orleans Daily Crescent*, November 24, December 27, 1865, and January 9, 1866; *The Daily True Delta*, December 20, 1865. Carl Schurz had spent a few days in Louisiana on "an important mission" as the guest of the military authorities, during which time he had spent a few days along Bayou Teche and in the interior investigating conditions. His "model report," made as a result of this sojourn, was not so considered by the New Orleans press. The Northern papers had spoken of it as "able, calm, dispassionate and logical." Not so the *Crescent*. It concluded its observations: "To prove that black is white, has from very remote ages been considered a conclusive test of logical and dialectical skill. We do not know that any one ever succeeded in the attempt until Mr. Carl Schurz produced that extraordinary report. Until we read his report, we never conceived the amount of villainy by which we were surrounded. Hence this 'calm and dispassionate gentlemen' comes to the conclusion that negroes ought to be allowed to vote—indeed ought to be forced to vote, else they stand in imminent danger of being made to *work*." *The New Orleans Daily Crescent*, January 6, 9, 1866.

¹⁸ Moorefield Storey, *Charles Sumner* (New York: Houghton Mifflin Company, 1899), p. 307. The reading of such letters into the records seems to have been a favorite pastime of Sumner. *The Louisiana Democrat*, April 11, 1866.

¹⁹ McPherson, *op. cit.*, p. 74; Beale, *op. cit.*, p. 66; *Le Louisianais*, February 24, 1866; *The New Orleans Daily Crescent*, February 21, 1866; *The New Orleans Times*, February 21, 22, and July 19, 1866; *The Louisiana Democrat*, February 28, 1866.

²⁰ *The Southern Sentinel*, April 21, 1866; Blaine, *op. cit.*, II, 385; Stryker, *op. cit.*, p. 288; *Le Louisianais*, March 14, 1866; *The New Orleans Times*, March 29, 1866; *The New Orleans Daily Crescent*, March 28 and April 9,

10, 1866; *The Louisiana Democrat,* April 4, 18, 1866. *The Sugar Planter* of April 14 stated that the passage of the Civil Rights Bill over Johnson's veto "has cast a gloom over our community." It was declared unconstitutional shortly thereafter by Judge Abell. *The New Orleans Daily Crescent,* May 10, 1866.

[21] Stryker, *op. cit.,* p. 292; *The New Orleans Daily Crescent,* May 17, 19, 1866; *The New Orleans Times,* May 12, 17, 1866; *The Southern Star,* March 15, 1866.

[22] *United States Constitution,* Article V.

[23] McPherson, *op. cit.,* p. 151; Blaine, *op. cit.,* II, 217; Stryker, *op. cit.,* p. 269; *The New Orleans Daily Crescent,* July 18, 1866.

[24] Beale, *op. cit.,* pp. 66, 172, 195; *The New Orleans Daily Crescent,* November 1, 14, 15, 1865. He had no doubt just learned of the purpose of the state legislature to eject him from his senatorial seat.

[25] *The New Orleans Times,* August 15 and September 10, 1866; *The New Orleans Daily Crescent,* June 8 and August 15, 1866. His representations on the "riot" were denounced as "point blank falsehood." He was reported to have said that if the convention had known that the President had directed the military to sustain the civil authorities, it would not have met. He did not tell his audience that this dispatch from the President had been posted on the street. *The New Orleans Times,* September 10, 1866.

[26] Warmoth, *op. cit.,* pp. 42, 50; *The Opelousas Courier,* March 31, 1866; *The New Orleans Times,* August 15, 1866; *The New Orleans Crescent,* August 15, 1866. Warmoth and others published a lengthly report in September that was a bitter tirade against President Johnson. *The New Orleans Daily Crescent* of September 15, 1866, copied it from the Northern press. It held Johnson "responsible for the bloodshed" in Louisiana.

[27] *The New Orleans Times,* August 17, 1866.

[28] *The Daily Picayune,* August 9, 1866; *The New Orleans Daily Crescent,* August 18, 1866; *The Louisiana Democrat,* August 15, 1866. The *Crescent,* in commenting on this said: "It is scarcely possible to believe that such an address could have emanated from such a source." *The New Orleans Daily Crescent,* August 18, 1866.

[29] *The New Orleans Daily Crescent,* September 14, 1866; *The New Orleans Times,* August 31, 1866; *The Baton Rouge Tri-weekly Gazette* and *Comet,* August 16, 1866; *The Louisiana Democrat,* August 22 and October 10, 13, 31, 1866; *The Southern Sentinel,* August 18 and September 22, 1866. Parson Conway was reported to be especially adept in the art of manufacturing public opinion. He was a former official of the bureau, who had become *persona non grata* to Louisianians. His representations became so offensive that it was suggested that an indignation meeting be called to burn him in effigy. He had said among other things that the "Southern people hate the North, the Union, and the Freedmen almost as intensely as they did when the revolution was in its full career." *The Daily True Delta,* January 10 and February 14, 1866; *The New Orleans Times,* July 14, 1866.

[30] *The New Orleans Times,* August 31, September 3, and October 1, 1866.

[31] *Journal of the Convention of 1864,* pp. 170-71; *Chase Correspondence,* II, 443; Dennison says that "The President of the Convention, however, is authorized to call them together again, in case their action is not ratified by the people." He had added that "there is great danger that the Constitution will not be ratified." But that contingency had passed upon ratification, and the body had apparently become defunct.

[32] *Chase Correspondence,* II, 443-44. Dennison, himself a radical, had said of the defunct convention: "Probably never before has there been held a State Constitutional Convention which has been regarded with contempt by nine-tenths of the people."

[33] *The New Orleans Daily Delta,* Feb-

ruary 16, 1866; *The Baton Rouge Tri-weekly Gazette and Comet,* February 22, 1866; *The Southern Sentinel,* July 14, 1866; Beale, *op. cit.,* pp. 245-46; Kendall, *op. cit.,* I, 305.

³⁴ Gideon W. Welles, *Diary of Gideon Welles* (New York: Houghton Mifflin Company, 1911), II, 574; *The Louisiana Democrat,* July 4, 1866; *The Sugar Planter,* July 14, 1866; Beale, *op. cit.,* p. 346.

³⁵ *The Daily Picayune,* August 1, 1866. This conservative daily stated that "not 500 whites in Louisiana" supported the "Convention plot."

³⁶ *Johnson Papers,* XCVII, 11,661-62; Stryker, *op. cit.,* p. 317. This view was expressed in a letter that was written by Albert Voorhies, Lieutenant Governor of Louisiana, on July 13, 1866, to Honorable J. A. Rogers, who had been commissioned by the interested Louisianians to present the facts to President Johnson.

³⁷ *The New Orleans Times,* June 11 and July 8, 1866; *The Louisiana Democrat,* July 25, 1866; *The New Orleans Daily Crescent,* August 10, 1866. The full text of this is given in the *Report of the Joint Committee on Reconstruction. Report of the Joint Committee on Reconstruction at the First Session, Thirty-ninth Congress* (Washington: Government Printing Office, 1866), pp. 7-21.

³⁸ *The New Orleans Times,* April 24 and June 11, 1866; *The Southern Sentinel,* July 14, 1866; *The Louisiana Democrat,* July 25, 1866.

³⁹ *The New Orleans Times,* June 26, 27, 28, 1866; *The Louisiana Democrat,* July 4, 1866; *The New Orleans Daily Crescent,* June 29, 1866. The *Crescent* of June 29 states that "only the correspondent of the *New York Tribune* was admitted." According to the *Picayune,* protracted meetings had been going on in private, and anxious conferences with outside persons were being held. *The Daily Picayune,* June 28, 1866.

⁴⁰ *The Daily Picayune,* June 28, 1866; Chambers, *op. cit.,* I, 661; *The New Orleans Crescent,* July 9, 1866; *The New Orleans Times,* June 27 and July 12, 1866. Judge J. K. Howell had ceased to be a member of the convention. He had resigned some time before adjournment, and, therefore, had not affixed his signature to the Constitution of 1864. *The New Orleans Times,* July 13, 1866; *Johnson Papers,* XCVII, 11,662. This information was given in a letter written by Lieutenant Governor Voorhies, on July 13, 1866.

⁴¹ John W. Burgess, *Reconstruction and the Constitution* (New York: Charles Scribner's Sons, 1902), p. 93.

⁴² *The Daily Picayune,* June 28, 1864; Chambers, *op. cit.,* I, 661; *The New Orleans Daily Crescent,* June 28 and July 11, 1866; *The New Orleans Times,* July 3, 1866. The *Picayune* of June 28 gives a complete account of the proceedings of "The Rump of the Convention."

⁴³ *The Daily Picayune,* June 30, 1866; *The Louisiana Democrat,* July 18, 1866; *The New Orleans Times,* July 28, 1866. The President, who recognized the state government, was not to be consulted.

⁴⁴ *The New Orleans Times,* June 28, 1864; *The New Orleans Daily Crescent,* July 13, 1866.

⁴⁵ *The Daily Picayune,* June 30 and July 3, 11, 1866. The hope was freely expressed that Judge Abell, who was shortly to impanel a grand jury in his court, would charge the jury "in accordance with his usually outspoken character." Judge Abell, who, it will be recalled, had been a member of the 1864 convention, did charge the grand jury a few days before the time set for the convention to reassemble formally, stating in substance that the "rump convention" was an illegal body, and that any attempt to "reassemble the extinct convention of 1864 would be an act of disturbance of the public peace, and a conspiracy against the government, the laws, and the institutions of the state; that it would, in fact, be a violation of a law of the state, which makes all assemblies for the purpose of subverting the authority of the state, criminal and punishable with severe penalties."

For making this so-called "treasonable" charge the judge was "arrested and held to bail." But this did not silence him, for in a second charge he branded the majority of the convention members as "political apostates," "military deserters," and "perjurers." "The members of the late convention," he concluded, "claim to be loyal men; this I concede with a few honorable exceptions; they were loyal to the Confederacy under apparent prosperity— loyal to the United States while they could get ten dollars a day as members of the Convention. And after the division of offices among them, they became so exceedingly patriotic that they declared the Constitution of 1864 the best ever made. Some of these men were deserters from the Confederate army; others held offices under the Confederacy, military and civil. And yet, Gentlemen of the Grand Jury, these men claim to be of and represent the loyal people of the state of Louisiana, and boldly assert that they are to receive the aid of the arms of the United States to assist them in usurping the right to alter the fundamental law of the state of Louisiana, and that in direct violation of the Constitution they have made, and the laws they have adopted. This is the mere vapor of disappointed men."

"They say emphatically that they have *large sums of money.*—Can it be possible that these men in their desperation, expect to corrupt a great state with their money?" *The New Orleans Daily Crescent*, July 21, 23, 24, 1866; *The New Orleans Times*, July 24, 27, 1866; Dostie, *op. cit.*, p. 283.

[46] *The Daily Picayune*, July 14, 1866. Judge Abell charged the grand jury again after the riot. A number were indicted, and some were arrested. But, as will presently be shown, Baird released them. *The New Orleans Daily Crescent*, August 3, 1866; *The Louisiana Democrat*, August 8, 1866; Dostie, *op. cit.*, p. 301.

[47] *Johnson Papers*, XCVII 11,661-63. This interesting and enlightening information is found in a letter written by Lieutenant Governor Voorhies on July

13, 1866. It also gave a complete history of the convention, and of the restoration of Civil State government, which had been set up as a result of the work of the convention, and which was being "consummated beyond their most sanguine expectations." The concluding paragraph is given in full: "Such are the leading facts concerning this passing strange event. Such a disregard of the plainest rules of the law and order, such preposterous assumption of authority and barefaced attempt at revolution, would be a matter more of surprise and disgust, if it were not that these machinations, important in themselves, assume importance from the fact that it is an inspiration from an agency, bent on rule or ruin, and for that purpose, determined to paralyze that restoration policy which in such short time has made such remarkable progress in healing up past dissensions."

[48] *The Daily Picayune*, July 8, 10, 1866; *The New Orleans Times*, July 8, 1866; Stryker, *op. cit.*, p. 317; Dostie, *op. cit.*, p. 286. Editorials also appeared in these same papers denouncing the whole proceedings as a "shame and mortification," and a "selfish plot and scheme to regain office and patronage."

[49] *The Daily Picayune*, July 10, 12, 1866; *The New Orleans Daily Crescent*, July 9, 1866; Dostie, *op. cit.*, pp. 286-87. All these proceedings appeared as an advertisement in the New Orleans press. *The New York Tribune* had been selected as the official organ of this body. *The New Orleans Times*, June 27, 1866.

[50] Warmoth, *op. cit.*, pp. 47-48; *The New Orleans Daily Crescent*, July 27, 1866; *The New Orleans Times*, June 30, 1866; *Le Louisianais*, August 4, 1866.

[51] *Edward M. Stanton Papers*, XXX, 56,013. This is a letter from the Louisiana Attorney General, Herron, to Johnson, dated July 27, 1864. *The Daily Picayune*, July 27, 28, 1866; *The New Orleans Times*, July 27, 28, 1866; *The New Orleans Daily Crescent*, July 27, 28, 1866; *The Louisiana Democrat*, August 1, 1866; Beale, *op. cit.*, p. 348; Dostie, *op. cit.*, p. 288. This election order did not have the attestation of the

Secretary of State, one of the six state officers elected on the same ticket with Wells. *The New Orleans Times*, July 28, 1866; Dostie, *op. cit.*, p. 289.

[52] *Johnson Papers*, XCVIII, 11,801-06; *Johnson Telegrams*, II, 233; Beale, *op. cit.*, p. 348; *The Southern Sentinel*, August 4, 1866; *The New Orleans Times*, August 7, 1866; *The New Orleans Daily Crescent*, August 7, 1866; *The Louisiana Democrat*, August 16, 1866. This exchange of telegrams between Johnson and Wells took place on July 28, 1866. It is interesting to note Judge Howell's movements during the interval between the issuing of his proclamation and the assembling of the convention. *The New Orleans Times* of July 18 gives the following information: "Judge Howell is in Washington endeavoring to induce Congress to postpone adjournment until the '64 Convention can get up a Constitution. . . ." This same journal makes another report on July 24: "The Honorable Mr. Boutwell's 'distinguished gentleman from Louisiana,' the President pro. tem. of the defunct Convention relieved his anxious friends by his safe return to the city yesterday.

"There was last night a mid-night assemblage as secret and mysterious as that which the President p. t. was first ushered upon the political arena in the dark lantern Know Nothing times, to hear his report of his mission to Radicaldom at the Federal Capitol."

[53] *Johnson Papers*, XCVIII, 11,782; *The Southern Sentinel*, July 21, 1866; *The Sugar Planter*, July 24, 1866; *The New Orleans Times*, August 1, 1866; *The New Orleans Daily Crescent*, August 1, 1866; Beale, *op. cit.*, p. 347; Dostie, *op. cit.*, pp. 298-99.

[54] *Johnson Papers*, XCVIII, 11,783-85. Letter of Baird to Monroe, July 26, 1866; *The Southern Sentinel*, July 21, 1866; *The Sugar Planter*, July 24, 1866; *The Louisiana Democrat*, July 25, 1866; *The New Orleans Daily Crescent*, August 1, 1866; Beale, *op. cit.*, pp. 347-48. This must have convinced the mayor that if Baird was not in league with the revolu-

tionists he at least was hostile to the municipal authorities.

[55] *Johnson Papers*, XCVIII, 11,802-03; Beale, *op. cit.*, pp. 348-49; *The New Orleans Daily Crescent*, July 28, 1866; *The New Orleans Times*, July 28 and August 5, 1866. This telegram also informed the President that Wells was siding with the radicals.

[56] *Johnson Papers*, XCVIII, 11,804; *The New Orleans Times*, July 30, 1866; *The New Orleans Daily Crescent*, July 30, 1866; Beale, *op. cit.*, p. 349; Dostie, *op. cit.*, p. 301. This telegram, as has been stated, was posted on the street, and it was also published in the *Times*. Dostie, *op. cit.*, p. 301.

[57] *Johnson Papers*, XCVIII, 11,810; Beale, *op. cit.*, p. 349. This telegram was received at 10:20 P.M. the same day, and Stanton must have read it immediately.

[58] *House Report* No. 16, 39 Cong., 2 sess., pp. 529-36, 546-47; Beale, *op. cit.*, p. 349; Dostie, *op. cit.*, pp. 300-01; W. G. Moore, "Notes," *American Historical Review*, XIX (1913), p. 102. Moore says: "The President believed that the riot, which occurred in the City of New Orleans, July 30, 1866, would have been averted if an answer had been sent to General Baird's telegram of the 28th, asking the Secretary of War for instructions." Stanton attempted later to justify his action. *Stanton Papers*, II, 316, 324, 325.

[59] *The Daily Picayune*, August 1, 1866. They do not seem to have been able to appeal to the more intelligent negroes with any degree of success.

[60] *Johnson Papers*, XCVIII, 11,802; *The Daily Picayune*, July 28, 1866; Chambers, *op. cit.*, I, 662; *The New Orleans Times*, July 28, 1866; Dostie, *op. cit.*, pp. 292-95; Beale, *op. cit.*, pp. 348-49. Beale gives a fair treatment of this "riot" but from the evidence he had in hand, it seems that he should have placed the responsibility where it was due.

[61] *The Daily Picayune*, July 28, 1866; Stryker, *op. cit.*, p. 317; Warmoth, *op. cit.*, p. 48; *The New Orleans Daily Cres-*

cent, July 27, 28, 1866; *The New Orleans Times,* July 28, 30, and August 3, 1866; Dostie, *op. cit.,* p. 297. Warmoth, who was in the city, but does not seem to have participated in this call—at least publicly—says that "Doctor Dostie and others made violent speeches, which tended to increase the bitterness. . . ." Dostie, among other things, was reported to have "shouted," to the now greatly excited negroes: "I want the negroes to have the right of suffrage. We have 300,000 black men with white hearts. Also 100,000 good and true Union white men who will fight for and beside the black race against the 300.000 hell-bound rebels. . . . We cannot only whip, but exterminate the other party. . . . If interfered with, the streets will run with blood." Rhodes, *op. cit.,* V, 612; Fleming, *Documentary History,* I, 231-32. The speech of the radical agitator is given in full in Fleming.

⁶² *The Daily Picayune,* July 31 and August 5, 1866; Chambers, *op. cit.,* I, 662; *The Louisiana Democrat,* July 25, 1866; *The New Orleans Daily Crescent,* July 31, 1866; Dostie, *op. cit.,* p. 303. Welles, in making his usual observations on the passing events, wrote on August 2 of the revolution: "Violent and revolutionary proceedings have taken place in New Orleans. A fragment of an old Convention held in 1864 met for the purpose of overturning the government. Riot and bloodshed were the unavoidable consequences. There are indications that the conspirators were instigated by Radicals from Washington and the North to these disturbances." Continuing, he wrote the next day: "Stanton read telegrams in Cabinet from General Sheridan concerning New Orleans disturbances. Stanton manifested marked sympathy with the rioters, and the President and others observed it. There is little doubt that the New Orleans riots had their origin with the Radical members of Congress in Washington. It is part of a deliberate conspiracy and was to be the commencement of a series of bloody affrays through the States lately in rebellion. Boutwell and others have

stated sufficient to show their participation in this matter. There is a determination to involve the country in civil war, if necessary, to secure negro suffrage in the States and Radical ascendancy in the General Government. Stanton, in great excitement, repeatedly spoke of the Attorney-General of Louisiana and the Mayor of New Orleans as pardoned Rebels, who had instigated the murder of the people in the streets of the city, [said] that they were guilty of this terrible bloodshedding." Welles, *op. cit.,* II, 569-70; 567-68.

⁶³ *The Daily Picayune,* August 1, 1866; Chambers, *op. cit.,* I, 662; *The New Orleans Times,* July 31 and August 2, 1866; *The New Orleans Daily Crescent,* July 31, 1866; *The Louisiana Democrat,* August 8, 1866. The *Picayune* gives this account in an article entitled: "Beginning of Riot." The day after the riot the *Picayune* reporter said: "It is useless to trace the origin. It had been brewing all the morning . . . and a toss of the feather would have started it."

⁶⁴ *The Daily Picayune,* July 31 and August 2, 1866; *The New Orleans Times,* July 31 and August 31, 1866; *The New Orleans Daily Crescent,* July 31, 1866; *Le Louisianais,* August 4, 1866. Probably the most authentic and unbiased accounts of the events of the day are to be found in the earlier press reports on the following day, and the first few days thereafter, before the whole affair became a political football. The reports that reached the North were colored and apparently contained omissions, as well as exaggerations; the negroes were repeatedly represented as "innocent victims" of a "premeditated massacre." This seems to be true of the so-called "later investigations," and after the possibilities of exploiting the event, politically, became apparent. However, the *Picayune* reporter, who braved the dangers, reports that it was a pitched battle in which "balls whizzed by," and "firearms were handled as freely as on the battle field."

⁶⁵ *The New Orleans Times,* July 31, 1866; *The New Orleans Daily Crescent,*

July 31, 1866; *The Southern Sentinel,* August 11, 1866; *The Daily Picayune,* July 31, 1866; Dostie, *op. cit.,* pp. 312-15. Reed makes a martyr of Dostie. This book was, in fact, used as propaganda by the radicals in the campaign of 1868. Dostie died from the effects of his wounds. Dostie, *op. cit.,* p. 312. The *Crescent* gives the following interesting item on Dostie: "We saw a gentleman wearing the uniform of the United States, conspicuous among the gallant men who assailed the State House. Dr. Dostie was severely wounded, and his worst wound was from this soldier, a Massachusetts gentleman, who proclaimed the white should be the ruling race of this continent. The white soldiers and the white citizens sympathized with each other heartily." *The New Orleans Daily Crescent,* July 31, 1866.

[66] *The New Orleans Times,* August 28, 1866; *The Daily Picayune,* July 31, 1866; *Johnson Papers,* XCVIII, 11,847; *The New Orleans Daily Crescent,* July 31, 1866; *The Sugar Planter,* August 4, 1866; *The Louisiana Democrat,* August 4, 8, 1866.

[67] *Johnson Papers,* XCVIII, 11,856. Telegram of Baird to Stanton, July 30, 1866; Beale, *op. cit.,* pp. 105, 349-50. As has been stated, all of the official correspondence in possession of the War Department relative to the "riot" was sent to Johnson at his request. It was then discovered that Stanton had failed to answer the important telegram asking for instructions from the President. Since he had not even consulted the President, all of the official correspondence was now given to the press by President Johnson in order that a full understanding of his course and position on that matter might be arrived at. The correspondence revealed to the public for the first time that Stanton had withheld from the President General Baird's dispatch just before the riot asking for instructions. *The New Orleans Times,* August 25, 26, 29, 1866; *The New Orleans Daily Crescent,* August 25, 1866.

[68] *Johnson Papers,* XCVIII, 11,844; *The New Orleans Daily Crescent,* August 1, 1866. This telegram was sent by Johnson on the thirtieth to Attorney General Herron in answer to one sent during the "riot."

[69] *Johnson Papers,* XCVIII, 11,851, 11,976-86. Baird to Stanton, July 30, 1866; and Monroe to Voorhies; and Herron to Johnson, August 30, 1866; Beale, *op. cit.,* p. 350; *The New Orleans Times,* August 2, 1866.

[70] *Johnson Papers,* XCVIII, 11,976-86. Telegram of Voorhies and others to Johnson, August 30, 1866. The mayor had some few days before addressed a note to Baird, inquiring whether he would be interfered with by the military authorities in case he would proceed to disperse the convention as an unlawful assembly. Baird had answered that such a meeting could not be suppressed, and that the military would prevent such interference. *Johnson Papers,* XCVIII, 11,979.

[71] *Ibid.,* 11,979, 11,981-82; *The New Orleans Times,* July 30, 1866; *The New Orleans Daily Crescent,* July 30, 1866. Voorhies and others to Johnson, August 30, 1866. The state and city authorities were using other means to avoid the impending battle. On Sunday, the day before, they solicited the press to advise the people as to their proper conduct on the following day so as to avoid trouble. The press of New Orleans, with the exception of the *Tribune,* did give wise and salutary counsels to the public, admonishing all to refrain from congregating about the capitol, and advising that all demean themselves with prudence and discretion. *Johnson Papers,* XCVIII, 11,980; *The New Orleans Times,* July 30 and August 28, 1866.

[72] *The New Orleans Times,* August 1, 1866; *Johnson Papers,* XCVIII, 11,982. Voorhies and others to Johnson, August 30, 1866. Mayor Monroe's sworn testimony before the grand jury was: "I can confidently state that had it not been for the interference of the Military Authorities with the ordinary course of law, there would have been no riot and no bloodshed. The city police, prepared for the emergency, would have been amply sufficient to keep the peace. If

General Baird, when he undertook to protect the Convention from the operation of the laws, had complied with his promise [to furnish troops], he could by the use of a small military force have averted the disturbances which occurred." *The New Orleans Daily Crescent,* August 14, 1866.

⁷³ *Johnson Papers,* XCVIII, 11,852-56, 11,982. Baird to Stanton, July 30, 1866, and Voorhies and others to Johnson, August 30, 1866; *The New Orleans Times,* August 1, 28, 1866. The long telegram, sent by Baird, seems to have been sent in an attempt to keep the records straight. Among the reasons given for his inaction in this "special pleading," Baird said: "I thought the City intended to keep order"; "I thought the meeting was to be at six o'clock"; "I enclose herewith copy . . . of a dispatch which the Lieutenant-Governor *claims* to have received from the President." An examination of this and other documents reveals that he must have known that he was to assist the city in keeping order; and that he had no information that the convention was to meet at six o'clock. [The writer has found none. The time was advertised in the papers, and the hour is the same as that on which it met.] Baird states, finally, that he doubted the authenticity of the President's dispatch relative to his duty to assist and to be subordinated to the civil authority; and that the city authorities must be charged with the responsibility of the "riot." *The New Orleans Times,* August 7 and September 17, 18, 19, 1866.

⁷⁴ *Johnson Papers,* XCVIII, 11,982-85. It must be recalled that the colored population, as a body, did not participate, and that freedmen in the vicinity were unmolested. It was the armed and organized mob that was engaged. The fact that forty-two policemen and several citizens were killed or wounded by them is evidence that they must have been armed. *Johnson Papers,* XCVIII, 11,985. Monroe in his message to his Council placed the responsibility for the battle on Baird because he was not willing to suppress the riot, and because he freed from the jails the ringleaders "to make political capital for the radical enemies of the reconstruction policy of his commander, President Johnson." Beale, *op. cit.,* p. 352.

⁷⁵ *Johnson Papers,* XCVIII, 11,875. J. Hamison to Brown, member of the Cabinet, July 31, 1866; *The New Orleans Daily Crescent,* August 1, 1866; *The New Orleans Times,* August 2, 5, 1866; Beale, *op. cit.,* p. 352; Welles, *op. cit.,* II, 572, 573, 574. Baird was an obscure man, according to Welles. In a cabinet meeting on August 7 Welles asked who he was, and "how it came about that such a man as was now described happened to be at such a place at this juncture." Seward knew "nothing of him," and the President knew nothing, for he expressed dissatisfaction with what he "heard of Baird." Meanwhile, Stanton "kept silent." It seems that the conversation relative to Baird was resumed between Welles and Johnson later in the evening. At that time Welles expressed regret that the President "had not officers for the business required at this time in this quarter." Welles reports that the President "concurred with me and said that Baird, so far as he could learn, had caused the trouble or might have prevented it." A subsequent portion of this same conversation gives some additional light as to "who Baird was." " 'Who,' inquired I, 'placed Baird there? Was it not part of the Radical scheme to bring this difficulty upon us? It certainly is unfortunate that we have these men.' He said he believed Baird was attached to the Freedmen's Bureau. I said this might have been ordered otherwise and should have been; that the Administration could not get along intelligently and well without faithful and reliable agents. I inquired if he noticed the remarks of Stanton today respecting the convention, 'though probably you knew his opinions previously.' The President said he had not known them before, that it was the first intimation he had received, and he noticed the remark. 'This is wrong,' said I; 'we cannot get along

in this way.' 'No,' replied he, 'it will be pretty difficult.' " Welles, *op. cit.,* pp. 573-74.

[76] *The New Orleans Times,* August 25, 1866; Beale, *op. cit.,* pp. 352-53; Welles, *op. cit.,* p. 572; *The Louisiana Democrat,* August 22, 1866.

[77] *Johnson Papers,* XCVIII, 11,939. Sheridan to War Department, August 1, 1866; *The New Orleans Times,* August 5, 7, 1866; *The New Orleans Daily Crescent,* August 11, 1866; Beale, *op. cit.,* p. 352. Welles in comparing the first and subsequent telegrams records that: "Sheridan's dispatches are somewhat conflicting. Although a brave and excellent officer, Sheridan lacks judgment and administrative ability. He is impulsive, but his intentions are honest and his first telegram was an honest impulse. It struck me that he was tutored as regards the others, either from Washington or by some one at New Orleans duly advised." Welles, *op. cit.,* II, 570. Beale does not seem to have used this first telegram.

[78] *Johnson Papers,* XCVIII, 11,959-61. Johnson to Sheridan, August 4, 1866; *The New Orleans Daily Crescent,* August 8, 1866. The Lieutenant Governor, Attorney General, and Mayor gave Johnson a complete report in a long letter dated August 3 which he must have received before he received Sheridan's "answer." *The New Orleans Times,* August 8, 1866; *The Louisiana Democrat,* August 16, 1866.

[79] Welles, *op. cit.,* II, 572. The editor of the *Democrat* made the statement that: "If General Sheridan had got up this document avowedly as a Radical campaign paper, he could not have been more successful in accomplishing his object." *The Louisiana Democrat,* September 5, 1866.

[80] *Johnson Papers,* XCVIII, 11,964-72. Sheridan to Johnson, August 6, 1866; Beale, *op. cit.,* pp. 350-53; *The Louisiana Democrat,* September 5, 1866. It seems that this telegram was given much publicity. Sheridan's apparent reversal led *The New Orleans Times* to observe that: "The sabre is his weapon not the pen. . . . We were slow to believe that so . . . reticent an officer had at once abandoned that discretion which is the better part of valor." *The New Orleans Times,* August 25, 1866. Judge Abell, in a long letter which he made public, replied to the "unfounded assertions," as he designated the charges against him in Sheridan's telegram. *The Daily Picayune,* September 1, 1866; *The Louisiana Democrat,* September 12, 1866. The Louisiana press condemned Sheridan's telegram generally, and charged that "Sheridan's inaction was the cause of the Convention riots." The writer found telegrams among the *Johnson Papers* from a number of Unionists in New Orleans placing the blame on the military authorities. Judge Abell, in his charge to the Grand Jury on August 2, had placed the entire blame on both those who attempted to assemble and those who encouraged it to do so; and the Grand Jury report, which was made after a great number of witnesses had testified on the riot, was in line with the charge of the Judge. *The New Orleans Times,* August 3, 1866; *The Louisiana Democrat,* August 22, 1866; Dostie, *op. cit.,* p. 323.

[81] *The Louisiana Democrat,* August 15 and October 31, 1866; *The Baton Rouge Tri-weekly Gazette and Comet,* August 30, 1866; *The New Orleans Daily Crescent,* August 14, 17, 1866. The *Crescent* commented on August 17: "We hasten the press while we stop our breath to lay the following 'truthful and harrowing' dispatch before the readers of the *Crescent.* We have neither time nor heart for comment. We can only cry out in our utter despair: 'Where is General Sheridan, and, oh, where is General Baird, and where, where, where, is anybody that can help us in our sore distress?' Here is the horrible telegram: " 'Washington, August 12—The legitimate results of the Johnson policy at New Orleans are developing themselves rapidly. A number of Union refugees from that city have already reached here, having been compelled to leave their families and homes in order to save their

NOTES

lives. They state that the Monroe–Johnson rebels have appointed a committee to notify Union citizens to leave the city, and in proof thereof exhibit the following notice, which is now being served on loyal citizens:

" ' "Sir—you are hereby notified to leave this city within seventy-two hours. Your presence cannot be tolerated longer in this community.

By order of
The Committee" ' "

[82] *The New Orleans Times*, August 1, 25, 1866; *The New Orleans Daily Crescent*, August 25, 1866; Beale, *op. cit.*, pp. 4-5, 141-42. General N. P. Banks was reported to have commented as follows on the riot: "The more anarchy in the South the more thunder in the North." *The New Orleans Times*, August 3, 1866.

[83] *Johnson Papers*, C, 12,169-70. J. Jemison to Johnson, August 4, 1866. Jemison placed the responsibility for all the trouble on the military authorities. The New Orleans press took the same attitude. Jacob Barker, a prominent Unionist, made the same representations. He said that the soldiers did not arrive until "exactly 3:35." He added that "a dozen soldiers could have prevented the trouble"; "that Union men were not persecuted," since he held office by election; and that "perhaps one hundred" in all were killed. *Johnson Papers*, XCIX, 12,062-63. As a matter of fact, the radicals seem to have had little cause for complaint over treatment of Union men in New Orleans, for of the six district judges, four had always been Union men, and of the five supreme court judges, three had always been Union men and the other two had been Unionists in sympathy. *The Sugar Planter*, September 8, 1866.

[84] *Stanton Papers*, XXX, 56,050-51. Sherman to Grant, August 13, 1866; *The New Orleans Times*, August 1, 1866; *The New Orleans Crescent*, August 3, 1866. The report of the "New Orleans Riots Committee," appeared some months later. The following "remarkable dispatch," which appeared in the *New York Daily Tribune* of August 1, is typical of the many that the writer examined:

"The riot is progressing with frightful results. President Johnson telegraphed the military to support the civil authorities. Mayor Monroe and his police force, sympathizers with the rebel element, have broken up a peaceable assemblage of loyal men, killing and wounding a number of the convention. Governor Hahn is dangerously wounded and locked up in jail. An indiscriminate massacre of Union men is going on. God help the colored people. General Baird has forsaken them. No troops have as yet arrived. General Sheridan is absent and expected to return tonight. The Confederate flags have been raised, and the city is in their possession. Governor Wells is a prisoner in their hands."

"Except the statements that there was a riot in progress, that President Johnson had given instructions for the military to support the civil authorities, that no United States troops had arrived at the city at three o'clock, and that General Sheridan was absent, every assertion contained in the above telegram is absolutely and unqualifiedly false. Can it be possible that the radical journals instruct the correspondents to invent falsehoods for the purpose of exciting Northern passion and resentment against the South?" *The New Orleans Cresecent*, August 7, 1866. The first paragraph is the dispatch that was copied from the *Tribune* and the second is, of course, the comment of the editor of the *Crescent*.

[85] *The New Orleans Times*, August 19, September 18, and October 8, 1866; *The New Orleans Daily Crescent*, August 2 and September 18, 1866. Dostie's speech had not been published at first because of its alleged "incendiary character." In fact, the real version had not appeared until some days after the "prophecies of blood" were fulfilled. The full text is in Fleming, *Documentary History*, I, 231-32.

[86] *The Daily Picayune*, September 6, 1866. H. C. Warmoth and others made

[299]

a similar but more detailed report to the Philadelphia Convention, which was given wide publicity. They laid the "premeditated murder" to Andrew Johnson. It is interesting to note that Warmoth took two negro delegates with him to this convention, and that they were the first to participate in a body of this nature. *The New Orleans Crescent,* September 15, 1866; Warmoth, *op. cit.,* p. 49; *The New Orleans Times,* September 11, 1866; Beale, *op. cit.,* pp. 164-65.

[87] Cox, *op. cit.,* pp. 544, 547, 549; Fleming, *Documentary History,* pp. 442-43; *The New Orleans Daily Crescent,* August 1, 1866. Mayor Monroe, Attorney General Herron, and Judge Abell were officially removed from office by Sheridan on March 29, 1867, under the authority granted him in what is usually termed the "Military Bill." This bill had been passed two days before (March 27) by the Congress of the United States. Shortly thereafter Governor Wells was ousted under the power granted by the Congressional Reconstruction Acts. Dostie, *op. cit.,* pp. 331-34.

[88] The Daily Picayune, August 24, 1866; *The New Orleans Times,* July 31 and August 1, 5, 25, 1866; *The New Orleans Daily Crescent,* July 31 and August 25, 1866; Johnson Papers, XCIX, 11,950-51. Voorhies and Herron to Townsend, August 2, 1866; Kendall, *op. cit.,* I, 311. As a matter of fact, martial law had never been removed

technically, and Sheridan now enforced it with negro troops, which continued to exasperate the citizens. He did relieve the military governor from his duties on August 24, but the second paragraph of this order declared that martial law "will be continued and enforced so far as may be required for the preservation of the public peace and the protection of property." *The New Orleans Times,* August 25, 1866; *The New Orleans Daily Crescent,* August 25, 1866.

[89] The Daily Picayune, August 24, 1866; Chambers, *op. cit.,* I, 633; *The New Orleans Daily Crescent,* July 31 and August 3, 1888; *The New Orleans Times,* August 1, 1866. The rioters were not brought to trial, whereas those who had sought to suppress it were held under military duress. *The Daily Picayune,* July 31, 1866; *The New Orleans Times,* August 26, 1866.

[90] The New Orleans Daily Crescent, August 25 and September 3, 1866. This paper reminded Sheridan that he had not waited for the "overt act" in suppressing the Relief Associations that had organized to dispense "charities to destitute hungry women and children" in New Orleans.

[91] Documents of the Second Session of the Second Legislature of Louisiana (New Orleans: J. O. Nixon, State Printer, 1867), pp. 1-4; *Journal of the Louisiana Senate* (New Orleans: J. O. Nixon, State Printer, 1867), p. 141; *The Louisiana Democrat,* April 3, 1867.

BIBLIOGRAPHY

MANUSCRIPT MATERIALS

Johnson Papers. There are more than fifty volumes of "Bound Letters," three volumes of "Telegrams," a "Scrapbook," two volumes of "Messages," and one volume of "Executive Mansion Letters" in the Manuscript Division of the Library of Congress.

Stanton Papers. A few were located in the Library of Congress.

Thaddeus Stevens Papers. There are only a few in the Library of Congress.

GOVERNMENT DOCUMENTS

Congressional Globe, 36 Congress to the 40 Congress (1860-1867).

Congressional Documents, 36 Congress to the 40 Congress (1860-1867).

Congressional Directory (1860-1867).

Eighth Census of the United States (1860).

House Executive Documents (1860-1867).

House Reports (1860-1867).

Report of the Joint Committee on Reconstruction at the First Session, Thirty-ninth Congress. Washington: Government Printing Office, 1866.

Report of the Select Committee on the New Orleans Riot at the Second Session, Thirty-ninth Congress. Washington: Government Printing Office, 1867.

Senate Executive Documents (1860-1867).

LOUISIANA STATE PUBLICATIONS

Acts of the Legislature of Louisiana, Extra Session, 1860. New Orleans: J. O. Nixon, State Printer, 1861.

Constitution of the State of Louisiana. New Orleans: J. O. Nixon, State Printer, 1861.

Journal of the Proceedings of the Convention of the State of Louisiana. New Orleans: J. O. Nixon, State Printer, 1861.

Louisiana Constitutional Debates in the Convention. New Orleans: W. R. Fish, State Printer, 1864.

Journal of the Convention for Revision and Amendment of the Constitution of Louisiana. New Orleans: W. R. Fish, State Printer, 1864.

Acts Passed by the Twenty-seventh Legislature, Extra Session. Natchitoches Times, 1864.

Journal of the House of the State of Louisiana for 1864-1865. New Orleans: W. R. Fish, State Printer, 1865.

[301]

Journal of the Senate of the State of Louisiana for 1864-1865. New Orleans: W. R. Fish, State Printer, 1865.

Debates in the House of Representatives of the State of Louisiana, Sessions of 1864-1865. New Orleans: W. R. Fish, State Printer, 1865.

Debates in the Senate of the State of Louisiana, Sessions of 1864-1865. New Orleans: W. R. Fish, State Printer, 1865.

Acts Passed by the General Assembly at the First and Second Sessions, 1864-1865. New Orleans: W. R. Fish, State Printer, 1865.

Journal of the Senate of the State of Louisiana, 1866. New Orleans: J. O. Nixon, State Printer, 1866.

Acts of the General Assembly, 1865. New Orleans: J. O. Nixon, State Printer, 1866.

Louisiana Session Laws, 1866. New Orleans: J. O. Nixon, State Printer, 1866.

Journal of the Louisiana Senate. New Orleans: J. O. Nixon, State Printer, 1867.

Documents of the Second Session of the Second Legislature of Louisiana. New Orleans: J. O. Nixon, State Printer, 1867.

Report of the Secretary of State, May, 1902. Baton Rouge: News Publishing Company, 1902.

Journal of the House of Representatives of the State of Louisiana, Session, January, 1867. New Orleans: J. O. Nixon, State Printer, 1867.

Acts Passed by the General Assembly of the State of Louisiana at the Second Session of the Second Legislature. New Orleans: J. O. Nixon, State Printer, 1867.

NEWSPAPERS

The Daily Picayune (New Orleans), 1859-1866.

The New Orleans Crescent, 1860-1862, 1865-1868.

The Daily Delta (New Orleans), 1860-1862, 1866.

The Patriot (Opelousas), 1861.

The New Orleans Commercial Bulletin, 1861.

The Opelousas Courier, 1859-1860, 1865-1866.

The Sugar Planter (Port Allen), 1859-1861, 1866.

The Era (New Orleans), 1863-1864.

The New Orleans Bee, 1860-1862.

The Louisiana Democrat (Alexandria), 1859-1860, 1865-1866.

The Daily Gazette and Comet (Baton Rouge), 1860-1861.

The Weekly Gazette and Comet (Baton Rouge), 1860-1865.

The Baton Rouge Tri-weekly Gazette and Comet, 1865-1866.

The Louisiana Signal (New Orleans), 1860.

BIBLIOGRAPHY

The Southern Star (New Orleans), 1865-1866.
The Southern Sentinel (Opelousas), 1865-1866.
New Orleans Price Current, 1860-1861.
The New Orleans Times, 1863-1867.
The New Orleans Tribune, 1865.
The Daily True Delta (New Orleans), 1859-1860, 1862-1866.
The Constitutional (Alexandria), 1860-1861.
The New Orleans Sunday Delta, 1861-1862.
The Weekly Delta (New Orleans), 1861.
The Morning Advocate (Baton Rouge), November 21, 1937.
New York Herald, 1860-1866.
New York Tribune, 1861-1865.
Le Louisianais (Convent), 1865-1866.

BIOGRAPHIES, MEMOIRS, AND WRITINGS OF PUBLIC MEN

Barrow, C. J. *Biographical Sketches of Louisiana's Governors.* Baton Rouge: The Advocate Book and Job Office, 1893.
Bartlett, N. *A Soldier's Story of the War.* New Orleans: Clark and Hofeline, 1874.
Basso, Hamilton. *Beauregard, The Great Creole.* New York: Charles Scribner's Sons, 1933.
Blaine, James G. *Twenty Years in Congress: From Lincoln to Garfield, 1861-1881.* 2 vols. Norwich, Conn.: The Henry Bill Publishing Company, 1886.
Bland, T. A. *Life of Benjamin F. Butler.* Boston: Lee and Shepard, Publishers, 1879.
Blessington, J. P. *Campaigns of Walker's Texas Divisions.* New York: Lange, Little, and Company, 1875.
Brown, William G., *The Lower South in American History.* New York: The Macmillan Company, 1902.
Butler, Benjamin F. *Butler's Book: Autobiography and Personal Reminiscences.* Boston: A. M. Thayer and Co., 1892.
Butler, Pierce: *Judah P. Benjamin.* Philadelphia: Jacobs and Company, 1907.
Cable, G. W. *The Creoles of Louisiana.* New York: Charles Scribner's Sons, 1901.
Chambers, Julius. *The Mississippi River.* New York: G. P. Putnam's Sons, 1910.
Cox, Samuel S. *Three Decades of Federal Legislation, 1855-1885.* Washington, D. C.: J. M. Stoddard and Company, 1885.

[303]

Dorsey, Sarah A. *Recollections of Henry Watkins Allen, Brigadier-General Confederate Army, Ex-Governor of Louisiana.* New York: M. Doolady, 1866.

Dubose, John W. *The Life and Times of William Lowndes Yancey.* Birmingham: Roberts and Son, 1892.

Flint, H. H. *Life of Stephen A. Douglas.* Philadelphia: John E. Potter and Company, 1863.

Foote, H. S. *War of the Rebellion.* New York: Harper and Brothers, 1866.

Fortier, Alcéi. *Louisiana Studies.* New Orleans: F. F. Hansell and Brother, 1894.

Greeley, Horace, *A Political Textbook for 1860.*

Hart, Albert B. *Salmon Portland Chase.* Boston: Houghton Mifflin Company, 1899.

Hunt, W. H. *Randell Hunt.* New Orleans: F. F. Hansell and Brother, 1896.

Irwin, R. B. *History of the Nineteenth Army Corps.* New York: G. P. Putnam's Sons, 1892.

Julian, George W. *Political Recollections, 1840-1872.* Chicago: Jansen, McClury, and Company, 1884.

King, Grace. *New Orleans, The Place and the People.* New York: The Macmillan Company, 1907.

Lothrop, Thornton K. *William Henry Seward.* New York: Houghton Mifflin Company, 1896.

McHatton, P. E. *From Flag to Flag.* New York: D. Appleton and Company, 1889.

Merrick, Caroline E. *Old Times in Dixie Land.* New York: The Grafton Press, 1901.

Pollard, E. A. *Echoes From the South.* New York: E. B. Treat and Company, 1866.

Reed, Emily Hazen. *Life of A. P. Dostie.* New York: Wm. P. Tomlinson, 1866.

Roman, Alfred: *Military Operations of General Beauregard.* 2 vols. New York: Harper and Brothers, 1884.

Sears, Louis Martin. *John Slidell.* Durham: Duke University Press, 1925.

Southwood, Marion. *Beauty and Booty: The Watchword of New Orleans.* New York: M. Doolady, 1867.

Stanwood, Edward. *A History of the Presidency from 1785 to 1897.* 2 vols. New York: Houghton Mifflin Company, 1898.

Storey, Morefield. *Charles Sumner.* New York: Houghton Mifflin Company, 1899.

Stryker, Lloyd Paul. *Andrew Johnson, A Study in Courage.* New York: The Macmillan Company, 1930.

Taylor, Richard. *Destruction and Reconstruction: Personal Experiences of the Late War.* New York: D. Appleton and Company, 1879.

Trowbridge, J. T. *The South: A Tour of Its Battle Fields and Ruined Cities.* Hartford: L. Stebbins, 1866.

Warmoth, Henry Clay. *War, Politics, and Reconstruction: Stormy Days in Louisiana.* New York: The Macmillan Company, 1930.

Wisner, Elizabeth. *Public Welfare Administration in Louisiana.* Chicago: The University of Chicago Press, 1930.

OTHER PRIMARY SOURCES

Annual Cyclopaedia for years 1861-1867. New York: D. Appleton and Company, 1869.

Bates, Edward. *The Diary of Edward Bates, 1859-1866.* Washington: Government Printing Office, 1930.

Butler, General B. F. *Department of the Gulf; General Orders 1862.* New Orleans: E. R. Wagner, Publisher, 1862.

Butler, General B. F. *Private and Official Correspondence of General Benjamin F. Butler During the Civil War.* 5 vols. Norwood, Mass.: The Plimpton Press, 1917.

Chase, Salmon P. "Diary and Correspondence of Salmon P. Chase," *Annual Report of the American Historical Association, 1902.* 2 vols. Washington: Government Printing Office, 1903.

Clarke, H. C., *Diary of the War for Separation.* Augusta: Press of Chronicle and Sentinel, 1862.

Dumond, Dwight L. *Southern Editorials on Secession.* New York: The Century Company, 1931.

Fleming, Walter L. *Documentary History of Reconstruction.* 2 vols. Cleveland: The Arthur H. Clark Company, 1906.

Moore, Frank (Comp.). *Speeches of Andrew Johnson.* New York: Little, Brown, and Company, 1886.

Nicolay, John J., and Hay, John. *Lincoln's Works.* 2 vols. New York: The Century Company, 1907.

Richardson, James D. *A Compilation of the Messages and Papers of the Presidents, 1789-1897.* 10 vols. Washington: Government Printing Office, 1906.

Smith, G. G. *Leaves From a Soldier's Diary.* New York: G. P. Putnam's Sons, 1906.

Smith, G. G. *Confederate War Papers.* New York: Atlantic Publishing and Engraving Company, 1884.

The Constitution of the United States.

Welles, Gideon W. *Diary of Gideon Welles.* 3 vols. New York: Houghton Mifflin Company, 1911.

ARTICLES IN PERIODICALS AND PUBLICATIONS OF LEARNED SOCIETIES

Bone, Fannie Z. Lovell. "Louisiana in the Disputed Election of 1876," *The Louisiana Historical Quarterly,* XIV (1931).

Bonham, Milledge L., Jr. "The Flags of Louisiana," *The Louisiana Historical Quarterly,* II (1919).

Bonham, Milledge L., Jr. "Louisiana's Seizure of the Federal Arsenal at Baton Rouge, January 1861." *Proceedings of the Historical Society of East and West Baton Rouge,* VIII (1917-1918).

Bonham, Milledge L., Jr. "Financial and Economic Disturbances in New Orleans on the Eve of Secession," *The Louisiana Historical Quarterly,* XIII (1930).

Booth, A. B. "Louisiana Confederate Military Records," *The Louisiana Historical Quarterly,* IV (1921).

Caskey, W. M. "The Second Administration of Governor Andrew Johnson," *The East Tennessee Historical Society's Publications,* II (1930).

Dart, W. K. "The Justices of the Supreme Court," *The Louisiana Historical Quarterly,* IV (1921).

Greer, J. K. "Louisiana Politics, 1845-1861," *The Louisiana Historical Quarterly,* XIII (1930).

Hart, W. O. "The New Orleans Times, and The New Orleans Democrat," *The Louisiana Historical Quarterly,* VIII (1925).

Kendall, L. C. "The Interregnum in Louisiana in 1861," *The Louisiana Historical Quarterly,* XVI (1933).

Moore, W. G. "Notes," *American Historical Review,* XIX (1913).

Renshaw, James A. "The Hunt Family," *The Louisiana Historical Quarterly,* V (1922).

Tompkins, Florence C. "Women of the Sixties," *The Louisiana Historical Quarterly,* I (1919).

Wheaton, C. C. "The Secession of Louisiana, January 26, 1861," *Proceedings of the Historical Society of East and West Baton Rouge,* VIII (1917-1918).

GENERAL HISTORIES

Brasher, Mabel. *Louisiana.* New York: Johnson Publishing Company, 1929.

Chambers, Henry E. *A History of Louisiana.* 3 vols. New York: The American Historical Society, 1925.

Fortier, Alcéi. *A History of Louisiana.* 4 vols. New York: Manzie, Joyant, and Company, 1904.

Kendall, John S. *History of New Orleans.* 3 vols. New York, The Lewis Publishing Company, 1922.

King, Grace, and Ficklen, J. R. *A History of Louisiana.* New York: University Publishing Company, 1897.

Magruder, Harriet. *A History of Louisiana.* Boston: D. C. Heath and Company, 1909.

Oberholtzer, E. P. *History of the United States Since the Civil War.* 3 vols. New York: The Macmillan Company, 1917.

Phelps, Albert. *Louisiana: A Record of Expansion.* New York: Houghton Mifflin Company, 1905.

Rhodes, James Ford. *History of the United States From the Compromise of 1850 to the End of the Roosevelt Administration.* 9 vols. New York: The Macmillan Company, 1928.

Rightor, Henry. *Standard History of New Orleans.* Chicago: The Lewis Publishing Company, 1900.

Schouler, James. *History of the United States Under the Constitution.* 7 vols. New York: Dodd, Mead, and Company, 1894-1899.

Special Monographs

Beale, Howard K. *The Critical Year.* New York: Harcourt, Brace, and Company, 1930.

Banks, General N. P. *The Reconstruction of States.* New York: 1865. (A copy will be found in the Howard Memorial Library, New Orleans.)

Barker, J. *The Rebellion: Its Consequences and the Congressional Committee.* New Orleans: Commercial Print Shop, 1866.

Beckles, Henry Wilson. *John Slidell and the Confederates in Paris, 1862-65.* New York: Minton, Balch, and Company, 1932.

Bledsoe, A. B. *Is Davis a Traitor, or Was Secession a Constitutional Right Previous to the War of 1861?* Baltimore: Innes and Company, 1866.

Bowers, Claude G. *The Tragic Era: The Revolution after Lincoln.* Cambridge: Houghton Mifflin Company, 1929.

Burgess, John W. *Reconstruction and the Constitution.* New York: Charles Scribner's Sons, 1902.

Coulter, Ellis Merton. *The Civil War and Readjustment in Kentucky.* Chapel Hill: The University of North Carolina Press, 1926.

Denman, Clarence Phillips. *The Secession Movement.in Alabama.* Norwood, Mass.: J. S. Cushing Co., 1933.

Dodd, W. E. *The Cotton Kingdom.* New Haven: Yale University Press, 1919.

Dumond, Dwight L. *The Secession Movement, 1860-1861.* New York: The Macmillan Company, 1931.

Dunning, William Archibald. *Reconstruction, Political and Economic, 1865-1877.* New York: Harper and Brothers, 1917.

Ettinger, Amos A. *The Mission to Spain of Pierre Soulé, 1853-1855.* New Haven: Yale University Press, 1932.

Ficklen, J. R. *History of Reconstruction in Louisiana.* Baltimore: The Johns Hopkins Press, 1910.

Fleming, Walter L. *Civil War and Reconstruction in Alabama.* New York: The Columbia University Press, 1905.

Fleming, Walter L. *The Sequel of Appomattox; A Chronicle of the Reunion of the States.* New Haven: Yale University Press, 1921.

Garner, James W. *Reconstruction in Mississippi.* New York: The Macmillan Company, 1901.

Hall, Clifton R. *Andrew Johnson, Military Governor of Tennessee.* Princeton: Princeton University Press, 1916.

McCarthy, Charles H. *Lincoln's Plan of Reconstruction.* New York: McClure, Phillips, and Company, 1901.

McMaster, John Boch. *A History of the People of the United States During Lincoln's Administration.* New York: D. Appleton and Company, 1927.

McPherson, Edward. *A Political History of the United States of America During the Great Rebellion.* Washington: Philp and Salmons, 1864.

Milton, George Fort. *The Age of Hate: Andrew Johnson and the Radicals.* New York: Coward, McCann, Inc., 1930.

Owsley, Frank L. *King Cotton Diplomacy.* Chicago: The University of Chicago Press, 1931.

Parton, James. *General Butler in New Orleans.* New York: Mason Brothers, 1864.

Pierce, Paul Skeels. *The Freedmen's Bureau.* Iowa City, Iowa: Published by the University, 1904.

Ramsdell, Charles W. *Reconstruction in Texas.* New York: Columbia University Press, 1910.

Shanks, Henry T. *The Secession Movement in Virginia.* Richmond: Garrett and Massie, 1934.

Simkins, Francis Butler, and Woody, Robert H. *South Carolina During Reconstruction.* Chapel Hill: The University of North Carolina Press, 1932.

Staples, Thomas S. *Reconstruction in Arkansas: 1862-1874.* New York: Columbia University Press, 1923.

INDEX

Abell, Judge, opposes emancipation, 125; defeated for Congress, 156; Sheridan reports on, 228.

Alabama, "Black Code" of, 191.

Allen, Gov. H. W., 175; departed for Mexico, 163; is a candidate for Governor, 176-177.

Amendments, Thirteenth ratified by the Legislature of 1864, 148; Fourteenth opposed by Johnson, 210.

Atocia, Judge A. A., Nominated Auditor on two tickets, 102.

Baird, General Absalom, Bureau agent in Louisiana, 195; in command in New Orleans during "riot," 218; is in sympathy with revolutionists, 219; sends telegrams to Stanton, 220; derelict in his duty, 224; acts with revolutionists, 225-226.

Baker, Joshua, claims seat in Congress, 85.

Baltimore, Constitutional Union Party sends delegates to, 5.

Banks, General N. P., relieves Butler, 70; reveals plans of restoration, 70-71; manifests a spirit of conciliation, 71-72; delays reorganization, 74; attitude towards Unionist factions, 79; attempts to fix negro status, 87; attempts to appease all factions, 97-98; indorses Hahn for Governor, 99; makes promises to loyal slave holders, 102; requires the qualified to vote, 106-107; speaks at inauguration of Hahn, 109-110; orders election of delegates to constitutional convention, 116; defeats of, 119; advises President Johnson, 166-167; regulates employment of negroes, 141; results of his forced labor policy, 142; establishes schools for negroes, 143-144; practises law in Louisiana, 179.

Barker, Jacob, a Unionist candidate for Congress, 64.

Baton Rouge, 7, 17, 88, 141; secession convention assembles in, 29; Hahn speaks in, 104.

Beauregard, General P. G. T., believes South will be coerced, 28; exploits of, 41.

Belden, Dr. James G., State Treasurer, 108.

Bell, John, great ratification meeting of, 6; supporters of hostile to Yancey meeting, 9; appeal of his supporters, 10-11; final rally for, 11.

Benjamin, Senator J. P., 32, 157, 161; speaks on the right of secession, 27-28; believes the South will be coerced, 28; writes joint letter to secession convention, 30; farewell address of to United States Senate, 34-35.

Bienvenu, C., proposes popular vote on secession, 33; calls for election returns to secession convention, 36.

"Black Codes," Legislature of 1864 fails to repeal 1855 code, 151; two real "Black Codes" defeated by legislature, 184; cause of reaction against the South, 208.

Blaine, James G., attacks the "Black Code" of Louisiana, 188.

Bonzano, M. F., author of the article of emancipation, 156; is elected to Congress, 156.

Bouligny, John E., 64, 65; Louisiana Congressman, 56.

Boyce, Henry, elected United States Senator, 192.

Breckinridge, John C., support in Louisiana, 8-9; the vote of his ticket, 12.

Bullitt, Cuthbert, serves on Conservation Committee, 79-80; expresses faith in Johnson, 167.

Bureau, Freedmen, history of in Louisiana, 193-197; many complaints against, 194-196; Howard, Fullerton, Sheridan report on, 196-198; Johnson vetoes the Bureau bill, 209.

Butler, Dr. A. J., brother of B. F. Butler, 68; grows rich, 68.

Butler, General B. F., enters New Orleans, 45; first proclamation of, 45-46; his address to working men, 46; charity of, 47; treatment of foreigners, 48-50; relationship with consuls, 49; treatment of citizens, 50; purges schools, 51-52; first assessment of, 52-53; acts of "renovation," 53; the negro enlistment policy of, 53-54; results of negro enlistment, 54-55; be-

Fullerton, General, reports on "Bureau" in Louisiana, 197.
Fuqua, J. O., opposes separate state action in the convention, 32.

Gayarré, Charles, urges immediate secession, 22.
Germans, receive aid from Butler in Louisiana, 48; appeal of Unionist to, 57; vote in congressional elections, 63; support Banks, 80; support Hahn for Governor, 99.
Graham, James, 154, 181; prominent Unionist, 73.
Grant, General U. S., says the South accepts the situation, 209.

Hahn, Michael, 72, 129, 140, 145, 223, 228; Unionist candidate for Congress, 64; elected to Congress, 65; pleads for recognition of Louisiana, 73; states Lincoln's restoration views, 74; creates Free State sentiment in the North, 80; a leader of the Conservative Free State faction, 98; logical choice of Free State conservatives, 99; Confederate record of, 99-100, 112; nominated for Governor, 101; his platform and campaign speeches, 104; elected Governor, 107; earlier history of, 108; inaugural address of, 109; recognized as Governor by Lincoln, 110; his "Bill of Inauguration" is excessive, 114-115; advocates negro education, 128; Lincoln writes him regarding negro suffrage, 130; removes an offending judge, 134; his message to the Legislature of 1864, 145-146; opposes negro suffrage at first, 147-148; requests adoption of the Thirteenth Amendment, 148; tells the North that negroes are re-enslaved, 210, 211.
Herron, A. S., 179; supports Douglas, 7.
Hope and Company, Citizens Bank owes a large sum to, 48-49.
Howard, O. O., 193, 196, 197; chief of the Freedmen Bureau, 143.
Howell, Judge R. K., 100, 124, 218; prominent member of Congress of 1864 Convention, 120; resigns judgeship, 134; appointed a District Judge, 154; appointed an Associate Justice,

155; tells a credulous north of "Massacres" in Louisiana, 211; elected President of the convention at caucus, 214-215; reconvokes 1864 Convention, 217.
Hunt, Randell, supports Bell, 6, 11; elected United States Senator, 192.
Hyman, W. B. Chief Justice, 155.

Irish, receive charity from Butler, 48; appeal of Unionists to, 57.

Johnson, President A. J., 196, 198, 229; follows Lincoln's restoration policy, 160-161; Republicans oppose his Southern policy, 161; issues important proclamations, 162-163; many citizens advise him, 164-167; Andrew Johnson clubs are active, 167; orders city election to be held without military interference, 201; pardons Mayor Monroe and others, 201; inherits the radical war upon Lincoln, 208; vetoes the Freedmen Bureau bill, 209; makes "Lincoln Day speech," 210; informed of "incendiary speeches," 219; Stanton withholds telegram from, 220; holds Stanton responsible for "New Orleans Riot," 224; instructs military to sustain the civil authorities, 225; Sheridan gives him a complete report on the "riot" 227-228; restored state government of overthrown by radicals, 230-231.
Johnson, Reverdy, 140; investigates and prefers charges against General Butler, 67-68.
Johnston, Brandish, on conservative committee to see the President, 75-76.
Judiciary; see Courts.

Kennedy, Hugh, 165, 205; Mayor of New Orleans, 166.

Lafourche, all property in district of sequestered by Butler, 62.
Landrum, J. M., Louisiana Congressman, 30.
Legislature, call of into special session in 1860, 17-18; the 1860 members vote for a convention, 20; war measures of in 1861 session, 29; organization of the "Free State Legislature" of 1864, 145; members of 1864 body

"Black Republicans," 3; President of Louisiana Secession Convention, 29.

Negroes, Butler's enlistment of, 53-54; results of enlistment of, 54-55; Butler requires oath of them, 60; demand their "rights," 86-87; early regulation of by Banks, 87; retained as troops by Banks, 89-90; hold "equal rights" meetings, 90-91; not included in Lincoln's "Ten Per Cent Plan," 96; suffrage of becomes an issue, 104-105; desire to register and vote, 105; action on education of by 1864 Convention, 126-128; suffrage of debated in convention, 128-131; appeal of to Lincoln for the privilege of suffrage, 129; debates in convention on legality of slavery, 134; regulation of employment by Banks, 141; suffrage for is debated in the legislature, 146-148; suffrage demanded for by radical leaders, 170; register and vote for Warmoth, 180-181; urgent need of regulations for in 1865, 185-186; are taught to distrust former masters, 186; laws passed for regulation of, 190-191; are advised by Howard, 196; suffrage for advocated by Chase-Sumner-Phillips school, 208; inflamed by "incendiary speeches" of radicals, 220-221; march armed to the Convention, 222-223; a number killed and wounded in battle of July 30, 223-224.

Neville, Julian, appointed Auditor, 170.

New Orleans, 14, 16, 23, 24, 25, 36, 67, 72, 82, 91, 109, 112, 129, 139, 142, 145, 150, 167, 178, 189; supports action of seceding delegates, 3-4; surrenders to Farragut, 43; charity of, 47; desolation of, 57; friction between citizens of and delegates to the convention, 121-122; the "New Orleans Riot," 204; beginning of "riot" in, 223; the authorities attempt to prevent the "riot" in, 229-230.

Opelousas, 141, 194; Ordinance of, 184.

Palmer, Dr. B. M., a strong advocate of Southern rights, 19-20.

Party, organization of by Constitutional

Unionists, 5, 6, 16; organization of by Southern Rights champions, 19; see Elections; see Unionists.

Peabody, Judge Charles A., presides over Lincoln's "Provisional Court," 153-155; resigns as Judge of the "Provisional Court," 156.

Phelps, General, objects to being a "slave driver," 54.

Picayune, a conservative daily paper, 25; opposes "immediate secession," 36-39; makes charges against the secession convention, 38.

Pinchback, P. B. S., a prominent negro leader, 54; demands "political equality," but not "social equality," 90.

Press, conservative journals hostile to Yancey meeting in New Orleans, 9; hostility of a number of Northern journals to the South, 23; controversy in over convention election returns, in 1861, 35-40; Northern papers criticize acts of the secession convention, 39; defies Butler, 43; denounces the proceedings in the Republican mass meeting, 182-183.

Radicals, fewer than five hundred white radicals in Louisiana, 220; derive great advantage from "reports" on the "riot," 228-229; overthrow of the restored Lincoln–Johnson state government by, 230-231.

Republicans, 12, 178, 201; oppose Johnson's policy, 161; enter the Congressional election in Louisiana, 179-181; platform and nominee of in 1865, 180; proceedings in mass meeting of in 1865, 181-183; Louisiana press denounces mass meetings of, 182-183.

Restoration, a strong movement for, 73-74; completed in Louisiana, 203; bill to annul, 205-206; overthrow of in Louisiana, 230-231; see Elections.

Riddell, Dr. J. L., president of a Unionist club, 73; reported elected Governor, 85; heads Louisiana delegation to National Republican Convention in 1864, 149.

Roselius, C., 6; serves on Conservative Unionists committee to Washington, 79-80.

Rozier, J. Ad., urges co-operative secession, 31-32; leader of Conservative Unionists, 102-103; candidate of Unionists for Governor, 103; refuses to participate in Convention of 1864, 117-119; drafts a platform for National Democrats in Louisiana, 174; appointed mayor by Canby, 202.

Schurz, Carl, makes unfavorable report after visit to Louisiana, 209.
Secession, debated by Louisianians, 12-13; arguments of "co-operative secessionists" and "immediate secessionists," 21; results of election on for delegates to convention, 24-26; analysis of election returns for delegates to the convention, 25-27; solidification of sentiment for, 27; Ordinance of, 31; the Ordinance of repealed, 123; see Elections.
Shepley, General, Military Governor of Louisiana, 72; requested to call an election, 75; report of Unionist committee to, 77; agrees to register citizens, 78; writes Lincoln regarding registration, 92-93; assists in registration, 94.
Sheridan, General P. H., says Confederates "accept the situation," 197-198; absent in Texas during "riot," 218; places responsibility for in first telegram, 226-227; the Sheridan-Johnson telegrams relating to the "riot," 226-228; makes a second attempt to place responsibility for the "riot," 228.
Slidell, John, 12, 33, 157, 161; followers of control Louisiana convention in 1860, 1-2; opposes Douglas, 8-9; urges immediate secession, 22; believes South will be coerced, 28; writes joint letter advising the secession convention, 30; was not a member of the 1852 Convention, 133; delivers farewell address to the United States Senate, 33-34.
Smith, Charles, 147; elected United States Senator, 157.
Smith, Kirby, capitulates, 163.
Soulé, Pierre, ardent supporter of Douglas, 1, 4; states position of "co-operative secessionists," 21-22; imprisoned by Butler, 51.
Stanton, E. M., withholds telegram in-

tended for Johnson, 220; Johnson says he is responsible for "New Orleans riot," 224.
Stevens, Thaddeus, 7, 161; protests against admission of Louisiana congressmen, 85; correspondence of Durant with, 111.
Suffrage; see Negroes.
Sumner, Charles, 161, 208; is vigorous opponent of the readmission of Louisiana, 158-159.

Taliaferro, Judge, 176, 179; nominated for Lieutenant Governor by Conservatives, 177.
Taylor, Miles, manages the Douglas campaign, 7.
Taylor, Richard, Confederate General, 119.
"Ten Per Cent Plan," instructions in regard to by Lincoln, 94-97; oath included in, 93; negro is excluded, 96; based on 1860 vote, 90; elections results on, 107; inauguration of officers elected under, 109-110; difficulties encountered by government established under, 111; election expenses of government established under, 113-114.
Terry, J. R., registrar of voters, 172.

Unionists, very few per se in Louisiana, 40-41; oppose using of negroes in army, 54; the associations of, 55-57; the appeals made by, 57; make complaints against Butler, 62; division of among themselves, 65; pass restoration resolutions, 73-74; two schools of thought, 74-75; the Free State party of plans restoration, 77-78; influence on of fall of Vicksburg, 78; break between factions of, 79-80; conservative faction of holds election, 81-84; Free State faction of opposes the conservative faction, 82-85; Free State conservative faction gains ascendency, 92; the conservative ticket, 103; conservatives are handicapped, 105-106; defeated factions of attack Hahn's record, 112; some refuse to participate in 1864 election, 118; enlisted as soldiers from Louisiana, 146; oppose Wells, 165; report on the "riot," 229.

INDEX

Voorhies, Judge Albert, elected Lieutenant Governor by Democrats, 177; tries to prevent reassembling of 1864 Convention, 216-217; informs Johnson of "incendiary speeches," 219.

Wade, B. F., opposes Lincoln's Louisiana Government, 159; appeal of Louisiana citizens to, 158; opposes the restoration policy, 203; issues Wade-Davis Manifesto against Lincoln, 206-207.

Warmoth, Henry Clay, a Republican leader in 1865, 179; elected by the Republicans as a "delegate" to Congress, 180-182; speaks before ratification meeting of Republicans, 182; goes as a "delegate" to Washington, 183; informs North regarding conditions in Louisiana, 184, 211.

Weems, Judge James I., imprisoned by a Bureau agent, 195-196.

Wells, James Madison, 163, 166, 171, 173, 183, 214, 218; nominated for Lieutenant Governor on two Unionist tickets, 101; early record of, 107-108; advocates education of negroes, 127; opposed by Louisiana Unionists, 165; is confident that Johnson will crush the radicals, 169-170; opposes negro suffrage, 170-171; exposes registration frauds, 172-173; orders on election for fall of 1865, 173-174; nominated for Governor on two tickets, 175-176; elected Governor on Democratic ticket, 178; message to the legislature in 1865, 187; opposes restoration of local and city governments, 199-201; Johnson orders him to hold an election in New Orleans, 210; gravitates towards radical camp, 204-205; supports reassembling of convention, 218.

Whigs, former strongholds of in Louisiana, 25-26.

Wickliffe, Governor Robert C., supports Douglas, 7; president of the Democratic State Convention in 1865, 174.

"Woman Order," issued by Butler, 50; Mayor Monroe protests against, 51; a cause of Butler's removal, 67.

Yancey, William L., speaks in New Orleans, 9.

[318]